BEETHOVEN AND HIS NEPHEW

1. Karl van Beethoven

BEETHOVEN
AND HIS NEPHEW

A Psychoanalytic Study
of their Relationship
By EDITHA STERBA
and RICHARD STERBA, M.D.

TRANSLATED BY WILLARD R. TRASK

LONDON: DENNIS DOBSON

First published in Great Britain in 1957 by
Dobson Books Ltd., 80 Kensington Church St., London W.8
All rights reserved. Original edition published in America
by Pantheon Books Inc., 333 Sixth Avenue, New York 16, N.Y
Printed in Great Britain by Jarrold and Sons Ltd., Norwich

CONTENTS

LIST OF PLATES

BEETHOVEN AND HIS NEPHEW

I

INTRODUCTION

IN Heiligenstadt, a lovely suburb of Vienna, many of the houses
bore commemorative tablets with the inscription:

IN THIS HOUSE LIVED
LUDWIG VAN BEETHOVEN
IN THE YEAR 18. .

Our own residence there was a small villa in a short, narrow
side street named after the Roman Emperor Probus, who, in the
course of his campaigns in Pannonia, had brought viniculture to
this land of the Danube. The street consisted almost entirely of
one-storey houses, most of them wineshops; it ended in a small
square, on the farther side of which stood the house in which
Beethoven had lived in 1804 while working on the Eroica Symphony. Hence it was known as the "Eroica House." The lodging
which he had occupied was open to visitors. We remember the
charming courtyard, the outside stairway, and Beethoven's low-
ceilinged, two-room apartment. One could not look about the bare
rooms without a feeling of reverence, as if the place had been consecrated by the great man's creativity. We could imagine the Titan
as he lived in these rooms, possessed by his creative urge, unapproachable, in solitary struggle with all the difficulties which fate
meted out to him, until, in a gigantic act of creation, he freed himself from everything earthly and rose into the transcendent realm
of his great works. Everything that we had read about him, everything that his works told us of him, crystallized into this concep-
tion of the Hero of the Spirit, whose presence and touch had imparted something of his own immortality to the shabby rooms.

9

All that the old woman who showed the apartment seemed to know about him was that he had been very strange and not at all lovable. We can still hear her saying: "He must have been a terrible man. He could never stay anywhere and nobody could put up with him." Somehow, the tradition which had been preserved in the neighborhood seemed to contradict the image of Beethoven which we had created — or, better, which our education and our early and continuing experience of his music had formed in us. We knew, of course, that he had been "difficult"; but we could understand his keeping others, even his intimates, at a distance: his genius needed this solitude to create the works through which he established a bond of the deepest experience between himself and all those who are responsive to his music. The old woman at the Eroica House, unaffected by any knowledge of his creations and by the ideal image which the educated world had formed of Beethoven, seemed to be talking about a different person, kept alive in popular tradition as "that terrible man" whom nobody had ever been able to stand.

We had another similar experience in Heiligenstadt. Across the street from us was a modest house in which a baker had his shop. For us, this too was a consecrated place, for it was there that, in 1802, Beethoven had written the "Heiligenstadt Will." At some time, the baker must have read the document in a newspaper; for he had cut it out and pasted it to the glass of his small show-window. There, above the rolls and the cheap pastries, it bore witness to the sorrow and despair of the great musician, who, about that period, had begun to lose his most important sense, his hearing.

From our window we could see into the baker's courtyard, where he kept his chickens. The baker's mother fed them regularly and with great solicitude. The old woman almost never left the house, but we once encountered her in the street and struck up a conversation. "Yes, that Herr von Beethoven — he must have been terrible," she said. When she was still a little girl, her grandmother had told her about the strange man who once, when the grandmother had herself been a child, had lived for a time in the house. He had been unapproachable, almost savage, and she had been afraid of him.

These two descriptions, both coming from simple people, forcibly conveyed the strong impression which Beethoven had left in Heiligenstadt. The lingering effect of his personality, which made people still talk of him after more than a century, clearly contained an admixture of dislike and fear. These brief contacts with remains of the local Beethoven tradition left a vague sense of the contradiction between the image which we had formed of him and the image which persisted among the simple people in Heiligenstadt. But it was not long before this impression died away and our concept of the personality of the great composer was once again in harmony with his magnificent works.

Yet it was strange how little we knew about his personality. We have since learned that, in this respect, we were no exception among educated people: indeed, practicing musicians know remarkably little about the strange man whose works mean so much to them. In general, the educated person knows far more about the personalities and lives of Mozart, Haydn, or Schubert, than he does about Beethoven. Yet a great deal more has been written about Beethoven. It is as if those who loved his music were prevented, by some inner block, from becoming better acquainted with Beethoven the man. But there is every reason why his personality should excite the most intense interest.

Many years later, long after we had left Vienna, we again became aware that our ideal image of Beethoven did not seem to be in harmony with his real behavior. More or less by chance, we read an article on Beethoven, from which we learned what an extraordinary relationship the composer, then in his forty-sixth year, suddenly developed toward his nephew — a relationship which, because of its strong emotionality, its permanence, and its catastrophic outcome, could not fail to arouse the liveliest interest in a psychologist. We decided to learn as much as possible about this relationship, and, to that end, turned to the well-known biographies of the great composer.

It is hardly credible how many thousands of volumes have been written about Beethoven; each year sees at least one new book on him in every Western language. There are periodicals whose issues for many years have been devoted entirely to Beethoven. So strong and enduring is the fascination which this strange man has ex-

ercised upon the minds of later generations! We were soon forced
to recognize that the earliest writings on Beethoven's personality
already presented a highly idealized picture of him — a picture
often in obvious contradiction to the documentary evidence, even
where the documents were given in the very same book.

The idealization of such a personality by his biographers is
well motivated, as depth-psychology has shown. A primitive urge
constrains the Romantic biographer to purify his "hero" from all
the dross of human failings, to tolerate nothing imperfect in him,
and to represent him in a halo of glory. This ideal personality now
joins the ranks of heroes, demigods, and gods, as they have been
created in legend, myth, and religion. These figures satisfy a deep
inner need for the superhuman and for moral perfection. The
typical biographer, "fixed on his hero in quite a peculiar manner," [1]
does everything possible to represent him in such a way that he
approximates these ideal figures. From our study and the documents we present, it will appear that idealizing Beethoven's personality has been no easy task.

There is no doubt that a psychoanalytical study of a historical
personality is bound to encounter certain difficulties. The classical
analytical method is founded upon the technique of free association, which presupposes cooperation on the subject's part. If we
attempt to understand a historical personality psychoanalytically,
we are obliged to forego this most important of technical tools.
We try to draw our conclusions concerning the deeper motivations of the behavior of the historical personality from the available documentary material. These conclusions are reached in
analogy with the results which the classical analytical method has
attained, in countless cases, with the cooperation of the subject.
Often the available material in respect to a historical personality
can be interpreted with considerable certainty, since its deeper
significance and motivation are obvious to the experienced practi-
tioner; in other cases the conclusion drawn will be doubtful, and
must be guardedly tendered as a mere possibility. We shall endeavor, in our presentation, to make a clear distinction between
comparatively certain conclusions and conjecture.

The frequent paucity of source material led Freud to outline
the limitations of psychoanalytic biography. "Psychoanalytic in-

vestigation has at its disposal the data of the history of the person's life, which on the one hand consists of accidental events and environmental influences, and on the other hand of the reported reactions of the individual. Based on the knowledge of psychic mechanisms it now seeks to investigate dynamically the character of the individual from his reactions, and to lay bare his earliest psychic motive forces as well as their later transformations and developments." [2] In his celebrated pathographical study of Leonardo da Vinci, in which these sentences occur, Freud has certainly chosen a personality about whom very little pertinent material exists. The interval of time between the period when Leonardo lived (1452–1515) and the year when Freud wrote of him (1910) is roughly four centuries. Statements about Leonardo by his contemporaries are few, his own writings are restrained and often seem intended to conceal more than they reveal. The situation is entirely different in the case of Beethoven. Little more than a century has passed since his death. (As a child, one of the authors of this book knew a lady, a Fräulein von Frech [3] — to be sure, she was then over a hundred years old — who had known Beethoven personally and still remembered him.) Contemporary accounts of him are to some extent already written with the interest in psychology which was characteristic of early Romanticism. But, above all, the personal material which has come down to us is unusually various and informative. The impulsiveness — not to say complete lack of self-control — which was one of Beethoven's most marked personality traits, often led him to make statements (frequently in writing) from which it is easy to recognize his varying emotional states. There are hundreds of his letters extant, many of them mere notes, which such friends as Baron Nicolaus Zmeskall von Domanovecz preserved for posterity. Beethoven also left a series of notebooks containing diary entries. And, finally, there are the unique documents known as the "Conversation Books."

The Conversation Books date back to the time when, as a result of Beethoven's increasing deafness, oral conversation with him became impossible. Beethoven's partner in conversation had to write, while Beethoven, as a rule, spoke. At home, a slate was generally used for the purpose, and what had been written was immediately erased. Away from home, small notebooks were em-

ployed. Sometimes Beethoven also wrote his part of the talk, especially when the conversation occurred in a public place, where he
feared he might be overheard by busybodies, since he was unable
to determine the loudness of his voice. Hence, on such occasions,
he always took along a notebook and a big carpenter's pencil, with
which the entries were made. Quite often he also used the notebooks for personal jottings. He preserved a large number of these
books; at the time of his death over four hundred of them were
found. The Conversation Books represent a unique and irreplace-
able source of information. They take the reader straight into the
composer's life and often let him share directly in his experiences,
important or trivial, in his interests, his outbursts of emotion, his
fears and hopes, and above all in his personal relationships with
relatives, friends, and servants. To be sure, we often have to
divine Beethoven's part in the conversations, for we find only
the other person's entries in the notebook; but in many cases this
is not difficult to do; at least we can deduce the subject of the
conversation, and the general nature of what Beethoven said, from
the other's reactions. It is as if we were to overhear someone talking over the telephone. We can reconstruct a considerable part
of the whole conversation.

No other historical personality has left such a source of information. The Conversation Books tell us not only about Beethoven himself; but his friends too reveal themselves very clearly.
In short, the Conversation Books would be the most precious
source of information concerning the composer's later years, if
we possessed all of those which were found in his lodging after
his death. But unfortunately, the information which they could
have supplied would seem to have been too contrary to the aims
of his earliest biographers.

Beethoven's first biographer was Anton Schindler.[4] He had
been a pupil of Beethoven's and counted himself among Beethoven's most intimate friends. We shall later have much to say
about his personality. His reverence for Beethoven was of the
fanatical type which we find when a negative undercurrent is to
be suppressed and concealed by the intensity of positive attitudes.
He was determined to present Beethoven as a figure harmonizing
with the legendary approach and with his own hero-worship of

the master, to whom he refers as "our hero." The contents of many of the Conversation Books must have stood in the way of this undertaking. Schindler circumvented the difficulty by an act of *force majeure* unique in the history of modern biography. He destroyed 264 of the 400 Conversation Books. The remaining 136 he sold to the Royal Library in Berlin, where they were preserved until quite recently. Before 1941, only extracts from them had been printed; there had never been a complete edition. In 1941, at the request of the Prussian State Library, Georg Schünemann began a complete and carefully edited chronological edition of the extant Conversation Books, to be completed in ten volumes.[5] After three volumes, comprising the years 1819–1823, had appeared, Schünemann died; and his work was not continued. We attempted to obtain a written or photostatic copy of the still unpublished Conversation Books from the Berlin Library. Shortly afterward, we read in the New York *Times* that both the Conversation Books and the librarian responsible for them had vanished from Berlin.[6]

Fortunately, an edition of the Conversation Books in French[7] exists (although it is incomplete and inadequately translated), and numerous passages from the unpublished notebooks are given in various biographies.

Schindler, in his fanatical zeal to keep his ideal concept of his great master's personality free from anything unbecoming or contradictory, would have preferred to suppress whatever interfered with such a portrayal. Thus, in his biography, he writes concerning Beethoven's letters during the period of his greatest emotional tension over his nephew: "Yet the greater part of these letters could well be destroyed, since, in and for themselves, they have no interest save as mere holographs of a great man, and many of them are likely to give an unprepossessing impression of their author if the reader is not willing to excuse them as products of momentary ill-humor . . ."[8]

The Conversation Books were in Schindler's possession; he could destroy them or remove pages from them. The letters were no longer within his reach, and thus escaped his fanatical efforts to represent Beethoven as flawless. Hence he attempts to deny their significance, or gives them an interpretation which forcibly twists

their content to fit his views. He has yet another method of defend-
ing his purpose from being defeated by facts of Beethoven's behavior which are incongruous with it. He transfers their motivation, and, with it, what he calls Beethoven's "guilt," to others. He
cannot do this without sometimes charging Beethoven with weakness and oversusceptibility. But this seems to him less injurious to
his ideal figure than finding the real motivation for many actions in
the master's own personality structure. At the same time Schindler
himself reports that the dying Beethoven, when the subject of his
biography was brought up, said to him and Stephan von Breuning:
"There are papers here and papers there, gather them together and
make the best use of them, *but the strict truth in everything,* I make
you both responsible for that." [9] If Schindler quotes this statement,
at the beginning of his biography, as a guiding principle, we
cannot but observe that he followed it in a most arbitrary manner.

We have entered rather fully into Schindler's purificatory activities because they exemplify the way in which most of the later
biographers have gone to work. Even Alexander Wheelock Thayer,
the most important, accurate, and devoted to truth among them,
is not entirely guiltless of trying to present an ideal portrait, even
though in general he limits his distortions to his interpretations
of the master's motives; sometimes he presents the truth only with
considerable hesitation, and it is obvious how painful the admission is to him.

Furthermore, when Thayer reached the point where he had
to deal with Beethoven's relationship to his nephew — at the
beginning of Volume IV of his biography — he was obliged to
give up the work, in all probability because it went too much
against the grain. He developed intolerable headaches, which
lasted all day, even if he worked on the biography for only an
hour. At the same time he could devote himself to other work
without ill-consequences, and he wrote two scholarly books during
the period when he had to renounce work on his Beethoven biography. It was only after his death that Volumes IV and V, written from Thayer's notes by Hermann Deiters and Hugo Riemann,
saw the light. Such conflicts recording the truth about Beethoven
were aroused in the most important of his biographers! Beethoven's human relationships in general, and especially his relation-

ship with his nephew, must, to be sure, have seemed exceedingly strange and incomprehensible to Thayer.

Sigmund Freud first supplied the key to an understanding of innumerable psychological forms of expression and modes of behavior which until then had been completely inexplicable. We owe him our knowledge of psychic drives, of their content and intensity, of psychic conflicts as they arise from drive and defense, of the possibility of their resolution, and of the structural organization of the psychic realm in general. The psychological discoveries of psychoanalysis influence the most various fields. Their effect on biography is revolutionary; a far-reaching revision of its methods will be indispensable. Such a revision must first of all be applied to the portrayal of psychological relationships and motivations. In the process it is inevitable that the persons who are the subjects of biographical technique will appear more human than they did in earlier biography — that is, less superhuman, less heroic, less godlike.

We have no intention of making a psychological study of Beethoven's works or of his creative gift or activity. Psychoanalysis as at present constituted is inadequate for such an undertaking. Our guiding principle in this study is to reach the psychological truth concerning the behavior of this fascinating human being, without whose works our cultural world would be so much poorer. We shall not escape the painful necessity of sacrificing many an illusion to truth. Nothing can diminish the greatness which speaks from Beethoven's immortal works. Ferdinand Ries, a pupil and friend of Beethoven's, to whom we owe some very valuable recollections of the composer, expressed the opinion that, in the case of a great man, everything could be told and that nothing could hurt him.[10] If by "everything" Ries meant "everything that is *true*," we are in complete agreement with his view. For a man's greatness is not the result of the legend which is built up around him; on the contrary, it is his greatness which gives rise to the legend.

II

BEETHOVEN'S BROTHER KARL

BEETHOVEN'S relationship to his nephew will most readily be understood if we follow it in its development, so far as the available material permits. This cannot be done without examining his relationship to the boy's parents, for his attitude to his nephew grew out of his relationship to them. We shall first describe Ludwig's relationship to his brother Karl, as we conceive it from the psychological point of view.

Almost nothing of psychological interest has come down to us regarding his relationship to his brothers during childhood. Ludwig had two brothers, Karl and Johann. Both were younger than himself, Karl by four years, Johann by six. After his mother's death, a period of increased activity began for Beethoven, then seventeen, during which he established important social contacts and markedly increased his reputation as pianist and composer. His father — who, like Ludwig, was a musician at the Electoral Court in Bonn — lost his voice about this time (he was a tenor) and, soon after his wife's death, was pensioned. He had a proclivity for drink, which got him into trouble with the authorities. Hence, a year and a half after his mother's death, Ludwig petitioned the Electoral Treasury to pay over part of his father's stipend to himself, and the petition was granted.[1]

This made Ludwig, at eighteen, the head of the family for all practical purposes, its three surviving members, his father and his two younger brothers, being financially dependent on him. It is impossible to determine if Ludwig's petition to the Electoral Treasury was simply a step rendered inevitable by his father's conduct, or if it should be regarded, at least to some extent, as an aggressive action satisfying a deep need on his part to make himself head of the family. In the latter case, the step would have to be viewed as a precursor of the later act of *force majeure* through which he obtained possession of his nephew. However this may be, in 1789, by the granting of his petition concerning the payment of his father's stipend, the son became the head of the family.

Ludwig's talent and his musical successes were so striking that the Elector Max Franz, in whose service he was, sent him to Vienna to complete his education under Joseph Haydn, the great old master of composition.[2] It was on November 10th, 1792, that the young musician arrived at the capital and imperial city of Vienna. Except for a few short journeys, he never left Vienna and its immediate vicinity again during the thirty-five years of life which remained to him.

A few months after he had settled in Vienna and begun his studies with Haydn, troops of the French Revolutionary Army invaded the Electorate and occupied Bonn; the Elector Max Franz was forced to leave his capital, at first temporarily, then for good. Nevertheless, Beethoven's stipend of 50 ducats a quarter was paid until March, 1794.

In Vienna Ludwig soon obtained the recognition of the musical world by his phenomenal piano-playing, but even more by his unrivaled art of improvisation, which, according to all descriptions, profoundly moved his audiences and held them for hours by an almost hypnotic spell, under which they were constrained to follow the master through the whole gamut of emotions expressed in his playing. His compositions too became more and more highly regarded. His musical success and the social connections which his playing brought him among the musically inclined members of the Viennese nobility gave him adequate financial security, even after the payment of his stipend from the Elector was discontinued. As soon as Ludwig reached this position of security, he urged his brothers to follow him to Vienna, since he was able to provide for them there until they should become independent in their own professions. Karl had already received a certain amount of musical instruction in Bonn; hence, with his brother's help, he could hope to make his way as a professional musician. The youngest of the three van Beethoven brothers,

Johann, was serving his apprenticeship with the Court Apothecary in Bonn. Their father had died rather suddenly in 1792, a few months after Beethoven left Bonn. We have no information concerning Ludwig's reaction to his father's death. His brothers responded to his summons, and reached Vienna in 1795, a few months after Ludwig had published his Opus 1, the first three piano trios.

From then on, his two brothers assumed an important place in Beethoven's life; or probably it would be more accurate to say that they re-assumed it, for the relationship as we learn of it in Vienna is doubtless only the continuation of the relationship established in Bonn in the period immediately following the mother's death. Since, as we said, nothing is known of Ludwig's earlier pattern of relationship to his brothers — in childhood, for example — we can only point out that, according to universal psychological experience, the relationship to brothers and sisters which prevails in later life is normally determined in the nursery. In any case, Ludwig had been appointed Assistant Court Organist in the Electoral Chapel and Cembalist in the Court Orchestra at thirteen, and at sixteen had begun to give music lessons. Thus he very early contributed to the support of the family.

It is not too easy to reconstruct Beethoven's real relationship to his brothers, as it existed in later times, from the biographies. It was precisely in presenting, or rather in misrepresenting, this relationship, that the biographers found their coveted opportunity to purge the composer's personality of the impurities which they found repellent. They had only to lay upon his "profligate" and "avaricious" brothers the "blame" for much in his behavior which they must otherwise have judged severely, and the great man could only be reproached with loving his brothers too dearly and hence allowing their evil influence to sway his conduct. Fortunately there exists enough documentary material concerning his brothers and Beethoven's conduct toward them to permit the unprejudiced investigator to recognize that, in many important behavior-patterns, the three brothers were not so wholly different as the biographers make them out to be. From these documents it is also possible to deduce Beethoven's relationship to his brothers with considerable certainty, and thus to correct the biographers' misrepresentations of it.

Beethoven was especially devoted to his brother Karl. But this affection cannot be described simply as "fraternal love" — Beethoven's relationship to this brother was too intimate, too blind, too indulgent, too emotional in general, to answer to such a definition. The unconscious homosexual factor in his relationship to Karl is unmistakable and we shall have occasion to return to it. Yet there was another unconscious attitude which had a determining influence on Ludwig's behavior toward Karl. What this attitude was, the remainder of this chapter will document.

Karl is described as ugly, short, and red-haired.[3] From what we are able to learn of his behavior toward his great brother, and from his own letters and other documents, we can draw reasonably certain conclusions in regard to his personality. He was a commonplace man, of narrow views and little education, rather primitive in his emotional life and possessed of a violent temper. No one would have taken any particular notice of him had not his brother given him the role which he played in the latter's life. It must be emphasized that Ludwig conferred this role on Karl, for there can be no possible doubt that Beethoven himself raised his brother to the significant position — both positive and negative — which he held in the composer's life.

When his brothers came to Vienna in 1795, Beethoven at once took charge of them. The younger, Johann, soon found a position in the "Zum Heiligen Geist" apothecary shop; thereafter, for a time, he played a comparatively minor role. Karl, on the other hand, became more and more the object of his older brother's anxious, tender, and protective interest. Ludwig appears at first to have interested himself in Karl's further musical education, and during this period helped him financially; before long, he found him pupils — his own increasing recognition among the music-loving society of Vienna making this easy for him to do. Little by little, he tried to make Karl a collaborator in his own work; thus, he entrusted him with the string-quartet and piano arrangements of some of his compositions. In 1800 Karl decided to take up a new career. He entered the public service and, through

Ludwig's influence,[4] obtained a minor official post as "Praktikant" in the Imperial Treasury. The relationship between the brothers continued to be very intimate, and Ludwig increasingly entrusted Karl with the conduct of his business dealings, especially with publishers. In 1803 Ludwig even persuaded Karl to share the apartment which the management of the Theater-an-der-Wien had placed at the composer's disposal in the theater building.

We have scarcely any direct testimony concerning the emotional relationship between Ludwig and Karl. Indeed, they lived in such intimacy that there was little occasion for them to write to each other. Among Beethoven's 1470 letters, not one is to his brother Karl. How strong and blind Ludwig's feeling for this brother was, can be deduced partly from Karl's conduct, especially as revealed in his management of Ludwig's business affairs, and partly from the reactions of Ludwig's friends, in whom Ludwig's relationship to Karl caused many forebodings. From a later period, in which Ludwig, after a long interval of alienation, had again become intimate with Karl, we have numerous expressions and reports of his great and indeed exaggerated tenderness for this brother. We shall in all probability not be wrong if we assume that his relationship to Karl before their alienation was of the same irrational nature and of equal intensity.

The role of protégé, confidant, collaborator, and business-manager which his great brother conferred on him puffed Karl up far beyond his proper size. It must not be forgotten that at this time Beethoven was on terms of familiarity with the highest aristocracy, that princes and counts called themselves his friends and courted him, that interest in him had spread far beyond the boundaries of Austria, that publishers everywhere were eager for his works — in short, that Beethoven was gradually becoming a personage of European fame. Karl basked in his brother's radiance; but the consideration which Beethoven showered on him was too much for a man of such illiberal and in every sense limited mind. It went to his head and led him to a ridiculous presumptuousness at the expense of his brother, as we can see from a letter which Karl wrote to Johann André, a music publisher at Offenbach, who had applied to Beethoven for new manuscripts:

But at present we have nothing except a symphony, with a grand concerto for pianoforte, the first would be 300 fl,[5] the second the same, if you wanted 3 pianoforte sonatas, I could not give them for less than 900 fl, all at the Vienna standard, only you cannot have them all together, but one every 5 or 6 weeks, because my brother no longer bothers with such trifles and only writes oratorios, operas, etc.[6]

As a matter of fact, Beethoven was working at this time on neither an opera nor an oratorio, nor did he ever regard his piano sonatas as "trifles."

Karl finally became so arrogant that he behaved as if Beethoven's works were his own. He wrote to the publisher Simrock at Paris in Beethoven's name as "we," and referred to Ludwig's compositions as "our works." Simrock, who had known the brothers from their days in Bonn, answered the younger brother's puerile presumptuousness in a sarcastic letter:

. . . What you are really after is expressed, I believe, principally in the following lines: 'from each of our publishers we receive 6 copies. Have the goodness to have 5 more sent here, directed to the Ind. Compt.' [7] — It is hardly possible that, in the few years since I have become a Frenchman, I should so completely have forgotten my native language, especially as the greater part of my business is still with Germans. I still understand German, but I cannot understand what you mean by the expressions *our* publishers and *we* . . .[8]

Simrock was not the only person to be irritated by Karl's behavior. Almost all of Ludwig's friends adopted a hostile position toward Karl or toward both of Ludwig's brothers; nor was this due only to the brothers' arrogant behavior but also to Beethoven's own attitude. His friends recognized, or, rather, felt, how exaggerated, unjustified, and unreasonable Beethoven's tender love for his brothers was, and how wasted upon two such insignificant petty bourgeois. His friends found it particularly incomprehensible that Beethoven was blind to the damage, both moral and material, which Karl's arrogance did him among both his friends and his publishers. Karl had little capacity to understand the greatness and significance of Beethoven's creations; his mental horizon was far too limited for that. He respected them chiefly as a source of income, and he endeavored to exploit them as such. He did not hesitate to sell unimportant works behind the composer's back.[9] Beethoven himself complains, in a letter of 1803 to Breitkopf & Härtel, that "unfortunately so many unlucky things of mine have been sold and stolen."[10] Karl offered publishers works which Ludwig had already sold elsewhere; he sold arrangements of Beethoven's works, made by Ferdinand Ries, under Ludwig van Beethoven's name.[11]

What particularly angered his friends was that Ludwig so quickly forgave Karl when Karl's unscrupulous conduct could not escape his own notice or was pointed out to him by his friends. Ferdinand Ries, whose father had known Beethoven from childhood, and who himself, between 1800 and 1805, was constantly with him as his pupil and friend, writes in his "Biographical Notes on Ludwig van Beethoven":

> His brothers were particularly concerned to keep all his more intimate friends at a distance from him, and whatever harm they did him, even when his friends had completely convinced him of it, cost him only a few tears and then he immediately forgot all about it. At such times he would say, 'After all he is my brother,' and the friend would be reproached for his good intentions and his frankness.[12]

Undoubtedly his friends were also jealous because Karl held such an important place in both the business and emotional life of the master whom they so greatly revered. Karl certainly was not backward in asserting his importance to his brother. Prince Moritz Lichnowsky, another faithful friend of Beethoven's, also deplored Karl's influence over him.[13]

Schindler, the fanatical purifier, is particularly bitter in his remarks on the brothers. It is true that he knew only the younger brother, Johann, personally, for Karl was already dead at the time Schindler became acquainted with Beethoven.[14] But Schindler was able to collect a great deal of information concerning the period now under discussion (1795–1805) from Stephan von Breuning, another intimate friend of Beethoven's, who, during this period, shared a lodging with Beethoven for some time, and as a result had occasion enough to be exasperated by the relationship between Ludwig and Karl. Schindler writes of the brothers:

What was it, then, which, despite so strong a bulwark about the person of the great master, was nevertheless able to confuse things and draw even him into the entanglement which it had created? What was it that could frustrate the good and disinterested influence of such true friends as we knew them to be, and finally, after a shorter or longer time, alienate them from Beethoven? It was a pair of brothers, bound to the master by ties of nature. In them, crooked purposes, deliberate contradiction, hypocrisy, and intrigue gave rise to a power which, through its malevolent efforts, could easily undo these men's solicitude for their friend, and in fact often did so, although not always without open and aggressive conflict between the two sides.

Clearly, Nature was playing a strange game when she gave the high-minded Beethoven, consecrated as he was by the muse of music, yet weak in certain respects, a pair of brothers who, entirely governed by the meanest spirit of gain, were incapable of any loftier feeling. In these two brothers we see the two guardians to whom reference was made earlier . . .

To express in brief the character of these two brothers in contrast with the above-mentioned circle of friends, they may well be termed the 'evil principle.' [15]

But here Schindler overlooks the fact that Beethoven did not simply permit his brothers to assume this importance but actively bestowed it upon them, and that his bestowal of it was the expression of the blind, overvaluing, indulgent, and forgiving love which he cherished for them. Ludwig was infatuated by his affection for his brothers. Schindler, in his zeal to present the "hero" of his biography with as few faults as possible, makes the "evil principle" — the brothers — guilty of all the many unpleasant situations into which Ludwig's own character difficulties precipitated him. But his brother Karl was at this period no especially evil principle. He was a rather weak, rather childish, rather characterless man, who exploited his great brother's overfond love and tried to get as much money as possible for his compositions — which, indirectly, benefited himself. In principle, Karl's dealings were no different from those of many a not overscrupulous art-dealer who tries to sell inferior works of a master at the same price as the best. Karl's conduct will have to be viewed even more leniently when we learn that Ludwig himself, at a later time and entirely uninfluenced by his brothers, engaged in the same sort of traffic with his own works.[16] Anyone who uses the concept "guilt" in investigating human conduct will find this behavior far more unpardonable in Ludwig, for Ludwig was aware of the greatness of his own work. As early as 1802, Ludwig had himself sold his C major string quintet, Opus 29, twice, and despite all his efforts and his outbursts against the firm of Artaria, which brought an action against him, he was unable to show in court that the simultaneous publication of his quintet by Breitkopf & Härtel and Artaria was not his own doing.

How Beethoven at times himself used the celebrity which his name had already gained at this period in order to reap material profit from unimportant works is indicated by the episode of his sale of three overtures to the London Philharmonic Society. This took place in 1816, hence immediately after Karl's death. By this time Beethoven had written his overtures to "Fidelio," to "Egmont," to "Coriolanus," and the three "Leonore" overtures, all of them masterpieces unsurpassed in greatness and beauty. The Philharmonic Society, obviously deeply impressed by these magnificent works and by the Fifth Symphony, which had just had its first performance in London, commissioned Beethoven to write three concert overtures, for an honorarium of 75 guineas. Beethoven sent them the overtures to "King Stephan" and the "Ruins of Athens" and the "Namensfeier" overture, all compositions much earlier in date and relatively of little importance, so that "in view of Beethoven's great name and the character of these concerts, not *one* could be performed." [17] This shabby dealing made such a bad impression on the London publishers that one of them wrote to their colleague Neate, who was trying to promote Beethoven's works in England: "For God's sake don't buy anything of Beethoven!" [18]

From all this it is clear that, in such matters, Karl was no more an "evil principle" than was Beethoven himself. We refer to this darker side of the great master's conduct only to show how unjustified it is to present his brother Karl as the evil principle whose sordid avarice corrupted Beethoven's pure soul. In money matters, the brothers were not very different from each other.

Beethoven's great love for Karl did not prevent occasional violent scenes between them. Both brothers had a lack of self-control such as is seldom found among cultivated people, and Ludwig, whose distrust was easily aroused, was quick to burst out and accuse Karl of all sorts of evil intentions toward him. But he would soon repent of his irascibility and would try, through redoubled affection and tenderness, to make up for his accusations and reproaches. Ries reports that the brothers even came to blows. He writes:

Beethoven had promised the three solo sonatas (Op. 31) to Nägeli in Zürich, while his brother Carl (Caspar), who, alas! was always actively concerned in his business, wanted to sell the sonatas to a Leipzig publisher. There had been frequent heated discussions between the brothers on the subject, for Beethoven wished to keep the promise he had given. When the sonatas were on the point of being sent away, Beethoven was living in Heiligenstadt. During the course of a walk, the brothers fell to quarreling again, and finally came to blows. The next day he gave me the sonatas, with instructions to send them to Zürich immediately, together with a letter to his brother, which was enclosed in another to Stephan von Breuning so that the latter could read it. No one could have preached a more beautiful moral, nor with a kinder heart, than did Beethoven to his brother concerning his conduct on the previous day. First he displayed it to him in its true, despicable light, then he forgave him all, but at the same time predicted an evil future for him if he did not completely change his life and conduct.[19]

Unfortunately this letter to Karl is not extant, but Beethoven's readiness to forgive is clearly apparent from Ries's report.

We shall subsequently have occasion to describe another scene, from a later period, which can in all probability be regarded as exemplifying similar incidents in Beethoven's relationship to his brother during the time now under discussion.

In 1805 an estrangement developed between Ludwig and Karl. Karl took lodgings of his own, after having lodged with Beethoven for two years in the Theater-an-der-Wien. Why Karl gave up living with Ludwig is not difficult to conjecture. For, a few months later, on May 25, 1806, Karl married Johanna Reiss, the daughter of a prosperous upholsterer. Five months later, Johanna gave birth to a son, the much-discussed nephew. The brief interval between the marriage and the birth of the child implies that Karl's interest in Johanna was already strong before their marriage—a circumstance of which his brother Ludwig could hardly have been unaware. We have no information that Beethoven was present at his brother's wedding, but it is unlikely that he took part in the festivities, for all his reactions indicate that he was opposed to the marriage and angry at his brother for entering into it. If his reaction to Karl's interest in Johanna was even approximately as violent as his later reaction to his brother Johann's relationship with a woman, he must have indulged in violent outbursts against Karl. In any case, we have every reason for assuming that Karl's marriage was the cause of the estrangement. Ludwig withdrew the management of his business affairs from Karl and entrusted it to his younger brother Johann and to friends. Karl, who had meant so much to him, was eliminated; so that Thayer, the most accurate of the composer's biographers, feels justified in saying that Karl vanishes from Beethoven's life for years. Evidently, the fact of his brother's entering into a relationship with a woman profoundly disappointed and embittered Ludwig, who was unwilling to share his brother with his brother's wife. He was hostile to Johanna from the beginning, and after the marriage refused to have anything to do with either of them. It is characteristic of the few deep relationships which the composer developed, that their objects became his property, which he could share with no one. Elimination of all other relationships was one of the most insistent demands which he made upon those whom he loved. Partial renunciation, forbearance, respect for the right of the person he loved to make his own decisions, to bestow his affection where he chose, were impossible to Beethoven. For him, love and sole possession were inseparably connected.

As further details of Ludwig's relationship to Karl are given, much will become clearer. Yet our survey up to this point already reveals characteristics which correspond to a typical human relationship: the relationship of a mother to her child. We may even say that Ludwig's relationship to Karl resembles that of a certain type of irrational, emotionally primitive mother to her son. Everyone knows this type of mother, who idolizes her son, babies him, gives in to all his demands and is blind to all his faults, always makes excuses for him and forgives him everything, so long as he more or less complies with her wishes and so long as she feels sure of possessing him. When her son displays independence, this type of mother feels deeply hurt, and is often most unjust and bitter in her reproaches against him, accusing him of ingratitude, as the worst of sins — for, after all, she has sacrificed everything for him. Such a mother believes that, by this readiness to sacrifice herself, she fully compensates her son for his obligation to belong to her entirely. When her son seems to be slipping away from her, she very frequently reacts by increased reproaches, culminating in the threat that her son will bring her to the grave by the grief he is causing her — and then he will see what he has lost in his mother!

A number of such threats, involving his own death, are extant, from a later period of Ludwig's life and in relation to another dear relative, with the typical content: "You are driving me to the grave, and when I am dead, you will see!" We have no direct report of his threatening his brother Karl in this way; but one of the most celebrated among Beethoven's writings can, at least as regards many passages, be interpreted as an indirect threat addressed to Karl. We refer to the "Heiligenstadt Will." The text of this holograph, which was found among Beethoven's papers after his death, runs:

For my brothers Carl and   [20] Beethoven.
     O ye men who think or say that I am malevolent, stubborn or misanthropic, how greatly do ye wrong me, you do not know the secret causes of my seeming, from childhood my heart and mind were disposed to the gentle feeling of good will, I was even ever eager to accomplish great deeds, but reflect now that for 6 years I have been in a hopeless case, aggravated by senseless physicians, cheated year after year in the hope of improvement, finally compelled to face the prospect of a *lasting malady* (whose cure will take years or, perhaps, be impossible), born with an ardent and lively temperament, even susceptible to the diversions of society, I was compelled early to isolate myself, to live in loneliness, when I at times tried to forget all this, O how harshly was I repulsed by the doubly sad experience of my bad hearing, and yet it was impossible for me to say to men speak louder, shout, for I am deaf, Ah how could I possibly admit an infirmity in the one sense which should have been more perfect in me than in others, a sense which I once possessed in highest perfection, a perfection such as few surely in my profession enjoy or ever have enjoyed — O I cannot do it, therefore forgive me when you see me draw back when I would gladly mingle with you, my misfortune is doubly painful because it must lead to my being misunderstood, for me there can

be no recreation in society of my fellows, refined intercourse, mutual exchange of thought, only just as little as the greatest needs command may I mix with society, I must live like an exile, if I approach near to people a hot terror seizes upon me, a fear that I may be subjected to the danger of letting my condition be observed — thus it has been during the last half year which I spent in the country, commanded by my intelligent physician to spare my hearing as much as possible, in this almost meeting my present natural disposition, although I sometimes ran counter to it yielding to my inclination for society, but what a humiliation when one stood beside me and heard a flute in the distance and *I* heard *nothing* or someone *heard the shepherd singing* and again I heard nothing, such incidents brought me to the verge of despair, but little more and I would have put an end to my life — only *art* it was that withheld me, ah it seemed impossible to leave the world until I had produced all that I felt called upon to produce, and so I endured this wretched existence — truly wretched, an excitable body which a sudden change can throw from the best into the worst state — Patience — it is said I must now choose for my guide, I have done so, I hope my determination will remain firm to endure until it pleases the inexorable parcae to break the thread, perhaps I shall get better, perhaps not, I am prepared. Forced already in my 28th year to become a philosopher, O it is not easy, less easy for the artist than for any one else — Divine One thou lookest into my inmost soul, thou knowest it, thou knowest that love of man and desire to do good live therein. O men, when some day you read these words, reflect that ye did me wrong and let the unfortunate one comfort himself and find one of his kind who despite all the obstacles of nature yet did all that was in his power to be accepted among worthy artists and men — you my brothers Carl and

[21] as soon as I am dead if Dr. Schmid is still alive ask him in my name to describe my malady and attach this document to the history of my illness so that so far as is possible at least the world may become reconciled with me after my death. — At the same time I declare you two to be the heirs to my small fortune (if so it can be called), divide it fairly, bear with and help each other, what injury you have done me you know was long ago forgiven, to you brother Carl I give special thanks for the attachment you have displayed towards me of late. It is my wish that your lives may be better and freer from care than I have had, recommend *virtue* to your children, it alone can give happiness, not money, I speak from experience, it was virtue that upheld me in my misery, to it next to my art I owe the fact that I did not end my life by suicide — Farewell and love each other — I thank all my friends, particularly *Prince Lichnowsky* and *Professor Schmid* — I desire that the instruments from Prince L. be preserved by one of you

but let no quarrel result from this, so soon as they can serve you
a better purpose sell them, how glad will I be if I can still be
helpful to you in my grave — with joy I hasten towards death —
if it comes before I shall have had an opportunity to show all
my artistic capacities it will still come too early for me despite
my hard fate and I shall probably wish that it had come later —
but even then I am satisfied, will it not free me from a state of
endless suffering? Come when thou wilt I shall meet thee bravely.
— Farewell and do not wholly forget me when I am dead, I deserve
this of you in having often in life thought of you how to make
you happy, be so —

Ludwig van Beethoven

Heiglnstadt, [*sic*]
October 6th
  1802.[22]

What brought forth this most moving document, this outburst
of harrowing despair, has long been a riddle to Beethoven's biographers. Its depressive content can very well be attributed to his
gradual loss of hearing, his distress over which is, indeed, its
principal subject. But the composer's auditory malady was a
process which developed very slowly, and the biographers are
perplexed over the immediate occasion to which they should attribute this outburst of somber thoughts of death on the part of
the then thirty-two-year-old composer. In any case, Ludwig's productivity during this period testifies against his having suffered
a more than usually deep and lasting depression at this time. It is
the period during which he wrote the three violin sonatas Opus 30,
the three piano sonatas Opus 31, and the Bagatelles Opus 33. At
Heiligenstadt, he was working on his Second Symphony (in D
major), and he soon afterward set about publishing his third
Pianoforte Concerto (in C minor, Opus 37). This abundant productivity makes a simultaneous depression of a serious nature
improbable, especially if we compare it with Beethoven's inability
to create during later periods of psychological disturbance.

It seems permissible to explain the "Heiligenstadt Will," as the
document has come to be called, on the basis of Ludwig's relationship to Karl. We have already said that Ries reported a violent
argument which took place between the two brothers at Heiligenstadt in the summer of 1802 and which ended in blows. Many
such quarrels may well have arisen between the brothers at this

time. It is conceivable that Ludwig wrote the document after such a dispute with Karl, when his agitation over his brother's conduct acutely reinforced the natural depression caused by his gradual loss of hearing. This would explain why, both in the superscription to his brothers and again later, in the body of the document, only the name "Karl" is mentioned. The "Will" was directed, as an aggrieved and threatening warning, to Karl who, during these years, played so preponderant a role in Beethoven's emotional life. Whether, for one reason or another, he was at the same time so angry with Johann that the latter's name could not be mentioned, must be left undetermined.

Many strange characteristics of his relationship to Karl become explicable if we bear in mind that Beethoven's emotional attitude toward this brother can be understood as a mother-child relationship, and indeed as the relationship of a highly irrational, impulsive mother toward her son, whom she regards as her private possession and consequently seeks to bind to herself forever by showering him with affection and at the same time making him feel guilty. Like many a mother of this type, who will have nothing more to do with her son after she has "lost" him to a woman, Ludwig shut himself off from Karl for a long period.

Those unfamiliar with psychoanalytic problems will doubtless find this interpretation of Beethoven's relationship to his brother Karl surprising. But in the course of this study we shall cite a great deal of material by which such an interpretation is substantiated and confirmed.

III

KARL'S WILLS

LUDWIG turned from Karl in anger and disillusionment; but this did not end the relationship for him psychologically. At first he tried to transfer his love to Johann, his youngest brother. He made an attempt to entrust him with the management of his business affairs. But Johann soon parted from his brother, for in 1807 he bought an apothecary shop in Linz, a city on the Danube, about a hundred and twenty miles up the river from Vienna. He appears to have saved enough money for the purpose. Of these savings he had once — it is not known when — lent Ludwig 1500 florins. When he was planning the purchase of the apothecary shop, he naturally asked Ludwig to return the money. Ludwig answered this demand by anger and aggressions which can hardly be referred to Johann's entirely justifiable request. The violence of Ludwig's reaction shows how deeply he was affected by the fact that this brother too was forsaking him, after Karl had so greatly disillusioned him a year earlier by marrying. In desperation over the threatened loss of his second brother, Ludwig turned to Karl, asking him to plead with Johann to withdraw his demand. Karl refused, probably in none too friendly fashion, since he was embittered by Beethoven's aggressive and censorious interference in his own personal affairs. How violently Ludwig reacted to Johann's demand and Karl's refusal to intercede for him with Johann, is shown by the following passage from a letter to his friend Ignaz von Gleichenstein, to whom at this period he entrusted many of his business dealings:

> . . . You may tell my brother that I shall certainly not write to him again. — The cause of it, I know already; it is this: because he lent me money, and has spent some on my account, he is, I

know my brothers, already concerned, since I cannot yet return it to him, and presumably the other, who is possessed by the spirit of revenge against me, and to him too.[1] — But the best thing would be, — that I should collect the whole fifteen hundred gulden (from the Industriecomptoir) and pay him with that, and then the matter will be ended. — Heaven preserve me from having to receive benefactions from my brothers.[2]

In any case, Johann bought the apothecary shop in Linz and thus for the next five years withdrew from Beethoven's immediate circle. He was to reappear under highly dramatic circumstances.

So now Ludwig was forsaken by both his brothers, whom he nevertheless loved so dearly and regarded as his children. At first he transferred his animosity to the place in which all this had befallen him, to Vienna. He indulged in highly unjust attacks on the inhabitants of that city of music, where he had received such encouragement and recognition as had never been accorded to another musician there. Thus Rust[3] reports that, during this period, Beethoven often spoke of leaving Vienna on the ground that "they are forcing me to." Who "they" were was not specified. When Jerome Bonaparte, whom his brother Napoleon made king of Westphalia at this time, summoned Beethoven to come to his court at Cassel as conductor, Ludwig, in his embittered frame of mind, decided to accept the position. The decision was hardly justified by the real circumstances. For Beethoven's deafness had by this time progressed so far that he could no longer perform the duties of a conductor. The motivation behind his decision to accept the proposal clearly appears from a letter of January 7, 1809, to Breitkopf & Härtel. It reads, in part:

. . . At last I am forced by intrigues and cabals and base actions of all kinds to leave the only remaining German fatherland. On an invitation from his Royal Majesty of Westphalia I am going there as conductor with a yearly stipend of 600 ducats in gold. I have this very day sent by post my assurance that I will come . . .[4]

Commenting on this, Karl Czerny, who knew the situation in Vienna and Beethoven's circumstances very well, remarks in the notes which he prepared for the Beethoven scholar Otto Jahn: "The truth is that, even as a youth, he enjoyed every possible sup-

port, as well as a consideration and respect, on the part of our
aristocracy, such as hardly another young artist has ever received." [5] How great the music-loving aristocracy's goodwill toward Beethoven and interest in him were, is shown by the efforts
made by three members of the high aristocracy to keep him in
Vienna by providing a fixed income for him, when they learned
of his intention to leave the city. Archduke Rudolf (brother of the
Emperor Ferdinand and Beethoven's pupil), Prince Lobkowitz,
and Count Kinsky bound themselves jointly to pay Beethoven
4000 florins a year from March 1, 1809, in return for which the
composer was obligated only to remain in Vienna and to give the
Archduke music lessons. This action, singularly generous for the
period, persuaded Beethoven to remain. But his bitterness against
Vienna never diminished. We shall only allude here to the fact
that the city in which one is born or resides bears, in the unconscious, the signification of the mother. Towns are personified as
women. Ludwig's frequent outbursts against Vienna may very well
have been expressions of his unconscious hatred of his mother, of
which many other indications will be cited as we proceed.

After Beethoven decided to remain in Vienna, he apparently
made an attempt toward a reconciliation with Karl, to which the
latter would not seem to have responded with any great readiness. For Beethoven wrote at this period to his brother Johann,
on the cover of a letter: "May God only give my other brother,
for once, instead of his insensibility — feeling. I suffer infinitely
through him . . ." [6] The letter itself has been lost.

When the French neared Vienna in 1809, a number of the composer's aristocratic friends left the city, among them Count Kinsky,
Prince Lobkowitz, Prince Lichnowsky, Count Palffy, and Count
Waldstein. For the few days of the siege, Ludwig moved to his
brother Karl's, who was living with his family in the Rauhen-
steingasse. We are told that, during the bombardment, he sat in
the cellar, with a pillow tied around his head [7] — whether to protect himself from the danger of falling fragments of mortar or to
shut out the roar of the cannon, we are not informed.

This was the only period during which Beethoven lived in Karl's
family circle, even for but a few days. What his feelings were in
this situation is not known. It may be assumed that his resentment

of Karl's family life made him an unpleasant guest. About this time Ludwig decided for the first time to set up a household of his own — that is, to engage servants who should live in his lodgings and provide his meals. Hitherto he had taken his principal meal at an inn. The new arrangement was inaugurated in 1809, but it is not known whether the idea of setting up a household came to him after his brief stay with Karl or had been in his mind before. At any rate, it marks the beginning of the difficulties with servants in which Beethoven was involved until the end of his life. There is no doubt that these difficulties were largely precipitated by Beethoven himself. His unconscious motives for doing this will be explained later.

Beethoven persuaded Karl to attend to some further business matters for him. This appears from a letter of February 4, 1810 to Breitkopf & Härtel, in which there is a reference to "the 'Gesang in der Ferne' which my brother recently sent to you." [8] On July 2, 1810 Ludwig wrote to Breitkopf & Härtel: "Since you are so fond of round sums, I will let you have the two works named for an honorarium of 250 ducats in gold, which amount, however, I cannot reduce, for I can get more here through my brother." [9] But we learn nothing of a more personal contact between the two brothers.

In 1811 there was a general devaluation of currency through a decree of the Ministry of Finance. In consequence Beethoven's yearly stipend from the three princes immediately depreciated from 4000 florins to a value of 1600 florins. Beethoven was greatly disturbed and unnecessarily alarmed by this financial loss. In general, he had a very strange attitude toward money and displayed excessive anxiety as to his financial security. To be sure, it may be objected that his increasing deafness, which made it impossible for him to accept a secure post at a princely court and which put an end to his career as a concert artist, would sufficiently explain his frequently very peculiar behavior in money matters. But there is testimony that this fear of poverty appeared long before there were any really disquieting indications that his hearing was affected. In 1792, when Beethoven was sent by the Elector to study with Haydn in Vienna, he was, as we mentioned earlier, allowed 50 ducats per quarter, which sum he regularly received until 1794. Together with the additional amounts which he was soon able to earn in Vienna, this assured him a modest but adequate income. Now in one of Beethoven's diaries we find, under the year 1792, the following note: "22 kr., chocolate for Haidn and me." [10] Hardly a biographer leaves this note unmentioned, for it is regarded as touching proof that Beethoven, comparatively poor as he was at the period, still spent money on "Papa Haydn." Only one biographer mentions a letter which Haydn wrote to the Elector and in which he stated that, on one and another occasion, he had advanced 500 gulden to his pupil Ludwig during the latter's first year in Vienna. Haydn's letter refers to Beethoven in terms of the highest praise and begs the Elector to increase his stipend, as he can hardly make ends meet in Vienna on *100 ducats* a year.[11] But it is known that Beethoven was allowed the sum of *200* ducats a year, which, according to the extant receipts, he received quarterly until 1794. Beethoven, then, had misrepresented the amount of his income to Haydn. Presumably the chief reason for this misrepresentation of his situation to Haydn was fear of poverty. This fear, then, had made its appearance at a time when there could as yet be hardly any question of a loss of hearing.

The devaluation had considerably decreased Beethoven's income. At the same time, most unfortunately, Prince Lobkowitz was forced to discontinue his payments, his debts having caused the sequestration of his estates. He was not able to resume payments until four years later. Count Kinsky who, like the Archduke Rudolf, declared himself ready to pay Beethoven's allowance in "notes of redemption" (which had the value of currency before its devaluation), lost his life by an unlucky fall from his horse, and a considerable time passed before his estate was settled and the payments to Beethoven were resumed (at their full value, be it said). The Archduke had begun to pay his share in "notes of redemption" as early as 1812. But these unfortunate events did not really impoverish Beethoven, for his great productivity during this period brought him in considerable sums for his works.

The years 1806–1813 were the most fruitful in Beethoven's life. During this period he composed, among many others, the following works: Opus 59, the three Rasoumowsky Quartets; Opus 60, the Fourth Symphony; Opus 61, the Violin Concerto; Opus 67, the Fifth Symphony; Opus 68, the Sixth Symphony; Opus 70, two Pianoforte Trios; Opus 73, the E-flat major Pianoforte Concerto; Opus 74, the "Harp" Quartet; Opus 84, the incidental music for Goethe's *Egmont;* Opus 92, the Seventh Symphony; Opus 93, the Eighth Symphony; Opus 95, the F-minor Quartet. An inquiring mind may speculate if the loss of his son-brother drove him to more intensive artistic creation. Such an opinion could find confirmation in the fact that, at a later period, Beethoven's attainment of a substitute for his brother Karl was accompanied by a striking decrease in his musical productivity for almost five years.

In any case, through his income from his works, Beethoven was in a position to give financial aid to Karl, who, like all civil servants, had been reduced to real poverty by the devaluation. We do not know what sums Ludwig advanced in this manner. He may well have found it a not unwelcome opportunity to put his brother under an obligation and thus to renew his hold upon him. Yet it appears that Ludwig had no great success with Karl and was again disillusioned. For he began a letter of 1812, to Count Brunswick, with whom he was then especially intimate, "Dear Friend, Brother!" . . . and ended it, "Farewell, dear Brother, be such to me; I have none to whom I could give that name . . ."[12] Soon after thus venting his complaint that his brothers had forsaken him, he was to receive a new blow. This time it came from his brother Johann.

We have said that in 1807 Johann bought an apothecary shop in Linz. The year 1809 brought him a certain prosperity there. He obtained contracts to supply medicines to the army, and, even as in our day, the profits from such transactions with the state were high. Johann was able to buy a large house, in which he rented an apartment to a doctor. The doctor's wife had a sister named Therese Obermeyer, who came to live with her sister and brother-in-law in the house. She became Johann's housekeeper, "and something more" as Thayer decorously puts it.[13] Johann was then thirty-five years old and unmarried. Ludwig learned of this relationship — how, we do not know. In a letter to Baron von Gleichenstein he wrote: ". . . What is the quickest and cheapest

way to get to Linz? — Please go into this matter thoroughly for
me . . ." [14]

In short, Ludwig went to Linz, resolved under any circumstances
to put an end to the relationship between Johann and Therese.
Concerning what followed, Thayer obtained information in Linz
in 1860 from "perfectly reliable sources." Ludwig, at whose disposal Johann had placed a large room with a view of the Danube,
began insisting that he must give up his relationship with Therese.
Johann considered this an unwarranted intrusion into his private
affairs and presumably said so to his brother; in any case he
refused to accede to his brother's demand. Hard words may have
passed, which embittered Ludwig and determined him to leave
no means untried, and to regard no means as beneath him, which
should lead to the accomplishment of his purpose. He called on
the Bishop of Linz (Ludwig's name apparently opened all doors
to him), he applied to the civil authorities, that is, presumably,
to the City Magistracy, and pushed the affair so earnestly that
he finally obtained a police order that the girl was to be taken
to Vienna if, by a certain day, she should still be in Linz. We
learn from Thayer that Johann was brought "almost to desperation" by Beethoven's action. He entered Ludwig's room and
showered him with reproaches and upbraidings, whereupon Ludwig too became angry. Thayer continues: ". . . and a scene followed — on which we shall draw the curtain. It was, unhappily,
more disgraceful to Ludwig than to Johann." [15] Here too Beethoven is spared by his biographer; Thayer lets the curtain fall,
so that we do not learn what was disgraceful to his hero. It may
be conjectured that Ludwig, in his blind fury, struck his brother
and was thrashed by Johann, who was big and strong. Blows between the brothers were not unusual, as we have had occasion to
mention earlier.

Johann now took extreme measures — how much from love of
Therese, how much from stubborn resistance to his brother, we
do not know. On November 8, 1812, he hastily married Therese,
just before the official order would have forced her to leave Linz.
Ludwig was beaten and had to give up the fight. On November 10
he returned to Vienna — we can imagine in what a state of bitter-

ness and disillusionment. Johann vanished from Ludwig's life for
many years. Ludwig had turned from him completely. A tragic
irony of fate brought it about that, fifteen years later, Therese
was the only member of the master's family to be present at his
deathbed.

After his return to Vienna, Beethoven was in a highly troubled
state; he had now lost his second brother to a woman. He felt alone
and forsaken by his "children." We have a comparatively reliable
means of gauging his state of mind during these years. His one
duty was the lessons which he was obligated to give to the Emperor's brother, Archduke Rudolf. When he was in a depressed
or disturbed condition, he repeatedly cancelled his appointments
with the Archduke.[16] From the period after his return from Linz,
we have an almost continuous series of such cancellations on flimsy
grounds; he usually says that his health is bad. In one such letter,
of January 1813, we find: "So far as my health is concerned, it is
about the same, the more so as it is influenced by moral causes,
which show no indication of ceasing so very soon . . ."[17] The
moral causes are presumably related to the unsuccessful outcome
of his journey to Linz.

His resentment against Karl may well have been increased by
his disappointment in his brother Johann. We are informed that,
during this period, Ludwig precipitated a violent scene with Karl.
Karl's son told his wife about it in later years. Beethoven, who
was in perpetual fear that his compositions would be stolen from
him, occasionally gave his manuscripts to Karl for safekeeping.
The composer was appallingly disorderly and often did not know
what notes he had entrusted to his brother. In any case, Karl's
son remembered that, when he was a boy of seven, the family
had been sitting at table; suddenly the door had opened, and
Beethoven had burst in with the words: "You thief, where are
my notes?" A violent scene had followed, and his mother had
had all she could do to reconcile the brothers. They had come
to blows; finally the notes were taken from a drawer and flung
down before the composer. Beethoven had then calmed himself
and had asked his brother to forgive him; but his brother had
refused to listen to him, and indeed had violently reviled him,
whereupon Beethoven had rushed out of the room without taking

the notes. The boy's father (i.e., Beethoven's brother Karl) had continued to revile Ludwig, saying that he would no longer have that "dragon" in his house, etc.[18]

This scene can be dated, for Karl's son says that at the time his father was already ill. It was at the beginning of 1813 that Karl was taken ill with tuberculosis. Ludwig may not yet have known how serious his brother's illness was. But shortly afterward, Karl's son reports, Ludwig happened to meet his brother on the Ferdinandsbrücke, one of the bridges that spanned the branch of the Danube which flows through Vienna (now the Danube Canal) — "and Ludwig was suddenly aware how ill Karl looked. He fell on his brother's neck and covered him with kisses in the public street, so that people watched in amazement. Then he conducted him to a fiacre [the Viennese term for a two-horse hackney carriage] to take him home with him, and almost overwhelmed him with kisses in the carriage." [19]

This animated description by Karl's son strikingly reveals the reversal in Beethoven's attitude toward his brother which began with the latter's illness and for which there is abundant testimony elsewhere.

Karl's tuberculosis was of a very serious nature and at first made rapid progress. When Ludwig recognized its seriousness, his concern for his brother's life caused the tender motherly relationship which had been latent for seven years to flare up again. What will not a mother do when her child is mortally ill! From this time on, then, we find increasing indications of a solicitous, pampering, and anxious love for his brother. At first Ludwig helped with money; Karl could not perform his official duties and had to furnish a substitute. The salary of civil servants had not at this time been raised to compensate for the devaluation of currency, so that they lived in poverty. In a letter written early in 1813 to Princess Kinsky, in which Beethoven asked that payment of the yearly income which the late prince had allowed him be continued, he explained the urgency of his request by referring to his financial expenditures for his brother:

. . . For you can easily imagine, when once one has counted upon something certain, that it is painful to be deprived of it for so long, the more so as I am obliged wholly to support an un-

fortunate sick brother together with his family, and have expended
my all without any consideration for myself, since I could hope
that, by the collection of my stipend, I could at least defray my own
livelihood.[20]

Even Thayer considers that Ludwig's statement that he had
"wholly to support an unfortunate sick brother together with his
family" must be taken with a grain of salt.[21] For Karl's family
still had the usufruct of the house which Karl had bought with his
father-in-law's legacy and the rents from which, coming from
eleven apartments, were certainly not inconsiderable.[22] Beethoven
not infrequently exaggerated adverse circumstances, if it was to
his advantage to do so. But it is certain that, during the earlier
period of his brother's illness, Ludwig had to provide pecuniary
support for Karl and his family. The rapid progress of the disease
gave Karl reason to fear that his end was near. He was concerned
for his son's material future, and, as he had realized that Beethoven's old love for him had revived, he attempted to make Ludwig's financial assistance extend to his son. To this end, on April 12,
1813, he executed a will which concludes as follows:

> Inasmuch as I am convinced of the open-hearted disposition of my
> brother Ludwig van Beethoven, I desire that after my death he
> undertake the guardianship of my surviving minor son, Karl Bee-
> thoven. I therefore request the honorable court to confer the
> guardianship upon my said brother after my death and beg my
> dear brother to accept the office and to aid my child like a father
> with word and deed in all cases. — Witness my hand and seal.
>
> > Karl v. Beethoven
> > R.I. Cashier [23]

Karl's signature is followed by Ludwig's and those of three witnesses.

With the exception of his birth registration in 1806, this is the
first time that Ludwig's nephew Karl is mentioned in the extant
documentary material. No letter, no diary, not one of the scores
of reminiscences of Beethoven left by various persons, mentions
his nephew before the date of this document. At the time of his
father's illness, the boy was seven; yet we receive the impression
that he now enters Beethoven's life for the first time. Beethoven's
brother Karl himself opened the way for Ludwig's relationship
to his nephew by appointing him the boy's guardian in this docu-

ment. To be sure, as we shall see later, Ludwig interpreted the appointment very differently from Karl and extended the relationship far beyond what Karl had intended for his son.

As often happens, even in cases where tuberculosis makes rapid progress at first, the process was arrested, Karl recovered, and was able to go back to work. He was even made cashier of the "Universal-Staats-Schuldenkassa," a promotion which brought with· it an increase in salary. Ludwig provided the security which had to be deposited in connection with this promotion. Soon afterward, it was arranged that public officials should be paid in silver, so that Karl's salary now sufficed for the needs of his family, and, during the next two years, he was hardly in need of Ludwig's support.

Karl's illness had revived Ludwig's maternally solicitous love for his brother. His visits to Karl's sickbed brought him into touch with his brother's family life, and perhaps awakened in the lonely bachelor a longing for similar relationships. On May 13, 1813 he wrote in his diary: ". . . Fearful circumstances, which do not suppress my feeling for domesticity . . ." [24] His numerous letters of excuse to the Archduke, who represented the only duty to which he was obligated, also show that he was in a disturbed state of mind. In one of them we read: ". . . if I fail, or have failed in anything, may Your Highness most graciously bear with me, for so many unhappy events in succession have really put me into a state verging on distraction. . . ." [25]

Early in 1815, after eighteen months of comparative improvement, Karl's condition became worse again, and now Ludwig's tenderly solicitous love for his brother gushed forth. As a mother would gladly fulfill even the most unreasonable wishes of her sick child, so Ludwig tried, for example, to obtain some peacocks for his dying brother, Karl having expressed a wish — certainly a strange one for a man in his condition — for these birds. In a letter to Varena, who was organizing charity concerts in Graz and to whom Beethoven had sent some compositions to be performed for the benefit of the Ursulines there, he wrote, under date of February 3, 1815:

> One of my brothers is ailing and, as such people commonly have fancies, hearing that I am acquainted with you, he asks me to send

you the enclosed; perhaps our good Ursulines can help in the matter.

Forgive me for burdening you with such a commission; if the creatures he mentions should be available to you without effort, I beg you will inform me at once; I will assume all the expenses, in order to procure him a pleasure; as I said, he is ailing and hankers after such things.

In haste, with true respect, your friend

Ludwig van Beethoven.[26]

A letter to Antonie von Brentano, who was in Frankfurt and whom he addresses as "respected friend," speaks for itself. In it we read:

> . . . Another matter which I must bring to your attention. It concerns a pipe-bowl! A pipe-bowl! — Among the persons (their number is infinite) who suffer, is my brother, who has been forced by ill health to retire on pension. This is a very difficult situation in these days, I do whatever I possibly can, but it is not enough. — He owns a pipe-bowl, which he thinks he can sell to the best advantage in Frankfurt. It is difficult to refuse him anything in his ailing condition, and in view of this I take the liberty of asking you to allow him to send you this pipe-bowl. You have so many visitors, among whom you may perhaps have the luck to dispose of it. My brother [thinks] you would perhaps get ten louis d'or for it. I leave this to your wisdom. He needs a great deal, has to keep a horse and carriage, in order to be able to live (for his life is very dear to him, even as I would gladly lose mine!!) [27]

As we see, Ludwig can refuse his sick son-brother no request; indeed he goes so far as to suggest that he would gladly give his own life to save his brother's, just as a mother is willing to do for her dying child. Once when he used his brother's horses to go to Jedlersee, not far from Vienna, he apparently left them there and took another conveyance for the return trip. Immediately afterward, he wrote to Brauchle, tutor in the household of the Countess Erdödy, whom he had visited in Jedlersee:

> Dear Brauchle! I had scarcely got home before I found my brother making lamentable inquiries about the horses. — Please do me the favor to go to Lang-Enzersdorf about the horses; take horses at my expense in Jedlersee, I will most gladly recompense you. — His sickness (my brother's) is accompanied by a sort of unrest, let us be of help where we can, I am obliged to act thus and not otherwise! I await a speedy fulfillment of my request and a

friendly answer on the subject from you. — Spare no expenses, I
will gladly bear them. It is not worth while to let someone suffer
for the sake of a few beggarly gulden.

In haste your true friend Beethoven [28]

Karl apparently asked Ludwig's friend and patroness, Countess
Erdödy, for money behind his brother's back. What motivated
him is not known; perhaps, in momentary need of money, he
wished to procure the necessary sum without having to pay for
it by a mortifying dependence upon his brother. To Ludwig, a
love relationship and possession were one and the same, and
financial dependence on the part of the love object was for him
one of the most effective means of gaining possession. Under
other circumstances, Beethoven would doubtless have reacted by
accusing and reviling his brother upon learning that the latter
had approached the Countess for money without his knowledge.
But his sick child must be forgiven for everything. So he wrote
to the Countess on February 29, 1815: "My brother has written
to you. You must be tolerant with him, he is really an unfortunate,
suffering man." [29]

These few surviving examples clearly reveal solicitous and
anxious maternal love for a sick child. Ludwig finally made a last
effort to help his brother, and doubtless also to bind him yet more
closely to himself. In a contract which he signed with S. A. Steiner
& Co., he stipulated that Karl should make pianoforte arrangements of Beethoven's works for the firm, under Beethoven's supervision. However, the progress of Karl's disease prevented him
from fulfilling this clause of the contract.

Ludwig's intimate relationship with Karl during the latter's
last illness brought him into closer contact with Johanna, Karl's
wife, and with Karl's son, whom, since his first name was the same
as his father's, it is convenient to call simply "the nephew" here.
Mother and son were to play the leading role in Beethoven's life
thereafter.

We know nothing concerning Ludwig's attitude to Johanna
before 1815. However, his reaction to Karl's marriage, and above
all his breaking off relations with Karl, lead to the inescapable
conclusion that Ludwig was thoroughly hostile to Johanna. We
have already seen that he opposed his brother Johann's marriage

with Therese and how he campaigned against her. It is unlikely that his feeling toward Karl's wife was any more friendly; probably only her premature pregnancy prevented him from insisting that the relationship be ended. The earliest document expressing Ludwig's hostile attitude to Johanna dates from 1815. We find it, in his own hand, on a sketch sheet; it is not clear if it was to be developed into a letter or if it represents a notation of the thoughts which he harbored against her. It reads:

> To Johanna van Beethoven
> As you have lived in great error concerning yourself, I consider it necessary to take up my standpoint here [sic], for it has often happened hitherto that, after you have vented your spiteful tricks on me, you have then tried to make up for them by a certain friendliness. — You were not absolved from your punishment — order is fitting to the momentousness [? of the occasion] in view of your sacred dead — and mine. . . . Apparently you believe I have not noticed all this, but, only to disabuse you of this error, I will merely state to you that, if perhaps you are anxious to make a better impression on me, this is precisely the method of doing the opposite. For that very reason I am again reluctantly forced to regret that my brother has saved you from your just punishment, that your dealings not I alone thus . . .[30]

At least we can deduce from this fragment that there had been disagreements between Johanna and Ludwig, that Johanna tried to smooth things over, which only increased Beethoven's distrust, and that Karl had taken his wife's side in the matter, certainly to Beethoven's renewed displeasure. What sort of incident occasioned the quarrel, the fragment does not tell us.

Johanna was by no means a good housekeeper, she was incapable of spending money thriftily, and this gave rise to many quarrels between husband and wife. Nohl reports that Karl had once become so angry over her inability to handle money that he had run a knife through her hand at table. She still showed the scar as an old woman.[31] Yet in general we get the impression that, in the altercations between Ludwig and Johanna, Karl took his wife's side and defended her. We never hear that Karl complained of his wife; on the whole, he appears to have been satisfied with her and to have forgiven her the difficulties in which her incompetence sometimes involved the family. Johanna's lack of good sense in money matters may, furthermore, have been the reason why, in the will of 1813 cited above, Karl appointed Ludwig guardian, partly as security for his son's financial future. How greatly Beethoven was disturbed by his contact with Karl's family, and doubtless more especially with Johanna, appears from a letter to Brauchle, which dates from this period. He wrote: ". . . The most miserable, most ordinary unpoetic scenes surround me — and make me ill-tempered." [32]

At the same time that his bitterness against Johanna was increasing during Karl's illness, he developed a growing interest in her son, the nephew.

Beethoven himself mentions his nephew for the first time in a letter of February 1, 1815, to the firm of Steiner, whose proprietor he playfully addressed in letters as "Lieutenant-General":

> . . . In addition you might well give my brother the collections of Clementi's, Mozart's, Haydn's pianoforte works, he needs them for his little son; do this, my dearest Steiner and be not of stone [Stein], however stony your name may be. Farewell, most eminent Lieutenant-General; I am always
>
> Your most obedient Generalissimo
Ludwig van Beethoven [33]

In a letter to Czerny, of 1815, we read:

> . . . Be so good as to tell me at what hour of the evening you get home on the day when you give Karl a lesson, you often give him more than an hour, so I hear, for which kindness I cannot sufficiently thank you; . . .[34]

Ludwig, then, took an interest in his nephew's musical education.

On May 1, 1815 Ludwig wrote asking Dr. Johann Kanka, a lawyer in Prague, to demand payment of the arrears of Count Kinsky's share of his yearly stipend. He explains the urgency of his request in the following terms: ". . . *My situation has meanwhile become worse; I have to provide entirely for my brother's son.* . . ."[35] At this time the boy was living with his parents, and his father was receiving his full salary, so that there was little real basis for such a statement. The sentence quoted, especially the word "entirely," acquires a deeper significance if we take later events into consideration; it sounds like a premonition of the future, like a resolve which Ludwig later put into execution.

In November, 1815 Karl's condition became rapidly worse; he felt his end approaching and, on November 14, decided to make another will. The significant portions of it for our presentation read:

> 5. I appoint my brother Ludwig van Beethoven guardian. Inasmuch as this, my deeply beloved brother has often aided me with true brotherly love in the most magnanimous and noblest manner, I ask, in full confidence and trust in his noble heart, that he shall bestow the love and friendship which he often showed me, upon my son Karl, and do all that is possible to promote the intellectual training and further welfare of my son. I know that he will not deny me this, my request.
>
> 6. Convinced of the uprightness of Hrn. Dr. Schönauer, Appellate and Court Advocate, I appoint him Curator for probate, as also for my son Karl with the understanding that he be consulted in all matters concerning the property of my son.[36]

Ludwig was not among the signers this time, nor was his friend Oliva, who had signed the previous will. The witnesses were the owners of houses in the immediate vicinity and a neighbor. This second will is longer than the first, the provisions are set forth in numbered paragraphs and obviously drawn up by a lawyer. Karl appoints a lawyer as curator, to see that the testamentary provisions are carried out and to look after his son's property. It is especially striking in this second will that Karl makes particular reference to his wife's property, which she brought to the marriage as her dowry, and separates it from his estate. He further designates certain objects as Johanna's property — hence not forming part of his estate — among them the aforementioned peacocks. Johanna, then, had paid for the peacocks, although in the letter to Varena quoted earlier, Ludwig had told him that he would undertake any expense to give his brother pleasure.

These differences from the first will leave the impression that Karl wished to protect Johanna's property from some threat. It is not difficult to divine from what direction the threat came. Ludwig's behavior had probably left no doubt regarding his bitter hostility toward Johanna, and since Karl knew Ludwig's impulsive nature only too well, he attempted to protect Johanna through the provisions of his will. Even so, the will made no provision against the greatest danger of all. Apparently at the insistence of

the mother, who was concerned for her most precious possession
— her son — Karl added a codicil to his will on the same day,
November 14. It reads:

Codicil to my will. —

Having learned that my brother, Hr. Ludwig van Beethoven,
desires after my death to take wholly to himself my son Karl, and
wholly to withdraw him from the supervision and training of his
mother, and inasmuch as the best of harmony does not exist between my brother and my wife, I have found it necessary to add
to my will that I by no means desire that my son be taken away
from his mother, but that he shall always and so long as his future
career permits remain with his mother, to which end the guardianship of him is to be exercised by her as well as my brother. Only
by unity can the object which I had in view in appointing my
brother guardian of my son, be attained, wherefore, for the welfare of my child, I recommend *compliance* to my wife and more
moderation to my brother.

God permit them to be harmonious for the sake of my child's
welfare. This is the last wish of the dying husband and brother.

Vienna, November 14, 1815.
                    Karl van Beethoven [37]

The next day, Karl van Beethoven died.

IV

THE ACQUISITION OF THE CHILD

KARL'S death came with unexpected suddenness, as some-times occurs in advanced cases of tuberculosis. Ludwig himself describes his first reaction to it, in a letter of excuse to the Archduke: ". . . Ever since yesterday afternoon I have lain exhausted by many efforts occasioned by my unhappy brother's so sudden death . . ." [1]

Yet he was soon to arouse himself to feverish activity. First, the suddenness of his brother's death gave him the opportunity to cast a terrible suspicion on his sister-in-law Johanna. He expressed the opinion that Karl had died so suddenly because his wife had poisoned him. So far as we can ascertain, this is the first time that the idea of poisoning arose in Beethoven's mind. We shall find him harboring it frequently hereafter.

Beethoven must have expressed his suspicion in no uncertain terms; for his friend Dr. Bertolini, who was his physician at the time, felt it necessary to examine the body of Karl in order to calm him. We do not know if the examination consisted in a regular post-mortem; in any case it showed that the suspicion "was unfounded." [2]

Unfortunately Dr. Bertolini later destroyed all the documents in his possession either emanating from or concerning Beethoven, in order to spare the composer their publication.

In any case, despite Bertolini's finding, Beethoven was by no means willing to drop his accusation that Johanna was guilty of her husband's death. To be sure, he abandoned the idea of poison, but he continued to hold that Karl had met death at his wife's hands. Thus on November 22, 1815 — a week, that is, after Karl's death — he wrote to Ferdinand Ries, who was now in London:

. . . My poor unfortunate brother has just died; he had a
bad wife . . . The poor man had changed greatly in his last
years and I can say that I heartily pity him, and I am glad now
that I can say to myself that I neglected nothing in respect of care
for him.[3]

In the first sentence quoted from this letter, Beethoven informs
his friend that his brother, whom he describes as poor and unfortunate, has died, and immediately afterward, in the same sentence,
separated from this statement only by a semicolon, he says that
he had a bad wife. Psychological experience shows that statements which thus stand side by side belong together. The connection must therefore be taken as psychologically a causal one, somewhat as follows: "My brother was poor and unfortunate and died
because he had a bad wife." In addition, Ludwig's observation
that his brother had changed in his last years, so that he could not
but sincerely pity him, can only refer to Karl's marriage, which,
in Ludwig's opinion, was the cause of his destruction. This assumption is confirmed by a few lines written in Ludwig's hand on a
sketch sheet of this period:

O look down, Brother! Yes, I have mourned you and mourn you
still. Oh, why were you not more upright toward me! You would
still be alive and would surely not have died so miserably, had
you sooner turned away . . . and come wholly to me.[4]

There is little doubt that the points of suspension which Beethoven
used here are to be replaced by "from Johanna"; Karl, then, would
not have died so miserably if he had turned from Johanna and
come wholly to Ludwig. Ludwig does not write the name "Johanna," just as one is afraid to pronounce the name of an evil spirit,
for fear of thus conjuring it up.

Similarly, in his letter to the singer Anna Milder-Hauptmann
in Berlin, dated January 6, 1816, we read:

My poor unfortunate brother has died . . .[5]

Ludwig is filled with pity for his brother, for he regards his sufferings and death as the result of the disastrous influence which Johanna exercised upon her husband.

In Ludwig's view, his brother Karl had been destroyed by
Johanna; three years earlier, he had lost his brother Johann to

a woman. But he still had a close male relative whom he could save from woman's fatal claws. This was his nephew. The nine-year-old boy entered perfectly into the pattern of a continuation of Ludwig's struggle against Johanna for his brother Karl. As Karl's son, the boy was the natural heir of Ludwig's relationship to Karl. There was a further circumstance which strengthened the equivalence of the two. They bore the same name, "Karl." In the unconscious, such a coincidence of names is of great signifi-cance, for it often establishes an identity between the bearers of the name; thus the child Karl was a suitable substitute for Lud-wig's brother as an object of maternal love. Hence the child must be wrested from his real mother.

Karl's will, with the codicil, was delivered to the Landrechte (General Court) on November 17, 1815. The Landrechte were the courts for the nobility. In those days in Austria there was still a sharp distinction between the nobility and non-noble persons, and it was among the privileges of the nobility that legal matters in which they were involved were heard before a different court from that of ordinary mortals.

When Ludwig came to Vienna, he was introduced into the aristocratic society of the city by Count Waldstein, who had be-friended him from his days in Bonn and who, now a Knight of the Teutonic Order, was living in Vienna. It appears that the "van" was useful in this connection. Now, the Dutch "van" is by no means a title of nobility if it indicates origin from a par-ticular place. "Beethoven" means "beet field," and the "van" indi-cates the local origin of the family. In Bonn, which is close to the Dutch border, everyone naturally knew that the "van" Beethovens were not of noble blood. This was not so in Vienna, where Lud-wig was apparently accepted as noble. In any case, he seems not to have denied it, and his brothers too behaved as if they were noble — as the depositing of the will with the Landrechte, the court for the nobility, shows. On November 22, 1815, the I.-R. Lower Austrian Landrechte "appointed the widow of the de-ceased, Johanna van Beethoven, guardian, the brother of the de-ceased, Ludwig van Beethoven, co-guardian of the minor son Karl." [6]

First of all, then, the court took into consideration the expressed will of the "dying husband and brother." As co-guardian, it was Ludwig's principal right and duty to supervise the financial affairs of his ward and to advise his mother in matters concerning his education. Ludwig, however, had resolved to make the boy his own. On November 28 he submitted an appeal to the Landrechte to transfer the guardianship to himself alone. The next day, the court ordered the petitioner and Dr. Schönauer to appear before it on December 2. On that date the matter was deferred to December 13. On December 13 Ludwig declared before the court that he "could produce weighty reasons for the total exclusion of the widow from the guardianship." On December 15 he was ordered by the court to produce these reasons within three days, "failing which, the preparation of the guardianship decree to the widow would be proceeded with at once." On the same day Beethoven petitioned the City Magistracy for an official certificate concerning the "condemnation of his [the nephew's] mother, Johanna van Beethoven, on an investigation for embezzlement." The Magistracy informed Ludwig that the "necessary disclosures" would be officially communicated to the court.[7] Now it is true that Johanna had once been subjected to "police punishment." In 1811 she was condemned to a month of "house arrest" by action of the Vienna Landesgericht (Circuit Court), on the ground that she had been guilty of embezzlement against her own husband.[8] We have already mentioned that she was incompetent in handling money, and that this had caused many quarrels between herself and her husband. As related above, Karl's anger once expressed itself by a knife-wound in Johanna's hand. A similar outburst of anger may have led to the denunciation which resulted in the month of "house arrest."

We encounter almost insuperable difficulties when we attempt to obtain a picture of Johanna's personality. Beethoven, in his burning hatred of the woman, has represented her in his statements as abysmally evil, and the power and influence of his own personality have forced everyone to see her as he wished her to be seen. Unfortunately, we have no document from Johanna's own hand which would help us to see her objectively. The biographers almost all adopted Beethoven's view of her — after all, it gave them yet another welcome opportunity to represent their "hero" in a better light. They frequently take over, word for word, the humiliating and insulting terms which Beethoven applied to Johanna.

We know almost nothing of Johanna's childhood and girlhood. In a Conversation Book dating from 1823, the nephew writes of his mother:

> I remember that she [Johanna] often told me that, whenever she wanted money, her father said: I won't give you any, but if you can *take* money without my knowing it, it belongs to you. Naturally, in this way she learned to steal without retribution.[9]

This was doubtless said in explanation and excuse on one of the many occasions when Ludwig inveighed against Johanna in his nephew's presence. We cannot assume that Johanna received any higher education; her degree of education doubtless corresponded to that of her husband. She was a poor manager, and her sense of honor in money matters was apparently very lax. The attitude of her father, who, as witnessed above, practically taught her to steal, may have been responsible for this. As for the rest of her character, it can hardly be reconstructed from the prejudiced material available. As we proceed, we shall attempt to point out at least all the obvious slanders upon Johanna. It must be emphasized that there is no evidence that Johanna was a bad mother, that she neglected or mistreated her son; she was concerned for her child, and she suffered under the inhuman cruelty with which Beethoven kept him from her for many years. In addition, the surviving descriptions of the boy during the time succeeding his father's death indicate that he was well behaved and exhibited no pathological traits; this supports the assumption that Johanna was not a bad mother. Nor would the dying father have entrusted his son to an unworthy woman.

On January 9, 1816 the court decided to confer the sole guardianship upon Beethoven. On January 19 Beethoven appeared in court to "take the vows for the performance of his duties." The official record reads:

> Today appeared Ludwig van Beethoven as the legally appointed guardian of his nephew Karl, and vowed with solemn handgrasp before the assembled council to perform his duties.[10]

So now he was sole guardian of the nine-year-old boy. We may assume that influence was brought to bear upon the court to induce it to take this decision. It has been shown what influence Beethoven had with official circles in Linz when he applied to the bishop and the town officers and obtained the banishment of his brother's sweetheart. How much more could he not do in 1815 in Vienna, where he was surrounded by influential friends belonging to the highest aristocracy! Without such patronage, the court would hardly have considered a "police punishment" sufficient reason for excluding the boy's mother from the guardianship.

After this short struggle, then, Ludwig entered into sole possession of the boy. His reaction to this turn of events was literally overwhelming. A feeling of joy possessed him, such as nothing in his life before or after ever aroused in him. We may say that the acquisition of the boy was the most significant experience of which we have any knowledge throughout his life. From then until his death, his relation to his nephew remained his most important emotional experience. There is no doubt that it gave him such a sense of joy because it unconsciously allowed him to become the boy's mother.

The child's real mother, Johanna, who thus became his rival, he thenceforth persecuted with relentless hatred. His aim was to be the boy's only mother. Hence he exerted every effort in a systematic attempt to destroy the boy's relationship to his real mother. On a sketch sheet dating from 1816 he admonished himself:

> You regard Karl as your own child. Heed no gossip, no pettinesses, in comparison with this sacred goal.[11]

The "sacred goal" is his own motherhood!

On February 29 he wrote to his friend Ries in London:

> . . . I have been unwell for some time; the death of my brother affected my disposition and my works. — Salomon's [12] death greatly grieves me, for he was an upright man whom I remember from my childhood. You have become testamentary executor,[13] and I at the same time guardian of the child of my poor dead brother. You will hardly have had as much vexation as this death has brought me; yet I have the sweet consolation of having rescued a poor innocent child from the hands of an unworthy mother.[14]

Here the idea of "rescuing" the boy from the danger of Johanna is clearly expressed. In reality, there is nowhere the slightest suggestion that the boy had suffered through his mother. All indications show that he was devoted to her. For Ludwig, his nephew represented a continuation of his brother. Since he believed that the latter had been destroyed by his wife, he inevitably considered Johanna a terrible danger to his nephew too, a danger from which he must rescue him. But it was precisely this "rescue" which also made the nephew his own child. In Ludwig's unconscious, the rescue was experienced as a birth-act.

On May 13, 1816, he wrote to Countess Erdödy:

> My respected, dear friend! You might well, and with reason, suppose that your memory had become utterly extinguished in me. However, this is mere appearance; my brother's death caused me great pain, and immediately afterward great exertions to rescue my dear nephew from his vicious mother. They were successful. However, until now I have not yet been able to do anything better for him than to put him in an institute,[15] hence at a distance from me. And what is an institute compared with the direct sympathetic care of a father for his child? For as such I now regard myself, and I am casting about for some way of having this dear treasure closer to me, so that I may influence him more quickly and beneficially. But how hard that is for me! — My health too has been in a shaky condition for six weeks now, so that I often think of my death, yet not with fear, only for my poor Karl should I die too soon.[16]

Here Beethoven speaks of the great effort which the rescue cost him, but through which he became the boy's father. His whole future behavior shows, however, that through the effort of the rescue he became the boy's *mother*. Almost always, when he calls himself the boy's "father," we have to substitute "mother," for it was as such that he experienced his possession of the boy.

The following letter confirms our interpretation that the rescue was unconsciously experienced by Ludwig as a birth-act. On September 6, 1816 he wrote to Councillor Kanka at Prague:

> I am furthermore full of cares, for I am *truly* the *bodily* father of my dead brother's child, and in this connection I *could also have brought* the second part of the Magic Flute *into the world,* for I have to deal with a Queen of the Night.[17]

Concerning the name "Queen of the Night" for Johanna, we shall have something to say later. Here it will be enough if we remind the reader that in Mozart's *Magic Flute* the "Queen of the Night" represents the evil principle. In this letter to Kanka, Beethoven says that he has become "truly the bodily father" of his nephew. "In this connection" (i.e., "on this occasion") — when he won the boy — he could "also have brought the second part of the Magic Flute into the world." But only the mother can "bring into the world." "This occasion," then, was the act of rescue, or of birth, which gave him possession of the boy. In this indirect form, he himself says that he has become the *bodily mother* of the boy. If we take into consideration the fact that in Ludwig's unconscious his nephew Karl was equated with his brother Karl, we shall realize that the act of rescue represents a rebirth of the brother in the nephew through Ludwig as mother. Such fantasies of rebirth form part of the archaic common property of mankind; the psychoanalyst is as familiar with them as is the mythologist or the student of religions.

If his brother Karl, before his death, was Ludwig's spiritual child, so in Ludwig's unconscious he was, through the act of rescue, reborn in Ludwig's nephew Karl as Ludwig's bodily child. Only if we grasp this deeper meaning of the rescue and taking possession of the boy — only if we see it as a birth-act through which, in his unconscious, his nephew becomes his bodily child — will all the aspects of Ludwig's future relationship to his nephew become comprehensible.

V

"MOTHERHOOD"

BEETHOVEN was not completely satisfied by the exclusive guardianship awarded him by the court — first of all, because the nine-year-old boy was still living with his mother and attending a public school.

He would have liked to take the boy home with him at once; but he realized that his "domestic establishment," if the term can be applied to his living quarters, was not suited to house and care for a child. His friends too doubtless pointed out to him the impossibility of such an undertaking.

The dreadful condition of Ludwig's lodging was described, for example, by Baron de Trémont, who visited him in 1809:

> . . . His lodging consisted, I believe, of only two rooms. The first contained a closed alcove with his bed, but was so small and dark that he had to make his toilet in the other room.
>
> Picture to yourself the extreme of dirt and disorder: pools of water decorated the floor; a rather ancient grand piano, on which dust competed for room with sheets of written or printed notes. Under it — I do not exaggerate — an unemptied chamber-pot. Beside it a small walnut table, well accustomed to having the contents of the inkwell overturned on it. Numerous quill pens full of dried ink, compared with which the proverbial inn pens would have been excellent. Most of the chairs had straw seats and were decorated with clothes and dishes full of the remains of the previous day's supper.[1]

Gerhard von Breuning has this to say of the lodging which Beethoven occupied during the last years of his life:

> . . . yet his furniture remained in disorder, his papers and various goods and chattels dusty and in confusion, his clothes unbrushed despite all the dazzling whiteness and cleanliness of his linen and

despite his frequent bodily ablutions. . . . He had always, when he had sat at his table composing for some time and felt his head heated by it, been in the habit of hurrying to the washstand, splashing pitchers of water over his heated head, and after these coolings off, followed by only a hasty drying, to go back to work or sometimes to take a short walk in the fresh air. In what haste all this was done, so that he should not be torn from his flights of imagination, and how little care was taken to really dry his soaked mop of hair, is shown by the fact that, all unknown to him, the water he had splashed over his head sometimes poured freely onto the floor, and indeed soaked through it, appeared on the ceiling of the lodgers below, and in turn occasionally led to unpleasant recriminations on the part of the latter, of the janitor, and finally of the landlord, and indeed to notice to vacate the premises.[2]

Into such a household he could not at once take his child. But at this period there was a very well-known and, it would seem, deservedly celebrated private school for boys, conducted by its proprietor, Kajetan Giannatasio del Rio. The family, in addition to Giannatasio, consisted of his wife and two daughters, Fanny and Nanni. The daughters were musically gifted and ardent admirers of the composer. Beethoven visited Giannatasio's Institute with a friend, the writer Karl Bernard; his nephew accompanied them. The school and the family made a most favorable impression on the visitors. Ludwig decided to put the boy in the Institute as soon as possible. At the end of January, 1816, he wrote to Giannatasio:

> I did not properly read your letter until I reached home yesterday; I am ready to confide Karl to you at any moment, but I think it should not be until Monday after the examination, — but earlier if you find it proper. In any case, later will certainly be best to send him away from here to Mölk [3] or elsewhere, there he will hear and see no more of his bestial mother, and where everything around him is strange, he will find less support and can gain love and respect only through his own courage. In haste your
>
> Beethoven [4]

It is easy to imagine what sort of a picture Ludwig gave Giannatasio of the boy's mother Johanna when, in his letter to him immediately after the first visit, he refers to her as a "bestial mother" of whom the boy is to hear and see no more. If the director of the school was only half as impressed by Beethoven's

music and personality as his two daughters were, Beethoven's
hostile attitude toward Johanna must have had a decided influence upon him.[5] Giannatasio's later behavior shows that he soon
became the tool of Ludwig's burning hatred of Johanna.

Ludwig's next letter to Giannatasio is dated February 1, 1816.
He announces that his nephew will enter the school the following
day:

> I tell you with great pleasure that tomorrow at last I shall bring
> you the precious pledge which has been entrusted to me. — Fur-
> thermore, I beg you once again to permit his mother no influence
> at all [as to] how or when she is to see him; all this I will discuss
> with you in greater detail tomorrow. — You may well even have
> your servants watched to a certain extent, for mine, although in
> regard to another matter, have already been bribed by her! Full
> particulars by word of mouth tomorrow, though silence would be
> preferable to me in the matter, — but for the sake of your future
> citizen of the world this grievous communication is required.
>
> With great respect, your most obedient servant and friend Bee-
> thoven

[In Karl's hand:]

> I am very glad to come to you and am your
>   Carl van Beethoven [6]

As we see, Beethoven is anxious to prejudice Giannatasio still
further against Johanna and to implant in him the ugly suspicion
that she may bribe his servants.

On February 2 the boy entered the Institute. His mother, apparently in despair over parting with her son, came to the school
to see him every day, or sent a messenger to fetch the boy and
bring him to her during his free time. It is easy to see that this
was disturbing to the regular conduct of the school. But Thayer,
the biographer, is influenced just as Giannatasio was by Beethoven's hatred of Johanna, when he describes the mother's attempts to see her little boy every day as an "intolerable annoyance."[7] In a note dated February 11 — that is, when the boy had
been in the school only nine days — Giannatasio demanded of
Ludwig "a formal authority in a few lines for refusing without
further ado to permit her to fetch her son." Ludwig wrote in
reply: "In regard to the mother I beg you for a few days, on the

pretext that he is busy, not to let her approach him at all." 8 At
the same time he went to see Joseph von Schmerling, a member
of the court which had given him the exclusive guardianship;
there was now a connection with Schmerling: Nanni Giannatasio
was engaged to Leopold von Schmerling, a brother of Joseph's.
Ludwig expected that Joseph von Schmerling would advise him
what measures he could take to exclude Johanna from any communication with her son. He imparted the result of this conversation to Giannatasio in the following letter:

February 17, 1816

This, my worthy friend, is the substance of my day-before-
yesterday's conversation with Herr von Schmerling: Without the
permission of his guardian, Karl is upon no excuse to be taken
from the Institute, his mother can never visit him there. If she
wishes to see him, she must apply to the guardian, who will make
arrangements therefor.

A document in these terms will be issued for me by the Landrechte. Until then, you can regard this as authoritative for your
treatment of the woman; today about twelve o'clock I and my
friend Bernard must trouble you, for we must at once draft the
document in your presence, and also so that what you wish will be
included, S[chmerling] wants to be sure that your letter is attached too. Last night the Queen of the Night was at the Artists'
Ball until 3 o'clock, exposing not only her mentality but also her
body — for 20 florins, people whispered, she was to be had! O
horrible! And are we to trust our precious treasure to those hands
even for an instant? No, certainly not! I embrace you heartily as
my friend and at the same time as Karl's father   Your
                                        Ludwig van Beethoven 9

This is the first extant document in which Ludwig calls Johanna
"Queen of the Night." From the context it is clear that he means
by this to brand her a whore, obviously to the end of making her
appear as bad as possible to Giannatasio. To be sure, we cannot
ascertain if Johanna really attended a masquerade ball so soon
after her husband's death. But material will be produced in due
course which clearly testifies against any assumption that Johanna
could be bought for money, and which makes it extremely improbable that she was generally regarded as a "bad woman."

Ludwig, Bernard, and Giannatasio now drew up a formal application to the Landrechte petitioning the court to grant the

guardian full authority "to exclude the widow and her agents from all or any direct communication with the boy." [10] On February 20, the Landrechte, doubtless influenced by Schmerling, granted the application, but with a proviso. Apparently the court found it too inhuman to exclude the mother from all contact with her son. Hence it added that the mother might visit her son "in his leisure hours, without disturbing the course of his education or the domestic routine, in the company of a person to be appointed by the guardian or the director of the educational institution." [11] To be sure, this put the arrangement of such visits into the uncle's hands. Ludwig triumphantly communicated the court's decision to Giannatasio:

> . . . A decision of the Landrechte just brought to me orders that in regard to visits by the mother of my nephew or to his being taken from the house, absolutely nothing must be done that I have not myself appointed, assented to, and approved, and that any arrangement and decision in these matters is at all times left entirely to me. Hence the boy's mother has only to apply to me if she wishes to see him, whereupon I will in my discretion decide when and how and whether it may take place. [12]

We shall see how mercilessly he employed this right against Johanna.

So now Ludwig had the boy all to himself. From this time on, we find his own frequent expressions of his joy plentifully confirmed by the observations of others.

Fanny Giannatasio, the elder of the headmaster's two daughters, later described the effect of the nephew on the uncle at the time when the boy entered the Institute:

> . . . When Beethoven's brother, an official in Vienna, died, B[eethoven] was appointed co-guardian of his son, the boy's mother was alive, but after a legal action she was excluded from the guardianship. The boy was, I believe, nine years old. And now, if I may use the expression, a new emotional life flowered in Beethoven; he seemed to wish to dedicate himself to the boy body and soul and, according as he was happy through his nephew or involved in troubles or subjected to grief, he wrote, or could write nothing. — It was in 1816 that he first came to our house to put his beloved Karl in the school which my father had started in 1798. This event was a particular pleasure to the daughters of the house, and I can still see the lively way in which Bee-

thoven turned from side to side and how we, disregarding his
companion and interpreter, Herr Bernard, later editor of the
Wiener Zeitung, addressed ourselves directly to Beethoven's ear;
for even then one had to be extremely close to him to make oneself understood by him.

From that time on we had the pleasure of seeing him frequently,
and later, when my father moved the Institute to the suburbs,
Landstrasser Glacis, he too took lodgings nearby and the following winter he formed part of our family circle almost every evening.[13]

Another account of the relationship between uncle and nephew
reads:

In the Streichers' house, there was commonly a musical enter-
tainment once a week in a room especially built for the purpose
acoustically, and during the years 1816–1818 Beethoven seldom
failed to be present. Usually, pianoforte compositions were performed. On these occasions Beethoven had often brought his
nephew Karl with him. Once the boy, then nine or ten years
of age, fell asleep on Beethoven's lap in front of the instrument
during the performance of a composition. Immediately afterward
something of Beethoven's was played, and at the first chord Karl
quickly waked and looked up with a smile. He was asked how he
could sleep and what had caused his sudden awaking, whether he
too knew who the piece was by; and he answered quickly: That
is music by my uncle. This behavior of the boy's contributed not
a little to Beethoven's constantly increasing affection for him.[14]

Friedrich Wähner says in his reminiscences of Beethoven:

His love for his nephew must also be mentioned as manifest proof
of his goodness of heart. As a lioness fights for possession of her
young, so he strove for the happiness of influencing the boy's upbringing, which, it seems, had for a time not been in the best
hands. His eyes shone with joy when he looked at him; all the
love in his rich and deep nature seemed to concentrate on this
one object. The most tender father can take no more interest in
his son's development than did Beethoven in the progress of his
nephew.[15]

The happiness of a mother finds voice in these reports.

According to descriptions by contemporaries, young Karl was
a handsome, prepossessing, and intelligent boy, whom people
liked on sight. Apparently he at first enjoyed his uncle's overflow-

ing love and the general consideration which the famous man's affection brought him.

He was lovingly received into Giannatasio's family, and in the beginning, the orderly school and family life would seem to have had a beneficial influence on him. At first, too, he was still allowed to see his mother. But this did not last long. His uncle's unrelenting efforts to exclude Johanna from his life and to extirpate every thought of her from his heart, could not fail to have an increasingly disturbing effect on the nine-year-old boy. The jealousy with which Ludwig sought to make the boy wholly his own resulted in his sensing a threat not only in Johanna but also in every other person to whom the lad showed affection. Hence he was anxious to keep Karl from developing other relationships, and, when he could not prevent them from arising, he attempted to undermine them. The poor child soon showed an obvious attachment to the Giannatasios, so that Ludwig found himself obliged to contend against it.

Fanny Giannatasio kept a diary, in which Ludwig's relationship to his nephew and to the Institute plays a large part. It is clear from her entries that Fanny developed a deep, though unreciprocated fondness for Ludwig. She was herself a person of great emotional sensitivity; the deep love which she felt for Ludwig made her particularly receptive to his direct and indirect utterances. Her judgment on the relationship between uncle and nephew can be trusted. To be sure, her judgment of Karl varies with Ludwig's feeling toward him; here she simply adopted Ludwig's attitude, with all its fluctuations. As has frequently been observed, in a love relationship the lover makes the beloved's value judgments and attitudes his own. As early as April 3, Fanny Giannatasio wrote in her diary:

. . . Our dear Beethoven, whom of late we have only seen for a few minutes in the presence of the Schönauers [friends of the Giannatasios], yesterday wrote his little one a very dear letter, in which he again says so many beautiful and true things to him that it gave me real joy to read it; yet I find it not quite right that he does not let him go on living in his natural ingenuousness but requires a trust whose advantages and value the little boy is as yet quite unable to appreciate, and thus might cause him to worry if there be not something lacking in him or, in consequence of his not too strong love of truth, might even lead him to tell him lies. But all this no doubt comes from his wish to furnish a substitute for his love of his mother and to be everything to him.[16]

Here it is clear that Fanny recognized Ludwig's wish to be a mother to the boy. But she is also aware that Ludwig's treatment of his nephew is not good for his development. On May 4 Fanny wrote in her diary:

> . . . the stern appearance of Beethoven, whose cold behavior toward us gave me a most unpleasant feeling, which will now be with me in my dearest preoccupation. My anxiety that he will not long leave his precious pledge in our care has not left me since I asked the boy why he had cried and he answered that his uncle had forbidden him to tell and it would seem that the cause of his bad humor was not, as Nanni and I had believed, that he had not written to him for so long. God knows what will happen in this matter, but I know that it will be as painful to me to see the loosening of the tie which brought us into relation with that eminent man as it once gave me joy.[17]

The uncle's unfavorable influence on his nephew, and Fanny's justified anxiety lest Ludwig might disturb the boy's relationship with her family, are here clearly apparent. We may assume that Beethoven now began to undermine the family and the school to Karl. On May 8, 1816 he wrote to Ries, in a letter in which he complains — unjustifiably — of his bad financial situation:

> Moreover, I have to care wholly for my little nephew; he is still in the Institute; this costs close to 1100 fl[orins] and is bad besides, so that I must set up regular housekeeping so that I can have him with me. How much one must earn, in order to live here; and yet there is never an end, for — for — for — you know it already.[18]

Similarly in the letter of May 13 to Countess Erdödy, quoted in the previous chapter, he complains that a school is nothing "compared with the direct sympathetic care of a father." According to all that we know of Ludwig's character, he was incapable of concealing from the boy the negative attitude toward the Institute which finds expression in these passages from letters.

At the end of July, Ludwig went to Baden, some fifteen miles south of Vienna, for a stay in the country and to take the cure. Distance heightened his fear that he might lose the boy to Gian-

natasio. Hence, the day before his departure, he wrote to Giannatasio as follows:

Worthy friend!
Several circumstances induce me to take Karl to live with me; in
view of which kindly permit me to send you the amount for the
coming quarter, at the end of which Karl will leave; — do not
ascribe this to anything disadvantageous to yourself or to your
respected Institute, but to many other pressing motives connected with Karl's welfare. It is an experiment, and as soon as
it is in execution I shall ask you to give me the support of your
advice, and indeed to permit Karl to visit your Institute from
time to time. We shall be eternally grateful to you, nor shall we
ever forget your solicitude nor the care of your worthy wife,
which can be compared only to that of the best of mothers. — I
should send you at least four times as much as I do, if only my
situation permitted it; in any case, in a better future, I shall seize
every opportunity to honor and preserve the memory of your laying the foundation of my Karl's physical and moral well-being.
— In respect to the 'Queen of the Night,' things are to remain as
hitherto, and even if K[arl] is to be operated on at your establishment, as he will be ailing for a few days and thus more sus-
ceptible and irritable, she is all the less to be allowed to see him,
since all impressions might easily be renewed in K[arl], which
we cannot permit. To what extent we can count upon her improv-
ing, the insipid scrawl herewith will show you; only to this end
do I impart it to you, that you may see how right I am in per-
sisting in the procedure adopted against her, but this time I did
not answer her like a Sarastro but like a sultan. — In case, however gladly I would spare you from it, Karl's operation should be
performed at your establishment, I beg you to inform me of anything that causes you additional expense and trouble in your
house, and I shall recompense you for it with the greatest gratitude. And now fare well, all good things to your dear children
and your excellent wife, to whose continued care I now commend my Karl. I leave Vienna tomorrow at five in the morning,
but I shall frequently come in from Baden.
     As always with respect your
                    L. v. Beethoven.[19]

Karl had suffered a hernia which appeared to make an operation
necessary. Beethoven feared that, at the time of the operation
and during the ensuing convalescence, the boy would particularly
miss his mother and want to see her. Hence the "Queen of the
Night" is "all the less to be allowed to see him." Child and mother

were kept apart with redoubled precautions, and the mother, who had apparently sent Beethoven a letter asking permission to be with her poor child during this period, was refused with the in-humanity — and doubtless the abusive language — of an oriental sultan. But Giannatasio's family also felt this letter to be a slap in the face. They had taken particular pains with the boy, had become fond of him, and had succeeded in making him begin to feel happy with them. Of course they did not understand that this was the very reason why Ludwig must snatch his child from them. Fanny wrote in her diary, on July 28:

> . . . Beethoven's letter and her [20] enclosure struck us like a bolt from the blue when we got home. Hurt as I was when I had read his letter I found some comfort in it, for mother's saying 'He has given notice,' together with her miserable letter, had made me fear that some misunderstanding, etc. was the cause. During the first hours I was infinitely saddened by the thought of so quickly losing all connection with a man whom I so greatly prize and who, ever since we became acquainted, has become more and more dear to my heart, but today I find it less painful, when I think how wholly heartfelt his letter is and that he is not ill disposed toward me. His course of action appears to be inconsistent: but I do not trust myself to pass any judgment upon it. For he does say that there are serious reasons which impel him to this step. Yet is it not perhaps that he is too anxious that no one, not even the boy's mother, should be able to reproach him, even upon no foundation, with not looking after the welfare of the boy? I do not know, but I think that, firm as he is in other respects, I have often observed such weaknesses in him. But I do know how grieved this makes me for his sake; for it seems unlikely to me that his step will advance the boy's welfare; then again it also makes me very sad that most people will criticize him again and those who do not will blame our family. Which can only lead to harm. There may still be a little hope that Papa's letter will dissuade him from his plan; but I really do not know whether this is desirable, for then if anything at all went wrong with the boy, we should perhaps be blamed. And yet I consider him so upright, and in his letter he says that he will be eternally grateful for what we have done, and how sincerely and gratefully he refers to motherly care. I could not easily think of anything which would make me so deeply heartsick! Yet who knows what good may come of it . . .[21]

As Ludwig wanted "to have the boy always around him," as Fanny correctly observed, he returned to the idea of setting up

a household for himself and his nephew in the fall. A letter to
Baron von Zmeskall, dated September 5, carries a postscript:

> Perhaps I shall be keeping my servants only a few months more,
> since I must take a housekeeper for my Karl's sake.[22]

For the present, however, the boy remained at the Institute,
and at the end of September was operated on by Dr. Smetana;
the operation was successful. Beethoven was still in Baden at the
time. Just before the operation, he wrote to his nephew:

> My dear K.!
> It is imperative that, in accordance with Hr. v. Smetana's direc-
> tions, you should bathe several more times before the operation, to-
> day the weather is favorable, and right now is the best time, I
> will await you at the entrance to the baths. —
> Needless to say, you must first ask H. v. G[iannatasio] for permis-
> sion. — Put on a pair of underdrawers, or bring them with you
> so that you can put them on immediately after the bath, in case
> the weather should turn cooler again. — Has the tailor been there
> yet? When he comes, he is to measure you for linen underdrawers
> too, you need them; if Frau v. G[iannatasio] knows where he
> lives, my servant could bring him to you. —
> My son, fare well! I am — and indeed through you
> Your trouser-button
> L. v. Beethoven [23]

This is the first letter from Beethoven to his nephew which has
been preserved. As we see, he gives him motherly advice; the
most striking thing about the letter is the signature: "Your
trouser-button." Much later, Ludwig gave an explanation of this:
"Because he clung to him like button to trousers." [24] Apparently,
then, he uses the term "trouser-button" playfully, as a tender expression of a feeling of particular physical and doubtless also
spiritual closeness. This intimately close feeling for his child found
especially clear expression in the letter which Ludwig wrote to
Giannatasio after the operation:

> Sunday, Sept. 22, 1816
> Certain things cannot be expressed. — In particular, my feeling
> of thankfulness when I heard from you of Karl's successfully with-
> standing the operation. — You will excuse me from uttering, or
> even from stammering, words here. — But you will say nothing
> against the homage which my feelings would gladly pay you, hence

silence. — That I wish to hear what progress my dear son is now making, you can well imagine; at the same time do not forget to give me your correct address, so that I can write to you directly myself. Since you left here, I have written to Bernard asking him to make inquiries at your house, but I have received no answer; for after all you might take me for an indifferent half barbarian, since Herr B. has presumably no more called at your house than he has written to me. — Your excellent wife being present, I can have no apprehensions, it would be quite impossible. That it causes me grief not to be able to share the sufferings of my Karl and that I at least wish to hear frequently of his condition, you will understand very well; since I have been mistaken in so unfeeling and unsympathetic a friend as Herr B., I must count upon your friendship and obligingness in this matter; I hope to receive a few lines from you soon and beg to express my best wishes and a thousand thanks to your honored wife

In haste your L. v. Beethoven [25]

His need to share the sufferings of his child like a mother is clearly expressed in this letter; how aggressive he is against his friend Bernard, whom he accuses of having neglected Karl!

We receive the impression that, his apprehensions for the boy being happily surmounted, his triumphant maternal feeling was only intensified. He wrote to Antonie von Brentano:

. . . You shall learn how I have become a father and really have a father's cares. — My poor nephew had a rupture and was recently operated on, and very successfully. . . .[26]

Soon afterward he wrote to an old friend in Bonn, Dr. Franz Wegeler:

. . . You are a husband, a father, — I too, but without a wife . . .[27]

According to all that we know of Ludwig at this period, this is an outburst of triumph over the fact that he had acquired a child without the participation of a woman.

Yet his "motherhood" was of a doubtful nature, "a trembling joy" as the Austrian expression goes. For the boy's real mother was still alive, and the poor child's heart longed for her. During the operation, or during the period of pain which followed it, the child had doubtless asked about his mother, perhaps even cried and called for her. Ludwig learned of this, and it shocked him

deeply. Thus, in his next letter to his nephew, dated early in the
autumn of 1816, when he was still at Baden, he wrote:

> To my nephew Karl! So far as I can see, a certain poison is still
> present in you. Hence I only ask you to write down your spiritual
> and bodily needs. It is growing colder; do you need another
> blanket or your coverlet? — Herr von Smetana [28] will have been
> to see you at my request. The surgical mechanic went once too,
> but to no purpose, he had promised me to go again and give you a
> new truss and take the old one to be washed. He has been paid
> for everything already. — Fare well, God enlighten your soul and
> your heart.
>   Your uncle and friend Beethoven.[29]

The idea of poisoning here reappears in connection with Johanna, if only in a spiritual sense. It is easy to imagine what torment and damage it produced in the poor child's mind when his
uncle, who had complete authority over him and in whose hands
he was helpless, described his mother as "poison." Evidently,
Ludwig was deeply hurt by the fact that the boy still clung to his
mother, and wanted Karl to know it. In contrast with the tenderness of his first letter to his nephew, the second is cold and reproachful. It does not begin with an affectionate salutation but
like a royal decree, and, because of the alleged "poison," is confined to ordering Karl to state his needs. And may God enlighten
the sinner's soul and heart and teach him to love only his uncle,
not his real mother! Ludwig signs the letter as "Your uncle and
friend," no longer as the physically close "trouser-button."

Ludwig now began making real efforts to set up a household
for himself and his Karl. At first the attempt was a lamentable
failure. He wrote to Giannatasio:

                              [Presumably October or November, 1816]

Valued Friend!
My housekeeping looks almost exactly like a shipwreck, or in-
clines to; as you know, I have been so swindled with these people
by a would-be expert, at the same time my health does not appear to be mending with any speed; to engage a tutor whose inward and outward man is unknown under these circumstances and
to trust my Karl's education to chance, I can never do, great as
are the sacrifices to which I shall in many respects again be subjected by it, hence I beg you, my worthy G., to keep Karl with
you again this quarter, your proposal as to his cultivation of

music I shall accept to the extent that, two or perhaps three times a week, Karl will leave you about 6 o'clock in the evening and remain with me until the following morning, when he can be back with you about 8 o'clock. Every day would be too taxing for K., and for me too, since it would always have to be about the same time, too tiring and restricting. During this quarter we will discuss in more detail what would be most suitable for Karl and in which at the same time I too can be considered, for in view of the fact that the times are steadily growing worse, I must unfortunately say: if your house in the garden had been suitable for my state of health, everything could easily have been straightened out. — [30]

As we see, Ludwig had to make the best of a compromise. The plan of moving into the Giannatasio's garden house had also to be given up because of his health.

Until now, the only flaw in Ludwig's happy motherhood had been the occasional manifestations of Karl's relationship to his real mother. Yet he yielded to the deceptive hope that, with time and his unremitting attacks upon Johanna, the boy's feeling of belonging to his real mother would weaken and finally cease. He was to suffer disillusionment not only in this hope but also in many other expectations he cherished for his child.

The lad was intelligent and alert enough to justify hopes for his future. In Ludwig these hopes were exaggerated to the pitch of illusion. He was convinced that — if only the right kind of upbringing should prevent all influence from the mother — the boy was destined for extraordinary things, that he would certainly become a great scholar or artist.[31] This further evidences to what a degree he felt the boy to be his own, for it is characteristic of many infatuated parents that they cherish the highest hopes for their children — especially for an only child — and expect extraordinary things of them. We feel the inevitability of tragedy in the fact that Ludwig himself, through the very violence of his efforts for his child, destroyed the hopes which he cherished for him. For the psychological shocks which the boy underwent from the measures taken against his mother and from his uncle's treatment of him began to reveal their disturbing effects. Fanny's observation that the boy had a tendency to lie is the first indication of his waywardness.[32] The next sign is diminishing diligence. It appears that, in consequence, Giannatasio advised Ludwig to be sterner with

the boy. How clumsily the composer followed Giannatasio's suggestion appears from the following letter to him, dated November
14, 1816:

> . . . I must ask to take Karl tomorrow, for it is his father's death-
> day, and we wish to visit his grave. I may come to get him about
> 12 or 1 o'clock. — I should like to know what effect my procedure
> with Karl after your recent complaint has produced. Meanwhile,
> it touched me very much to find him so sensitive as regards honor;
> even before we left your establishment, I made allusions to his
> lack of diligence, we walked along together more gravely than
> usual, he pressed my hand timidly, but received no response. At
> table, he ate almost nothing and said that he was sad, but I could
> not get him to tell me why; finally, when we went out for a walk,
> he explained that he was so sad because he had not been able to
> be as diligent as usual. I now played my part, but more affection-
> ately than before. There is certainly delicacy of feeling to be seen
> in this, and these very traits make me hope that all will be well.
> — If I do not come myself tomorrow, I beg you only to write me
> a few lines concerning the success of my meeting with
> Karl. — . . .[33]

As we see, Ludwig expected an immediate effect from his "procedure" with Karl. At the same time he unconsciously aggravated
the trouble from which the boy's difficulties arose. For, on the
anniversary of his father's death, the boy was obliged to visit the
grave with his uncle, whereas his mother would have been his
natural companion there. How painfully he must again have
missed her on this occasion!

Ludwig also interfered with the schedule of the Institute, in
order to have the boy with him as much as possible. Thus he
writes to Giannatasio during this period:

> . . . Although you have accorded me permission to take Karl out
> twice, I must still beg you to let me send for him tomorrow about
> eleven o'clock for the reason that I want to take him to an inter-
> esting concert; besides, I want him to come to my lodging to play
> tomorrow, this having been intermitted for a long time. — In ad-
> dition I ask you to keep him even more constantly busy today than
> usual, so that, in a manner of speaking, he will make up for the
> holiday. — I heartily embrace you and am your Ludwig van Bee-
> thoven.[34]

As we see, Ludwig wanted to have the boy with him three times
this week, whereas he had agreed with Giannatasio to have him

only twice. Nor can the boy have been very happy over being kept "more constantly busy" — i.e., having to study longer — because his uncle wanted to see him oftener. The lack of self-control which we have earlier remarked in Ludwig, his impatience when he wanted something, his inability to master himself when he encountered opposition — all these traits led to great inconsistency in his behavior toward his nephew, to which the boy could not but react unfavorably. On another occasion, though protesting that he disliked disturbing the school routine "in the least," he wrote to Giannatasio asking that Karl be sent to him "immediately, by the bearer," for the whole day and possibly the following night.[35] On the other hand, principally because at this period he was becoming increasingly concerned over his own health, Ludwig repeatedly excused himself from appearing when his nephew was expecting him.

Let us consider the boy's psychological situation. He was now ten years old. He dared love his mother only in secret, and was constantly under the apprehension that any expression of his longing for her would be regarded as poisonous and evil. His attachment to Giannatasio's family was undermined and finally broken off by his uncle, who had complete control over him. His uncle himself was erratic in his behavior, exaggeratedly affectionate and tender when the boy reacted as his uncle wished, hard and reproachful when he realized that the boy had not wholly forgotten his mother. It is astonishing that young Karl's difficulties with his studies and his behavior in general were not worse than the documents show them to have been. But Ludwig met even these slight manifestations of the lad's disturbed state with psychological clumsiness, with swift alternations between love and stern disapproval, so that, under the circumstances, the boy's waywardness could only increase. Yet another factor contributing to his inner insecurity was his uncle's increasingly bad health.

To what point Beethoven had cultivated the illusion that his being with Karl had a particularly beneficial pedagogical influence, is shown by two passages from his "Diary":

1817

Karl is an entirely different child when he has been with you for a few hours, therefore hold to the plan of taking him to live with you. — And your own state of mind will cause you less concern.

A thousand beautiful moments vanish when children are in wooden institutions, whereas, at home with good parents, they could be receiving the most soulful impressions, which endure into the extremest old age.[36]

It was not only for the nephew but also for the uncle that Ludwig's relationship to young Karl gave rise to enduring and increasing difficulties which soon began to destroy the joy which possession of the boy had brought him and to change it into bitter grief. Doubtless Ludwig was always conscious that his possession of the boy was in large part illusory. This can be deduced from the severity of the measures by which he at first reduced contact between Johanna and her son to a minimum and finally stopped it altogether. At first he decided that the mother might see her son only once a month, for a short time and in his own lodging, and he was inexorable in his insistence that this condition be carried out. Two passages from letters to Giannatasio clearly reveal his attitude:

. . . In regard to the mother, I beg you, upon the pretext that he is busy, not to let her approach him at all; no one can know and judge this better than I, all my well-considered plans for the child's welfare have been to some extent deranged by this already. I will myself discuss with you how his mother can in future see Karl; the way it happened yesterday I can in no case wish repeated. All responsibility for this I take upon myself, and, so far as I am concerned, the Landrechte have given me full power and authority to obviate, without consideration, anything that is contrary to the child's welfare. Had they been able to regard her as a fit mother, they would certainly not have excluded her from the guardianship. Whatever nonsense she may talk, nothing was put over on her — the entire Council was unanimous in the matter. I hope that I shall not have any trouble over this; the situation is difficult enough without that. According to my conversation of yesterday with Adlersburg . . . it may still be a very long time before it is even definitely known what belongs to the child. With these cares, am I again to be visited by the apprehensions which I believed your Institute had wholly banished for me?

Fare well. With respect your devoted
L. v. Beethoven [37]

We can deduce from this letter that Johanna, on a visit to the Institute, had expressed the opinion that legal procedure had not

been strictly adhered to in Ludwig's appointment as sole guardian
and that, through his connections, he had influenced the decision
— a not unjustifiable assumption.[38] Giannatasio conveyed this
statement of Johanna's to Ludwig, who — conscious of his guilt —
responded by intensified aggressions against the mother.

The following passage from another letter to Giannatasio shows
that Ludwig intended, before very long, to exclude the mother
from all contact with her son:

> . . . As to Karl's mother, I have now decided that in this matter
> your wish to see no more of her at your establishment will be
> conformed with. It is more expedient and safer for our dear Karl,
> inasmuch as experience convinces me that every visit from his
> mother leaves a bitter echo in K.'s mind, through which he can
> only lose but not gain. — I shall soon see to making arrangements
> for her to see him at my lodging, and this will certainly result in
> everything being broken off with her entirely all the sooner. —
> Since we are in complete agreement in our views concerning
> Karl's mother, in regard to the details we need only our-
> selves . . .[39]

Gradually, however, these and other aggressions against the
boy's real mother reacted on the composer's own psyche. They
caused feelings of guilt in him. As early as 1816 he had said to
Fanny Giannatasio: "What will people say, they will take me for
a tyrant." [40]

Here it is apparent that, hearing the voice of conscience within
him, he projected it into other people's opinion of his conduct.
For, in general, the opinion of other people left him wholly indifferent, indeed he despised it. A few months later, when he was
also demanding money from Johanna, we find a real outburst of
his direct feeling of guilt toward the widow. He wrote on a
sketch sheet:

> My part, O Lord, I have performed.
> It might have been possible without hurting the widow, but it
> was not so. Only Thou, All-powerful, lookest into my heart, know-
> est that I have neglected my own good for my dear Karl's sake;
> bless my work, bless the widow! Why can I not wholly obey my
> heart and help her, the widow?
> God, God, my refuge, my rock, O my all, Thou seest my inmost
> heart and knowest how it grieves me to cause anyone to suffer
> through my good work for my dear Karl!!! O hear, ever Ineffable,
> hear me, thine unhappy, unhappiest of all mortals! [41]

As we have seen earlier, he frequently responded to feelings of guilt by intensified aggression, particularly against the person toward whom he felt guilty. This gave rise to a vicious circle, which continually aggravated the composer's unhappy psychological state, already most adversely affected by his loss of hearing.

In the following letter to Giannatasio Ludwig's being "unstrung by the evil woman's talk" is doubtless also to be interpreted as a guilt reaction:

> The talk of that evil woman has so unstrung me that today I cannot answer everything; tomorrow you will be informed of everything, however do not let her see Karl under any circumstances, and hold to it that it is to be only once a month; . . . In haste your L. van Beethoven.[42]

But such conscious guilt-feeling reactions are only very occasional in Beethoven. We must assume that his feeling of guilt toward Johanna was for the most part repressed, but was then given indirect expression by his unconscious. One such indirect expression is the collapse of all his efforts to set up an orderly household for his Karl. Thus an inward impediment prevented him from permanently having with him the child whom he so dearly loved. A sketch sheet carries the despairing reaction to this unconscious prohibition to take the boy to live with him:

> Help, God! Thou seest me abandoned by all mankind, for I will not commit injustice. Hear my cry, that I may yet in the future but be with my Karl, for no possibility points to it now. O hard fate! O terrible doom! No, no, my unhappy state is unending! [43]

Another effect of his feeling of guilt is his increasing hypochondriac preoccupation with his health, perhaps also the intestinal disturbance in the form of diarrhoea which began to trouble him more and more. Thus an inward retribution mechanism was added to the external difficulties in his relationship to his child, with the result that his maternal joys were brief and precarious, extinguished again and again in inner conflict and suffering.

VI

REBEL AND TYRANT

LUDWIG'S psychic condition deteriorated soon after he assumed the guardianshp, as is first of all clearly evident from the considerable number of his letters of excuse to the Archduke.[1] One of them reads:

> Your Imperial Highness! My condition became worse again, so that I was able to go out only a few times during the daytime. Meanwhile it has improved again, and, at least three times a week, I can have the happiness of again waiting upon Y.I.H. In addition the cares which one [undergoes] in these terrible times, which go far beyond anything ever experienced before, are so great and are, furthermore, so much increased by the fact that since November of last year I have become the father of a poor orphan, that all this too prevents my entire recovery. I wish Y.I.H. all imaginable good things and beg your graciousness not again to misjudge Your Imperial Highness's most obedient servant
>
> Ludwig van Beethoven [2]

Ludwig's state of health cannot be judged with certainty from these letters, for he perpetually used it as an excuse to escape his duty to the Archduke when he felt psychically unwell. Yet it is worth noting that he ascribes the prevention of his recovery to his fatherhood (i.e., "motherhood"). From many other letters which he wrote after his brother's death, it appears that at this period he really did feel physically unwell. Fanny Giannatasio, too, frequently mentions Beethoven's "ill-health" in her diary. At the same time she recognized the hypochondriac nature of his malaise, his complaints and fears, for she wrote:

> Then sometimes he would sit for whole evenings with us at the round table, seemingly sunk in thought, though often he would smile and put in a word, meanwhile continually spitting into his

77

handkerchief . . . and looking at it each time, so that I often
thought that he feared he would find specks of blood.[3]

We have another account of this hypochondriac examination of
his spittle. Joseph Blöchlinger, whose parents Beethoven often
visited, for his nephew later boarded with them, relates that his
mother was in despair

> . . . when Beethoven pulled out his gaily colored handkerchief,
> laid it in the palm of his hand, cleared his throat, spat on it, then
> looked at the spittle for some time before he refolded the hand-
> kerchief and put it in his pocket.[4]

Ludwig, then, was concerned lest he should find symptoms of
tuberculosis in himself, especially traces of blood in his sputum.
That an almost conscious longing for this disease lies behind this
concern, appears from a letter to Nanette Streicher, in which he
tells her, with a certain satisfaction:

> . . . So long as I am ill, my relations with other people must needs
> be different; fond as I am of solitude in general, it is now all the
> more painful to me since it is almost impossible, what with all
> this taking of medicines and baths, to keep myself as occupied as
> usual; add to this the trying prospect that perhaps I shall never be
> better, that I even have doubts of my present physician, *only now
> at long last* does he tell me that my condition is consump-
> tion . . .[5]

This long-awaited and imaginary consumption was connected
with two persons who had been close to him and who had died
of the disease; it is difficult to avoid the thought that Ludwig's
"consumption" was an unconscious punishment for his having so
badly fulfilled his dying brother's last wish. Yet this hypochondriac fear must have had a deeper basis, for it had appeared, years
before Karl's death, immediately after the death of Ludwig's
mother. And his mother, as we have said, died of tuberculosis.

She died on July 17, 1787. On September 15, Ludwig, then
seventeen years of age, wrote to Dr. von Schaden, of Augsburg,
who had lent him money:

> . . . I must admit to you that, since I left Augsburg, my joy
> and with it my health have begun to cease; the nearer I came to
> my native city, the more letters I received from my father, telling
> me to travel faster than usual, for my mother was not in a good

state of health; hence I hurried as much as I could, for I myself was indisposed; the longing to be able to see my sick mother once again made me disregard all impediments and helped me to overcome the greatest difficulties. I found my mother still alive, but in the most wretched state of health; she had consumption and finally died, about seven weeks ago, after undergoing a great deal of pain and suffering. She was such a good, lovable mother to me, my best friend; oh! who would be happier than I if I could still speak the sweet name of mother, and it were heard, and to whom can I say it now! To the dumb images of her which my imagination puts together? Since I have been here, I have enjoyed few happy hours; I have been afflicted the entire time with *shortness of breath*, and I cannot but fear that a *consumption* will develop from it; and, to fill the measure, there is melancholy, which for me is almost as great an evil as my sickness itself. —
Now consider my situation, and I hope to receive forgiveness from you for my long silence. Your very great kindness and friendliness in lending me three Karolin at Augsburg, I must ask you to show me yet a little further consideration [*sic*]; my journey cost me a great deal, and I can expect no compensation here, not even the slightest; fate is not favorable to me here in Bonn . . .[6]

This letter may give an exaggerated description of his condition, for its purpose is to explain why Beethoven does not fulfill his obligation to pay back borrowed money, and under such circumstances he was not overscrupulous about the truth. Yet his fears for his health and his complaint over his depressed mood sound genuine. As we saw in Chapter II, however, in other respects he reacted to his mother's death by increased activity, assuming the role of sole parent in the family, for his father was very soon out of the picture and indeed was obliged to turn over half of his pension to his son.

The psychic mechanism by which Ludwig experienced his mother's symptoms and imagined himself to be suffering from tuberculosis, is known to psychology as "identification." This kind of identification, after the loss of a close relative or friend, takes place with particular frequency when the emotional relationship to the lost object was a mixture of love and hostility. Such an emotional attitude, which consists of both positive and negative elements, is termed "ambivalent." Particularly when a disease symptom is adopted to express the identification, we can safely assume that the relationship to the object was highly ambivalent. Ludwig's relationship to his own mother must have been of this two-fold nature.

The surviving documentation concerning Ludwig's mother and his relationship to her is extremely scanty. To be sure, the biographers exert themselves to depict the relationship between mother and son as wholly affectionate. But the mother's personality justifies the assumption that the son's feelings toward her were not all of them positive.

The few descriptions of Ludwig's mother which we owe to contemporaries make it clear that she was by no means a cheerful and equable person. She was born in simple circumstances — her father had been head cook in a castle. At seventeen, Maria Magdalena (as Beethoven's mother was named) married a valet in the service of the Elector of Treves; but her husband died after two and a half years of a childless marriage. Of Maria Magdalena's relationship to her first husband, we know nothing. Two years after his death, the young widow, then twenty-two years of age, married the future father of the great composer, Johann van Beethoven. Johann's father, Ludwig's grandfather, a respected musician at the Elector's court, opposed his son's marriage to a woman of inferior station. Two years after the celebration of her second marriage, Maria Magdalena gave birth to a son, Ludwig Maria, who lived only six days. A year later, 1770, a second son was born and was also baptized Ludwig. Then followed, four years later, a boy, Kaspar Karl; two years later again, a boy, Nikolaus Johann; in 1781 a boy Franz, who died at two and a half; and, in 1786, a daughter, Maria Margaretha Josepha, who died at one and a half, two months after the death of her mother. The mother, Maria Magdalena, was obviously disillusioned by her marriage. Speaking to Caecilie Fischer, a girl who had received a proposal from a musician, she said: "If you take my advice, you will stay single, that way you have the quietest, nicest, most comfortable life. For what is marriage? A little joy, but after that a chain of griefs . . ." [7]

Caecilie Fischer, in whose father's house the Beethovens lodged, reports that Madame van Beethoven often expressed similar ideas: "How unreflectingly many young people married, without knowing what lay before them; but even the best did not escape suffering." [8] Ludwig may have been present when his mother thus expressed herself upon marriage; he repeated almost the same view to Fanny Giannatasio years later.

This impression of a depressive woman, disillusioned by marriage, is strengthened when Caecilie Fischer, who was much with the Beethovens, reports that she never remembered having seen Madame Beethoven laugh; "she was always serious." But this depressive attitude, which she was apparently able to conceal in the presence of strangers, occasionally gave place to aggressiveness, for Caecilie Fischer describes her as "hot-tempered and quarrelsome." [9]

Ludwig is said to have been his mother's favorite, but we have no further details. On a journey by ship to Holland she is said to have kept the five-year-old boy's feet warm in her lap.[10] We do not get the impression that she especially protected the boy from mistreatment by his father; and she often left her children to the care of maidservants. We are told that she did not bring up her children to be neat. All this is too scanty to permit conclusions concerning her relationship to Ludwig. Yet Ludwig's attitude and conduct toward women, not least his bitter hatred of Johanna, show that his love of his mother, which is so stressed by his biographers, had a large admixture of hostility and negativism. The cause of this negative element remains obscure. Yet the fear, so clearly apparent in Ludwig, of being poisoned by a woman points to a very early origin for it. Clinical experience shows that the content of such an idea of poisoning goes back to the child's earliest relationship with its mother. It is true that we know nothing of Ludwig's experiences, failures, and disillusionments at this early period. We do not know at what age he learned that a child named "Ludwig" had died before him and how he reacted to the knowledge, nor what his reaction to the birth of his younger brothers and sisters was. These were born when he was, respectively, four, six, eleven, and sixteen years old. We cannot even make conjectures concerning Ludwig's psychic experiences on these occasions.

By those who knew him as a child, Ludwig is described as peculiar. He was serious and engrossed in himself; ordinary children's games never amused him.[11] He was particularly conspicuous for his uncleanliness, and once, when Caecilie Fischer reproached

him for it and said that he ought to keep himself "tidy," the child
answered: "When I'm a grown man, no one will pay any attention
to that." [12]

With his brothers he once stole a runaway rooster, wrung its
neck, and had the maid cook it, while his parents were out of the
house.[13] He also stole eggs laid by Frau Fischer's hens — Frau
Fischer had long wondered about the disappearance of the eggs,
until she caught Ludwig stealing them.[14] As a boy, he cared little
for friends or companionship. He was happiest alone, "free from
his parents," when they went out and he could devote himself to
music.[15]

His father, Johann van Beethoven, is more clearly defined as
a character than his mother. He was the son of a well-known court
musician at Bonn, whose name, "Ludwig," was given to the great
composer. Our information concerning the composer's father sets
him in no very favorable light. Johann was unstable, hot-tempered,
and, especially in his later years, so given to drink that, at his
death, the Elector remarked: "The liquor excise has suffered a
loss in Beethoven . . ." [16] Johann's mother was also an alcoholic
and had to spend her last years in an institution. When Closson,
in his biography of Beethoven, describes the composer's father
as: "inconscient, inconsistant, léger, instable, incapable de régler
son tempérament, bayeux aux corneilles et apparemment d'une
faible moralité," [17] he may somewhat overshoot the mark; yet we
know beyond doubt that Johann was harsh and unaffectionate to
his son. When he recognized the boy's musical talent, he tried to
exploit it as a source of revenue instead of developing it systematically. Presumably he was thinking of the example of the child
Wolfgang Amadeus Mozart, who had amazed the world by his
virtuosity at the age of six, when he toured Europe with his father
Leopold. So Johann very early forced his little Ludwig to long
hours of piano practice. The boy Beethoven received his first piano
and violin lessons from his father, and they were given with a strictness which left him little freedom for the exercise of the musical
imagination which had early awakened in him. Caecilie Fischer
has this to say on the subject:

> Ludwig was once playing without notes; his father, happening
> to come in, said: 'What silly stuff are you scraping there, you know

I cannot abide it, scrape according to the notes, or your scraping won't be much use.' —

When Johann v. B. had visitors, and Ludwig came in, he usually hung around the piano and touched the keyboard with his right hand. Said his father: 'More of your tomfoolery? — go away, or I'll box your ears.' — His father, hearing him play the violin, finally became aware that he was again playing according to his own invention, without notes. Then his father came in: 'Won't you obey yet, after all I have said?' He played again, then asked his father: 'But isn't it beautiful?' — Said his father: 'It's just something more out of your own head; you aren't ready for that yet, work hard at the violin and the piano, tackle the notes quickly and right, that's more to the point; after you've got that far, there'll still be plenty that your head will do and must do. But I won't have you doing it now, you're not ready for it yet.' [18]

Caecilie Fischer also reports that Ludwig's father locked him in the cellar. When Ludwig was nine he was given piano lessons by the tenor, pianist, and oboist Tobias Pfeiffer. No set time was arranged for the lessons:

> . . . often, when Pfeiffer had been drinking with Beethoven's father in a tavern until eleven or twelve o'clock, he went home with him, where Ludwig would be in bed asleep; his father furiously shook him awake, the boy collected his wits, weeping, and went to the piano, where Pfeiffer remained sitting with him until early in the morning, for he recognized the boy's unusual talent. [19]

No one can mistake the inhuman sternness with which the two half-intoxicated men went to work on the boy. We hear nothing of his mother's protecting him from them.

His father's clumsy and harsh treatment of him certainly exercised a decisive influence on the development of Beethoven's character. An early inner rebellion against his father's arbitrariness and unjust strictness laid the foundation for the revolt against every sort of authority which appears in Beethoven with an intensity which can only be described as highly unusual. He could tolerate no kind of constraint. He rebelled against every political authority, against every pressure of social forms, and even against the slightest obligation — as is repeatedly shown, for example, by his behavior toward the Archduke. He was a revolutionary in almost every relationship. Undoubtedly this is why no one could better incarnate and more forcefully represent the spiritual principle of the revolution of his period. In this sense he is, above all others, the spiritual "hero" of the modern cultural age, for in both his direct and his spiritual rebellion he foreboded and pre-experienced the tremendous revolutions of our time.

The few accounts we have of his relationship to his father do not show that he rebelled against him directly. Caecilie Fischer reports:

> Herr Johann van Beethoven's three boys, Ludwig, Kaspar and Nikola [Johann], were very much concerned for their parents' honor. When their father had occasionally drunk a little too much in company — though this did not often happen — and his sons heard of it, they all three came at once and tried, in the nicest way, so that any sort of scene would be avoided, to take their father home quietly; they coaxed him: 'O Papächen, Papächen!' And he would do as they said.[20]

And Gerhard von Breuning, the son of the friend of Beethoven's younger days, Stephan von Breuning, reports that, as a young man, Ludwig got into trouble with the Bonn police by desperately attempting to save his father from being arrested when, in his drunkenness, he would go reeling and shouting through the streets at night.[21] Long afterwards, when someone "spoke harshly" of his father, he was very much upset and would not permit it.[22] But he himself seldom spoke of his father and avoided recalling him; however, Czerny reports that Beethoven mentioned the harsh treatment and inadequate instruction he had received from his father.[23]

At eleven, Ludwig received organ lessons from Van der Eeden, then seventy, who was court organist to the Elector. The old man soon let the boy take over his duty of playing the organ in church — which, among other things, obliged little Ludwig to be present at early Mass. We do not hear that he objected to this. But soon afterwards, as a youth, he rebelled against such duties with almost insurmountable aversion. He regarded having to give lessons as a particularly intolerable constraint.

Before he was seventeen — that is, before his first visit to Vienna — Ludwig, through his friend Wegeler, was introduced to the von Breuning family in Bonn as a piano teacher. His pupils were Eleonore von Breuning (some two years younger than himself) and her younger brother Lorenz (Lenz). He was soon on terms of friendship with the family, and some of its members remained his intimates to the end of his life. At the time of Ludwig's introduction to the Breunings, the family consisted of the mother, Hofrätin Helene von Breuning, Christoph (the eldest son), Eleonore, Stephan, and Lenz. The father had died in 1777 in attempting to save the electoral archives from destruction during a fire at the castle. We shall probably not go wrong in assuming that the absence of a father in the Breuning family made it possible for Ludwig to feel so at ease with them. He was soon treated as a son of the house, and spent a great part of the day, and often the night as well, with the von Breunings. He developed a strong affection for Madame von Breuning, and the intelligent, cultivated, and understanding woman tried to use her influence over him to improve the wild, intractable lad's education and manners. Because he had lost his own mother, his relationship to Madame von Breuning as to a substitute mother was particularly congenial to Ludwig. But even Madame von Breuning could not break his stubborn resistance to the duty of giving lessons. Wegeler recounts that Ludwig was engaged as music-teacher in Count Westphal's family. The Count's house was diagonally across from the Breuning house. Madame von Breuning sometimes tried to force him to fulfill his obligation of giving lessons at the Count's house. "Then, knowing that he was being watched, he would go, 'ut iniquae mentis asellus' (like a stubborn donkey), but sometimes at the very door would run back and promise that tomorrow he would give two lessons, but today he could not." [24] When he had thus "come flying back" to the good-hearted motherly woman who had been watching him from the window, she would shrug her shoulders and say: "He has his *raptus* again today." [25]

In Vienna he soon assumed a very arrogant attitude toward his teacher Haydn; the latter was well-disposed toward him, as appears from the letter, cited earlier, in which he asked the Elector to double Ludwig's allowance. But Ludwig's behavior toward Haydn soon put an end to this well-wishing attitude and changed it into lasting resentment. Because of Ludwig's arrogance, Haydn called him the "Grand Mogul." In any case, Ludwig's attitude of rebellion against all authority must have been known to the Elector, for his answer to Haydn's application on Ludwig's behalf was a highly ungracious refusal.[26] After Ludwig had ceased to be dependent on the court at Bonn, he openly expressed his opposition to all authority and to the governmental and social hierarchy. He was embittered by the higher position which his aristocratic friends held in the order of society. They had to treat him with the utmost circumspection and submission, to avoid awaking his suspicion that they regarded him as a kind of inferior or stressed their higher position as members of the aristocracy. It is hardly credible how badly he treated his highly placed friends and patrons. From a long series of examples, we shall cite only a few:

> . . . Mähler remembered that at one of the general rehearsals [of *Fidelio*] the third bassoon was absent; at which Beethoven raged and fumed. Lobkowitz, who was present, made light of the matter: two of the bassoons were present, he said, and the absence of the third could make no great difference. This so enraged the composer that, as he crossed the Lobkowitz Place, on his way home, he could not restrain the impulse to turn aside and shout in at the great door of the palace: 'Lobkowitzian ass!' [27]

In order to realize what an unprecedented lack of respect such behavior represents, we must bear in mind what a dominant place was held, in the Austrian monarchy of the period, by the high aristocracy, to which Prince Lobkowitz belonged, and what profound reverence ordinary mortals showed, and indeed were obliged to show, to a prince. Ludwig was particularly bitter against the highest authority in the country, the imperial house and the government.

A scene at Teplitz, recounted by Bettina von Arnim, has become famous, although her description probably contains a certain amount of poetic coloring: Beethoven, out walking with Goethe, strode through the retinue of the Empress and the Archdukes, so that those illustrious personages had to step out of the way, while Goethe stood aside with his hat off until the company had passed.[28] This was an affront not only to the imperial family but also to Goethe, whom Beethoven in other respects greatly admired. Goethe's judgment of the surly rebel Beethoven may have been based upon this or other occurrences similarly painful to him. He wrote of the composer:

I made Beethoven's acquaintance in Teplitz. His talent amazed me; unfortunately he is an utterly untamed personality, not altogether in the wrong in holding the world to be detestable, but who does not make it any the more enjoyable either for himself or others by his attitude.[29]

Once, encountering the Emperor and his suite out walking on a narrow path at Baden, Beethoven kept straight on, so that the Emperor had to step off into the grass. The Emperor merely said to his suite: "There have to be such people." [30]

Baron de Trémont reports that one morning when the Empress sent to ask Beethoven to come to her, he answered that he was busy all that day but would try to come the next.[31] Hence he was regarded at court as a republican, and the court circle stayed away from his concerts and his opera. He had a bad name with the police too, and was on the list of political suspects. Nevertheless, he took every opportunity to rail at the Austrian government. Thus Potter reports:

> Even politics had a place in the conversations [of Beethoven and his circle]. The very first day we were together, Beethoven fell upon the subject and gave the Austrian government every possible bad name.[32]

Simrock writes:

> He especially delighted in railing at the Austrian regime, unrestrainedly and at the top of his voice, in the street.[33]

Schindler, to explain his destroying more than half of the Conversation Books, says that they were full of calumnies against persons of the highest station.

The tyrannical way in which, as a child, he had been forced to practice the piano, both by his father and his teacher Pfeiffer, makes it understandable that his resistance was particularly strong when he was urged to play for anyone. His friend Wegeler, who was studying at Vienna from 1792 to 1794 and was much in Beethoven's company during that period, describes his disinclination to play for others:

> Later, when Beethoven had already attained a high standing in Vienna, a similar, if not even stronger resistance to requests to

play in public developed, so that every such occasion took all the
joy of life out of him. More than once he came to me gloomy and
depressed, complaining that people would force him to play even
if it made the blood burn under his nails. Gradually we would fall
to talking and I would try to encourage and soothe him. If I was
successful in this I would let the conversation drop, and sit down
at my desk; then, if Beethoven wanted to go on talking to me, he
had to sit down at the piano. Very soon, sometimes still turned
away from the keyboard, he would hesitantly strike a chord or
two, from which, little by little, the most beautiful melody would
develop . . .

Yet the resistance remained, and was often the source of Beethoven's quarreling violently with the foremost among his friends
and patrons.[34]

An unprecedented incident, in which Ludwig showed himself
implacably rebellious when asked to play, occurred in 1809, when
he was a guest at Prince Lichnowsky's castle, near Troppau. The
prince, to whom Beethoven was greatly indebted at the time, had
several French officers of rank as guests at his castle, among them
a music-loving general, to whom he rashly promised that he would
hear Beethoven play after a soirée at the castle. When the time
came, Beethoven had retired to his room; the prince repeatedly
sent for him, but in vain; finally he went to the master himself, to
persuade him to play. Ludwig refused, picked up a chair, and
threatened to strike the prince with it.[35] "A repulsive, not to say
vulgar scene followed," writes Anton Weiser, to whom Beethoven
recounted the incident soon afterward. Beethoven immediately
had his belongings packed, and hastened to Troppau on foot,
despite a terrible rain, and from there returned to Vienna the next
day.[36] Ley also reports that, upon his return home, Beethoven
broke the bust of Prince Lichnowsky which the latter had given
him.[37] Beethoven tried to insist that Prince Lichnowsky should
make him a public apology, and a reconciliation did not take place
until 1811.

Beginning in 1800, Prince Lichnowsky had provided Beethoven
with an annuity of 600 florins, which was to be paid until he obtained a secure post; even after this scene, he remained faithful
and devoted to him. Such was the spell which Beethoven's powerful personality cast upon him, as upon many others.

Ludwig gave lessons only so long as he had to for monetary

reasons; it was an obligation which he found unbearable — again, no doubt, because it awakened painful memories of his own days of study. Yet this did not make him any the gentler with his pupils; indeed, we get the impression that he used them as outlets for the irritation and ill humor which giving lessons aroused in him. For example, he insisted that a little boy under six years old, Emanuel Alois Forster, should "come for his lesson at six in the morning," thus making his pupil repeat what he had himself experienced as a child when he was dragged from sleep and made to sit at the piano. He also struck his little pupil's fingers with a coarse steel knitting needle, so that the child ran home screaming.[38] When he was angry he pinched his pupils and sometimes bit their shoulders. He once tore up a pupil's music. Nor did he spare his august pupil and patron the Archduke Rudolf. Thus he is reported to have said to Goethe, when the latter told him of his devotion to the Empress:

> 'Nonsense' (said he), 'you mustn't go about it like that, that's no good, you must keep throwing it in their faces what they have in you, or they won't realize it at all; there's no such thing as a princess who recognizes a Tasso any longer than the shoe of vanity pinches her; — I've handled them differently; when I had to give lessons to Duke Rainer [Archduke Rudolf], he made me wait in the anteroom, I paid him back by wrenching his fingers apart for him; when he asked me why I was so impatient, I told him that he had wasted my time in the anteroom and I couldn't squander any more of it on patience now. After that he never kept me waiting . . . I said to him: "You can hang an order on someone, but he's none the better for that; you can make an Aulic Councillor or a Privy Councillor, but you can't make a Goethe, or a Beethoven, so what you can't make, and what you yourself are far from being, you must learn to respect, it's good for you." ' [39]

Yet in his letters to the Archduke, Ludwig was extremely submissive and made it appear that serving His Highness was his greatest happiness. We cite a few of the many examples.

> . . . I am truly inconsolable to be unable to wait upon Y.I.H.; although at first I accused myself, it seems that the weather is to blame for my suffering, I only hope and wish that Y.I.H. will not likewise succumb to it. However, I hope soon to be able to come to my most revered and exalted pupil, through whose gracious sympathy I feel soothed in many sufferings and recent events which have been painful to me.[40]

. . . My heart is constantly with Y.I.H., and I certainly hope that circumstances will at least change in such a manner that I can do far more than hitherto to perfect your great talent. I think that Y.I.H. is at least already aware of my very good intentions in this, and will certainly be convinced that only insuperable impediments are able to keep me from my most revered and amiable prince, who is dearer to my heart than all else . . .[41]

But we must bear in mind that these are all letters in which — usually for no valid material reason — he excuses himself from giving the Archduke a lesson, and that he compensates for this failure to fulfill his obligation by these expressions of deep devotion.

That he felt his obligation to the Archduke to be an intolerable constraint, and inwardly rebelled against it almost as if it were a monstrous injustice, is apparent from the manner in which he represents it to others. Schnyder von Wartensee, for example, reports:

. . . He speaks harshly of Vienna and wants to leave it. 'From the Emperor down to the bootblacks,' he says, 'all Viennese are worthless.' I asked him if he was not going to take a pupil. No, he answered, it was irksome work; he had only one, who kept him very busy and whom he would be glad to get rid of if he could. 'And who is he?' 'The Archduke Rudolf.' [42]

Passages from his letters also show his real attitude toward his obligation to the Archduke. For example:

This morning I am slave to the Archduke.[43]

It has become too bad, I am worse irked by the Cardinal [the Archduke] than ever. If I don't go, lo and behold, a crimen legis [sic] majestatis, my bonus consists of the obligation to pay for a tax stamp when I get my miserable salary.[44]

. . . My situation is so hard and embarrassed . . . thank God, the blame for it is not mine. It is my too great devotion to others, especially to the weak Cardinal, who has brought me into this morass and does not know how to help himself . . .[45]

. . . I wish and hope for you that your circumstances become better every day; unfortunately I cannot say so of myself; my unhappy connection with this Archduke has brought me almost to beggary.[46]

His violence and lack of control in all his emotions also characterized his resistance to all authority and to every restriction and constraint. How far this went we see from Gerhard von Breuning's report of an incident which occurred when Ludwig was staying in the house of Baron Pronay at Hetzendorf:

> The Baron, who entertained the highest respect and reverence for Beethoven, had freely placed the great park at his disposition, and had made but one stipulation — that Beethoven should make no noise at night in one of the rooms which he occupied, and which faced the garden, because he [the Baron] slept directly beneath it and was, moreover, a very light sleeper. At first all went well. But when the Baron, in his extravagant reverence for Beethoven, began bowing deeply to him whenever he met him, and Beethoven noticed it, he began to feel uncomfortable in the house. To convey this to the Baron, he tried to make himself as annoying to the latter as possible: from then on he purposely supped over the Baron's bedchamber, and when Schindler, who came to pay him a visit for several days, called his attention to the stipulation concerning that particular room, he at once became really noisy, banged on the table with his fists, pushed it back and forth, and so on. Schindler disapproved of this behavior and left the room. The following morning he told Beethoven that he wanted to return to Vienna, and all that Beethoven answered was: 'But you'll take coffee first, won't you?!' . . .[47]

Here Beethoven's rebellion exhibits an unmistakable element of sadism, which cannot be denied elsewhere in his behavior. For example, asked to play at a gathering, he said that he would comply only if the well-known composer Wranitzky, who was also present, would crawl under the table on all fours — which the latter actually did.[48] Again, he wrote to Baron von Zmeskall concerning a new servant: ". . . If he is a little humpbacked, I shouldn't mind, because then one knows immediately what is his weak side to attack him on . . ."[49]

It is to the rebel's titanic resistance to all political and civil order, his disregard of all social norms and customs, and the fearlessness and lack of hesitation with which he set himself against authorities and obligations, that we must ascribe a great part of the fascination which Beethoven's personality exercised and still exercises upon many people.[50]

Personalities like Baron von Zmeskall-Domanowecz and Prince

Karl Lichnowsky were practically his slaves. Upon such natures he had the sinister effect which a certain type of Führer-personality produces. The influence exercised by such men is due to the fact that they themselves rebel against all authority and thus embody the unconscious revolutionary tendencies of others. Toward themselves, however, they require absolute submission, and they obtain it because such submission appeases the unconscious feelings of guilt which accompany rebellion against legal or conventional authority in the average person. Beethoven, it would seem, exercised this influence upon others consciously, as appears from a letter to his nephew:

> Our age requires strong-minded men, who will flog these petty, treacherous, miserable scoundrels of human beings.[51]

In addition, his powerful personality, so prone to terrible outbursts of irritation and anger, inspired fear in weaker natures, and he never hesitated to use threats to obtain the submission which he required. Thus he wrote to Baron von Zmeskall:

> . . . I don't want to hear anything about your morality, strength is the morality of men who distinguish themselves above others, and it is mine too; and if you start in again today, I'll plague you until you come to the opinion that everything I do is good and praiseworthy . . .[52]

Or to Kanka, whom he had charged to arrange for the further payment of his annuity after the death of Prince Kinsky:

> . . . If this business turns out badly through the behavior of the K. family, I'll have the story made public in all the papers, exactly as it is, — to the shame of the family.[53]

There is no doubt that his circle feared him. In addition, now that he had become a personage of European fame, he had influence and prestige enough to carry out many of his threats.

Another psychological attitude which is requisite if such a Führer-personality is to influence many people, Beethoven possessed in a high degree. Basically, such men love none of the many who submit themselves to them, for they love themselves more than anything. Beethoven kept on his desk a sheet with the following lines, which he had copied from Schiller's essay, "Die Sendung Moses": "I am that which is," (inscription on an ancient monument of Isis) and "I am all — what is, what was, what will be; no mortal has lifted my veil" (inscription on a pyramid at Saïs).[54] We may assume that he chose these particular passages as his mottoes because, consciously or unconsciously, he identified himself with these statements and thus applied the words to himself. Grandiose narcissism of this sort is typical of the great genius. By its transfer to his work, the latter acquires for its creator the immense significance which justifies him in expending every effort to accomplish it. The enormous importance which the work thus gains for the artist makes it at the same time of such significance to its audience.

When Beethoven wrote on a sketch sheet, addressing himself, "Never let people see any outward sign of the contempt which they deserve, for there is no knowing when they may be needed," [55] he betrayed one of the secrets of his sinister influence over so many small personalities — namely, the very scant respect which he felt for them.[56] Add to this the effect which his magnificent works produced and which shed a glory upon his person such as hardly a composer had enjoyed before him, and we can understand the almost religious reverence which many people felt for him. An example of this is the minor poet Ludwig Rellstab, who owes the survival of his name almost entirely to the fact that Schubert set his poems to music. He describes his first visit to Beethoven in the following terms:

> . . . So one morning, with throbbing heart, I resolved to set out for No. 767 Krugerstrasse where Beethoven was then living . . . When I had climbed the considerable number of stone stairs to the fourth floor, I found at the left a bell-pull with a half-obliterated name; yet I thought I could make out 'Beethoven.' I rang, steps were heard, the door opened: my pulse raced, I really cannot say whether it was a maid who let me in or a young man, Beethoven's nephew, who was living with him at the time and whom I saw once or twice later. My great emotional tension had entirely deprived me of awareness of outward things. All that I remember is that I could hardly bring out the question: 'Does Herr Beethoven live here?' How the gigantic weight of such a great name breaks down the pygmy barriers and laws of convention, behind which boundless mediocrity safeguards its idle rights!
>
> Yet these forms would not surrender their petty rights even here, and I was announced, sent in my letter of introduction from Zelter, and stood waiting in the anteroom. I could still paint it,

in its desolate half emptiness, half disorder. On the floor stood a quantity of empty bottles; on a plain table a few plates, two glasses, one of them half filled. 'Could Beethoven have left that half-glass?' I thought. And a desire came over me to drink the remainder, like a secret theft of bosom-brotherhood, as German custom pledges it.

The door of the adjoining room opened; I was invited to enter. As I stepped timidly over the sacred threshold, my heart beat audibly! I had already stood in the presence of great men, whom youthful poets saw at the same immeasurable height above them; I name only Goethe and Jean Paul. — Yet I had not experienced this kind of feeling toward these two . . .[57]

So great was the reverence and fear with which people approached him! The glory which enveloped him was at the same time largely based upon terror of him. The ungovernable nature of his outbursts of wrath left the deepest impression on those who witnessed them, to say nothing of those upon whom they were directed. There was nothing to do but to submit. The poet Grillparzer, who was often in Beethoven's company, said of him: "When he was angry, he was a wild beast."[58] Terror of him simply forced his intimates to agree with him. He tolerated no contradiction, and no admonition to reason, in matters which had a strong emotional coloring for him, such as his relationship to his nephew or to Johanna. This is clearly apparent from the remarks and answers of his friends in the Conversation Books. Hence the similarity in the accounts of Johanna by all who were under his fascinating and commanding influence. This includes practically all of his biographers.

The titles which Beethoven jokingly bestowed upon himself, such as "Commanding General" or "Generalissimo," are significant of his attitude toward those whom he used for his purposes.

The sense of Beethoven's greatness as a man — of a greatness which, though inseparably connected with his works, is something over and above their aggregate effect, and which casts its spell on us all, even today — is based upon the personality traits which we have just described. In his *Moses and Monotheism*, Freud, in connection with the personality of the prophet Moses, investigates the concept of the "great man." His point of departure is the fact that we do not immediately call *every* man with extraordinary ability in some field, even an outstanding artist or scientist, a "great man": ". . . When we declare, for instance, Goethe, Leonardo da Vinci, Beethoven to be great men, something else must move us to do so beyond the admiration of their grandiose creations . . ." [59]

We see that even Freud, who, as he himself tells us, had scarcely any sympathy with music, could not escape the influence of Beethoven, so saturated was the atmosphere of Vienna with his powerful personality after more than a century. Otherwise Freud would not have coupled his name with those of two other great men who were of extraordinary significance to him. After making the statement quoted above, Freud explains why we call such men "great":

. . . Why the great man should rise to significance at all we have no doubt whatever. We know that the great majority of people have a strong need for authority which they can admire, to which they can submit, and which dominates and sometimes even illtreats them. We have learned from the psychology of the individual whence comes this need of the masses. It is the longing for the father that lives in each of us from his childhood days, for the same father whom the hero of legend boasts of having overcome. And now it begins to dawn on us that all the features with which we furnish the great man are traits of the father, that in this similarity lies the essence, which so far has eluded us, of the great man. The decisiveness of thought, the strength of will, the forcefulness of his deeds, belong to the picture of the father; above all other things, however, the self-reliance and independence of the great man, his divine conviction of doing the right thing, which may pass into ruthlessness. He must be admired, he may be trusted, but one cannot help also being afraid of him. We should have taken a cue from the word itself; who else but the father should in childhood have been the great man? . . . [60]

Almost all of the traits which Freud here describes in the great man can be found in Beethoven; Freud had good reason to name him in this context. In so doing, he puts him on a plane with the powerful Führer-personality of Moses, with whom Beethoven has in common, among other things, lack of self-control, violence of wrath, rebellion against civil authority, and the inexorable insistence that others submit to him. The similarity in the character and influence of these two great men has led W. J. Henderson too to a like conclusion: "We do not hesitate to set him [Beethoven] in the foremost rank beside Moses and the Prophets." [61]

His rebellion against all authority and his ruthlessly dominating behavior toward others made Ludwig a hero and leader, and the fascination of his personality is based upon the combination of the rebel with the terror-inspiring father-figure. His Promethean masculinity had a profound and enduring effect.

Yet there was an important area of life in which, for inner reasons, he could not assert this outspoken masculinity; namely, in his relation to the female sex.

VII

CONFLICT WITH WOMEN

BEETHOVEN'S love-life was already a riddle to his contemporaries, and, like his biographers after them, they filled this gap in their several descriptions of Beethoven's personality each according to his viewpoint — some by imagining erotic relationships for the great master, others by explaining his asexuality on the ground of his strict and lofty morality. Thus Wegeler tells us that all through the time that he (Wegeler) remained in Vienna, Beethoven was involved in love-affairs and made occasional conquests; [1] whereas Wähner, who knew Ludwig equally well, asserts that love appears never to have had any power over him. [2] Ries says that Beethoven frequently fell in love, but generally only for brief periods. [3] At the same time he does not report a single specific love-affair observed by him during his intimate relationship with his friend and master. Bertolini, Ludwig's physician and friend, says that Beethoven habitually had one or another "flame"; [4] on which Dolezalek comments that if he was in love, no one ever saw any signs of it. [5] Ignaz von Seyfried says: "Beethoven was not married, and, remarkably enough, was never involved in a love-affair either." [6] As we see, the statements of Beethoven's contemporaries are in such disagreement that our best procedure will be to draw no far-reaching conclusions from them concerning his relationship to women or to a particular woman. In any case, we have no evidence that he ever pushed to fulfillment any of the love-affairs ascribed to him by his biographers. On the other hand the documents furnish many indications from which we can read the negative side of his relationship to women. Of the *defensiveness* which he exhibited in this relationship, there can be no possible doubt. It can be traced through every stage of his development, from his youth to the end of his life.

97

Outside of his own family, the first member of the opposite sex in whom Ludwig appears to have shown any marked interest was Eleonore von Breuning, the daughter of the lady in whose house Ludwig served as piano-teacher and was received as a member of the family during the five years preceding his final removal to Vienna. Two letters from Ludwig to Eleonore, who was two years younger than himself, are extant. The first, presumably written in 1791, reads:

> I beg you, however little I may deserve belief in your eyes, believe me, my friend (let me still call you so), I have suffered greatly and still suffer from the loss of your friendship. I shall never forget you and your dear mother. You were so kind to me that I shall not soon be able to make good your loss, I know what I have lost and what you were to me, but — to fill up this blank, I should have to return to scenes which are unpleasant for you to hear and for me to describe.
>
> As a small return for your kind remembrance of me, I take the liberty of sending you herewith some Variations and the Rondo with violin . . .
>
> Fare you well, my friend. It is impossible for me to call you otherwise, however indifferent I may be to you, pray believe that I still honor you and your mother as much as formerly. If I am in a position to contribute anything further to your happiness, I beg you not to pass me over; it is the only way still remaining for me to show my gratitude for the friendship which I have enjoyed.
>
> Have a happy journey and bring your dear mother back completely restored to health. Think sometimes of your
>
> Friend who still and ever honors you,
Beethoven.[7]

There had, then, been a breach in the friendship; and Ludwig felt that he was responsible for it. What he had done to lose this friendship does not appear, either here or in his second letter to Eleonore. He wrote it two years later, from Vienna, in an attempt to dispel the unpleasant impression which his conduct must have left in her:

> Honored Eleonore, my dearest Friend,
> I shall soon have been in this capital a whole year, yet only now do you receive a letter from me, but you were certainly constantly in my thoughts. Frequently, indeed, did I hold converse with you and your dear family, but, for the most part, not with the

tranquillity of mind which I should have liked. Then it was that the fatal quarrel hovered before me, and my former behavior appeared to me so abominable. But the past cannot be undone, and what would I not give if I could blot out of my life my former conduct so dishonoring to me, so contrary to my character. Many circumstances, indeed, kept us at a distance from each other, and, as I presume, it was especially the insinuations resulting from conversations on either side which prevented all reconciliation. Each of us believed that he was convinced of the truth of what he said, and yet it was mere anger, and we were both deceived. Your good and noble character is indeed a guarantee that I have long since been forgiven. But true repentance consists, so it is said, in acknowledging one's faults, and this I intended to do. And now let us draw a curtain over the whole story, and only learn from it the lesson that when friends fall out it is always better to have no go-between, but for friend to turn directly to friend . . .

> Your true friend,
> L. v. Beethoven.

P.S. — The V[ariations] will be somewhat difficult to play, especially the shakes in the Coda. But don't let that alarm you. It is so arranged that you need only play the shake; the other notes you leave out, as they are also in the violin part. I never would have written anything of the kind, but I had already frequently noticed that there was some one in V[ienna] who generally, when I had been improvising of an evening, noted down next day many of my peculiarities in composing, and boasted about them. Now as I foresaw that such things would soon appear [in print], I resolved to be beforehand with them. And there was another reason for perplexing the pianists here, viz., many of them are my deadly enemies, so I wished in this way to take vengeance on them, for I knew beforehand that here and there the Variations would be put before them, and that these gentlemen would come off badly.[8]

From Ludwig's explanation of the cause of the quarrel, we see that he lays the principal blame on "insinuations resulting from conversations on either side," thus admitting that he had talked about Eleonore to others, and that he had believed the gossip others had brought to him. The one is explained by the passionateness and primitive lack of self-control which were so characteristic of him, the other by his readiness to distrust people, including his intimates. This distrust is also apparent in the postscript to the letter. It is one of his most striking characteristics. He feels himself perpetually taken advantage of and robbed — and this, as the letter shows, long before his hearing was threatened. Hence his distrust cannot have been *caused* by his deafness, but only strengthened by it. Such distrust is the expression of the individual's own hostile feelings, which are projected into the outside world, a process which results in an increased preparedness against imaginary dangers from without. The causes of such a heightened readiness for hostile aggression are disillusionments in the first exemplary love-object, especially the mother.[9] That Ludwig's early relationship to his mother was highly ambivalent must be concluded from his extremely troubled attitude toward women. From the course of the relationships which, after his friendship with Eleonore von Breuning, he developed to other women, we can conclude with considerable certainty that inner causes impelled Ludwig to destroy his friendship with her. Eleonore later married Beethoven's loyal older friend Dr. Wegeler, who had introduced him to the Breunings. Ludwig never saw her again.

From 1793 to 1798, there is no known letter from Ludwig to a woman in whom he was personally interested, although dozens of other letters are extant. In 1798 he wrote two letters to the poetess Christine von Gerardi. In the first he thanked her for verses she had sent him in his praise, and expressed the wish to make her acquaintance. The second letter reads:

> Dear Ch. You made some remarks yesterday about the portrait of me. — I could wish that you would nevertheless proceed somewhat cautiously in the matter; I fear that, if we decide upon returning it through F., the annoying B. or the arch-fool Josef might interfere, and then too the thing might have been intended as a trick on me and that would really be annoying; I should have to defend myself again and the whole *populasse* does not deserve it. Try to get hold of the thing as well as may be; I assure you that, after this, I will ask all painters, in the press, not to paint me any more without my knowledge, I did not think that my own countenance could still get me into an embarrassing situation.
> As to the matter of lifting the hat, it is too stupid and at the same time too impolite for me to have dared to do such a thing, so set him to rights about the walk. — Adieu, the devil take you.[10]

Obviously, his relationship with the poetess is already strained; what the "annoying" matter referred to in the letter may be, it is impossible to guess; in any case, a portrait of him, painted without his knowledge, figures in it. The conclusion of the letter speaks for itself. Christine disappeared from Beethoven's life.

All the relationships which Ludwig developed to women took the same or a similar course. They all led to non-fulfillment, to a dead end, to a quarrel; more and more they terminated in a withdrawal to a womanless solitude. This was the case with Therese von Malfatti, with Countess Giulietta Guicciardi, with Countess Therese Brunswick. His interest in these women of so much higher social position than his own was doomed from the beginning. How ready Ludwig was to draw back when he had ventured a little distance, appears from a very warm letter to Therese von Malfatti, which clearly betrays a certain intensity in the relationship between him and the young woman, who was soon to leave for the country. It ends:

> Commend me to the good will of your father, your mother, although I can yet lay no rightful claim to it, — likewise to that of your cousin M. [?]. Now fare well, honored T., I wish you everything that is good and beautiful in life. Keep me in remembrance, and fondly — *forget that wild behavior* — be convinced that no one can wish you a freer, happier life than I, even though you take no interest
>
> in your most devoted servant and friend
Beethoven.[11]

The "wild behavior" which he wanted Therese to forget is obviously an eruption of his positive feeling for her, some expression of it which he regarded as too daring and outspoken.

Among papers which Beethoven had carefully preserved, and which were found in a "secret drawer" after his death, is the celebrated letter to the "Immortal Beloved." We do not know in what year this letter with two postscripts was written. We give it in full:

July 6, morning.

> My angel, my all, my self. — Only a few words today, and indeed in pencil — (with yours); my lodgings will not be definitely settled upon until tomorrow; what a useless waste of time over such matters! — Why this deep sorrow where necessity speaks? — Can our love endure otherwise than through sacrifices, through not demanding everything. Can you alter it that you are not wholly mine, I not wholly yours? Oh God, look upon beautiful Nature and

calm your heart concerning what must be; — love demands everything, and rightly so, thus it is for me with you, for you with me
— only you so easily forget that I must live for myself and for
you; — if we were wholly united you would feel this painfulness
as little as I. — My journey was terrible. I did not arrive here
until four in the morning yesterday; as there was a shortage of
horses, the mailcoach took another route; but what a terrible road;
at the stage before the last I was warned against traveling by
night, told that the forest was to be feared, but that only spurred
me on and I was wrong, the carriage must needs break down what
with the terrible road, bottomless, a mere country road; without
such postilions as I had, I should have got stuck on the way. —
Esterhazi, traveling the other road here, the usual one, had the
same fate with 8 horses as I with four. — Yet I had some pleasure
from it, as always when I successfully get through something. —
Now quickly from outward things to those within; we shall
very probably soon see each other, besides, I cannot impart to
you today the observations I have made during the last few days
concerning my life. — If our hearts were always close together, I
should probably not make any such. My heart is full with much
to say to you; — ah, there are moments when I find that language is nothing after all. — Be of good cheer — remain my true,
my only treasure, my all, as I to you; the rest, the gods must
send, what must be and shall be for us. —

Your faithful
Ludwig. —

Monday evening July 6.

You are suffering, you, my dearest creature. — I have only just
learned that letters must be posted very early in the morning.
Mondays, Thursdays — the only days when the post goes from
here to K. — You are suffering. — Ah, where I am, you are with
me, I talk with myself and you, make it possible that I can live
with you, what a life!!!! thus!!!! without you — pursued hither
and thither by the goodness of men, which I think — I as little
care to deserve as I deserve it. — Humility of man towards man —
it pains me. And when I consider myself in the context of the
Universe, what am I and what is he who is called the greatest?
— And yet — herein again lies the divine in man. —
I weep when I think that you will probably not receive the first
news from me until Saturday. — However you love me — I love
you more strongly. — But never hide your thoughts from me —
good night. — As I am taking the baths, I must go to bed [two
words obliterated]. Oh God — so near, so far! is not our love a
true heavenly mansion, yet as firm as the firm vault of heaven. —

Good morning on July 7 —

Even in bed, my thoughts press toward you, my immortal beloved, now and then joyfully, then again sadly, waiting to learn if fate will hear our prayer. — I can live either wholly with you or not at all; yes, I have resolved to wander in distant lands until I can fly into your arms and can say that I am wholly at home with you, can send my spirit, enwrapped in you, into the realm of spirits. Yes, unfortunately it must be so, — you will gain self-command, the more so as you know my loyalty to you, never can another woman possess my heart, never, never! O God, why must one go far [from] what one so loves; and yet my life in V[ienna] as it is now is a miserable life. — Your love made me at once the happiest and unhappiest of men. — At my age now I need a certain regularity, equability of life; — can these exist in our circumstances? Angel, I have just learned that the post goes every day, — and hence I must close, so that you may receive this letter at once. — Be calm, — only through calm consideration of our existence can we attain our goal, living together. — Be calm, — love me. — Today — yesterday — what longing and tears for you — you — you — my life — my all, — fare well — oh, continue to love me — never misjudge the most faithful heart

      Of your beloved

           L

ever yours
ever mine
ever us.[12]

This is the only letter of Beethoven's in which he uses the intimate form "Du" in addressing a woman. Volumes have been filled with subtle hypotheses as to the identity of the mysterious woman who inspired the great man to these passionate utterances. None of these hypotheses has remained uncontested. Nor has anyone been able to prove that any woman ever received the letter.

What is of far greater interest to the psychologist is what the letter reveals concerning the writer of it. There is no doubt that it was written under the immediate impression of an agitating emotional experience with the beloved one. The writer is brimming with it. We get the impression that he here made what was apparently a bolder advance into the realm of love of the opposite sex than at any other time in his life. How far it went, we cannot judge; but in any case it was too far for him. For the letter, despite all its ardent expressions of love, is to be understood as a refusal and as a summons to the beloved to renounce. From this standpoint it is possible, without doing violence to the data, to reconstruct the essentials of the occurrence to which the letter represents Beethoven's reaction. In whatever way the emotional coming together of the two lovers may have found expression, there can be no doubt that the beloved disclosed her affection to him. She refused to accept his objections to a lasting relationship; she was obviously suffering from his insistence upon them at the moment of parting. This elucidates the first sentences of the letter, which refer to what had taken place: "Why this deep sorrow, where necessity speaks? Can our love endure otherwise than through sacrifices, through not demanding everything?" The painful agitation which his lack of initiative has aroused in her, he tries to counter with a not very effective piece of consolation: "Oh God, look upon beautiful Nature and calm your heart concerning what must be." He expresses his intention or hope of soon seeing her; yet he does not propose doing anything to bring it about; the gods must send "what must be and shall be for us."

A psychologist cannot but consider it symbolically significant that this part of the letter, which sets forth the necessity for renunciation and urges it, also includes a description of the dangers of Ludwig's journey. Ludwig had disregarded the warning he had received, he had braved the darkness, had tried not to be afraid of the forest; but the road was terrible and bottomless, so the carriage had to break down. He had been rescued only with difficulty, and was now happy to have got through the danger.

The first postscript dwells upon the beloved's sufferings, but the writer says nothing about suffering himself or that her suffering inspires him to any concrete action which might end it. It is probably in compensation for his inner necessity to make the beloved suffer through his inhibition and defensiveness that, at the end of the letter, he compares their love to a heavenly mansion; and his emphasis on its firmness seems to represent a vehement denial of his awareness that it is failing in himself.

The final postscript shows that his renunciation and turning away have progressed overnight. He no longer expects or hopes to see her soon; instead, he has made up his mind to "wander in distant lands" until he can fly to her arms — an outcome which any amount of such wandering about would certainly never have made possible. "Yes, unfortunately it must be so," he writes, and laments his inner need to give her up: "O God, why must one go far [from] what one loves . . ." He even gives reasons for his retreat. "At my age now I need a certain regularity, equability of life; — can these exist in our circumstances?" His final admonition — "Be calm, — only through calm consideration of our existence can we attain our goal, living together" — is a tragic admission of his inability to deal with women.[13] Significantly enough, he ends his letter, "your *beloved* L." — not "your *loving* L."

The check to his erotic impulse and the defensive reaction within him also find expression in a minor detail which is nevertheless significant. He is not sufficiently careful in inquiring when the mail leaves for K., and twice corrects himself on the point. It is not going too far to assume that the letters were never sent at all, and that the "Immortal Beloved" never laid eyes on them.[14] Beethoven could not bear to part from anything in writing; so, with everything else, he kept these letters until his death. If the year in which they were written is 1812, as the majority of the biographers assume, a remark which Beethoven made in 1816 to Giannatasio del Rio may well refer to the "Immortal Beloved." Fanny Giannatasio wrote in her diary:

> . . . My father asked him if he did not know anyone, etc. I listened with the utmost attention, at some distance, and learned something which threw my inmost soul into turmoil, which confirmed a long foreboding — he was unhappy in love! Five years ago he had become acquainted with a person, a more intimate union with whom he would have considered the greatest happiness of his life. It was not to be thought of, almost impossible, a chimera. Nevertheless, it was still as on the very first day. 'I have not been able to get it out of my mind,' were the words which affected me so painfully . . .[15]

And on May 8, 1816 he wrote to Ries:

> . . . All good wishes to your wife; alas, I have none; I found but one woman, and her I shall never possess, but that has not made me a woman-hater.[16]

However, the statement that he was not a woman-hater cannot be allowed to stand uncontradicted, as later events will show.

If Ludwig developed an erotic interest in women who were beyond his reach, this choice in itself served his defensiveness. An exception is his relationship to Amalie Sebald, a most attractive and gifted singer from Berlin, whom Ludwig met in 1811 at Teplitz. In a letter to the poet Tiedge, he sends Amalie "a fiery kiss when no one sees us." Yet the lady's presence at Karlsbad the following summer does not seem to have helped the relationship along. We have seven letters from Ludwig to Amalie, written during the period of their second encounter. They are letters in which he excuses himself from seeing Amalie because he is ill. We quote sentences from five of them: "I was not quite well even yesterday, since this morning it has grown worse; I think I must have eaten something indigestible." — "Since I parted from you yesterday, my condition has become worse, and I have not left my bed since yesterday evening." — "I only announce to you that the tyrant [Ludwig himself] is chained to his bed like a slave." — "My illness seems not to be making strides, but still to be creeping along, at any rate it is not yet arrested!" — "I cannot yet tell you anything definite about myself, at moments I seem to have improved, then to have fallen back into the old course, or I might be taking a turn toward a long illness, — I still must stay in bed today." [17]

In addition, the letters show that the relationship was superficially a playful one; yet, behind this, one senses the possibility of a deeper affection which the writer feels as a danger against which he must guard himself. In any case, Ludwig's defensiveness gained the upper hand; again and again he used his illness as an excuse to avoid seeing Amalie and after the summer of 1812 we hear no more of her in Ludwig's life. Probably the struggle to protect himself which finds expression in the following diary entry of 1812 refers to his relationship to Amalie:

> Submission, the most devout submission to your fate, only this can give you the [self-] sacrifice — for your obligation. O hard struggle! . . .
> You must not be a man, not for yourself, only for others. For you there is no more happiness except in yourself, in your art. — O God, give me the strength to conquer myself; nothing must chain me to life. In this way with A. [Amalie?] everything goes to ruin.[18]

This exhausts the biographical material which demonstrably refers to an erotic relationship with a woman. Ludwig's defensiveness against falling in love with a woman may be the reason why the material is so scanty. Of course, he had relationships with other women, but these were in the nature of friendships. The high social position of these women and the fact that they were married and had children excluded them from the first as objects of conscious erotic aspirations. He respected them, and showed it, even though it was often in his cross-grained and sometimes almost boorish way. Nevertheless, he succeeded in gaining their good will and arousing a motherly fondness in them. They tried to take care of him and protect him from his own imprudences. Madame von Breuning was the first of these motherly friends. His relationship with Princess Lichnowsky was of the same kind. It is to this remarkable woman that we owe the revision of *Fidelio,* which Beethoven undertook with a heavy heart after the Princess had made him swear by his mother's memory that he would rewrite the opera. Beethoven said of her later that in her household he was "fostered with a grandmotherly love that went to such lengths that the Princess was often not far from having a glass bell made and put over me so that no unworthy person could touch me or breathe on me." [19] Years later, he expressed his gratitude for the Princess's affectionate care with unusual warmth. [20] Countess Erdödy may serve as a third example. In one letter he addressed her as "Dear, dear, dear, dear Countess." [21] Ludwig lived for some time in her house, until he learned that she was secretly paying his servant an extra five florins a month, and had given him twenty-five florins, to keep the man from leaving him. [22] Other differences arose between himself and the Countess, and it was not long before he left her house. Later, however, he was reconciled with her, and he continued to write to her even after she had been banished from Vienna, for reasons which are not known, and was living on her estate in Croatia.

Both Princess Lichnowsky and Countess Erdödy were semi-invalids; Princess Lichnowsky had had both breasts amputated and was obliged to spend the greater part of the day in bed. Countess Erdödy had suffered an incurable injury in giving birth to her first child. She could be out of bed only three months in the year, and then she "limped from piano to piano with enormously swollen feet." [23] These women's invalidism doubtless made it easier for him to re-experience his own mother in them, and they treated him like a dearly loved, if difficult and irritable, son.

A striking trait is revealed in Beethoven's relationship to another type of married woman. Careful as he was to give no occasion for the slightest suspicion that he might have an erotic interest in the wife of a friend, and sternly as he judged extramarital relationships in others,[24] he was apparently not averse to making ostensibly playful allusions to the possibility of his having a secret erotic relationship with the wife of one of his more intimate friends whose social position was the same as his own. This seems to have been the cause of a regrettable misunderstanding between himself and his friends the Bigots. One fine morning in the summer of 1808, Beethoven had urgently invited Frau Bigot and her little daughter Caroline to go driving with him, despite the fact that, only the day before, Herr Bigot had said that he did not want to let his wife go out with Ludwig. Frau Bigot therefore refused, and Herr Bigot took offense at Ludwig's invitation to her. Ludwig immediately wrote a letter full of regrets and excuses. He says: "Moreover, it is one of my first principles never to stand in other than friendly relations with the wife of another man," and, further: "It is possible that I may have jested with Bigot a few times in a way that was not too refined" — "but how can good Marie put so bad a construction on my actions . . ."

> . . . With regard to my invitation to go driving with you and Caroline it was but natural that I should believe, Bigot having opposed your going with me alone, that both of you deemed it unbecoming or objectionable — and when I wrote I had no other purpose than to make you understand that I saw no *harm* in it, and when I declared that it was a matter of great importance to me that you should not refuse it was only to persuade you to enjoy the gloriously beautiful day. I had your and Caroline's pleasure in mind more than my own and I thought to compel you to accede to my wishes when I said that *mistrust on your part or a refusal would really offend me* . . .[25]

It remains sufficiently strange that Ludwig, despite all his care to avoid showing the slightest appearance of interest in a married woman, should get himself into a situation where he was forced to apologize for having urged a woman to do something of which her husband disapproved. Yet such indications of any display of interest in another man's wife are very rare. Further accounts by contemporaries of manifestations of interest in women on Ludwig's part are few, which is significant of his sexual conflict. We learn from Ries that, during the period when the latter was his pupil, Ludwig liked to go to masked balls; Ries could be sure of finding him at such gatherings.[26] And on one occasion a friend writes, in one of the Conversation Books, that he had seen Ludwig in a street where prostitutes were looking for customers.[27] From an anecdote told by the Austrian poet Grillparzer, who knew Ludwig personally and wanted to write an opera libretto for him, it is clear that he was once attracted by a woman of questionable reputation:

> During one of the following summers, I often visited my grandmother, who had a country house in the nearby village of Döbling. Beethoven too was staying in Döbling at the time. Across from my grandmother's windows stood the dilapidated house of a peasant celebrated for his slovenliness; his name was Flohberger. This Flohberger, in addition to his run-down house, was also the proud possessor of a very pretty but not too well-famed daughter named Lise. Beethoven seemed to take a great interest in the girl. I can still see him come up the Hirschengasse, his white handkerchief held in his right hand and dragging on the ground, then stop and stand before the gateway to Flohberger's yard, in which the frivolous beauty, perched on a hay wagon or manure cart, would be vigorously plying her fork and laughing all the time. I never saw Beethoven speak to her, he stood silently staring in until finally the girl, whose taste ran more to peasant lads, sometimes by a mocking word, sometimes by stubbornly ignoring him, roused his anger, then he would turn quickly and rush away, but, for all that, did not fail to stop at the gateway again the next time. Indeed, his interest went so far that, when the girl's father was sent to the village jail . . . in consequence of a drunken brawl, Beethoven went in person to the village council to demand his release and, in his usual way, accorded Their Worships such rough treatment that he came very close to becoming the unwilling companion of his imprisoned protégé.[28]

Yet in contrast to these scant indications of approaches to the opposite sex, we have abundant testimony to Ludwig's aversion to women. We also have observations by contemporaries which clearly show Beethoven in the role of rejecting an erotic relationship. Nikolaus Simrock, the horn player, writes, for example:

> One noon at an eating-place some young fellows bribed the waitress to conquer Beethoven with her charms. Beethoven received her provocations with disdainful coldness and when, encouraged by the others, she refused to desist, he lost patience and put an end to her importunities by a box on the ear.[29]

Holz reports that the violinist Schuppanzigh "after a gay gathering once took Beethoven to a girl, and then did not dare to appear before him for many weeks." [30] In addition, as we have seen, he tried to induce other men, particularly his intimates, to adopt the same defensive attitude toward women. The first of his extant letters to his brother Johann, who was then twenty, warns him: "Only beware of the whole tribe of bad women." [31] Ludwig's unsuccessful attempt, in Linz seventeen years later, to save Johann from his future wife has been described in Chapter III. His letters to his friend Zmeskall frequently contain warnings such as: ". . . I need no longer warn you to beware of expenditures before certain fortresses. There is now profound quiet everywhere!!!" [32] The "fortresses" symbolize women, as appears from the following passage from a letter: ". . . fare well, keep away from decaying fortresses; assaulting them is more costly than assaulting well-kept ones." [33] This is a reference to the greater danger of venereal infection from women of doubtful reputation.

Again:

> . . . So far as the fortresses are concerned, I thought I had informed you that I have no wish to maintain myself in swampy ground . . .[34]
> . . . Fare well, but not lustfully. Owner, Commandant, Pasha of sundry decaying fortresses!!!!! [35]

Beethoven's "moral purity," as his defensive attitude toward women is termed by many of his biographers, went so far that he rejected two of Mozart's operas on the ground that their librettos were lascivious. He said to Rellstab: "I could not compose operas like Don Juan and Figaro. They are repugnant to me. — I could not have chosen such subjects, they are too wanton for me." [36] In his only opera, Fidelio, composed in 1809 and subtitled "Conjugal

Love," the principal part is played by a woman, Leonore, who, disguised as a man, saves her husband Florestan from prison and from destruction by the evil principle incarnated in the governor of the prison, Pizzaro. Leonore, after whom the opera was originally named, since she plays the principal role, appears throughout the opera in male attire; she triumphs by her courage and daring; she rescues Florestan and brings him from the darkness of the deepest dungeon to the light of day. It is unmistakable that, years later, when he saved his nephew from destruction by the evil principle — Johanna — Ludwig assumed the role of Leonore himself. And in doing so, he too was a woman in man's clothing, as Chapters IV and V have sufficiently shown.

After Ludwig gained possession of his nephew, we find no further signs in him of any erotic interest in a woman. His total renunciation of the idea of a union with a woman received expression in a conversation with Giannatasio's daughters:

> He said that he had never known of a marriage in which, after a time, one or the other partner had not regretted the step, and that, of the few young ladies whom he had in earlier days wished to make his own, considering that the height of happiness, he had later remarked to himself that he was very lucky that none of them had become his wife, and what a good thing it was that the wishes of mortals often remain unfulfilled.[37]

The conflict which raged within him between desire and defensiveness was brought to a temporary conclusion by his conquest and possession of his nephew. The positive element in his extremely ambivalent relationship to the female sex was absorbed into his identification with woman. His masculine love of woman was transformed into maternal love of his nephew. The hatred and hostility which his positive feelings had hitherto neutralized could now emerge with undiminished violence. They found their expression in his embittered and relentless campaign against his child's real mother. The exaggerated intensity of his hate shows, at the same time, that the psychic equilibrium which Ludwig attained through his conquest of his nephew was highly unstable and could only be maintained through constant effort.

VIII

DISQUIET BEFORE THE STORM

MORE than passing mention must be accorded to another woman who, during the years 1816–1818, played a very important part in the great master's life. Her role was not that of a love-object, but of motherly protectress and counsellor. Her name was Nanette Streicher. She was the wife of the pianoforte-maker Johann Andreas Streicher, who made several pianos for Beethoven, attempting to adjust them to his increasing deafness. Frau Streicher, who was herself an excellent pianist, had first taken Beethoven under her wing at Baden in 1813, when she found him "in a desolate state" in respect to his physical and domestic needs.[1] His active relationship to her, however, did not develop until 1817, and lasted a year and a half. Frau Streicher deserves great gratitude, not only for her unwearying efforts to help the master with advice and services in the increasing difficulties which his "motherhood" brought upon him, but also as the most important source of our knowledge of Beethoven's outward circumstances and psychological state at this time. For during those eighteen months the composer wrote her a great many letters, sixty-five of which are extant. It was the period when he was thinking more and more of setting up a household for himself and his Karl. This was a harrowing undertaking; even the thought of it upset and terrified Ludwig; and he used all sorts of excuses to put off establishing a home for his nephew. One of the reasons for his hesitation was the necessity of taking on a housekeeper if he was to have Karl with him. All through the previous years, Ludwig had had constant difficulties with his servants, as is shown by the numerous letters to Zmeskall in which he asks or orders him to procure other maids or menservants for him, because he found the old ones unbearable or had already dismissed them. It was when he had resolved to take Karl to live with him that his dislike of servants reached its climax. As we showed at the end of the previous chapter, his "motherhood" intensified his hostility to women in general. But if he took Karl to live with him, a woman in the household would be particularly unwelcome, for there was the danger that Karl would become fond of her and then Ludwig would have to share his child with a woman. This jealousy tormented him in advance, and led him to defer setting up a household.

We cite two passages from letters to Frau Streicher written during this period of indecision:

> As to a housekeeper, I will give it further consideration; if only, in this state of utter moral corruption of the Austrian nation, one could be at all convinced that one might expect to find an honest person, it would be easy, but — but — !!! [2]
> Tomorrow I will come to you at noon, if you will be so good as to have the housekeeper present at the same time, I shall be greatly obliged to you. — Yesterday I reckoned up future expenses with someone; — he reckoned 2 florins for servants and 2 for the housekeeper simply for food, does this mean that the manservant with 20 florins a month and the housekeeper with 120 florins a year would cost a total of 1704 florins just for the two? — Must this be? — God have mercy on us. — [3]

The second passage also reveals that he did not entirely trust Frau Streicher and checked her estimate of household expenses by consulting someone else, thus only increasing confusion and intensifying his fear of setting up housekeeping. For at this period Ludwig was also tormented by another imaginary danger. He feared that he would be reduced to poverty.

This idea of impending poverty appeared immediately after his brother Karl's death. On November 22, 1815 — six days, that is, after he lost his brother — he wrote to Ries:

> . . . I beg you most urgently, my dear Ries! to take charge of this matter, and to see that I receive the money! it is costing a great deal, until everything comes in, and I need it.
> I have lost 600 florins per year from my salary; at the time of the bank-money notes it was nothing; — then came the redemption notes, and through those I lost the 600 florins, with several years of vexations and complete loss of my salary. Now we have reached

the point where the redemption notes are worse than the bank-
money notes were then; I pay 1000 florins for rent . . .[4]

And again on May 8:

> . . . my salary amounts to 3400 florins in paper, I pay 1100 for
> rent, and almost 900 to my manservant and his wife. So you can
> reckon what is left over. In addition I have to provide entirely
> for my little nephew, he is still in the Institute. This costs as much
> as 1100 florins, and is poor at that, so that I must set up a regular
> household and bring him here to live with me. How much one
> has to earn merely to be able to live here! . . .[5]

Ries himself writes in his reminiscences:

> . . . Since almost all the letters which I received from him in
> England concerned his financial straits, — why should he not like-
> wise have sent me manuscripts, if he had had any? [6]

But manuscripts were the very thing which he could not produce after his conquest of his nephew. On May 16, 1816 he wrote
to Charles Neate at London, in English:

> . . . hardly I can live alone three months upon my annual salary
> of 3400 florins in paper and now the additional burden of main-
> taining a poor orphan . . .[7]

These letters, especially the one to Ries in which he complained
of losing all his money, have led many writers to conceive that
Ludwig was miserably poor. Fry, for example, writes: ". . . as
anyone acquainted with his career knows, he lived a necessitous
life, corresponding to his poverty and to his inferior position as
a composer . . ."[8]

Thayer, in his meticulous way, calculated Beethoven's receipts
at this period and found his complaints over his financial situation
unjustified and incomprehensible. In 1813, Ludwig had received
the sum of 3,400 florins in redemption notes from the princes. Arrears to April, 1815, to the amount of 4,987 florins, were paid to
him in full. Neate had paid him 75 guineas, and the publisher
Steiner had settled his account in full. Birchall sent him 65 pounds,
and the publisher Thompson had likewise fulfilled his obligations.
During the period of the Vienna Congress, he had been able to
save 4,000 silver gulden, with which, in 1819, he bought seven
shares of bank stock, which were found in a secret drawer of his

desk after his death. Nor had his nephew been left entirely without means; he had a claim to part of a house in Vienna and to part
of another in the little town of Retz in Lower Austria. The widow
Johanna's yearly income amounted to 1,500 florins.

The constant concern over impending poverty which becomes
so marked in Ludwig after his brother Karl's death must, then,
be attributed to a psychological cause. Such a cause is not hard to
find. His income, aside from his annual salary, consisted of the
proceeds from the sale of his works to publishers. If his productivity had been only moderately satisfactory, his European fame
at this period would have assured him an ample income. The
music publishers of Vienna, Leipzig, Paris, and London were
eager to have their imprint upon each new work of the famous
"tone-poet," as he preferred to call himself; and he was well versed
in playing off the rival houses against one another to obtain higher
fees. The prices he demanded were unusually high for the period.
But he could usually only demand them when he produced new
compositions. Yet during his struggle for the boy, his creative
power had diminished in a way which justified grave concern. The
years 1816–1819 are the most unproductive of his life. In 1816 he
finished the Piano Sonata, Opus 101, and the song cycle "An die
Ferne Geliebte" (begun in 1815), and composed a little cantata
for Prince Lobkowitz's birthday, and the D-major March for military band. No sketches for new works are traceable to this year.
Thayer calls 1817 "the most unfruitful year of his life." [9] During
the first six months of it he did not even sketch a work, during the
second he wrote nothing but the trio for three male voices "Rasch
tritt der Tod den Menschen an," the Fugue in D major, a short
piece for five stringed instruments, and, the greatest musical accomplishment of the year, the arrangement of the C-minor Trio,
Opus 1, for quintet (Opus 104). All three works are of minor importance, as their unfamiliarity shows. In 1818 he worked on the
sketches for the Sonata in B major, Opus 106, on variations and
songs which he was getting ready for Thompson in London, on
sketches for the Missa Solemnis, and on the first sketches for the
Ninth Symphony. In 1819 he continued work on the sketches for
the Missa and the Ninth Symphony (which was not finished until
1823), on more folksongs for Thompson and on the Variations,

Opus 107. All this is a very small output for four years, if we consider that Beethoven was then in the prime of life, devoted himself
entirely to composition, and had no obligations of a practical nature. Composition in itself was a great labor, and he had an entirely
different way of working from such other masters as Bach, Handel,
Haydn, and Mozart. A thorough student of Beethoven's music,
Nottebohm, writes of his method of working:

> Beethoven is the only one of our great composers in whose case
> we have the advantage . . . of being able to use his sketch-
> books. It is not known that any of our other great composers
> sketched and kept sketchbooks in the way Beethoven did. We may
> safely assert that they did not sketch at all, or sketched very little
> in comparison with Beethoven. That Beethoven used sketchbooks
> accords with his way of composing. Beethoven worked slowly and
> laboriously. His ideas erupted volcanically and had to be used
> again and again before they reached final form ... . Sketching,
> keeping sketchbooks, became a habit, a necessity, the smallest piece
> had to be sketched before it was fairly copied out . . .
>   Beethoven kept a sharp eye on his sketchbooks, that is, he later
> read through what he had written at previous times. Passages which
> attracted him were then copied, and compositions which had been
> abandoned were resumed and partly completed . . .
>   It is understandable that Beethoven wrote comparatively few
> works. He was continually active for at least thirty years, but
> during that time he produced less work than any of our other
> great masters in a shorter period. Had Beethoven worked as
> easily and rapidly as, say, Haydn or Mozart, his compositions would
> number at least half as many again as they actually do. Without
> betraying the secret of his genius, Beethoven's sketchbooks give
> us an idea of his method of production. They exhibit the frag-
> mentary genesis and slow growth of a composition. For us, this
> manner of creating has an element of mystery. The mystery lies,
> first and last, in Beethoven's struggle with his daemon, with his
> genius. His daemon dwelt in these sketchbooks. But the daemon
> has vanished. The spirit and mind which dictated a work does
> not appear in the sketches for it. The sketches do not reveal the
> law by which Beethoven was guided in his creation. Of the
> idea which attains to manifestation only in the work of art, they
> can give no conception. They cannot show us the entire process of
> creation, but only individual, disconnected incidents of it. What
> we call the organic development of a work of art is nowhere to
> be found in the sketches. This means that they contribute noth-
> ing to an understanding and just appreciation of a work of art.
> Certainly, they are superfluous to the understanding of a work

of art. But they are not superfluous to an understanding of the artist, if it is to be a truly comprehensive understanding. For they express something which finds no voice in the finished work of art, in which everything that recalls the past has been obliterated. And this something, this surplus, which the sketches afford, belongs to the biography of the artist Beethoven, to the history of his artistic evolution.[10]

As we see, in Beethoven the process of composition was accompanied by an immense struggle resulting from inner conflicts. In all probability it is to this struggle that we must attribute the unparalleled tension and emotional expressiveness which are such marked characteristics of his work. But his conquest of his nephew disturbed the equilibrium between these opposing tendencies to such a degree that composition became almost impossible.

During this unproductive period after his conquest of his nephew, his inability to work found yet another expression. He failed to follow up, or even bluntly refused, orders for compositions, despite the fact that they were to be extremely well remunerated. In September, 1816 his friend and physician Bertolini introduced one of his patients, the English general Alexander Kyd, to Beethoven. Kyd proposed that Ludwig should compose a symphony, for which Kyd would pay him 200 ducats. He undertook to have it performed in London and assured Beethoven that the proceeds would come to a thousand pounds. At the same time, he expressed the wish that the symphony should be comparatively short and simple, more in the manner of the first two symphonies. Beethoven bluntly rejected the commission. Some days later he and Simrock encountered General Kyd. Ludwig pointed to him and said: "There is the man I threw down my stairs yesterday." The incident caused a permanent break with Bertolini, who had introduced Kyd to Ludwig.[11]

The Viennese "Gesellschaft der Musikfreunde" wished Beethoven to compose an oratorio for its use. Zmeskall acted as the intermediary in the transaction. In this connection, Ludwig wrote to him in January, 1816:

> My respected Zmeskall!
> Not until today did I realize, to my dismay, that I have not yet replied to the proposal that I write an oratorio for the Society of Friends of Music of the Austrian capital.

The death of my brother two months ago, the resulting guardianship of my nephew, together with many other unpleasantnesses
and events are the reason of my writing so tardily. Meanwhile the
poem by H[err] v. Seyfried is already begun, and I shall soon set
the same to music. That the commission is a great honor to me I
certainly need not tell you; it goes without saying, and I shall
try, as far as my small powers will permit, to execute the same as
worthily as possible! [12]

But he never delivered the composition, although the "Gesellschaft der Musikfreunde" later (1819) gave him an advance of 400
florins on a new work.

Ludwig was himself troubled by this stoppage in his output. In
1817 he wrote on sketch sheets:

Something must happen — either a tour and writing the necessary works for it or an opera. If you remain here during the coming summer, the opera would be preferable in case your circumstances were only tolerable.

There is no other way of saving yourself except to get away.
Only thus can you again soar to the heights of your art, whereas
here you sink into the humdrum. Only one symphony — and then
away, away, away! . . .

Work during the summer toward a tour. Only through that can
you accomplish the great work for your poor nephew. —
Make plans and be confident for Karl.[13]

Nor did contemporary witnesses fail to perceive the poor state
of health to which possession of his nephew gradually reduced
him, despite the fulfillment which it brought. Bursy, for example,
thus describes a visit:

In general, he has not been well for some time and has composed
nothing new. I asked him about Berge's opera text (a libretto
which Amenda had sent him) and he said it was very good and,
with a few changes, would be well adapted for music. But his
illness, he said, did not yet permit him such work, and he would
write to Amenda on the subject himself. . . . He told me a great
deal about Vienna and his life here. He is full of bile and poison.
He disdains everything, is displeased with everything, and is particularly abusive on the subject of Austria and especially Vienna.
He speaks rapidly and with great vigor. He often pounded the
piano with his fist so hard that the room echoed. He is not at all
reserved, for he soon acquainted me with his personal circumstances and told me a great deal about himself and his family. —

He complained of the present times, citing numerous reasons. Art, he said, no longer stands as high above the common as formerly, is no longer as respected, and, particularly, is no longer valued as highly so far as compensation goes. Beethoven complains of bad times from the pecuniary point of view too. — 'Why do you stay in Vienna, when every foreign monarch must and would offer you a place close to his throne?' 'Circumstances chain me here,' he said, 'but things go boorishly and dirtily here. It could not be worse. From the highest to the lowest, they are all scoundrels. No one can be trusted. No one will do or observe anything that is not down in black and white, not even what he has agreed to. At the same time there is nothing for anyone to have in Austria, because everything *is* nothing, that is, paper.' . . . Beethoven seems to be very much concerned about money, and I must admit that it makes him more human, that is, it brings him more humanly close to us.[14]

Fanny Giannatasio, too, wrote in her diary that his genius was seriously affected. Schindler says of this period:

But instead of writing many notes as usual, our tone-poet during these years wrote many letters, some of which concern his household arrangements, others the law-suit, yet others the education of his nephew, and which in general are to be counted among the most unedifying and regrettable testimonies to his inner agitation and his passionate pursuit of these things.[15]

Schindler could have added that Beethoven also wrote a great many figures during this period, for he tried to counter his fear of poverty by increased economies in his housekeeping. This set him to figuring. But he found it a hard task, for he had only attended school for a short time in his boyhood, and his mathematical acquirements stopped short of multiplication. If he needed the product of 5 times 17, he had to write five seventeens in a column and reach the result through addition. Especially in the Conversation Books we find numerous calculations of this sort, and he does not always arrive at the correct answer. In all this we are struck by his almost miserly effort to watch over the most trivial household expenditures by writing them down. At the same time he became increasingly niggardly and exaggeratedly preoccupied with how much was spent for the housekeeping. For example, he wrote down the price of candles, took pains to find the cheapest source of economical boot-polish. He wanted to know how much oil and vinegar were needed to make one portion of salad, how often spice for the soup had to be bought. He became a frequent visitor and patron of the second-hand market in Vienna, known as the "Tandelmarkt." In the Conversation Books we see that whole pages of conversations with advising friends center on household utensils and concerns, on pots and pans, the carding of mattresses, thread, a chamber stool, the quantity and quality of food. He wanted the cook to take the flour-measure with her when she went marketing, so that she could check on the shopwoman. A patient friend, Oliva, who had a better sense of reality and who was well acquainted with Viennese shopwomen, advised against this: "for no cook ever takes one with her to market." [16] These are but a very few examples out of many. Ludwig was particularly anxious not to give the servants any more than was absolutely necessary. His letters to Frau Streicher document this. He is shocked by the annual cost of a daily roll for the kitchenmaid: "In addition to her 12 kreuzer of bread money, N[anni] also has a roll every morning, does the same apply to the kitchenmaid? A roll [a day] adds up to 18 fl[orins] for a year!" [17]

Numerous passages in the letters to Frau Streicher deal with "dish rags," the number of which ought to be determined, the lack of which is deplored, or the disappearance of which enrages the composer. He could not bring himself to part with the housekeeping money; the housekeeper had to fight for every kreuzer — he gave her, for example, only 24 kreuzer for the milk for three days. He checked the stock of supplies on hand — thus: "on April 9th there were 11 eggs, scarcely enough butter for one day, no salt." [18] He recorded what the cook had spent for a pound of salt — 5 kreuzer — in order to check on her; suspected that a new servant had paid more than necessary for salt. His friend Oliva had to remind him that salt was a state monopoly and cost the same everywhere. It can be imagined what resentment, and indeed what desperate resistance, such behavior must have aroused in the servants, and how impossible it made any harmony in the household.

These traits of petty economy, of exaggerated interest in figures and sums of money, and of heightened anxiety concerning the possession of objects scarcely important or even worthless, are

familiar to psychologists. It is well known that persons who have
reached the age at which their sexual interest slackens exhibit the
above-described attitude toward property to a far greater degree
than formerly. It corresponds to a psychological regression, and
often goes hand in hand with an increase of interest in their own
digestive processes. If Ludwig, after the death of his brother Karl,
showed a markedly heightened and petty interest in money and
possessions, if his defensive attitude toward all possible losses
increased, while at the same time his complaints of intestinal up-
sets became more and more frequent, we cannot but conclude
that, with his conquest of the boy, he had reached a period in
which, though biologically still in full possession of his virility,
psychologically he was regressing. His interest turned to possession
in general, the possession of a woman had lost all attraction for
him.

For Ludwig, his most important property was his nephew, whom
he repeatedly described as his "most precious possession." But
this possessiveness was by no means good for the relation between
uncle and nephew, nor, above all, for the boy's own development.
It inevitably led to abuses on the nephew's part, to whose later
rebellion against his uncle the latter reacted by becoming disillusioned and embittered. An endless chain of painful experiences
in regard to his nephew was the inevitable consequence of this
possessiveness in his relation to Karl.

In his violent attempt to be a "mother" to his boy, he summoned
Frau Streicher to support him with advice and help. His sixty-five
letters to her are sad and touching testimony to his efforts and his
ill success in the role of housewife. He turned to her almost desperately, begging her to teach him how to run the house and manage
the servants. He also looked to her to tell him how to take care of
his child's daily needs. If an inexperienced and incompetent girl
had written these letters to her mother for help, they would not
have sounded very different.[19] Ludwig sent her the kitchen ac-
countbook to give her an idea of his housekeeping. But this did
not suffice him:

> . . . The kitchen accountbook by itself cannot show you every-
> thing clearly, you must, like a saving angel, appear unexpectedly
> at meal-times, so that you can see for yourself what we have. — I

never eat at home now except when I have invited a guest, for I
do not want to buy, simply for one person, what would be enough
for 3 or 4 to eat. — I shall soon have my dear son Karl with me,
hence all the more need for economy. — [20]

And again:

. . . I send you herewith the two keys so that you can look everything over. Please tell me if it would be possible for the housekeeper to make herself available here early Tuesday at the latest?
— or even Monday afternoon? — There are no dish rags here —
though I have provided them two and even three times, the devil
keeps making off with my supply.[21]

The staff, then, were expected to serve two masters, who often
gave conflicting orders. It is easy to understand that the servants
frequently did not know where they were at, and, in their confusion, rebelled against such supervision and took advantage of
the double authority to justify lapses of which one master accused
them by laying the blame on the orders of the other. The resulting
confusion in the household was incurable. In addition, Ludwig
indulged in tale-bearing, as appears from the following passage
from a letter:

. . . What you say about gossip, I do not understand, I remember, on one single occasion, having forgotten myself for a
moment in respect to a third subject [sic], but it was among entirely different people. That is all I have to say on the matter.
For my part, I never listen to or heed the gossip of common people; I have even given you hints concerning this, without saying a word about what I have heard — enough, enough, enough
of such things — [22]

Frau Streicher, in her inexhaustible readiness to help, under-
took to look after the washing, which led to further developments.
The disappearance of a pair of socks produced great excitement;
Ludwig suspected one of the servants and instantly dismissed him.
A long passage from a letter refers to this incident:

. . . So far as a new servant is concerned, I think that, now that
I have finally got rid of that one, I will leave it at that for the
moment, to whomever we may ascribe all the lost things; his bad
behavior in other respects, the way he slandered [the remainder
of this clause is unintelligible] and took many other liberties, have
made me lose all confidence in him, and I consider him the mis-

doer rather than anyone else, I beg you to tell him that you
thought a pair of socks had disappeared, this appears from the
letter which you wrote me on the subject, he keeps sheltering himself by claiming that you had found the stockings; the washwoman
received two pairs of stockings, as the two laundry lists, yours and
mine, showed; if she had not received them she would either
have crossed out one pair or sent word that she had received only
one pair; as neither occurred, I am convinced that she delivered
two pairs of stockings to him, just as she certainly received the
same and that the same have simply disappeared through him,
wherever he goes now he complains loudly of my distrust and
invents things which never happened at all, to clear himself and
to get people to intercede with me to keep him in my service; it
was only casually that I wanted to ask you about the stockings,
however I had quite forgotten about it and it was only through
his gossip that you have had to hear anything about this trifling
matter. Furthermore, whatever he most protests that he does
not do, he is most certainly doing. I know his nature, and I do
not speak without being thoroughly convinced; — away with
him — . . .[23]

Frau Streicher impressed Ludwig as a model housewife who
knew how a proper household should be run. He made an effort to
learn from her and to imitate her. Her letters to him have not been
preserved, but, from the wearisome repetition of the same questions and demands in Ludwig's letters, we may conclude that she
stood by him and took care of him with tireless patience and touching concern, like a loving mother.

No document better reveals Ludwig's petty and niggardly concern for economical housekeeping, and Frau Streicher's generous
and patient helpfulness, than the following series of questions and
answers, written on sketch sheets:

What does one give two servants for dinner and supper.
Both in quantity and quality.
How often are they given roast meat?
Are they given it for dinner and supper too?
Is what the servants get the same as the master's meal, or do they
make one especially for themselves, that is, do they in addition
prepare other victuals for themselves than what the master gets?
How many pounds of meat is enough for 3 people?
How much bread money for the housekeeper and maid per day?
What is done about the washing, do the housekeeper and maid get
more?

What about wine and beer? are they given these and when?
Breakfast

Advisor:

On weekdays the 2 servants get two platefuls of soup, the same
amount of vegetables and a pound of meat. At night soup and
vegetables[;] if some of their meat is left over from dinner so
much the better for them, if not, they can lay no claim to it. They
get roast meat every Sunday and holiday. That is, counting one
pound for the two. Instead of roast meat, it is allowable to give
them five or six groschen. At night they get no roast meat. If an
ordinary vegetable is cooked for the master, such as red cabbage,
green cabbage, beets, potatoes, lentils, peas, etc., it is better to
have it all cooked together, because cooking two separate dishes
undoubtedly takes more fat. The same procedure is followed with
the soup. Meat is always kept in one piece.

N.B. But if a vegetable which is expensive and which does not
give much is cooked for the master, such as vetch, asparagus and
the like, the servants can cook a more ordinary vegetable for themselves.

N.B. In general it is only advantageous for servants to cook
separately when there are many of them or it is a large household.
As to [portions] for each person one reckons ½ lb. of meat [which]
makes 1½ lb. of meat for three people. The housekeeper gets 12
kr[euzer] bread-money a day, so does the kitchenmaid.

When a master alone has two womenservants, it is only reasonable that they should do his washing and their own, payment then
being unnecessary, provided that on such occasions each of them
is given a glass of wine. Every decent servant will regard this as a
token of good will.

N.B. The matter of washing and ironing must be stipulated when
hiring the person.

Neither wine nor beer are given to ordinary servants except in
token of good will and concern for their well-being now and
again on the occasion of washing, window-cleaning, scouring, etc.
There should be vegetables left over for the servants' supper. The
cook must be responsible for estimating that. Not all vegetables
are the same price, partly the season, partly the kind of vegetable
determines the differences; disregarding that, today 18 kr[euzer]
worth of vegetables will suffice on the average for three people.
Sometimes a few kr[euzer] more, sometimes a few less.

Today being the eve of a saint's day, the servants get soup-maigre,
vegetables, and each a portion of fish too, as well as a good piece
of gogelhupf [a kind of cake]. If they get this at noon — at night
they are each given a slice of butter or cheese or the other way
around because today is a fast day with only one hot meal eaten.

Tomorrow, being a saint's day, each, in addition to the roast, gets two *bratwürste* [a kind of sausage] on the vegetable and in any case a glass of wine.

Enough.[24]

It must be borne in mind that at this period Ludwig's deafness was rapidly increasing and that this made his dealings with servants more difficult; he should really have turned the management of his household over to a competent person. This he could not do — his jealousy of his nephew, his dislike of women, and the suspicion which increased with his deafness made it impossible. He assumed that the servants whom he sent to Frau Streicher complained of him to her, that they spied on him and told Frau Streicher what they found out. He wrote to Frau Streicher on the subject in great excitement.[25]

Ludwig was not chary of using strong words when he expressed his contempt for servants. "The vulgarity of both of them is unbearable to me, — for a housekeeper, she is too ill-bred, indeed swinish, and the other, despite her face, is swinish too." [26] Or: "I don't consider N. entirely honest, aside from the fact that she is also a frightful sow; — not love but fear is the proper way to handle such people, I see that clearly now." [27] When he felt too greatly threatened, he allowed himself to be provoked to physical assaults on the servants. Once he threw a heavy chair at the housekeeper. His behavior to male servants was the same. The servile and feminine nature of their tasks may have put them in a category with womenservants. Thus, he said to Josef Simrock, who visited him at Vienna in 1816:

Now we can talk, for I have given my manservant five gulden, a kick in the behind, and sent him to the devil.[28]

As we see, Frau Streicher was confronted with a gigantic task if she was to introduce and maintain order in Beethoven's household. She did what she could to defer the shipwreck.

But Ludwig had an inner compulsion to destroy this last relationship with a woman too. After the servants whom Frau Streicher had procured for him gossiped about him, his distrust of her became so great that he broke off the relationship entirely.

In addition, his relationship to Frau Streicher was not without erotic components; to be sure, his rejection of sex had increased to such an extent that they could find only an aberrantly negative expression. In his letters he frequently urges sexual continence upon her, in coarsely jocular terms — for example: "Furthermore don't let your husband seduce you into certain connubial tricks" [29] or: "Most esteemed Frau Streicher, don't play any tricks [Streiche] on your mate, but rather let every man call you Frau von Stein [of stone]!!!" [30] These are his last distant erotic allusions to a woman.

It is time to return to the principal theme of our study. We were discussing the conflict between Ludwig's efforts to gain sole possession of his nephew and the inward and outward obstacles which opposed the undertaking. His terror of impending poverty played an important role here. He feared that the costs of keeping house and of private teaching for the boy might easily prove more expensive than the Institute. Since his inability to compose was tormenting him at the same time, the desperate nature of the situation, as he saw it, gave him the idea of obtaining money from his child's real mother. Apparently he himself thought it improper to make the widow pay for the boy's education after he had wrested him from her, even though legally she was obliged to do so. Hence he first set about making it clear to her what large sums he had been obliged to expend for the boy. To this end, he asked Giannatasio to send him an accounting for his nephew's "trousers, stockings, shoes, underdrawers," [31] so that he could present it to Johanna. He also asked Giannatasio, presumably for the same purpose, for "a complete schedule of expenditures" [32] for Karl. He even went so far as to hold several conversations with Johanna on the subject. On one of these occasions, he failed to keep an appointment with Frau Streicher, as a letter to her, dated February 7, 1817, shows:

> . . . I ask a thousand pardons for yesterday. It was a meeting on the subject of my nephew which had been set days before and, on such occasions I am always in danger of losing my head, and that was what happened yesterday. I only hope you will not feel hurt and will give me the pleasure of a call some other day; I was busy yesterday afternoon with the same matter and again this morning at 10 . . .[33]

Finally, an agreement was reached between Ludwig and Johanna. Johanna received her husband's entire estate — including Karl's share — and, in return, was obliged to pay the sum of 2000 florins immediately and thenceforth contribute half of her pension, by regular quarterly payments in advance, toward the boy's education.[34]

At this time the nephew was still in the Institute. The Giannatasios had their troubles with the uncle. Once when he was in arrears in payments to the Institute, Giannatasio sent a message of reminder through Karl. The boy delivered the message in the presence of his piano-teacher Czerny, which greatly vexed Ludwig. He immediately wrote Giannatasio a sharp letter.[35] Giannatasio once expressed an unfavorable opinion of Ludwig's pedagogical procedures, and the latter challenged it with biting mockery.[36] Fanny Giannatasio had the greatest difficulty in restoring mutual confidence between Ludwig and the Giannatasio family and maintaining it for a while longer. In April, 1817 Ludwig moved to the Landstrasse suburb, where he was close to the Institute and to Frau Streicher. In May he went to the country, to Heiligenstadt, to cure the "inflammatory catarrh" with which he had been attacked. A plan to spend the summer with his nephew at Countess Erdödy's estate in Croatia came to nothing.[37]

The fact that Johanna had to pay to have her son brought up far from her, and in accordance with Ludwig's ideas, gave him feelings of guilt. Hence, instead of obliging her to meet the boy only in the presence of strangers, he allowed her to visit him at his own lodging in Heiligenstadt; though he still insisted that a third person should be present, he apparently regarded the new arrangement as a great concession. For he wrote to Zmeskall, on July 30, 1817:

Dear Zmeskall!
On reflection, I have changed my mind. After all, it might be painful to Karl's mother to see her boy at a strange house, and, without that, there is more harshness in all this than I like, so I shall let her come here tomorrow; a certain Bihler, Puthon's tutor, will be present too. If you would be here about 6 o'clock I should be vastly pleased, indeed I earnestly beg you to, for I like to inform the judges who is present on these occasions: a Court Secre-

tary, as of course you know, is more favorably looked upon there than a man without a label [Charakter] even though he be a man of character [Charakter]. — Now, all joking aside. Apart from your being truly dear to me, it will also be of great service to me if you come, — so I expect you without fail.

Your friend, who esteems you,
L. Beeth.

N.B. I insist that there be no misunderstanding of my joke.[38]

A certain transient mildness appeared in his attitude toward Johanna at this period. Indeed, before he left for the country, he seems even to have gone to see her once with Karl. He wrote to Giannatasio:

> . . . your friend will already have told you that I shall come for Karl early tomorrow morning: I want to give his mother a better standing in the eyes of her neighbors, so I am doing her the favor of taking her son to her tomorrow in company with a third person. — This will occur once each month. —
>
> In regard to all that has occurred, I ask you neither to speak nor write of it further, but, like myself, to forget it all.[39]

But this somewhat better relationship with Johanna put him in an uncomfortable situation so far as the Giannatasios were concerned. For almost two years, he had represented Johanna to Giannatasio as a fiend from hell, and he was now in a quandary to explain his altered behavior toward the "Queen of the Night." He could hardly tell Giannatasio the truth and explain that it was her money which made him feel more kindly toward her. In such embarrassing circumstances, his typical reaction was distrust and aggression. He suspected that the Giannatasios accused him of vacillation and had even expressed their opinion of him to his nephew. For his part, he did not hesitate to express his distrust of Giannatasio to the boy — certainly a highly unsound procedure pedagogically. Fanny wrote in her diary:

> . . . From then on little unpleasantnesses continued to pile up until the crowning quarrel with Beethoven. That Nanni's quick and skillful interventions saved us great annoyance and pain, testifies to the greater serenity and justness of her perceptions, for I should be afraid to interfere in another person's business as she did . . .
>
> When Carl returned from Czerny, he brought me a message from the uncle asking me not to give my father the letter which

2. *Beethoven*

3. *Nickolaus Johann van Beethoven*

he had written in rage and blindness. So far so good. Yesterday I was walking home in the rain, with Beethoven's letter to my father, in which he reveals such a mortifying opinion of me, hurting me to the quick and indeed making me furious. I could find neither peace nor rest, and I immediately wrote down the feelings of my heart. I have never undergone such a mortifying experience, and, coming from a man whom I esteemed so highly, it hurts the more. If Duncker [an acquaintance of Fanny's] knew that Beethoven regards me as so base! — for I cannot take it otherwise when he believes of me that I showed Carl my disapproval of his remarks to him and above all that I disapproved of what the uncle did or left undone in general, that I belittled him to the boy and other things of the sort which are unworthy of me . . .

I once found myself in very unpleasant conflict with Beethoven because he thought that I sided against him about his way of handling his nephew . . .

Once he mortified me very much because he thought that a negligence on my sister's part, which was due to the illegibility of his handwriting and was certainly somewhat excusable, was attributable to me! . . .

I found it strange that, after he had learned the truth from a very sincere letter on my part, and that I bore no guilt for the annoyance he had experienced, he did not give me one friendly word but only shook his finger at my sister and said: Just you wait, you've cooked up a pretty mess! [40]

In his resentment against Giannatasio, Ludwig went so far as to make derogatory remarks to Johanna on the subject of the Institute and the Giannatasio family; Johanna lost no time in regaling Giannatasio with them. Nanni Giannatasio, the elder daughter, wrote down what Johanna said to Giannatasio, and the latter conveyed her statements to Ludwig in a letter. Ludwig's answer reads:

Unfortunately I received your letter too late day before yesterday, for she had already been here; otherwise, as in duty bound, I would have shut the door to her. I heartily thank Fräulein N[anni] for her trouble in setting down the woman's chatter. An enemy to all other chit-chat and gossip, this is nevertheless important to us, for I shall write to her and also give Herr A. S[chmerling] a letter of hers to me tomorrow. It is possible that, on the recent occasion, I did let escape in her presence a remark about disorderliness in respect to you; but I have not the slightest recollection of having written about you. It was only an attempt on her part to provoke you against me, as a means of obtaining and getting more from you, just as she earlier purveyed to me all sorts of things against me on your part, but I pay no heed to her chatter. — This time I wanted to try and see if she could be improved by patient and gentler behavior; I imparted this intention to Herr A. S., but it has miscarried; for even by Sunday I had made up my mind to leave it at the old necessary sternness, for she had quickly imparted some of her poison to Karl. In a word, we must stick to the zodiac and only let her take Karl twelve times a year and then fence her in so closely that she cannot even smuggle a needle in to him, whether at your house or at mine or in some other place is all the same. This time I believed, now that I am acceding to all her wishes, that this would encourage her to improve herself and recognize my entire disinterestedness . . .

One thing more. She claims that she receives news from someone in your household. — In case you cannot have Karl brought all the way to the house by Czerny, it must be omitted, proved and tried, in him confide! Karl must get no other idea of her than the one I have already given him, namely to honor her as his mother but to imitate her in nothing; against that he must be strongly warned.[41]

Ludwig admits in this letter that "a remark about disorderliness" in respect to Giannatasio may have escaped him in Johanna's presence. Hence what he said about the headmaster to Johanna must have been quite severe, for in general he was only too ready simply to deny such slips. In any case, the incident marked the end of his brief phase of lessened hostility to Johanna. After this, Ludwig was better disposed toward Johanna only for one short period. From August, 1817 she was not even allowed to see her child for several months.

But this did not mean that Ludwig's dissatisfaction with Giannatasio decreased. He made the Institute responsible for Karl's mediocre progress in piano-playing. He wrote to Karl's piano-teacher Czerny:

. . . I beg you to deal patiently with Karl so far as possible, even if things are not yet going as you and I wish, otherwise he will accomplish even less, for (he must not be allowed to know this) he is under too much of a burden from the bad distribution of his study hours, unfortunately this cannot be changed at once, so as far as possible treat him lovingly but strictly. It will turn out better under these truly unfortunate circumstances for K. . . .[42]

"These truly unfortunate circumstances for K." refers to the Institute. Ludwig expressed his dissatisfaction with Karl's treat-

ment at the Institute to Giannatasio himself as well — Giannatasio's reminder that he was in arrears doubtless serving as sufficient incentive:

> . . . At least this is the first time that I have had to be reminded
> of my dear duty; extremely pressing concerns both in connection
> with my art as well as many other causes made me entirely forget
> the account, I shall never need to be reminded again. As for my
> servant's bringing Karl home in the evening, the arrangement has
> already been made; meanwhile I thank you for having been so
> obliging yesterday as to have him fetched by your servant, for I
> knew nothing about it so it might easily have happened that Karl
> would have had to stay at Czerny's.
>
> Karl's boots are too narrow and he has complained of it several
> times, indeed it troubles him so that he could hardly walk and
> how long would it take to have the boots fixed [sic]. This sort of
> thing ruins the feet, I implore you not to let him wear these boots
> any more until they are made wider. So far as his periods of piano-
> practice are concerned I beg you to keep him at it because other-
> wise his piano-teacher is of no use. Yesterday Karl was unable to
> play all day, I myself have found several times when I counted on
> going through [something] with him that I had to go away dis-
> appointed. 'La musica merita d'esser studiato' [sic].
>
> The few hours he is at present allowed for his music studies
> are insufficient as it is and hence I must insist all the more that
> they are adhered to. There is nothing unusual about attention
> being paid to this in an institute; a good friend of mine has his
> boy in an institute too who is destined for music and he is given
> all encouragement in it, indeed I was not a little surprised to find
> the boy in a distant room all by himself upstairs and he was neither
> disturbed nor disturbed anyone else . . .[43]

During the autumn of 1817 Ludwig would have had to be preparing for his journey to England, if he had really been thinking
of accepting the pressing invitation he had received from there.
The Philharmonic Society had offered him 300 guineas for two
symphonies. Since a new currency devaluation took place in Austria at this time, such a fee could not but have been extremely
welcome to him; however, he was much too busy planning his
housekeeping. His letters to Frau Streicher become numerous this
autumn, and show how excitedly and anxiously he looked forward
to the moment when his nephew was to come to him. On November 12, 1817, he wrote to Giannatasio:

Altered circumstances may well bring it about that I shall be unable to leave Karl at the Institute any longer than to the end of
this quarter; hence I am forced to give you notice for the coming
quarter. Hard as it is for me to give this notice, my straitened
circumstances do not permit me to spare you from it since otherwise I should with the greatest of pleasure have remitted you the
fee for an entire additional quarter, gladly and as a slight tribute
of my gratitude to you, at the moment when I take Karl from you.
I should wish that you would recognize my intention herein as
true and pure. If meanwhile I should be able to leave Karl with
you again for the coming quarter, counting from February, I shall
inform you of it at the very beginning of January, 1818; I must
ask you to show me this consideration and I hope that you will not
let me ask in vain. If I continue to enjoy good health, so that I can
again earn more, I shall demonstrate my gratitude to you further,
for I know only too well how much you do for Karl beyond the
most that could be expected of you; and I can truly say that to
be obliged to admit my inability at this moment is very painful
to me. — [44]

(Karl was ill at the time and causing the Giannatasios a good
deal of trouble.)

Giannatasio's attitude toward Ludwig and the boy appears from
his reaction to Ludwig's letter. As Ludwig alleged lack of money
as the cause of his giving notice, Giannatasio offered to keep Karl
for less. Beethoven did not accept the offer, and, in his letter of
reply, pointed out that he had previously decided to take Karl to
live with him. He left it open whether Karl should remain for a
few more months or not. The reason for this, he did not impart to
Giannatasio, but it can be gathered from other letters of this period: he was still looking for a tutor for his son. Early in January,
1818 he thought he had found a suitable person and wrote to Frau
Streicher to that effect. But he asked her "not to breathe a word to
anyone" concerning his decision "lest he [the tutor] or Karl be
injured by it."[45] Presumably he was afraid that Giannatasio might
hear something of his plans and take vengeance on either Karl
or the tutor. And while Karl was still living with the Giannatasios
at the Institute and, as we are justified in concluding from the documents, was being affectionately cared for by the whole family,
Ludwig wrote to Frau Streicher:

. . . Should you happen to meet these Giannatasians at Czerny's,
you know nothing about what is happening in respect to my Karl,

say that it is not my habit to talk about my intentions because an intention once talked about no longer belongs to one. They would be glad to interfere still further, and I want as little of these vulgar people for myself as for my Karl . . .[46]

On January 6, 1818 Ludwig finally wrote to Giannatasio informing him that he was about to remove Karl from the Institute:

In order that no mistake may prevail, I take the liberty of most respectfully informing you that unfortunately it must remain settled that my nephew will leave your excellent Institute at the end of this month. As for the other proposal you made to me, here too my hands are tied, since other plans for my nephew's welfare would be wholly defeated thereby; yet I thank you most cordially for your good intention.

Circumstances might demand that Karl be removed even earlier than the end of this month, and, since I shall presumably not be here, by someone whom I shall designate for the purpose. I mention this to you now so that you may not think it in any way peculiar; furthermore, my nephew and I will be grateful to you throughout life. I have observed in Karl that he is so already, and this is proof to me that, though he is frivolous, there is no evil in him, still less does he have a bad heart. I hope all good from him, the more so as, for almost two years now, he has been under your excellent direction.[47]

Ludwig did not go himself to take Karl from the Institute partly because he had a guilty conscience toward Giannatasio. He certainly knew himself that Karl had better care and better teaching at the Institute than he could offer him. The letter was a hard blow to the Giannatasios, who had not expected such treatment from the master they so revered. Fanny's diary records this for us under date of January 8:

On Sunday I was extremely hurt by what reached us from Beethoven. My father's proposal to keep Karl for very little money, he rejected on grounds which he hides from us, and at the end of the month we must part from him [Karl], and with him, as it seems, from every intimate connection with our most dear Beethoven, who however has caused us many troubles since our more intimate acquaintance with him. I did not understand at once what grieved me so in this matter. [It was] the manner of it. The formally extremely polite but uncordial letter which he wrote to Father, not the slightest mention of him, together with the announcement that a deputy would come to fetch Karl (because he will presumably have gone away at the time). This behavior, from which I see

only too clearly that he does not think of us as he should and as
we deserve, gives me real pain and makes our parting with Karl
all the more grievous.[48]

After his final decision to take Karl to live with him, Beethoven
became more sensitive and hostile toward women. For some reason he no longer wished to see Frau Streicher. "I cannot quite prevail upon myself to come to you, you will forgive me, I am very
sensitive and not accustomed to such things, all the more reason for not exposing myself," [49] he wrote to her, yet he asked
her to continue her supervision of his household. His aggressiveness toward servants also increased at this time. He seems to have
been especially prone to physical violence, as his letters to Frau
Streicher show: "Fräulein N. [the housekeeper] has changed completely since I threw those half dozen books at her head. Presumably some portion of them found its way into her brain or her evil
heart, at least we have a bosomy traitress!!" [50] The incident of his
throwing the heavy chair at the same housekeeper dates from this
period too.

It was under such circumstances, then, that, two years after Ludwig gained possession of him, his child was at last to be entirely his
own. On January 23 Ludwig wrote to Frau Streicher:

> . . . Karl comes tomorrow, and I was mistaken when I thought
> that he might after all prefer to remain there. He is in a happy
> frame of mind and far more alert than usual and he shows me his
> love and devotion every instant; in any case I hope you see now
> that I do not vacillate once I have firmly made up my mind to
> something, and it was good! [51]

He had, then, feared that the boy had become too attached to
Giannatasio and would not willingly come to him. So he was relieved when Karl showed love and devotion to him. Karl was taken
from the Institute on January 24; Ludwig did not go in person to
fetch him, probably also in order to avoid witnessing expressions
of the boy's attachment to the Giannatasio family. On the day of
Karl's departure, Ludwig wrote to Giannatasio:

> I shall not come myself, for after all it would be a kind of leave-
> taking, and I have long avoided such things.
> Pray accept my most sincere thanks for the zeal and the upright-
> ness and honesty with which you have undertaken the upbringing
> of my nephew. —

As soon as I come to myself a little, we shall pay you a visit; in any case, on account of his mother, I do not wish it to be too much known that my nephew is now with me. — I greet you all, and my particular thanks to Frau A. G[iannatasio] for the motherly solicitude she has shown to my child.[52]

As we see, his full possession of the boy increased his fear that Johanna might again approach her son. She had not been allowed to see Karl since August. It had been easy to keep her away from the Institute; in his own house, where he was surrounded by servants whom he always turned into enemies, Ludwig had to expect that the mother would find it easier to establish some connection with her child, if only indirectly. Hence his warning to Giannatasio to keep Karl's change of residence secret.

The twelve-year-old boy was now for the first time wholly exposed to his uncle's tutelage and to the influence of his personality and housekeeping. How variable his uncle's behavior was, these pages have sufficiently shown and will unfortunately be obliged to show further. From his letters to Frau Streicher it appears that Ludwig's incompetence and unreasonableness, with the concomitant chronic servant trouble, soon reduced the housekeeping to something very close to chaos. Nor did things go smoothly with the tutor, and Ludwig sent a call for aid to Frau Streicher in which we find the despairing sentence: "God help me, I appeal to Him as my last resort." [53]

Johanna was still kept from her child. In February Ludwig wrote in his diary: "Since August 10 his mother has not seen Karl." [54] We do not know if she was allowed to see him in March. About this time Johanna seems to have been in financial difficulties, for Beethoven, as guardian, gave permission for the sale of the house which belonged to Johanna; the 7000 florins which were Karl's share in it remained invested in the house.[55] The letter in which Ludwig gave this permission appears to have been the sole communication between Ludwig and Karl on the one hand and Johanna on the other during these seven months. To the mother, this banishment from her child gradually became intolerable. She was not even allowed to know what was happening to him and perhaps only learned indirectly that Karl was now living with Ludwig. It is understandable that she made every effort to find out how her child was, what plans his uncle had for him, where he

intended to take him for a stay in the country, and the like. She
bribed the servants to give her news. Doubtless the servants felt
for the poor mother who was so hard-heartedly kept from her
child, and at the same time their hatred of their hostile and over-
bearing master was served by the intrigue.

At the end of May Ludwig left Vienna for the summer, taking
Karl with him, and settled in Mödling, a village about ten miles
south of the city, at the foot of the limestone hills in which the
Alps terminate. From there he wrote to Frau Streicher concerning his discovery of what had been going on behind his back and
his "betrayal" by his servants. He reported, in substance: [56] Johanna had bribed the servants with coffee, sugar, and money and,
two days before they left Vienna, Karl had secretly visited his
mother. Karl had admitted everything, after Ludwig had several
times "shaken" him (by which Ludwig presumably means that he
"shook" him physically) and sworn that he would forgive him.
Ludwig had immediately dismissed the servants. The priest at
Mödling had been involved in the intrigue. The letter ends with
fearful threats against this "parson," whom he would "make such
a pitiful spectacle that the whole parish will be aghast."

The discovery of this intrigue was a shattering experience for
Ludwig and his heart was "terribly affected by this affair." Everything was in confusion. Yet in his letter he made an effort to excuse
Karl and to cling to the belief that the boy loved him and only fell
a victim to Johanna's wiles. To excuse Karl he even admitted that
there was a natural bond between a mother and child, and he made
this responsible for Karl's act: "Karl did wrong — but mother —
mother — even a bad mother is still a mother." Yet this blow was
but a prelude to the series of catastrophes which he was to suffer
for his nephew's sake.

The tutor had not accompanied them to Mödling. So Karl had
to go to school there. He was put into a private class conducted
by a priest named Fröhlich. He is the "parson" referred to in Ludwig's letter to Frau Streicher. It appears from the letter that Johanna, in her desperate attempt to obtain news of her son, had
applied to the priest. The judgment which the priest formed of
the uncle and nephew will appear as an important document in
the following chapter. In any case, after a month Father Fröhlich

refused to keep Karl in his school any longer, because the boy, whose capacity he admitted, showed himself indifferent to religious instruction and indulged in boisterous behavior in church and in the streets, eliciting complaints from the villagers. The priest also feared Karl's bad influence on his other pupils. It is clear that even the brief time during which he had lived with Ludwig had unfavorably affected Karl; there were no particular complaints concerning his behavior while he was with Giannatasio. The various influences to which he was subjected — uncle, servants, mother, school — all operating in different directions and laying contradictory commands upon him, but above all his daily life with his eccentric, almost deaf, suspicious, and pedagogically incompetent guardian, had brought about a rapid increase in the boy's waywardness.

So Beethoven had to engage a private tutor again to prepare the boy for his next school, the "Academic Gymnasium." For the months of July and August, we have no report of any particularly striking event in the relationship between uncle and nephew. The artist August von Klöber painted Ludwig's portrait during this Mödling period and has left an account of the first sitting. He reports that Beethoven entered and said:

> "You want to paint me but I am very impatient." He was already very deaf, and when I wanted to say anything to him, either I had to write it or he applied his ear-trumpet, if his famulus (a young relative of twelve years or so) was not present to shout the words into his ear.
>
> Beethoven sat down, and the lad was obliged to practice on the piano, which was a gift from England and equipped with a large tin dome. The instrument stood some four or five paces behind him and Beethoven, despite his deafness, corrected the lad's every mistake, made him repeat some passages, etc. . . .[57]

Meanwhile, however, Johanna had begun to lose her long-tried patience. She decided to resume her legal battle for her child.

IX

THE SECOND SUIT:
DEFEAT

JOHANNA not only — and quite understandably — longed for
her child, she was also troubled over his development. She
had learned what Father Fröhlich thought about Karl and his
uncle's handling of him and that the priest had felt it necessary to
expel him from his school. From the servants she knew the nature
of Ludwig's housekeeping and how he was bringing up the boy,
and she saw that, under his uncle's direction, her son was in danger. In her trouble, she applied to the guardianship authorities to
deprive his uncle of all influence over Karl's education. The petition, which was presented to the Landrechte in September 1818,
is not extant; it had no result. Apparently Johanna sought no advice in the matter and had no one to influence the court in her
favor. On September 18 she was notified that her application had
been rejected.

This time, however, Johanna exhibited more determination than
before; she presented a second petition, in which she asked permission to place her son in the "Imperial-Royal Konvikt," a state
educational institution. This second petition has also disappeared,
but its essential points can be reconstructed from Ludwig's answer. Following upon it, Johanna and Ludwig were summoned
to appear before the court on September 23, the date being subsequently deferred to September 30. Ludwig did not appear, giving the excuse that he had not received the summons. Instead he
wrote a letter to the court, in which he discussed Johanna's demands point by point. How he became acquainted with the contents of her petition is not known. Ludwig's letter is given in the
Appendix; [1] only the essential passages are summarized here.

THE SECOND SUIT: DEFEAT

The style of the letter shows that someone helped Ludwig draw it up. The conduct of the argument and the lucidity of expression both differ from his usual practice. Ludwig opens with his heaviest artillery, emphasizing Johanna's "moral incapacity," which had already furnished him with his chief argument in his struggle for the exclusive guardianship; and to show Johanna's "base-minded-ness," he asserts that his deafness and ill-health were sheer fabrications on her part, intended to justify her action. This time the mother had not insisted that the child be given to herself but had only asked that he be removed from his uncle's detrimental influence and educated in a state school. Ludwig sees this as an expression of her evil purpose of obtaining easier access to her child and occasionally taking him home. In his eyes this is a crime, which she had already had the audacity to commit by leading the boy into falsehood and deceit, although she had permission to see him and talk to him at his uncle's whenever she wished. He represents her financial contribution to the boy's education as a negligible amount in comparison with his own; it gives her no right to have a voice in his upbringing. He petitions the court to deprive the mother of all influence over the boy. The impropriety of which she was guilty in signing the petition as the boy's "guardian" serves him as an excuse to punish her by a final attack.

Johanna's second petition was rejected on October 3, 1818. Considering Ludwig's influence with the court, it had hardly any hope of succeeding. Presumably the following note from Ludwig to Councillor Tuscher dates from this time:

> Dear Tuscher: Since I have this Goethe in duplicate I beg you [to permit] that your charming wife accept the one I now send (to which the volume you had from me belongs) as a cordial memento from me. — I shall see you today by half past nine, do not forget about Schmerling, for through your acquaintance you can certainly do much in this matter.[2]

Von Schmerling, it will be recalled, was a member of the Landrechte, which had conferred the sole guardianship on Ludwig.

For the moment, then, Ludwig was guaranteed exclusive possession of the boy. Uncle and nephew returned from Mödling to Vienna. We know little of the occurrences of the next few months. The court records show that Karl attended the third class at the

Academic Gymnasium during November and December. He was tutored at home in piano-playing, French, and drawing.

Since the servants whom Frau Streicher had procured for him had "betrayed" him, Ludwig entrusted the Giannatasios with the task of finding him servants. Fanny Giannatasio wrote in her diary at this period:

> Yesterday Beethoven visited us again. We had found him a house-keeper. He remained for three hours, and since his hearing was particularly bad that day, we wrote everything down.[3]

On December 3, a severe misfortune befell Ludwig. Karl ran away to his mother's. The events which led up to this were as follows:

The housekeeper whom Fanny Giannatasio had found for the Beethoven household wrote her two letters on the subject of Karl's behavior, in which she said that Karl had talked abusively to the servants and had kept back money from them to buy sweets. After receiving this news, Fanny wrote in her diary, under date of November 30:

> . . . Day before yesterday Beethoven's housekeeper's account of the boy's baseness angered and touched me to the quick . . . But painful though it be to us and much as we must fear, in Beethoven's unhappy situation, to displease him, it is necessary that we reveal the sad truth of this to him, in all his [sic] mortifying reality . . . To write would be best! Oh, if I were only a man, I would wish to be his most intimate friend![4]

Fanny sent the housekeeper's letter to Beethoven, together with one from herself, to inform him of his nephew's behavior. The uncle took the nephew to task and was not sparing of reproaches. Shortly afterward the nephew vanished from the house, leaving a note "in which he bade farewell." The boy's actions, though reprehensible, are easy to understand. In abusing the servants, he was only imitating the example which his uncle all too frequently set him, and Ludwig's parsimony probably made it impossible for the boy to satisfy his natural childish appetite for sweets, so that he tried to obtain them by devious means.

That his child had run away from him was the hardest of blows for Beethoven. It is impossible to read Fanny's description of his state of mind without being deeply touched:

One day [Dec. 3] Beethoven came in great excitement and sought
counsel and help from my father, saying that Karl had run away!
I recall that on this occasion . . . he cried out tearfully: 'He is
ashamed of me!' [5]

Immediately after seeing Giannatasio, Ludwig went to Johanna
and demanded the return of his child. She refused to give him back
at once; she wanted to have him with her a little longer. But she
promised to bring him back the evening of the same day. Ludwig
was terrified lest she should smuggle the boy out of Vienna during
the day. So he applied to the police, who brought Karl back to him.
But Ludwig no longer believed the boy safe in his lodging, and
took him to Giannatasio to be cared for in the Institute. Fanny's diary contains an account of this — in which, however, her
judgment of Karl is strongly colored by her attachment to Ludwig:

> Never in my life shall I forget the moment when he came and told
> us that Karl was gone, had run away to his mother, and showed
> us his letter to prove his baseness. To see that man suffering so,
> *weeping*, was most touching! . . . a pleasant feeling that we are
> now *much* to Beethoven, indeed that at this moment we are his
> only refuge. . . . The bad child is back with him again; through
> the help of the police, the raven-mother! Oh! how terrible it is that
> that man must suffer so through such scum. He [Karl] must leave
> here, or she; that is the upshot. For the present Beethoven wants
> to leave him in our care, a great act of friendliness on my father's
> part, if it comes about, for he will have to regard him as a person
> under arrest.
>
> Nanni and I have just been writing several hours with Beethoven;
> for when he is so affected, he hears almost nothing. . . . he said
> that he was so smitten by the event that he must first collect his
> thoughts. . . . He complained that he did not know what would
> become of his housekeeping, if Karl were away.[6]

For her part, Johanna had been deeply impressed by the boy's
flight to her and her possession of him for a few hours. Doubtless
she realized how unhappy the child was with his guardian; and
she tried once again to remove him from his uncle's deleterious
influence. Again she petitioned the Landrechte to be granted a
voice in Karl's education and destiny. This time she was apparently advised by a lawyer. The court record yields the following
information:

. . . Johanna van Beethoven (residing at No. 238 Tiefer Graben) declares to the Imperial-Royal Landrechte of Lower Austria that her son Karl v. Beethoven, *without her knowledge and participation, ran away from his uncle and guardian Herr Ludwig van Beethoven, but was returned to him by her through the Imperial-Royal Police.*[7] She requested that, since, to judge from his proceedings, Ludwig van Beethoven intends to send her son to an educational establishment, entirely away from here, perhaps even abroad, he should be denied the sanction of the Supreme Guardianship Board thereto, and that she would again request permission to be allowed to put her son in the Imperial-Royal University Konvikt for care and education.[8]

This time the court took Johanna's petition more seriously; apparently Karl's running away was considered an indication that his uncle's educational methods were not the most suitable. On December 9, Beethoven was summoned to appear with his ward for a hearing. The same summons was issued to Johanna. The object of the hearing was to determine if Johanna's request to have Karl placed in the Konvikt was justified.

The twelve-year-old boy was heard first. The court record, dated December 11, 1818 begins:

The ward Carl van Beethoven, 12 years of age, student in the Latin class, appeared and was questioned: Did he have good marks?

In Latin he had received 'eminent,' in other studies 'first class.'

Why had he left his uncle?

Because his mother had told him she would send him to public school and he did not think he was getting on under private instruction.

How did his uncle treat him?

Well.

Where had he been staying recently?

He had been hiding in his mother's house.

Where did he prefer to be, with his mother or with his uncle?

He would gladly remain with his uncle if he had someone with him, because his uncle is hard of hearing and he cannot talk with him.

Did his mother persuade him to leave his uncle?

No.

When did he leave him?

A week ago.

How could he say that he was not getting on under private instruction when he had in fact made good progress?

Since he had studied in public school, this was the case; but before that he had received a 'second class' in mathematics, which he had not made up.

Had his mother ordered him to return to his uncle?

She had wanted to take him back to him; but he had resisted because he feared mistreatment.

Had his uncle mistreated him before?

He had often punished him but only when he deserved it; he had been mistreated only once and that had been after his return; his uncle had threatened to strangle him.

How long had he been with his mother?

Two days.

Who gave him religious instruction?

The same teacher who gave him the other subjects; before that the priest of Mödling, who, however, was not well disposed toward him because he did not behave properly in the streets and chattered in school.

Had he allowed himself to speak disrespectfully of his mother?

Yes, and it was in his uncle's presence, whom he thought he would please by it and who had in fact agreed with him.

Was he often alone?

When his uncle was not at home, he was left all alone.

Did his uncle exhort him to pray?

Yes, he prayed with him morning and evening.[9]

Here for the first time the nephew comes on the stage with words of his own. His statements sound simple and natural; but it is generally known that a child's statements in court must be received with extreme caution. They are greatly influenced by his relationship with the persons to whom he is emotionally bound or whom he fears. In Karl's statements the conflict which the struggle between his mother and his uncle had aroused in him can clearly be perceived. He tries not to let his love for his mother become apparent, for he knows how much it would offend his uncle, who had so often warned him to beware of his mother's poison. Hence, to excuse his running away to his mother, he falls back on her having promised him better success with his studies in a public school — certainly an insufficient reason. His true reason — his longing for his mother — was something he could not betray in the presence of his uncle. To deny his truest and strongest feeling was a heavy psychological burden on the child. The court too found Karl's alleged reason insufficient, for he had in fact made good progress under private tuition. Karl admits that his behavior

was influenced by his uncle when he says that he spoke disrespectfully of his mother to please him.

Beethoven was questioned next. His friend Bernard had come
to court with him to make comprehension easier. The record of
Beethoven's examination is given in the Appendix.[10]

In his first answer Ludwig expressed his suspicion that Johanna
had directly caused Karl's flight to her; but he admitted the possibility that it might have been the boy's fear that he would punish
him. All his other statements also reveal his intense hatred of
Johanna. He asserts that she had bribed the servants, so that he
could no longer trust the child to them; that she had previously
influenced the priest at Mödling; and that she would only too
easily have access to her child if he were put in the Konvikt. He
denies having expressed his hatred of Johanna in the boy's presence. Karl must either remain with him under the supervision of
a tutor or be entrusted to Giannatasio. At this point Ludwig committed a glaring error, by which he himself threw away the possibility of remaining sole guardian. He said that he would send
Karl to the Theresianum if only he were "noble." The Theresianum, founded by the Empress Maria Theresia, was a celebrated
and excellent establishment for the education of boys of noble
birth.

Such a glaring error in such an important matter is produced
by unconscious motives. We shall not go wrong if we assume that
one of the causes of Beethoven's revealing slip was his unconscious feeling of guilt. He had repeatedly told untruths in his examinations, as the record shows. His slip is obviously a self-punish-
ment for the lies he had told in court in his struggle for the boy and
against Johanna.

The judge — himself a nobleman of course — immediately took
up Beethoven's admission, "if only he [Karl] were noble," and inquired into the documentary proofs of the Beethovens' nobility.
Ludwig had to admit that neither he nor the other members of the
van Beethoven family were noble. This admission had a temporarily catastrophic effect on the disposition of the case. (Schindler's
account of the scene, according to which Beethoven pointed to his
heart and his head and proudly declared "My nobility is here —
and there," [11] is sheer invention.)

Johanna was examined last; the court record is given in the Appendix.[12]

Johanna's statements are simple, almost naive, without any particular animosity against her brother-in-law. She does not seem to have quite realized Ludwig's hostility to her. She denies that her son spoke disrespectfully of her, either to herself or to anyone else. She complains that she is not allowed to see her child, though her accusations on this point are rather mild; and that his residing with his uncle is unsuitable because he cannot talk with the deaf man and because his physical needs are not attended to. It is impossible to escape the impression that Johanna was intimidated and was unable to state her case emphatically and effectively. Her honest concern for her child clearly appears from her statements. Her last answer shows that she was acting in good faith when she regarded her son as noble: the brothers had told her that they were noble, and her husband had intimated that Ludwig was in possession of the documents of nobility, which in fact were never issued.

From the recorded testimony it is clear beyond doubt that it was Ludwig's statement in court which led to the discovery of his non-nobility. His blind hatred of Johanna is shown by the fact that he later accused his sister-in-law of having raised the question of his nobility out of ill-will toward him.

On December 10, Johanna presented a new application to the Landrechte in which she asked permission to put her son in the Imperial-Royal Konvikt. She supplemented her application by two documents which, as the observations of relatively disinterested persons, have an objective value. One document derives from Hofconzipient Jacob Hotschevar, who, as the husband of Johanna's mother's step-sister, was Johanna's step-uncle, and who served as tutor in several noble households. The other document derives from Father Fröhlich.

Hotschevar's observations are written in a tortuous legal style and are very detailed.[13]

He begins by describing the Beethoven brothers as eccentrics, a judgment which can hardly be contradicted. The document reveals the mercenary bargaining over the boy in which Ludwig and Karl had indulged. Karl had been forced (i.e., by financial pressure) into giving Ludwig the guardianship of the boy. Ludwig had insisted upon sole guardianship in return for his financial assistance during Karl's illness. Later Karl had demanded the return of the document, proposing, on his side, that he would not demand the payment of 1500 florins which Ludwig apparently owed him. Hotschevar emphasizes, much more strongly than had Johanna in her statement, that the mother was not allowed to see her son at all, and the curt unfriendliness with which Giannatasio had forbidden her to see the boy at his school. He brings out the enmity which existed between Ludwig and Johanna and which so increased Ludwig's bad influence on the boy. For Ludwig expressed delight when the boy, against his own will and merely to please his uncle, called his own mother a "raven-mother." When Karl ran away from his uncle and was with his mother for a short time, Hotschevar saw him and observed that he had "frozen hands and feet" (presumably chilblains), that his clothing was inadequate for the cold weather, that he had not changed his linen for a week, and that in general his cleanliness was neglected: "The child is forced to conceal his real feelings, make a hypocritical pretense of feelings which he does not have, and to lie." Hotschevar's report and his indignation over Karl's condition and treatment sound genuine and honorable.

The priest Fröhlich's statement may speak for itself:

> That Karl v. Beethoven, during his month of study with him, had shown that he was by no means lacking in the necessary aptitude for study, but that unfortunately his morals were totally corrupted, and this on the following grounds:
>
> 1. it is generally known that Ludwig v. Beethoven is almost totally deaf, consequently it is impossible that *as a deaf man he should be able to give a youth proper guidance*, for when one does not hear and understand the other the result is a Babel of confusion.
>
> 2. there is *great dislike between Ludwig van Beethoven and the mother of young Karl van Beethoven*, such indeed that the young v. Beethoven, to make his uncle fond of him, *reviles his mother with the vilest epithets in his presence*, sometimes in writing, sometimes shouting them into his ear, *at which Ludwig v. Beethoven expresses the greatest joy* and in addition cries bravo to the young breaker of the Fourth Commandment.
>
> This is *young Karl van Beethoven's own statement*, who several

times confessed to me *that he had to speak abusively of his dear mother,* greatly as he was aware that it was wrong, just as he never dared to tell his uncle the truth because he only believed him when he lied. This last he also once told his mother in my presence and would certainly have said more about his uncle in the proper place had he not had to fear being betrayed to his uncle and then mistreated by him.

Furthermore *Ludwig v. Beethoven* once came to me *with a joyful countenance and reported to me with malicious delight* that *his nephew could not bear his mother* and *had called her a raven-mother* that day.

This manner — to me despicable and contrary to all moral principles — of bringing up a youth of thirteen, together with the indifference which Karl v. Beethoven showed to my instruction in religion and to his compositions on the same subject as well as his unruly behavior in church and on the street, of which many of the inhabitants of this place complained to me, compelled me, after fruitless warning and representations to the boy's uncle, in order not to provoke my twelve other pupils, who openly asserted that 'they did not want to study any more with the unruly Karl v. Beethoven,' to dismiss him entirely.[14]

On December 15, Ludwig directed a memorandum to the Landrechte. It is given in the Appendix.[15]

At the beginning of this document Ludwig emphasizes that his disposition and his "publicly recognized moral character" guarantee the truth of his assertions. As has been shown earlier, it is safe to assume that he is about to present a gross distortion of the facts when he particularly emphasizes the truthfulness of his assertions. Apparently he was extremely concerned lest his nephew's having run away from him to his mother should produce a bad impression on the court. He represents the boy's flight as the result of his mother's machinations. The letters from the housekeeper, in which she complained of the boy's conduct to Fanny Giannatasio, were, he explains, dictated by the mother in the expectation that he, Ludwig, would scold the boy upon learning of his bad conduct; Johanna had thus created a pretext for the boy to run away. However, as an added precaution, Ludwig had mislaid the letters; so he could state that they contained only wretched and exaggerated vulgar gossip. (He does not explain why he nevertheless scolded the boy.) He connects the arrival of the letters and the boy's running away on the same day, as if they were both planned by the wicked mother and then maliciously staged. (We may be certain that Fanny Giannatasio would never have lent her support to any such plot.) By thus representing the incident which so vexed him, Beethoven attempted to exculpate himself and his nephew entirely and to put all the blame on the wicked mother. Yet the nephew now regrets his faults and "only begs to be allowed to remain with" his uncle. In contrast to Johanna and Hotschevar, who, in their statements, make an effort to bring out Ludwig's positive traits and regret that they cannot approve of everything in his education of his nephew, Ludwig expresses his enmity for Johanna without reserve. It also seems likely that his expressions of his hatred for Johanna are intensified by a secret fear that he may lose his nephew. Beethoven appears to have assumed that his presentation of the mother's evil character would convince the court and that she would be judged wholly unworthy to have her child with her. He emphasizes the large amount that he has expended for the boy, in contrast to the mother's contribution, as sufficient justification in itself for his claim to sole guardianship. He even refers to his dead brother's wishes, although he was doing exactly the opposite of what his brother had asked on his deathbed.

Beethoven's memorandum received no answer. For on December 18, 1818, the Landrechte, the court for the nobility, handed over the whole matter of the guardianship, together with all the pertinent petitions and records, to the Stadtmagistrat (Civic Magistracy), the court for commoners. "It . . . appears from the statement of Ludwig van Beethoven, as the accompanying copy of the court minutes of Dec. 11 of this year shows, that he is unable to prove nobility; hence the matter of guardianship is transferred to an honorable magistrate . . ." [16] reads the communication from the Landrechte to the Magisterial tribunal.

A letter to the Archduke — apparently the only letter Beethoven wrote in the first three months of 1819, during the troubled days of the suit — shows the state of profound despair, almost of shock, into which he was thrown by fear that the transfer of the case might cause him to lose his child:

> . . . a terrible event has recently taken place in my family affairs, during which I completely lost my mind for a time, and only this

is to blame that I have not waited upon Y.I.H. myself nor reported on the masterly Variations of my highly honored and exalted pupil and favorite of the Muses.[17]

In addition, he felt deeply mortified at no longer being considered noble. Schindler says of this:

As a result of the transfer of the suit to the Magistracy, Beethoven felt smitten as if by the hardest blow. Whether he set any value on being regarded as of noble birth in the common opinion, it would be hard to determine; after all, his descent and his family circumstances were sufficiently well known, the latter also through his brother's plebeian position. At any rate, it remains certain that he greatly valued being able to bring his case before the special authorities, partly because that court was better able to understand and esteem him (as Fräulein Giannatasio rightly observes), partly because the unfavorable reputation of the above-mentioned lower court inspired little hope in him of the outcome he wished. It may also be stated with no less certainty that neither his genius nor his works would have gained him the favored position he had so far held in aristocratic circles, had it not been for the presumption that he was one of their own. This was evidenced by numerous examples as soon as the action taken by the higher court became public. It was not among the middle class, but among the upper, that the little word 'van' exercised an obvious spell. The fact remains that, after this action of the Lower Austrian Landrechte, the great city of Vienna became too small for our offended master, and, had not the duties he had assumed in accordance with his brother's will restrained him, the frequently planned journey to England would have taken place and perhaps also a long stay there, for he was already most sympathetic to its political institutions.[18]

It is from this period that the first Conversation Books date. Beethoven's entries express his anger over the humiliation to which he had been subjected by being relegated to the lower class. Apparently he no longer remembered that it was he himself who had betrayed his non-nobility to the court. For in one of the Conversation Books from this period, he wrote:

. . . when it [presumably the court] learned that my brother was not noble. It is obvious, so far as I know, that there is a gap here which needs to be filled in, for, in accordance with my occupation, I do not belong with this plebeian mass.[19]

Later, in answer to a remark by his friend Peters concerning his bad mood, Ludwig wrote: "The bourgeois is to be excluded from higher men, and *I have fallen among the former.*" [20]

In his despair over the turn of events and his fear for the outcome of the case in the hands of the Magistracy, Ludwig could not bear to have his child away from him. The boy was still at Giannatasio's, where, according to Fanny's diary, he had to be regarded as "under arrest," for it was considered possible that he might run away to his mother again. Beethoven soon began to express all his dissatisfaction with the treatment Karl was given at the Institute — for example, that Karl's room was inadequately heated; when the boy had been with *him,* he had never had frozen hands and feet (!); [21] they must not carry things too far with the delinquent! Fanny wrote in her diary: ". . . his [Ludwig's] carping spirit and his weakness for the boy have gained complete possession of him and now he believes him, the *liar,* more than his proven friends . . ." and ". . . Father today wrote him his real opinion, perhaps one of these days he will know us. This afternoon B. himself took the boy from Nanni on the bridge when he left school. As to what will yet come of it, we can fear the worst . . ." [22] So once again he assumed complete possession of the boy; he now kept him at home with him. His joy was brief. For at the very beginning of the year, the Magistracy removed Ludwig van Beethoven from the guardianship and he was forced to resign his child to Johanna. The boy stayed with his mother and went to school at a private institute which was run by a certain Joseph Kudlich. In her tender sympathy for Beethoven, Fanny Giannatasio felt his grief — at the same time, of course, completely adopting Ludwig's judgment of Johanna:

> . . . The wicked woman has at last succeeded in triumphing over him. He has been removed from the guardianship and the evil son returns to the source of evil. I can imagine B.'s pain. Since yesterday evening he has been all alone, we hear . . . Yet he should know that Karl is happy with his mother, it would ease the pain of parting for him.[23]

On January 7, 1819, Ludwig, with Karl, Johanna, Hotschevar, and the attorney Schönauer were summoned to appear for a hearing on January 11. Unfortunately the record of the hearing has not been preserved. On February 1, Ludwig addressed the Magistracy in a letter [24] in which his excited concern, indeed his despair, at the threatened loss of his child is movingly apparent. As in the previously cited applications to the Landrechte, he principally stresses two arguments in his behalf — first, the various things he has done for his nephew, among which he emphasizes his financial expenditures, second, the immorality of the boy's mother. Ludwig apparently wrote this letter without assistance: the train of thought is confused, sometimes illogical, the orthography extremely faulty. His excitement and fear urge him to great exaggerations, in which he compares himself to Philip of Macedon and his nephew to Alexander the Great. Besides his studies under Kudlich,[25] he continues, his nephew will be instructed by a tutor, a "Reverend Father," a French master, a drawing master, and a music teacher. In addition, Karl will be inspired to virtue and industry by Ludwig's personal example. Life in the Imperial-Royal Konvikt is bad, for it corrupts the boys, and his mother would too easily have access to him. But his mother is a "plague" to Karl, "who had the misfortune to suck in this mother's-milk"; yet, even now that he has saved the boy from this corruption, there is still the danger that "the tender plant, my nephew, will be flawed by a poisonous breath." Here the idea of poisoning through the mother is clearly apparent. Furthermore, Ludwig continues, the mother tries to arouse lusts and desires in the boy and to bring him into evil company. Johanna is represented as a diabolical person bent upon luring the boy to corruption. Ludwig attempts to discredit the testimony of Hotschevar and Fröhlich by likewise impugning their moral character, sufficiently revealed, he asserts, by their association with Johanna. The priest Fröhlich is the particular object of his angry insults. He also makes it appear that he himself removed Karl from the school in Mödling because he (Ludwig) "oversaw" the priest — by which he presumably means "saw through" him. The whole letter betrays a rather childish intention of influencing the Magistracy by violent denunciations of the opposing side. In closing, he makes a great concession: he will permit the appointment of a co-guardian to be proposed by himself; but Johanna must be entirely excluded.

No reply from the Magistracy to this communication is extant;

we only know that, at the end of March, Beethoven informed the Magistracy that he resigned the guardianship of his nephew. The Conversation Books give us a striking picture of the depression which he felt after losing his child. We find his friends constantly trying to comfort him, assuring him that all is not lost, and advising him as to further steps, especially the choice of another guardian. In the Conversation Books for March and April, 1819, his friend Bernard, director and editor of the "Wiener Zeitung," writes:

> The thing is to choose as guardian a man who has your entire confidence, both morally and pedagogically, and with whom you could always remain in friendly relations in regard to these matters. Since Kudlich has a better effect on Karl than . . . Gian[n]atasio, I maintain that he should be preferred; if you cannot find anyone else who would be more suitable. Certainly, it is extremely difficult for you.
> If you hope to find some peace, I think it would be well for you to name a guardian, as you were willing to do yesterday. But if it were feasible to send the boy to Sailer at Landshut,[26] that would be even better, for, that way, your mind could be entirely at ease, for you would know that he was in the best of hands. Even if you have Tuscher as co-guardian, that would change nothing in your situation, for all the cares would still fall on you.
> Perhaps Tuscher and Kudlich could assume the guardianship together, which could also be very advantageous.
> Besides, everything remains as formerly, even if you send him away. . . . As long as you are guardian and Karl stays here, you not only have all the cares as hitherto, but you will still have to go on fighting against his mother and her intrigues.
> Let Karl be sent back to Kudlich only temporarily, meanwhile the matter can be set in order.[27]

It appears, then, that Kudlich, from whom Karl was receiving instruction, and Councillor Tuscher, were being considered as co-guardians. Tuscher himself was rather hesitant at first, when Beethoven imparted his wish to him. According to Schünemann's dating, this conversation must have taken place before March 12. The following entry in the Conversation Book is in Councillor Tuscher's hand:

> With the mother? But the mother will always find means to acquire influence
> Her personality —
> A few words from her on the boy's mind —

All communication with the mother must be made impossible
I shall take the liberty of calling on her one of these days.
    As co-guardian?
I am extraordinarily busy ex officio these days
This matter demands quiet consideration and consultation
It cannot be settled in a few words — It demands knowledge of
the persons and the circumstances
    The sole foundation of education is the home and personal influence [28]

We see how carefully and tentatively Tuscher inquired into the actual circumstances.

Tuscher was finally appointed guardian on March 26. The Magistracy charged the new guardian to place "the ward, now with his mother Johanna van Beethoven" elsewhere, and under proper supervision, for education and upbringing, and also to submit a formal opinion as to the advisability of entering the boy in a public school, as his mother and Hotschevar had proposed.[29]

Ludwig first considered taking Karl abroad without Johanna's knowledge. We learn this from conversations with Oliva,[30] a banker, who was in Beethoven's favor at this time as financial adviser and "errand-boy."

But if Karl was to go abroad, he had to have a passport. In the Conversation Book we find Beethoven's friend Bernard explaining the necessary steps to obtain one.[31]

These passages from the Conversation Books further show how the conversation kept returning to the nephew and the matter of the guardianship, how Ludwig was constantly tormented by worry over his nephew, and how his friends came to Ludwig's help with unwearying counsel and comfort.

Councillor Tuscher agreed to having his ward go abroad and Beethoven applied to the appropriate authorities for a two-year passport for Karl.

On April 23 the authorities inquired of the Magistracy if there was any objection to the passport being issued. The Magistracy declared against the boy's going abroad and asked Tuscher if he would not withdraw his application to that effect and instead name a school in Austria for his ward. Tuscher, however, insisted upon his proposal, dwelling upon the great hopes he had for the boy's education in the institute at Landshut in Bavaria, since its

director, Professor Sailer, "because of his reverence for the talents
of the composer Beethoven, was bound to him in particular respects," and could, if the boy were committed to his charge, give
him the strictest guidance and supervision, "which, in the case of
this boy who is extremely cunning and adept in every sort of crafti-
ness, is of the greatest importance." [32] Tuscher, acting on Beethoven's instructions, was obviously making every attempt to get
the latter's plan past the Magistracy.

We find the following entries in the Conversation Book under
date of April 29:

> Bernard: I do not believe that, after the guardian's written instruc-
> tions, Kudlich will permit another communication with Karl's
> mother. He has given his word of honor in the matter. [33]
>
> Even if he [Karl] was led astray for a time, he cannot but realize
> at once whose intentions toward him are good, as soon as he comes
> to his senses. It is a great fault that Kudlich allowed himself to be
> manipulated.
> Weakness. He is without independence of mind.[34]

According to this, Johanna had found access to Kudlich, and
this was now to be made impossible. The plan of sending Karl
abroad was pursued further, and it was hoped that the influence
of a prominent ecclesiastic, Provost Spandau, would ensure its
accomplishment.

When Ludwig learned that Johanna had applied for an audience
with Archduke Ludwig, he attempted to offset any possible support of her cause on Archduke Ludwig's part by applying to his
own patron, Archduke Rudolf.[35]

But this attempt to effect a permanent separation between
mother and son also failed. On May 7 the Magistracy answered the
inquiry of the passport authorities: Karl was to be removed from
his mother's influence, but there was no need to send him abroad,
since the mother objected and the curator of the ward, Dr.
Schönauer, had declared himself against it. Upon this, the authorities refused to give Karl a passport.

The Magistracy, then, had adopted a compromise solution, acceding to Ludwig's insistence that the boy be removed from his
mother but not finding it necessary to stop communication between them entirely. When Thayer writes, "the Vienna Magis-

tracy's narrow-mindedness and lack of judgment are clearly exhibited; any unprejudiced person must have seen what a good
thing it would have been to send the boy away and entrust him to
Sailer. The Magistracy was under the influence of the boy's mother
and Hotschevar," [36] he shows how greatly he was himself under
Beethoven's influence. For the Magistracy, in its decision, exhibited a wholly reasonable appraisal of the situation and remained uninfluenced by Ludwig's feelings, particularly by his
aggressions against Johanna. In any case, it did not agree with
Ludwig's condemnation of her. We must bear in mind too that the
Magistracy was on the whole composed of petty bourgeois, who
were much more ready to condemn a "bad" woman than a body
of noblemen would have been. The Magistracy's refusal to condemn Johanna is a strong positive datum in any estimate of Karl's
mother.

Upon this, Karl was permanently placed in Kudlich's Institute.

For Ludwig, the Magistracy's action was a veritable defeat.
Forced to resign the guardianship, he had lost his "motherhood"
of the child, and he had failed to remove Karl from Johanna's
sphere of influence. It is easy to understand that he was profoundly
affected. His only extant letters from this period are to his friend
Ries in London, and they contain touching evidence of his depression:

> I am exhausted by the hardships which have befallen me and
> which still continue; [37]

> Forgive these confused expressions. If you knew my situation, you
> would not wonder at them but rather at what I am accomplishing
> even so; [38]

> As to coming to London we will write each other further. It would
> certainly be the only salvation for me, the means of getting out of
> this miserable, tormenting situation, in which I am never healthy
> and can never do what, in better circumstances, would be possi-
> ble; [39]

> I have meanwhile been fettered by such cares as never in my life
> before, and all through going too far in doing good to others. [40]

Yet in none of these letters did Ludwig mention what the cause
of his disturbed state was; it would seem that he was ashamed of
his defeat and unwilling to admit that he had lost the child whose
conquest he had so joyfully communicated to all his friends.

Since this state of continual torment paralyzed his creative powers, he decided to go to the country, and on May 12 moved to Mödling. He wanted to make sure that, during his absence, Karl, who was now in Kudlich's Institute, would be kept from Johanna. He still had some right to determine Karl's destiny, for it was his money which made the boy's higher education possible. He therefore attempted to place the boy in Giannatasio's school again. On June 17 the Giannatasio family visited Beethoven at Mödling to tell him that they were unwilling to take Karl back. Upon this, Ludwig placed him in another school for boys, located in the Josephstadt quarter of Vienna and directed by Joseph Blöchlinger. Blöchlinger was a Swiss pedagogue, a pupil of Pestalozzi's, and his Institute had a good reputation.

On July 5 Ludwig suffered a new blow: Councillor Tuscher petitioned to be relieved of the guardianship on the ground that "both the multiplicity of his official duties and various other considerations did not permit him to continue the same." [41] Tuscher was annoyed because his colleagues in the Magistracy had decided against him in the matter of the passport; in addition, he had accepted the guardianship only hesitantly, upon Ludwig's insistence. Ludwig took Tuscher's resignation of the guardianship in very bad part and spoke of him most severely, as the Conversation Books show.

But meanwhile, it appears, Ludwig found the strength for renewed action. On the same day on which Tuscher resigned the guardianship — he had presumably communicated this intention to Ludwig in advance — Ludwig wrote a letter to the Magistracy in which, with no legal justification whatever, he reassumed the guardianship, alleging that Tuscher had been forced to resign it because of the "ceaseless interference of the mother," and asking that the Magistracy give Blöchlinger "the necessary instructions to prevent the untimely and disturbing interventions of the mother with the necessary firmness." [42]

Thus he resumed hostilities against Johanna. Indeed, his effort to keep mother and child apart now became almost a monomania. To accomplish it, he returned to the idea of sending Karl abroad. On July 15 he wrote to the Archduke:

. . . The continuing difficulties in regard to my morally almost completely ruined nephew are largely to blame. I myself had to take over the guardianship at the beginning of this week, for the other guardian resigned and has been guilty of many things, for which he asked my forgiveness; furthermore the referee has given up the refereeship, because since he interested himself in the good cause, he was cried down as partisan. And so this confusion continues without end, and no help, no comfort! All that I have built swept away as by a wind! The present proprietor of an Institute, a pupil of Pestalozzi's, in which I have placed my nephew, is also of the opinion that it will be difficult to attain an end desirable for himself and my poor nephew. — But he is likewise of the opinion that nothing could be more beneficial than for my nephew to be sent abroad! . . .[43]

We can guess why Ludwig regarded his child as "morally almost completely ruined." The boy had himself expressed the wish to remain in Vienna, which Ludwig interpreted as wanting to be near his mother.

Ludwig's pathological idea that Johanna was dangerous now went so far that he believed she intended to poison Karl every time she came near him. If Karl, on his side, showed attachment to his mother, it was, for Ludwig, because she had poisoned him.

In regard to the boy's feelings during this summer we know nothing, for the Conversation Books have not been preserved.

As the Magistracy was seeking further information in respect to the guardianship before making a final decision, it appears that Karl was to be summoned to make a statement. When Ludwig learned of this, he was terrified by the possibility that the statement might not be to his liking. In a letter to Councillor Piuk he strongly opposed the summoning of his nephew; the boy, he wrote, ought to be spared because of his wicked mother; it would be far better that Ludwig himself should make a statement instead (!); the chief thing was to keep his mother away from him; Ludwig insisted that mother and son should meet only every other month, for "this mother must be morally and legally dead for him." The letter repeats the familiar accusations and slanders against Johanna.[44]

These attacks on Johanna testify to Ludwig's increasing bitterness against her. When he learned that she had succeeded in approaching Blöchlinger, he even included Karl in his condemnation. He wrote to Bernard:

> Dear B! I called on you yesterday evening, when O[liva] brought me your letter, but you were out, though O. had certainly assured me that I should find you at home — naturally I at once wrote to Blöchl[inger] yesterday evening at the tavern, that he must on no account bring K[arl] to the Over-Arse-Behindship,[45] I had to give the letter to O[liva] so that he could see to it today, he will have done so early enough, I hope. — As to the mother, I knew it already, for she was seen when she went to B[löchlinger], I hastily sent Oliva to him and it was I who charged him — though without revealing that I knew it — to treat him rather roughly. With a man who has written me such a letter, one can certainly apply rather strong [methods]. On account of this plague-laden person I wish to waste not another word on H[err] Blöchl[inger], I am today sending him through Steiner the fee for the month to come, beginning August 22, in the situation in which we are at present, in which, so far as I can see, the bestial mother can spread her pestilential breath everywhere, I shall not let myself in for paying for an entire half year. Karl, I hear from Oliva, asked Blöchl[inger] for permission whether [sic] he should write me his Latin letter on my name-day — I am therefore of the opinion that you should explain to K[arl] in Herr B[löchlinger]'s presence that I want no letter from him, he ought to have done this long ago, and asked my forgiveness for his evil actions into which he allowed himself to be drawn partly through his mother and also partly of his own motion, his obduracy, his ingratitude, his heartlessness so rule him that, while Ol[iva] was there, he did not once ask after me, indeed when I took him to Blöchlinger for the first time, leading him by the hand, as soon as we got near them he took his hand away, and again later once when I was there with Ol[iva] — enough, my patience has an end, I have cast him from my heart, wept many tears over him, the good-for-nothing, only if he himself finds the way to approach me, and if I first have proofs that his bad heart has grown better, will I see if I can acknowledge him again, my love for him is gone, he needed it, I have no need of his, and since he has been in this plague-ridden neighborhood, and is so again, I want to hear no more of him except that I pay for him and otherwise provide for him. — [46]

This first part of the letter is an expression of Ludwig's despairing disillusionment and deep mortification over the "obduracy," "ingratitude," and "heartlessness" of his nephew because the boy had communicated with his mother and twice withdrawn his hand from Ludwig's. The letter shows in startling fashion how completely his nephew had absorbed all the great man's love-interest, and how greatly Ludwig's entire feeling of his own existence depended upon whether the boy turned to him or to Johanna.

At the end of the letter, his affection for his nephew breaks through despite everything, and we see the terrible tragedy of torturing jealousy to which his ill-fated love had brought him:

> You can now answer me about this, what concerns K[arl] is written thus so that he will hear it from you out of this letter, it goes without saying that I do not think thus (I still love him as before, without weakening and with great partiality, yes I can truly say that I often weep over him),[47] my situation with my closed senses is so hard in itself and what untoward events and abominable encounters for such great sacrifices, which too these wicked people have found ways to denigrate. — You know very well how I regard Oli[va], but unfortunately in my isolated situation I need such men, he is a burden to me in respect to money into the bargain, as it appears, he regards himself as in my pay, what can I do about it — resignation — my health is very much shaken, so that I can hardly manage to write. — Now go to Blöchl[inger] I do not want to go there again, because I will not tolerate these abominable encounters between myself with [sic] this person and do not wish to refute her low gossip against me.
>
> In haste your Beethoven [48]

He loved Karl as his own child with all the strength of which a mother's heart is capable; and he was to have it forced upon him again and again that the child felt closer to his real mother than to his uncle.

It was a comfort to Ludwig in his misfortune if he could cling to the idea that Karl's love of Johanna was an indication of the corruption, the evil, the poison which the "bestial" mother had instilled into her child. In this way, he could discharge all the fury of his disappointed motherly heart upon Johanna, and his letters show how profusely, emphatically, and tirelessly he did so. When he received Karl's letter written for his name-day, he wrote to Bernard:

> August 19, 1819.
> Karl's letter has just arrived, it goes back with this, I beg you, despite Herr B[löchlinger] to hand it back to him yourself. When you are there, have Karl show you his letter, so that you can read it too. There is no heart in it, not even the wish to see me or talk

with me, but he shall not see me again as long as I live, the monster, and his pestilential mother, who has made him such, has recently started her intrigues with the headmaster again.[49]

With this he enclosed a letter to Blöchlinger [50] in which, as guardian (!), he made him responsible for not allowing Johanna to set foot in his house again. He reproached him with having let her enter the school, as he (Ludwig) had learned. He complained of Karl's troubled behavior, which he attributed to Johanna's poisonous influence. His mother was to be shown to Karl in her true light. As in his letter to Councillor Piuk, he again urged the greatest consistency in keeping the mother away from the boy.

But even his friend Bernard became an object of aggression when he did not approve of everything that Ludwig did in relation to the boy, or was unable to tell him that the boy loved him.

Dear Friend! Long as we have known each other, I cannot refrain from saying that your nature has frequently caused me difficulties. You seem gladly to lend an ear to flatteries from poor miserable people, and to appear as their protector, thus you harm your friends, because in thus extending your protection you wish to find everything good and for the best, the present affair shows once again what a very wrong move you have made, and without consideration have added new vexation for me to the old. This man [Blöchlinger] is obviously a coarse, very coarse man — you have approved his pitiful ideas, and betrayed your friend, I saw this only too well, how carelessly everything was arranged in respect to the wicked person, Oliva was not subtle enough and you not crude enough for this un-Swiss boor, for he is, wherever he may come from, a boor. Out of respect for me he speaks of my unreasonableness, what logic, against which he again appeals to your friendliness — this should not take with you, nothing is honorable from such a creature. — But — I must say it dawns on me that you are as much my enemy as a piece of a friend. — So my nephew ought to feel wholly hostile to me, and, if so, he ought to be allowed to continue so, or inquiries should be made as to whether he loves his raven-mother better or me? To these miserable ideas of this wretched pedagogical creature you have given your approval, without even thinking of their complete unjustifiableness, you yourself only a few days ago in town gave me to understand clearly enough that my nephew hates me — I curse and damn the miserable human scum.

4a. Stephan v. Breuning

4b. Dr. F. G. Wegeler

4c. Anton Schindler

4d. Johann Baptist Bach

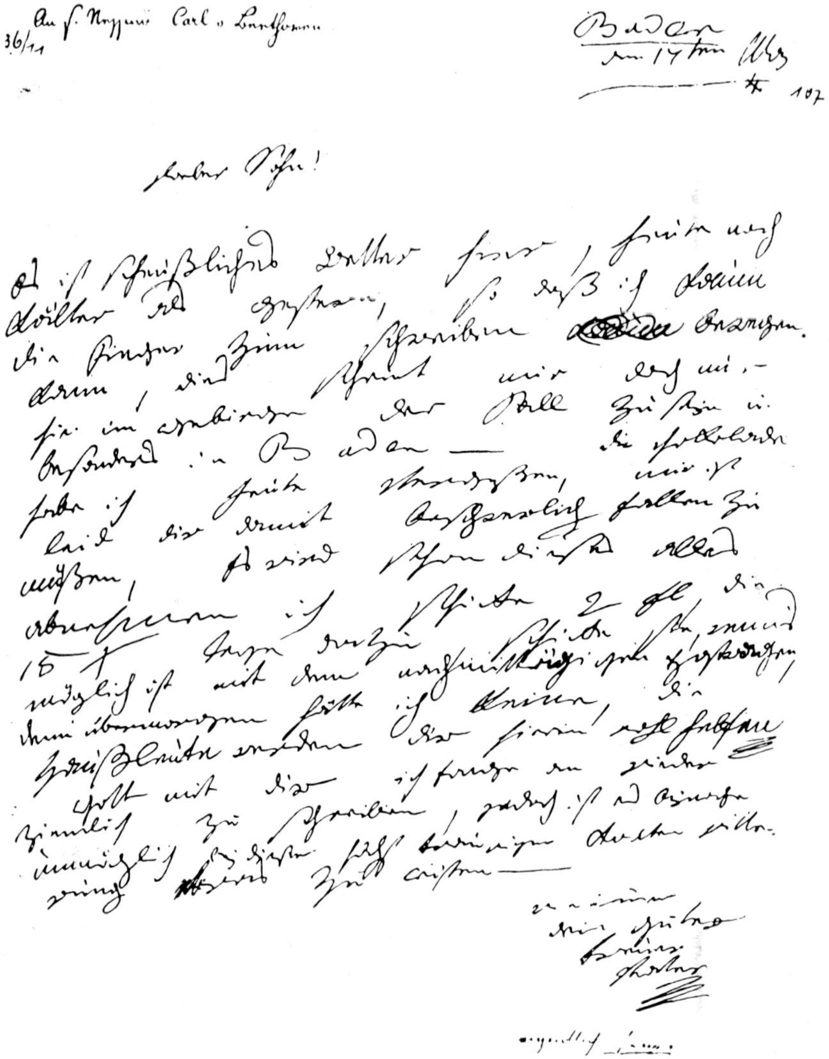

5. Autograph of a letter by Beethoven

More and more he took to himself the role of sole protector of the boy, and on September 14 he issued a formal ukase to Blöchlinger, to whom he wrote:

> . . . Only the following individuals have free access to my nephew: H[err] v. Bernard, H[err] v. Oliva, Herr v. Piuk, Referee. — In addition, whatever person has business with my nephew I will on each occasion inform you of the fact in writing through the same, whereupon you will be so obliging as to give him immediate access to him, for it is a long way to you, and it is already obliging to me when anyone does this for me, as, for example the truss-maker etc. —
>
> My nephew is never to leave the house without written notice from me. — From this it is also clear how the mother is to be treated. I insist that this be strictly adhered to, it being what the authorities and I have arranged. You, Sir, are too new in these circumstances, greatly as your other deserts are apparent to me, to be able to act of your own authority in this matter, as has happened before. Credulity in this case only produces confusion, and — and the result thereof might always speak more against you than for you, which I do not wish for your honor. — I hear that my nephew needs or wants several things from me, he should apply to me for them; you will only be so good as to see that his letters reach Steiner and Co. [the address follows].
>
> Your devoted L. v. Beethoven
exclusive guardian of my nephew Carl v. Beethoven
>
> N.B. Expenditures in this connection will be reimbursed each time.[52]

Although Beethoven here so explicitly assumes the role of sole guardian, he was still tormented by the fact that the Magistracy had not yet expressed itself on the guardianship. On September 15, he wrote to Karl Bernard:

> I have charged Oliva to inquire at my lodging if there is not some order or notice from the Magistracy there, I consider it necessary that Schmerling be asked whether, while the Magistracy gives no answer, I am guardian or not, or that Dr. Krause be asked, he lives in Singerstrasse. You can tell Schmerling everything that has happened so far. That I finally should have the principal reason that Karl is to see his corrupted mother as little as possible [sic]. Is it not crass, and like the majority of today's schoolmasters, that Karl has not written to me yet? Accursed, damned, execrable, wretched Viennese dogs! They may think that, because my brother is in

with them, something can be got from the Magistracy with money. Schmerling will know best how to attack the matter. Perhaps it would be necessary for us to go to the Referee again together. I hope for immediate cooperation and news. In haste

as ever your true friend Beethoven.[53]

How bitterly Beethoven here complains that Karl does not write to him, although he himself had sent his last letter back to him! His brother Johann, of whom we have long heard nothing, here reappears for the first time. He had bought a property, known as the "Wasserburg," in Gneixendorf; he was spending the winter in Vienna, where he had rented a lodging from his brother-in-law, the baker Obermeyer. Ludwig suspected that he had allied himself with Johanna and had bribed the Magistracy for her.

Then came the hardest blow. The Magistracy finally announced the result of its investigation into the guardianship. It concluded that "the boy had been subject to the whims of Beethoven and had been tossed back and forth like a ball from one educational institution to another" [54] — a summary of the situation with which, after an objective review of the facts, one is unhappily forced to agree. The Magistracy provided that Councillor Tuscher, in accordance with his request, should be relieved of the guardianship; that the guardianship should no longer be entrusted to Ludwig van Beethoven; but that the mother should remain as legal guardian, with a "capable and honest man" as co-guardian. Leopold Nussböck, Municipal Sequestrator, was appointed to this office.

So now it had happened, the thing that Ludwig had dreaded when, on August 2, he had written to Bernard, "I hardly believed that Karl would finally enjoy some peace, and I too — and is this monster to conquer at last?" [55]

Yet this time his courage was not shattered by the monster's victory. On the contrary, he reacted to the court's decision by continuing his fight against Johanna with increased alertness and vigor.

X

THE SECOND SUIT:
VICTORY

FROM a letter to Bernard, written on October 10, it appears that
Ludwig's first reaction to the shattering news that Johanna
had been named guardian was a plan to smuggle Karl out of
Vienna to Salzburg and put him in a school there; "but we must
first make sure that the mother cannot go there." [1]

However, the plan was dropped in favor of a new line of attack.
Ludwig had turned to his legal adviser, Dr. Bach, who undertook
to represent him in the matter. On October 23, he wrote Dr. Bach
a letter in which he set forth the circumstances of the guardianship — naturally with all the distortions of fact to which he was
led by his pathological relationship to the boy and his mother. He
begins by stating the goals which he wishes his lawyer to attain:

> The principal points are that I be immediately acknowledged sole
> guardian; I will accept no co-guardian; likewise the mother is [to
> be] excluded from communication with her son at the Institute,
> because there cannot be guards enough there for her immorality
> . . . But so that humanity be not lost from sight here, she can
> sometimes speak with her son at my lodging in the presence of
> his teacher and other honorable persons . . . I think, furthermore,
> that . . . it should be sought to obtain the Appellate Court as
> the guardianship authority; since I have put my nephew in a
> higher category, neither he nor I belong under the Magistracy,
> since only tavern-keepers, cobblers, and tailors belong under such
> a guardianship . . .[2]

A long enumeration of the financial sacrifices he has made for his
ward follows; the obvious intention is to show that he has paid a
high price for the boy, which entitles him to the sole guardianship.

In a postscript Ludwig carries his slandering of Johanna so far
that he asserts: "The intention of the mother is to have her son
with her in order that she may enjoy her entire pension." He
completely forgot that Johanna had originally asked only that her
son be brought up in a school instead of at his uncle's. But by now
he was too blinded to be capable of a reasonable judgment.

A note to Dr. Bach, written soon after this letter and urging him
to increased activity, has the following postscript:

> I will send you Frau Beethoven's address later today. She no longer
> owns a house, so we can only reimburse ourselves from her pen-
> sion. In this matter the word must be: veni, vidi, vici.[3]

Ludwig's financial situation must indeed have been critical at
this time, if he needed the widow's "pension" — presumably her
contribution to the expenses of Karl's education — to save himself. Several conversations during this period with Oliva, the
banker, show that Beethoven was also trying to raise money on
his shares of bank stock.

But this increased activity in the attempt to recover his nephew
was not his only reaction. His numerous letters to Bernard testify
to the deep grief, indeed the despair, into which the loss of the
guardianship had plunged him. We find most heart-rending expressions of his jealousy, usually provoked by news that Johanna
had seen her child or had done something for him. Thus he wrote
to Bernard:

> . . . what supervision at Blöchl[inger's], with the mother able to
> sneak in in this fashion, believe me, there is nothing there, very
> soon we shall be exactly where we were. — Why did he not in-
> quire of me or of you and what can be the matter with a man who
> wrote to me so crudely? — You can deal with Karl as you wish,
> let him write, but do not say anything about it, it will again con-
> tain heartless and unfeeling hypocrisy, cold gratitude, he already
> belongs to the adder breed of his bestial mother. — Find out how
> often she has been there, and perhaps without previous notifica-
> tion, which should be absolutely requisite in the case of this raven-
> mother, I will then at once issue orders as to how the matter is to
> be dealt with, my trust in him [Blöchlinger] is dead. — In the end
> he will even let him out of the house, but then let the devil take
> him.[4]

And again:

> . . . The first thing to do would be to resign the guardianship
> without choosing anyone and leave Karl wholly to his fate. For
> he is already too much of a good-for-nothing and is best fit for his
> mother and my pseudo-brother.[5]

The following letter to Bernard, written when Ludwig learned
that Karl was wearing a new hat which Johanna had bought for
him, sounds particularly anguished:

> Dear B. This for the glacier [6] . . . what information you may
> wish to impart to this ice-cellar, in a few lines, you are free to do.
> — But you will kindly add that *he is absolutely to accept nothing
> else from her;* he [Karl] *had on a hat yesterday which was again
> procured new by her.*[7] Spare me from this vulgar riffraff! It would
> have been best at Giannatasio's after all, I have to stand before
> such miserable riffraff like a poor sinner and all their twaddle is
> taken up and bandied about — from the present silence concern-
> ing everything that Karl especially through the influence of his
> wicked mother cooks up against me, K[arl] will believe that his
> activities against me are approved or tolerated — only a some-
> what delicate sensitivity would long since have ceased to listen to
> and accept the bilge both written and verbal, for we, yourself as
> well as I and I and you have after all the most experience of Karl.
> So it is best that H[err] B[löchlinger] Glacier guide himself by
> us — I keep having the impression that you have something else
> to tell me, which might horrify me, at one time you believe that
> I should leave Karl wholly to his fate, at another time that I should
> not do so. — Still perhaps you have concealed something horrible
> from me, it is not necessary. — *For me there is nothing more hor-
> rible than I have already — and through Karl, too — experienced,
> so out with it, my breast is strong, let darts and blows rain upon
> it.*[8] — I beg you to have the letter sent to Blöchl[inger] immedi-
> ately, herewith the tip. — God help me, I am so tired of dealing
> with mankind that I can hardly see and hear another.
>   Your Beethoven

> Dr. Weissenbach [9] has let me know that he will take Karl, but
> only temporarily — this between ourselves. This would be ex-
> cellent, to me this glacier and ice-cellar is hateful.[10]

On October 30, presumably under Dr. Bach's direction, Ludwig addressed the Magistracy in a letter which, for him, is extremely restrained. Alleging that, "being absent for some time on

account of a business journey," he had raised no objection to being "temporarily supplanted by a legal guardian" (Nussböck), he announces that he has now returned permanently to Vienna and wishes to be reinstated as guardian, "the more so . . . as I hear, that due to lack of money to defray the expenses his mother wishes to remove the boy from his former school, chosen by me, and take him to live with her." [11]

The letter was doubtless meant to serve as a trial-balloon, to discover whether the decision of the Magistracy was to be regarded as final. In answer, the Magistracy referred to its decision of September 17, which removed Beethoven from the guardianship.

Ludwig replied in another letter to the Magistracy which has not been preserved but which is referred to in a letter to Bernard. This letter gives full expression to his despair over the loss of his nephew and over the shattering of his illusion that the child whom he had believed to be his own would love him as another mother, and to the intensifying hatred of Johanna which this realization aroused in him:

> Karl has not yet written a word, as [if] in an institute the son can perpetrate whatever he pleases against his father without being punished for it?!! God better this! You can hardly believe how I suffer through it. What obduracy and ingratitude in the young villain?! When you go there, ask to speak with Karl to hear what, utterly misguided as he is, he will find to say about me. — My brother is absolutely not to be allowed access; and it is good to let him [Karl] feel that he is no longer to see his so criminal mother who, by who knows what Circe wiles or spells or conjurations, has bewitched him against me, [and] who in any case has sought only to promote his physical and moral corruption. — For he will only talk about what he can get from him, etc., the twaddle that always puts him off the track.
>
> Yours in haste.[12]

As we see, his brother Johann is here again included in his pattern of distrust; and he becomes a danger to Karl, Beethoven having already suspected him of being allied with Johanna and having bribed the magistrates.

At the end of October Ludwig returned to Vienna from Mödling. He moved to a lodging on the Josephstädter Glacis, close to Blöchlinger's Institute, so that he could see Karl frequently.

The Conversation Books reveal that Beethoven's thoughts at this period were concentrated on recovering the guardianship. Most of the talks are with his friends Oliva and Bernard. We can observe how, every time his friends started a new subject, Ludwig stubbornly brought the conversation back to the guardianship. It is clear that his friends did not dare to utter any opinions contradictory to Ludwig's on the subject; friendship would immediately have suffered shipwreck if they had not agreed with him in every respect. Oliva emerges as a rather colorless figure who simply says "yea and amen" to everything. Bernard, on the other hand, plays an active role by fanning the flame of wrath against Johanna and the Magistracy. His entries in the Conversation Book show that he brought Ludwig a great deal of gossip. In November he wrote:

> It seems to me that, after Schmerling's removal, the Landrichter [13] had connived it this way. For how would it ever have entered their heads to raise the question of nobility now, after two years.[14]

And:

> I say too that the Magistracy believes everything it hears, for example that she [Johanna] said that you were in love with her.[15]

Ludwig also used Bernard as intermediary between himself and Blöchlinger, which gave occasion for all sorts of tale-bearing; Bernard also dealt with Dr. Bach, Ludwig's lawyer, and brought Ludwig Bach's advice.

It is about this time that Councillor Peters appears in Beethoven's circle of friends. He was tutor to the Princes Lobkowitz, the sons of the Prince Lobkowitz who had been Beethoven's patron. Peters declared himself ready to assume the guardianship of Beethoven's nephew. He was extremely devoted to Ludwig, perhaps influenced in this by the late Prince's friendship and respect for the composer. As tutor in a princely household and an experienced pedagogue, he appeared to be highly suitable for the guardianship. His loyalty to Ludwig is especially manifest in the fact that, in judging and dealing with Johanna, he was in complete agreement with him. He also expressed the same derogatory opinion of the Magistracy as Ludwig.

After a conversation with Bach at the beginning of November, Bernard wrote:

> Bach says that without you the co-guardian is simply a figurehead, and all arrangements proceed from you. In addition no objections can be made to any such arrangements, because he [the co-guardian] has no relation to the matter and besides is himself a teacher. The present guardian Nussböck himself wants you to take over the guardianship, but because your deafness raises a difficulty, they want you to have someone with you. H[er]r v. Bach says that H[er]r Nussböck is a very reliable man for the purpose; but I said that I had already talked to you about Peters. H[er]r v. Bach says that it cannot be put through that you should get the guardianship alone because deafness is a legal reason.
> As Peters is an upright and circumspect man, no intrigues are to be feared on his part, especially since he has no ulterior interests. I can assure you that Peters has not changed his attitude in the least down to today. He is too noble to be dependent on petty things.
> Then you can at once make the most appropriate arrangements.
> A plan must be adopted for several years, so that Karl is systematically guided in his education.[16]

> The Magist[racy] ought to be ashamed to make such arrangements; for as the Doctor [Bach] says, H[er]r Nussböck has to look after horses and children all at once. Their Sapiences have let themselves be taken in by that woman.[17]

We see from this that Dr. Bach was cautiously trying to persuade Ludwig to resign the guardianship to others, and himself, as it were, to pull the wires from backstage. On another occasion Dr. Bach himself wrote:

> If we are willing to let the widow be named co-guardian, the matter will present fewer difficulties;

and in answer to Ludwig's immediate refusal to entertain such a proposal, Bach went on:

> As co-guardian, she really has no preponderant power but only the honor of sharing in the guardianship. She remains a mere figurehead — [18]

But Ludwig's emotional excitement, his inordinate wishes, and his sincere conviction of Johanna's corrupting influence on Karl, made it impossible for him to accept such compromise solutions.

He refused to allow Dr. Bach to propose the widow even as co-guardian. Ludwig insisted — and Bernard agreed — that Karl and Johanna must be completely separated. Thus Bernard wrote toward the end of November:

You must insist that she may not see Karl anywhere except at your lodging [19]

and, a little later:

All this must finally come to an end.
but that in everything she must apply to you as the guardian
In this way she will not pester him [20] again.[21]

We learn from the Conversation Books that Councillor Peters planned to visit Karl at Blöchlinger's Institute, and he promised that he would inform Ludwig of the slightest details and of any changes, on each such occasion. In any case, he was as convinced as Ludwig that Johanna must be kept from her child. He wrote, for example, during the course of a conversation:

The matter will be arranged in complete accordance with your wishes, and my humble self will deal with H[err] Plechlinger.[22] The mother must not enter the Institute unless you are present. Four times a year is quite enough.[23]

Thanks to Peters' accounts of his visits to the Institute, we have a considerable amount of information about Karl during the months of November and December 1819. Peters frequently brought highly encouraging reports, as the following extracts from conversations held in December show:

Much has already been gained, in that the boy has now caught up with his public school studies — and Plechlinger, if not a genius, seems to me to be good . . . Your nephew looks well, fine eyes — charm, an eloquent physiognomy and excellent bearing. I should like to have the teaching of him just for two years . . . The boy will be outstanding — he will spurn everything common — he was too young . . .[24]

And Karl successfully passed his examinations. Peters reported:

The Greek examination came off well, although he was only prepared for it a few days before — He really has a great deal of talent. The professor[s] showed him real respect.[25]

Bernard and Oliva also praised Karl's behavior and his success in school. From all this it appears that Blöchlinger and his Institute had a very good effect on Karl's state of mind. This was during a period when Karl had occasional contacts with his mother, and, according to Beethoven, was infected with all evil by her.

In the following passages from the Conversation Book, Peters exhibits real pedagogical understanding:

> The boys are too different
> ———
> Your nephew is the only one who is taking the second class — That means he has to have a teacher of his own, it would be better if there were at least three or four boys. The only one. [Peters refers to Karl.]
> ———
> He has nobody ahead of him and nobody behind him. Not good. If there were twenty and your nephew were the best or among the best, that would be better.[26]

The conversation turned to other subjects but, as usual, Ludwig brought it back to his nephew. Peters' judgment of Karl's schoolwork was, as we see, pedagogically sound.

During this period Karl's handwriting occasionally appears in the Conversation Books, so that little by little we get a clearer impression of him.

In December he had "frozen feet" again and had to stay in bed to cure them. Ludwig visited him at school, and on this occasion Karl wrote the following entries in the Conversation Book:

> She [Johanna] told me that she herself wants me to stay here, but that it is becoming harder for her to raise, instead of 900 florins — 1200 now.
> ———
> But cannot you get yours [27] until she draws her pension?
> ———
> I don't know where all these lice can come from.
> ———
> But it is healthy to have lice.
> How are the Magistrates behaving?
> ———
> Did the court sit yesterday?
> ———
> Schmerling is there.
> ———

Have you taken Peters as co-guardian yet?

———

Nothing of the kind can happen here, because there is the strictest supervision.

———

Secretly never [28]

———

I should be able to get up day after tomorrow. When my frozen feet *are all cured,* they will *never come again.*

———

On each foot I have — five corns.

———

He cut open the frozen toe today.[29]

A few remarks on these entries seem indicated here. In the first place, Karl's faultless spelling is in gratifying contrast to that of Ludwig and many of his friends. His answers are clear and concise; he is alert and intelligent. We get the impression that he was no unworthy object of the great man's love. It appears from the conversation that Karl was following the progress of the lawsuit for his possession and was well aware of Ludwig's intentions and moves. We may suppose that this being drawn into the decision of his own destiny gave the boy the opportunity to play the opposing parties off against each other; in his immaturity he could hardly resist doing so, and it must have influenced his character unfavorably. His love of his mother and his obligation to be grateful to his uncle, whose great fondness for him must have made a strong impression on him, aroused a conflict in him which was beyond his powers.

We learn from the Conversation Books that there was a hearing before the Magistracy, at which Ludwig was represented by Bernard while Johanna appeared in person. Bernard reported:

Peters is ill; so I was alone. The friendly Doctor [Bach] sends you his best wishes; it was a commission before which the Queen of the Night was summoned; she said that she would gladly accede to these arrangements; in any case she is very submissive and will gladly accede to everything. If the Magistracy should not agree, the Doctor will proceed with the greatest rigor in the appeal and put the Magistracy to shame. He sends you word that he will do everything to prove himself worthy of your confidence. You must only be patient for a few more days.[30]

Again the Magistracy found no reason for giving Ludwig the exclusive guardianship and wholly removing the boy from his mother. Dr. Bach's application was rejected on December 20. Dr. Bach appears to have expected this outcome, for, a few days earlier, Bernard had written:

> But if it comes to the Appellate Court, it will be all the better, because then their stupidity will be put to shame. Doctor Bach would prefer to have an appeal, because all the preliminaries are such that any reasonable person must approve them.[31]

Dr. Bach now moved to appeal from the decision of the Magistracy. The step gave all Beethoven's friends fresh hope, for the Appellate Court was much more accessible to the influence of Beethoven's highly placed patrons than the Magistracy with its bourgeois personnel.

On January 7, Ludwig applied to the Appellate Court to reverse the decision of the Magistracy. His appeal is brief, to the point, and moderate in tone.[32] Dr. Bach must have assisted in drawing it up, if he did not himself compose it. Ludwig repeated the arguments which, in his opinion, entitled him to the guardianship. The need that the boy's education be directed by a man is emphasized; little is said about the mother's immorality. Johanna is even conceded a sort of co-guardianship which entitles her to see her child and to be informed of the plans for his education.

Bernard reported to Ludwig on progress, and we learn from his statements that Schmerling, who had already been useful to Beethoven earlier, was now expected to influence the Appellate Court. Dr. Bach wrote in a Conversation Book: "I thought that you had already been to see the judges, [seen] Schmerling and Winter."[33] Bernard gave Ludwig instructions as to his behavior during the appeal. He wrote, for example:

> I think that, to eliminate all possible objections now, you ought not to take Karl to eat at a tavern, because then it is immediately said that you habitually take him to taverns, because everyone is watching you and everything is distorted by gossip and false interpretations.[34]

For his nephew often went to taverns with him, since at this time Ludwig had no meals prepared at home. It is to these visits to taverns that we partly owe the record of conversations, for at Beethoven's lodging chalk and a slate were generally used for the purpose. We have already mentioned that, in public places, Beethoven often wrote his part of the conversation too, since his deafness made it impossible for him to determine the loudness of his voice and he feared that he might be overheard by strangers.

In January, 1820, Karl wrote:

> She promised me so much that I could no longer resist her; I am sorry that I was so weak then, and beg you to forgive me for it; but I will certainly not let myself be led astray again now. — I did not know what consequences it could have when I spoke that way before the magistrates. But if there should be another investigation, I will take back everything that I *said then that was untrue.*[35]

Karl here refers to a statement before the Magistracy the record of which is not extant. Apparently his uncle had reproached him for the tenor of his testimony. Under the pressure of these reproaches he excuses himself for his statements and says that they were untrue. We see how each of the opposing parties tried to win Karl over to its side and, when the opportunity arose, was able for the moment to bias him in its favor. All the data leave no doubt of his love for his mother; it is deep and lasting, and from time to time breaks through the stratum of his relationship to his uncle. This relationship had various motivations. His uncle was clearly a father-substitute for Karl, and through this he was strongly bound to him emotionally; he owed him his higher education and his attendance at a private school for boys from well-to-do families, and he was very proud of this. His impoverished mother could not have done all this for him. He also shared in his uncle's fame. Claudius Artaria, one of the teachers in Blöchlinger's school, later remembered Karl as "highly talented by nature and a trifle conceited as Beethoven's nephew." [36] All this caused Karl to incline toward Ludwig. In addition, Blöchlinger and Ludwig's friends, under pressure from Ludwig, also influenced the boy. Oliva wrote in the Conversation Book:

> I told him [the lawyer] of Karl's change of heart; he wants very much to talk with him and believes that such a conversation could be of importance for the outcome of the matter.[37]

And again:

> the lawyer is very accommodating and particularly welcomed the
> idea that Karl himself is to contribute to undoing the iniquity.[38]

Dr. Bach sent for Karl, to obtain information from him. Karl
reported his interview with Dr. Bach in Ludwig's Conversation
Book:

> He asked me how old I am. If I want you for my guardian. If I am
> convinced that you want only my good. If I know the guardian
> [Peters]. If he has occupied himself with me. In what school I am.[39]

Following this, Peters wrote:

> You give your co-guardian (honorary guardian) nothing to do —
> I am jealous of Bernard [40]

from which we gather that Beethoven made particularly free use
of Bernard's services in the matter of the guardianship. A few lines
further on, Bernard wrote:

> The interpretation of the record does not fall to the Magistracy
> but to the Appellate Court; the Magistracy appears here simply
> as a party. The lawyer will bring that up; for he makes the reply
> as your representative. Perhaps there will also be a commission at
> which Karl will have to appear, and that is why the lawyer's ques-
> tions are good, for he must be informed of everything, including
> the workings of the boy's mind.
>
> After all that is his business. These men acquire a great readiness
> in comprehending a great variety of incidents.[41]

We see from this that Ludwig was beginning to distrust Dr. Bach
because the matter was not going fast enough for him and because Bach had applied to Karl personally for information. At
the same time his distrust of Karl never ceased; he was always
afraid that Karl would run away to his mother; he carefully inquired into the measures taken at the Institute to prevent this. In
answer to a question from his uncle, Karl wrote:

> the door of the next room, where H[er]r Blöchlinger sleeps, is
> always open.[42]

Meanwhile, despite the conflicting influences at the Institute, the
boy thrived most satisfactorily. Peters, the educator, was under-

standably concerned over Karl's teaching and soothed Ludwig's suspicions of the school:

> You will certainly get matters properly settled with Karl now, and Blöchlinger too is, so to speak, full of you and seems to be willingly and zealously heedful of Karl.[43]

On February 5 the Magistracy reported to the Appellate Court. It declined to revoke its decision of September 17, 1819, and added "certain further remarks in justification thereof." Since these remarks represent the view of the Magistrates, we give them in full:

> a) that the appellant, because of his physical defect and because of the enmity which, as the codicil to the will itself [shows], he entertains toward the mother of the ward, is held unfit to undertake the guardianship.
>
> b) that the guardianship by law belongs to the natural mother.
>
> c) that her having committed an embezzlement, of which she was guilty against her husband in the year 1811 and for which she was punished by a police house arrest of one month, is now no longer an impediment;
>
> d) that of all the harmful disturbances and interferences in the education of the ward with which it has been attempted to charge the mother nothing definite is alleged, still less proven. —
> If by harmful disturbances is to be understood that the natural mother wishes to see and talk with her child once every fortnight or four weeks, or to inform herself of the condition and cleanliness of his clothes, or to obtain information as to his behavior from his teachers, this can only appear a harmful influence in the eyes of the appellant; but everyone else would hold it against a natural mother if she did not inquire about her child at least once in a fortnight or four weeks.
>
> ad 2dum it appears that the appellant seeks to demand from the mother and the guardian that they also educate the boy in the sciences, since he finds neither of them fit to provide the boy a higher education; on this the Magistracy finds that the appellant is likewise unfit, at least he has not so far exhibited such fitness; he has entrusted the preparation of his nephew for a higher education to others; why should not the mother and the present guardian equally well do this, since they have in mind a better plan, namely to place the boy in the I.-R. Konvikt and to have him receive public instruction, where the boy will certainly make better progress with less expenditure. —
>
> ad 3tium. What the appellant has here written is not properly reconcilable with his [statement] that his nephew's welfare is dearest to his heart. He made, he says, the unwilling discovery that

the boy had lost a whole year and had to remain behind in his class; but certainly he cannot blame this on the mother or the present guardian but must ascribe it to his own direction; as the record *sub* D shows, after the first 2 months he removed the boy from public instruction at the University, kept him at home for 3 months, and only placed him in another school toward the end of June; so naturally the school year had to be lost for the boy, wholly or in part. — Finally, so far as the present education of the ward is concerned, it has been stated above that he is now in the educational institution of a certain Johann Blöchlinger in the Josephstadt and is being educated at the expense of the appellant and the mother, who contributes half of her pension, as suballegation d in petitioner's Exhibit A shows.

Herewith the Magistracy believes that it has dutifully performed its high charge, has justified its decision of September 17, 1819, and may with due deference propose that it be confirmed.

February 5, 1820

> Piuk
> Krall
> Miniberger
> Beranek [44]

The document is clear, concise, and to the point. Obviously the judges of the Magistracy had very reasonable views concerning the uncle's physical and psychological unfitness as guardian, Johanna's legal right to the guardianship, the fact that many years had passed since her misdemeanor, the untenability of the opinion that she had detrimentally influenced Karl's upbringing, and the attempt to turn her natural concern for her child into a reproach.

In his desperate compulsion to save his child from its wicked mother, Ludwig composed a long memorial to the Appellate Court, in which he attempted to set forth in detail his reasons for demanding that his nephew be entrusted exclusively to him.

The composition of this document occupied him for several weeks. Numerous passages in the Conversation Books for this period represent ideas to be incorporated in it or tentative drafts of various passages. We feel in them his agitation in the face of the great and solemn task which he saw his fight for his nephew to be. We reproduce one of these passages; it is characteristic of his obsession with the subject, and we see how his thoughts upon it keep recurring and demanding expression:

Since the Landrechte insisted that he should be put in a school, it is proper that, as soon as I am no longer to be guardian, I should be reimbursed.

Karl's own nature was to blame that he cannot be put just anywhere, as the professors themselves said, that he would not do well in the Gymnasium. —

He was put in the University because it was believed that the studies there [were] best for his nature . . .

I could do as little as others, for he remained the same there whether he was fetched away by Giannat[asio] or by me or by the tutor. —

In any case this person will receive little hearing as complainant, for anyone who has such a crime [as] reference deserves little confidence or none at all . . .

§191 [45] indicates this too, besides she is inspired by veritable wickedness, interest in enjoying her pension . . .

even if I erred here too, which has to be proved, I still deserve respect and consideration for the support and interest which I have always shown . . . even when Tuscher was g[uardian] I paid everything out of my own purse, had more worries than before, because she always worked to [influence] him against me and her son.

The various periods set forth,[46] this is the clearest; first Giannatasio could not and would not keep him — all the testimony I gave is good — how it went at Kudl[ich's] everyone knows, where he could be out whole days, strange that blows are rained down from every side on the doer of good, whereas the really evil can undertake everything criminal against the good —

I cannot go running everywhere like these idlers during the time when I was in Mödling [Beethoven adds in the margin below:] and Karl at Kudlich's

she [Johanna] ran to Tuscher, kept lying to him

on May 12th I arrived at M[ödling]. Tuscher had already resigned [the guardianship]. On June 22nd Karl went to Blöchl[inger's] — From November on 100 fl[orins] a month — blotting pap[er] candles

why is not Fr[au] Beeth[oven] mentioned as guardian in the first paper

the Magistracy showed itself prejudiced for her from the very beginning and only attacked me — and how

Several other counts and barons have gone from Giannata[si]o, all of whom went through the University

Cabinetmaker Housekeeper

Piano-tuner

Bank Karl —

Education absolutely requires an assured course
no sooner was she forbidden to see him than the opposite again
immoderate
Go with the lawyer to the Referee —
Juniper-wood
Dust broom and frying pan
2 times he went to her, where he perpetrated the worst.
since I give the money for his education to be advanced, it is natural
that this end too must be gained —
Night-lights
Blankengasse [47]
everything against her was not credited
G[iannatasio]'s letters only against me.
it is to be supposed that Smettana [48] would not in order to spare
me allow a bad thing to become worse by calling the whole thing
well taken care of.
Schlemmer [49]
Paper
to my nephew the character of his mother was never a secret, [but]
this the M[agistracy] out of ill-conceived immorality and partisanship refused to acknowledge, although my nephew was instructed
in the proper degree of respect for his mother
Blotting-paper [50]

The chaotic turmoil of Ludwig's thoughts is here unmistakable.
His friend Bernard finally had to assist in putting the Memorial
into shape. Ludwig wrote to him:

Dear Bernard! Since today I find myself alone again in these con-
fusing circumstances for me, there now first hovers before me the
real view of my Memorial, without wishing to deck myself in another's feathers, I nevertheless believe that I should leave [it] entirely to you, since you in a few words can say as much or more
than I roundabout, to treat it all according to your superior views,
the matter will thus be more impressive and understandable for
the judges. Of course it would have to be finished soon. Consider
that you are working and cooperating for Karl's happiness and
for my only possible satisfaction, and [doing so] for the last time —
once again deal with my raw material entirely as you see fit. In
any case you write more clearly than I do and the copy would soon
be ready.

Your friend and admirer Beethoven [51]

Thus, after weeks of effort, the many manuscript pages of the
Memorial were finally completed. Better than any other docu-

ment, it shows Beethoven's relationship to his nephew and to Johanna in all its pathological distortion. We will briefly review the principal points. The entire document can be consulted in the Appendix (p. 321).

The Memorial is divided into six sections. The first is devoted to presenting Johanna in the worst conceivable light. Beethoven again employs the primitive argumentation which he had used in earlier documents. The worse he represents Johanna to be, he thinks, the more he must be conceded to be right in regarding his nephew as his child. It is only to save his child that he makes a last attempt and incurs the "humiliation" of "sullying himself" with a person like Johanna. Johanna could develop her "evil propensities" very early, for her parents were only bourgeois upholsterers without education. Even in her parents' house she had accused a maid of a crime which she had herself committed. Although the Magistracy had declared that Johanna's embezzlement in 1811 had happened so long ago that it had no bearing on the guardianship,[52] Ludwig again presents it to the Court of Appeals as a "frightful crime." We hear for the first time that it was only by the greatest effort on the part of Karl and of Ludwig's friends that Johanna was saved from the most shameful punishment. The truth of this statement may be doubted.

And now Ludwig fabricated a connection which the dates of the events wholly belie. The "most frightful occurrence" (Johanna's embezzlement in 1811) had, he says, brought a severe illness on his brother Karl so that from thenceforth he had been an invalid and had only been able to survive for a time through Ludwig's pecuniary assistance. (In reality Karl did not fall ill until two years after Johanna's "frightful crime," and recovered from his first attack of tuberculosis in 1813, so that he was able to continue going to work until shortly before his death.) Next, in explanation of the codicil in which Beethoven's brother Karl expressly appointed Johanna co-guardian, Ludwig says that Karl was "misled" into adding it in his (Ludwig's) absence. Karl had asked him, and he had several times attempted, to get it back from the lawyer that same day, but in vain, since he could not find the lawyer.

Further, Johanna had taken a lover immediately after Karl's death, thus outraging the modesty of the innocent child. She went to all sorts of dances and amusements, while the child had not even the barest necessities and was left to a "miserable maid."

Later Johanna had revealed herself to be a corrupt and designing person. She gave her son "erroneous ideas" and brought him
to "everything abominable," to deceit and lies. She tried to lead
her son astray with money; she also gave him money to bribe
the servants who let her in to see him. Ludwig, the child's father
"in the true sense of the word," she tried to "vilify" through "most
abominable intrigues, cabals, and slanders," at the same time in-
fusing "her moral poison into the most innocent." (Ludwig cites not
one fact in proof of these accusations.) She had talked the boy
into wasting a school year, so that he would remain in Vienna. The
guardianship authority had enjoyed "certain infernal dainties"
with Johanna, for it recognized Johanna as guardian, whereby he,
Ludwig, the true and only guardian and father of his nephew, was
"abased in the basest, most vulgar way."

The second part of the Memorial is devoted to accusations
against the Magistracy as the guardianship authority. First, Ludwig bewails the "odious chance, full of evil consequences," that
his nephew and he, because of lack of nobility, had fallen under
the jurisdiction of the Magistracy. For Johanna's hypocrisy and
lies had found a ready ear there. This is the introduction to his
account of an event to which there is no allusion in any of the
extant documents before this. But it appears that the Magistracy
or the Appellate Court had knowledge of it and that Ludwig
feared the occurrence might testify against him. According to his
own description, Ludwig had fallen upon his nephew in anger,
pulled him from his chair, and, it seems, injured him so severely
that a doctor had to be called. This was two years after the operation for hernia — that is, when the boy was thirteen. He was still
obliged to wear a truss which, under his uncle's violence, caused
him "some pain at the most sensitive spot" — that is, presumably,
injured him in the genital region. In any case, Ludwig obliged
Dr. Smetana — the physician who had originally performed the
operation — to draw up a statement that the lad was not seriously
injured. Ludwig accounts for his act of rage by saying that he too
"is but a man," "harried on all sides like a wild beast," "misunderstood, often treated in the basest way by this vulgar authority
[the Magistracy]." This mistreatment of his nephew is probably

referred to in a passage in a Conversation Book from the period
when he was drafting the Memorial:

> I committed one single fault, but as little as a father (and such
> I was and am) has his children taken away from him, [or] as when
> there is a mistake made in an educational institution is the latter
> suppressed, even so little, I hope, could the guard[ianship] be
> taken from me for this reason.[53]

Johanna, the Memorial continues, had accused him of writing
a letter to Karl against confession, and this he attempts to deny.
In view of the anti-religious attitude which Ludwig frequently
expressed on other occasions, and especially in view of his hostility to the clergy, we cannot exclude the possibility that he did
declare himself against confession in a letter to his nephew, especially as he might well fear that the boy would, in confession, say
something about his uncle's conduct, particularly toward Johanna.
In answer to Johanna's accusation, Ludwig emphatically states
that the exact opposite was the case: he had written the boy a
letter in which, in a truly religious, moving, and fatherly way, he
had urged him to this solemn duty. But once, instead of going
to confession, the boy had gone to his mother.

From here on the distortions and perversions of fact in the
Memorial become truly outrageous. The Magistracy, Ludwig
states, had formed a false opinion of the matter *a priori* and had
regarded Ludwig as "the cause of a family squabble." Johanna had
enticed the boy to her a second time. Thereupon Ludwig, in view
of "the mother's machinations," had resigned the guardianship
and chosen Councillor Tuscher as guardian; he refused to have
his nephew with him any longer because, under the circumstances,
the difficulties were too great. Ludwig had wanted to entrust the
boy to Giannatasio, but because "it was known" that Giannatasio
was very much against the mother, the boy had been put in
Kudlich's school, where the mother hoped to receive better treatment. (We know that, in reality, Giannatasio had refused to keep
Karl on permanently.) The mother had prevented Karl from being
put in charge of Professor Sailer at the Institute in Landshut; yet
separation from his mother would have been the only way for the
boy to obey the commandment, "Honor thy father and thy mother,"
for being frequently with her rendered it impossible. When, shortly

afterward, Councillor Tuscher resigned the guardianship, the entire matter was placed in the hands of a Referee, who allowed the boy to see his mother freely; the result had been disastrous, for Karl had been so treated, mentally and physically, that he was no longer recognizable. What this "treatment" consisted in, Ludwig does not state.

Here Ludwig reports an event which throws a new light on his pathological idea of poisoning through Johanna. Karl was instructed — it is not clear by whom — to pay his respects to his mother on her name-day, and he had spent that day and the following night with her. His "corrupt" mother had so stuffed him with "food and strong drink" that, the next morning, he could not move. Nevertheless, sick as he was, he was forced to take the twenty-five-minute walk from the Tiefer Graben, where his mother lived, to Kudlich's school. In addition, the mother had sent him a "bungler of a doctor" — as if she had done so on purpose to make him even worse. Ludwig, just back from the country, visited him at the school. Karl was sick in bed; Ludwig considered the medicines unsuitable for his condition — by which he presumably intended to suggest that the doctor was cooperating in Johanna's plan to poison her son. Ludwig called in Dr. Hasenöhrl, and "there proved to be a hemorrhage." Ludwig had arranged for the boy to have the best of care, but the mother had rushed into the school "like a raging Medea" and had taken Karl home "at risk of life" (sic; the meaning is doubtless "despite the danger to his life"). The motive which Ludwig ascribes to Johanna is equally grotesque. She had, he says, feared that at the school the real cause of the boy's illness would be discovered — namely, that she had given him poisoned food and drink. (Ludwig's describing Johanna as a "Medea" is another expression of his delusion, for Medea murdered her children.) The boy had spent several weeks in bed at his mother's before he recovered. Ludwig does not explain how he could have recovered, for, according to him, the mother wished to take her son's life. But in this advanced stage of his pathological idea, all logic had vanished. In reality the boy's illness may have been a digestive upset, brought on by overeating on his mother's name-day. If Karl had been seriously ill at this time, we should certainly find some reference to it in letters or other documents.

The "hemorrhage" must be regarded as purely the product of Ludwig's imagination.

The pathological idea of poisoning by a woman, which continually reappears from the time of his brother Karl's death (as we reported, Ludwig believed him to have been poisoned by Johanna) found its clearest expression in the Memorial. We shall not be wrong if we find the origin of it in Ludwig's relationship to his own mother. In view of the lack of material, it is, of course, impossible to discover the infantile prototype for this idea. But a prototype for it exists in the events of the last weeks of his mother's life. During her last illness, Ludwig cared for her for seven weeks and hence was with her a great deal. She had presumably spat blood, as tuberculosis patients often do in the last stage of the disease. Her death forced him into the maternal role for which his infantile experiences had presumably predetermined him; but at the same time, in his unconscious, it predisposed him toward the disease of which his mother had died.

Ludwig's hypochondriacal idea, after his mother's death, that he was himself suffering from tuberculosis was, in Chapter V, traced back to the identification by which he provided a substitute for his lost mother. To this positive signification of the hypochondriacal idea we can, then, add another, which is negative. From the connection which he makes in the Memorial between hemorrhage and poisoning, we see that the hypochondriacal idea of having tuberculosis is psychologically associated with the idea of being poisoned by the mother-figure. Even at the time of his brother Karl's death, the association between poisoning and tuberculosis was so close in Ludwig that he explained Karl's death from tuberculosis as the result of being poisoned by Johanna. It is known from clinical psychopathology that the paranoiac's idea and fear of being poisoned represents a projection of hostile aggression toward the persecutor. The intensity of the hostile emotions can be gauged from the intensity of the defensiveness. There can be no doubt that Ludwig identified himself with his nephew to a high degree. This follows from the fact that, in the Memorial, he projects on his nephew the tuberculosis-hypochondria which he had himself twice developed — and connects it with poisoning by the mother. The idea of poisoning, which first appears as a form of anxiety for his brother and his nephew, he henceforth increasingly develops in regard to himself. But with this it becomes clear that Johanna represents a substitute-figure for his own mother. His whole hatred of Johanna and his passionately hostile attitude toward her must be regarded as originally applying to his mother. Unfortunately, the lack of material from his early childhood does not allow us to trace the origin of this hatred of his mother.

The name-day episode also explains why, the following August, Beethoven 'did not wish to receive a name-day letter from his nephew. The recollection that Karl had spent Johanna's name-day with her was too fresh and painful, and Ludwig was still too angry to welcome his nephew's good wishes on his own name-day. In this there is an element of resentment against his nephew which receives stronger expression in the future. It becomes more and more clear that, in his relationship to his nephew, Ludwig was repeating his relationship to his brother Karl. As Karl at an earlier period, so now his nephew must increasingly become his exclusive possession. The element of hatred in his ambivalent attitude toward his nephew, above all his jealousy of him, becomes more and more apparent. His two physical assaults on his nephew, of which we learn from the court records, are strongly reminiscent of the physical violence between the two brothers. His aggression against his nephew, especially the psychological torture to which he subjected him, plays an important part later; for it precipitates the final catastrophe.

The slandering of the Magistracy continues through several pages of the Memorial; many details are grotesquely distorted. It would be tiresome to enumerate them. Ludwig again discusses his nephew's character, which Johanna has ruined by teaching him to lie and deceive. Without his corrupt mother's machinations, Karl, under his uncle's guidance, might well have been able to become a great composer. At present, Blöchlinger is highly satisfied with his diligence and conduct, only the Magistracy passed "the most one-sided, injurious and unfeeling" judgment upon him. Next comes a long and detailed account of all his expenditures for his nephew, which give him a right to his possession, as if the boy were something to be bought and sold. After all the violently emotional attacks on Johanna and the Magistracy, it sounds almost

like irony when Ludwig adds: "Let no one believe that, as she
[Johanna] says, I am guided by private hatred of her or vengeance
against her." And it is a painful disavowal when he writes: "My
nephew needs me, not I him."

The Memorial is followed by a "supplement." This treats of
Father Fröhlich, who had once furnished the Magistracy with
such impressive testimony against Ludwig's guardianship and his
educational methods. Ludwig reviles the priest almost obscenely,
in an attempt to invalidate his arguments by counterattacks. He
describes him as a drunkard, sadist, and libertine, with whom
Johanna had had an intrigue. We know from Fröhlich's testimony
that Karl's fellow-pupils refused to go to church with him because
of his boisterous behavior. Ludwig turns this completely around:
he himself, he says, had become aware of the other boys' improper
behavior and had immediately forbidden his nephew to associate
with them. Father Fröhlich had said that he was obliged to expel
Karl from his school. Ludwig, on the contrary, asserts that he
had removed the boy from the school because he "saw through
the man's crookedness only too well"; this had wounded the priest's
vanity, who thus became "a new tool" against him in Johanna's
hands.

A final insult to the Magistracy and a threat to refuse to recognize it as the proper guardianship authority bring this extraordinary document to a close.

On February 21, 1820, the Appellate Court ordered the Magistracy to submit further documents and a more explicit report; we
may assume that this was in reaction to Ludwig's Memorial. The
answer, presented on February 28, shows what an intelligent per-
ception the Magistracy had of the unreasonable and exaggerated
feelings which motivated the Memorial. Ludwig, the answer sets
forth, had in December, 1816, obliged the Landrechte to hold a
special session, "as if the greatest peril were imminent" — a clear
recognition of Ludwig's panic fear of losing his child. For excluding the mother, he had produced no other reason

. . . than the misdemeanor of which the mother incurred the guilt
in 1811, for everything else which appears in appellant's statement *sub* F is unproven gossip to which the R. I. Landrechte could
give no consideration, but which is eloquent testimony to *how*

passionately and hostilely appellant has long since treated the mother and still treats her, how easily he falls to reopening her healed wounds, now when, after undergoing punishment, she is reinstated in her previous rights, *reproaching her with a misdemeanor* which she expiated many years ago, a misdemeanor which her wronged husband himself forgave her, in as much as he not only petitioned for leniency in the punishment meted out to her but also, in his testamentary dispositions, recognized her as fit and worthy to act as guardian of his son, and hence prescribed that he should not be taken from her; regardless of which, appellant last year attempted to send the boy abroad to Landshut to be educated, obviously not for the boy's good, for the best educational institutions are undeniably here, *but simply in order to mortify the mother and tear the heart from her bosom.* Fortunately, however, on the basis of an opinion demanded from this court, the government frustrated appellant's plan by refusing a passport.[54]

We do not know if the Appellate Court replied to the Magistracy; there is no record of such an answer.

Meanwhile Ludwig pushed his business with the Appellate Court. He did everything possible to influence the judges personally. On March 6 he wrote a letter to Judge Winter announcing the presentation of his Memorial:

> . . . I believed that I owed it to myself to show the baselessness of so many slanders against me, as well as to disclose Frau van Beethoven's intrigues against me to the detriment of her own child, as well as to set the conduct of the Magistracy in its proper light . . .

His accusations against Johanna and the Magistracy are repeated, including Karl's "hemorrhage." The letter closes with an expression of his trust

> . . . in a man as intelligent as he is full of feeling, and I hope all advantage therefrom. For I can never suppose that such treatment as, upon me, the benefactor of my dead brother, the support and stay of my nephew for five years, the Magistracy bestowed without any regard for all this, could be condoned, let alone approved, by any higher court.[55]

In whose favor the Appellate Court would decide remained uncertain for several weeks. The Conversation Books show that the question constantly occupied Ludwig and his friends. Blöchlinger and Peters especially reveal themselves as toadying to Beethoven;

in passing judgment on the Magistracy, they say exactly what he
wants to hear. A single example:

> Blöchlinger:
> The Magistrates are always trying to fish in troubled waters, anyone who has even the justest cause, but does not bribe, loses. If
> you had bribed, you would have won the case long ago. It is impossible to conceive of such beasts, advising a child, who can be
> subsidized to attain a higher cultural level, to learn a handicraft.
> They [the Magistrates] are sheer automatons. Such a court ought
> to concern itself only with marketwomen.[56]

And so on.

There is much information about Karl in the Conversation Books
of this period. Peters, who had been proposed as co-guardian,
praises Blöchlinger's Institute highly. His remarks on Karl are
also extremely positive. Karl is making great progress in Greek,
which he is studying as an elective subject; now that Ludwig had
given up the idea of making him a great musician, he should become a great scholar. Ludwig was forever doubting if the instruction at Blöchlinger's was good enough for Karl. Peters tried hard
to reassure him, and hence gave detailed reports of Karl's studies
and progress. He wrote, for example:

> The whole Institute was at work, I found the greatest order and
> quiet — Karl's teacher in Greek and Latin seems very skillful. He
> studies Greek zealously and could read Homer in 3 months. In
> mathematics they have three hours a week — They are at equations now — I am thoroughly satisfied with the Institute.
>
> ———
>
> It speaks well for the Institute that Karl learns a great deal more
> than is required in school.[57]

In one place Peters speaks of Karl with real enthusiasm:

> Karl pleased me extraordinarily today — A really splendid nature
>
> ———
>
> You must have had to struggle with yourself to be Karl's benefactor — It must be [told] to the boy, such love must be explained
> to him. It must bind him to you forever
>
> ———
>
> Such natures under pernicious circumstances often go to utter destruction — [58]
>
> ———

Blöchlinger will make it difficult for her [Johanna] to find any opportunity to see him, he says that Karl must not be disturbed and she must go away
The whole story is really interesting, for it contains almost unbelievable things; the Magistracy plays an awkward role — He did not understand you at all —

The Magistracy does not appear to be fit for unusual cases.[59]

There are frequent entries by Karl himself in the Conversation Books of this period. He reports on his examinations, in which Ludwig showed himself particularly interested, says that he has been having headaches, and takes an active part in Ludwig's eternal servant problem, as the following entries by him show:

She [obviously an acquaintance who recommended a servant to Ludwig] says that she knows a man who would do everything that *she* [60] does and of whose honesty she is convinced. She says the woman chatters incessantly and snuffs so much tobacco.

She says that you give the woman, together with bread-money, 14 fl[orins] a month; but the man will do it for 12, and you will be better satisfied with him than with the woman
Everything
better and more regularly

She will bring him tomorrow.

She [61] is so lazy that she only carried one tub.

The one who teaches me Greek does not live there but only comes daily from 10–12

After the midyear examination.

Tomorrow is the written examination.

I do that without a mistake

I have already done one from Greek but not in writing

But I am qualified for the fourth class now.

Yesterday I had a very bad headache. I get it often, I don't know why.[62]

As we see, the boy is outspoken in criticizing Beethoven's serv-ants. Further on, we learn that, during a brief illness which Karl suffered, Ludwig was extremely concerned that Blöchlinger keep him informed of Karl's condition, that Ludwig wanted to send the doctor to the boy even after the doctor himself considered it un-necessary; he was afraid that Karl might miss the semester ex-aminations.[63] During this period of anxious suspense about the outcome of his appeal, Ludwig was particularly concerned that nothing go amiss, so that nothing could be brought against him in court. Blöchlinger seems to have been thoroughly satisfied with Karl; thus, he said that Karl "must in any case get 'excellent' in all his subjects" and ". . . It would be a monstrous injustice if he did not get 'excellent' in all his subjects." [64]

Yet just before the decisive hearing before the Appellate Court, Blöchlinger became dissatisfied with Karl, in strong contrast to his positive remarks in earlier conversation. He wrote:

> Karl is unsettled and extraordinarily inclined to be lazy,
> every circumstance,
> which harms other boys harms him doubly, he can as little stand praise. I had a terrible time with him getting him to stick to work again, good words are often fruitless with him and do not pull him out of his rut.

> His understanding is far behind his memory and it is very hard to wean him away from being mechanical in his work.
> Since he has been with me, he has always been treated strictly, otherwise we should not yet have got where we are now; for ex-ample, if he has a bad mark in any subject, he is given nothing to eat at noon except soup and has to learn the failed subject in the presence of the other pupils.[65]

Possibly there was a connection between Karl's growing tension while his fate was being decided and this diminished interest in his studies. In any case, we learn from Blöchlinger's statements how strictly he was treated at the Institute.

The hearing was set for March 29, 1820. On March 28, Ludwig's lawyer, Dr. Bach, gave him detailed instructions as to what he was to say in court. Bach was ill and hence could not accompany him.[66]

The next day Beethoven, with his friend Bernard, appeared before Magistrates Piuk, Beranek, and Bayer. The record of Ludwig's declarations reads:

> Appeared Ludwig van Beethoven and Joseph Karl Bernard, editor of the *Wiener Zeitung*.
> After the strictest representations, in conformity with instructions received from above, had been made to the former, he declared:
> 1. that he desires the guardianship of his nephew according to his brother's will and according to law and persists in this,
> 2. that as co-guardian he asks for the Prince-Lobkowitzian Councillor von Peters,
> 3. he desires that Frau van Beethoven, as previously by the Landrechte, be excluded from the guardianship,
> 4. he alleges the data previously submitted to the Civil Senate of the Vienna Magistracy [to show] that he provides completely for his nephew and that he is willing to accept a co-guardian but absolutely not a guardian, in as much as he insists upon his right to have a share in the guardianship and is convinced that experience [had demonstrated] that another guardian would not care for the ward as appellant [has done].
>
> Ludwig van Beethoven [67]

Immediately after the hearing, Bernard wrote in the Conversation Book:

> Piuk was very humble. When I talked to him last July he said, We pay no attention to Herr v. Beethoven — we shall do exactly as we see fit. But when I explained everything to him for an hour after that, he at once changed.

Then he added:

> Schmerling helped a great deal.[68]

Schmerling was at this time a judge of the Appellate Court and had sufficient influence to obtain a decision in Ludwig's favor. Ludwig's friends were confident that he would win the case. Karl Czerny — Karl's piano-teacher — wrote after the hearing:

> I am delighted that the matter has turned out this way. For you have been vindicated and can in future bring Karl up according to your views without molestation.[69]

We learn further from the Conversation Books that on April 3 — a few days after the hearing, that is — Beethoven wanted to present Karl to one of his patrons among the Appellate judges, as

it were in a feeling of triumph over his success. This appears from
the following entry by Bernard:

> You can simply say that you want to bring Karl to him because,
> after all, in a way he owes him a great deal.[70]

Bernard advised Ludwig against telling Karl something concerning his mother, as Ludwig apparently wished to do:

> He really does not need to know that now, and anyway it will not
> particularly concern him. With time, when the things will no longer
> excite, he can still learn it in good time, and the impressions will
> be all the better.
> All these things only distract him now in a way that is bad for his
> state of mind and his application, without being of any essential
> moral benefit to him. Later it will be entirely different.
> It is simply an opinion
> There is nothing better to do now than to put the past wholly aside,
> since it is harmless; only the future is to be considered in respect
> to Karl's guidance and destiny — [71]

Ludwig also wished to remove Karl from Blöchlinger's school, of
which he had long been so deeply suspicious. Bernard advised
against this:

> You will find nothing better here. And he [Blöchlinger] really has
> a vocation for it.[72]

Ludwig's distrust of the school seems to have had two causes. He
always suspected that he was not getting enough for what he
spent. Money at this period was already of exaggerated importance
to him. But in addition, Karl was thriving at Blöchlinger's and
seemed to be happy there, which aroused Ludwig's jealousy.
Hence he sought for a reason for removing the boy from the Institute. Thus he asked a certain Kanne, who had been a protégé
of Prince Lobkowitz and wrote opera librettos, to report on Karl's
scholastic attainments. Kanne wrote:

> For arithmetic master they have a *cannoneer*. These people under-
> stand everything only mechanically. The boy, your nephew is never
> able to give a reason. The teachers here are too lazy. Your nephew
> is nothing less than developed. I cannot spare you this bitter con-
> viction.
> It would go better in the worst of a thousand schools. At the Uni-
> versity the instruction, especially in *Latin* is very thorough. I know

Professor Stein. He is a very fine man. I am against all ordinary institutes or private establishments. The directors are mostly speculators. Competent people do not go in for it. In Greek it is not going too badly. He seems to be strongest in Latin. — Only it all does not come from within, it is pure memorized material. But memory alone never makes a man. He declaims too. They have in fact — as he tells me — presented a play. With mathematics it looks bad. And yet it is the highest branch of learning.[73]

Ludwig himself spoke boastfully of his appearance in court to Kanne:

I was left free to choose Peters as guardian or co-guardian.

Kanne wrote in answer:

Hence complete vindication. What are the names of the Appellate judges? I will announce it in the *Morgenblatt*. That will please the Appellate Court too.[74]

Although Ludwig was certain of victory, the final decision of the Appellate Court was not yet in his hands. His impatience to enjoy the fruits of his victory was almost uncontrollable. He could hardly wait to inform Johanna that she could not see her child, and to receive her contribution to the expenses of Karl's education from her pension. In a conversation with Oliva he wrote:

Must the decision be put off on account of Peters [who was absent from Vienna at the time]? As to seeing the mother — cannot the Appellate Court be petitioned to hurry the decree, since there are such good testimonies to my guardianship. It must also be stipulated that she draws the money every quarter.[75]

Dr. Bach tried to soothe him:

We shall soon have the final decision — that will settle everything at once, including the matter of the mother.

To which Ludwig answered:

Meeting with the mother at Peters' — and how often depends upon *me*.[76]

His distrust of Blöchlinger seems to have increased at this time. He wanted to possess his child entirely by himself. Oliva argued against his accusation that Blöchlinger was in league with Johanna:

But B[löchlinger] — is after all apparently an honest man, who rather acts in accordance with false views perhaps, than is false himself — I believe he is timid and hence cannot act as authoritatively toward Karl's mother as he should.[77]

And on another occasion:

As a rising young pedagogue he [Blöchlinger] did not wish to quarrel with the court, fear made him equivocate.[78]

Oliva finally had to warn Ludwig specifically not to undertake anything against Johanna at the moment:

The lawyer says *first* that you must make absolutely no move in respect to the mother now, later on you can act as you please; anything that you did now would give her a new pretext for lodging a complaint, and that must be avoided. —
He will arrange that she must immediately draw her pension, what is in arrears, and in future regularly; — the Magistracy's decree on the whole matter cannot be expected for two weeks; — it is useless trying to urge the matter in that quarter for it must take its prescribed course.[79]

The Conversation Book for these weeks also shows why Beethoven was in such haste to act against Johanna. Karl wrote:

Mother came Friday.[80]

The possibility of meetings between mother and child was to be ended as quickly as possible.

Finally the Magistracy informed Ludwig of the Appellate Court's decision. The court

has seen fit to ordain that, with complete exclusion of the mother Johanna van Beethoven from the eventual guardianship over the minor Karl van Beethoven, whereby the appointment of a co-guardian in the person of Leopold Nussböck, brought about only by virtue of the law applicable to her, is automatically desisted from, the appellant, Herr Ludwig van Beethoven and Prince Lobkowitzian Councillor Karl Peters, proposed by him, are to be appointed joint guardians of the said minor Karl van Beethoven.

Vienna, April 20th, 1820.[81]

Beethoven had won complete victory. Johanna was entirely excluded from the guardianship; the co-guardian Nussböck had previously resigned; Ludwig and Peters were both appointed guardians. We will allow Ludwig himself to proclaim his triumph:

Dear Herr von Pinterics! [82]
I announce to you that the Civil Senate was charged by the High
Appellate Court to inform me of its decision, which affords me full
satisfaction. Dr. Bach was my representative in this matter and
to this Brook [Bach] was added the sea with lightning, thunder and
storm and the Magisterial brigantine suffered total shipwreck on
the same.

Your devoted Beethoven [83]

XI

FURTHER DEVELOPMENTS

SO now the Appellate Court had delivered the thirteen-year-old boy over, body and soul, to the strange, deaf genius. Yet this second rescue had certain painful after-effects, which must now be recorded.

Johanna submitted a petition to the Emperor, appealing from the court's decision. In addition, after her child was taken from her, she found a certain satisfaction in depriving his uncle of her stipulated share in the expenses of Karl's education, by refusing to draw her own pension. As we have seen, Ludwig frequently cited this as an argument against Johanna during the second suit. On the basis of the court's decision, he could now demand payment of this portion of her pension, but in order to do so he had to present a formal report on Johanna's circumstances. Oliva, Ludwig's adviser in money matters at this period, was charged to procure this report, which was to be drawn up by the priest of the parish in which Johanna lived. From the Conversation Books we learn that Oliva made numerous attempts to see the priest, but failed to find him at home.

During this time — the last weeks of April, 1820 — complaints about Karl make their appearance in the Conversation Books. It seems that the boy began to resist the pressure put on him, by the Institute and Ludwig's friends, to turn him from his mother. Oliva wrote:

> This is inexcusable both on the part of the pupil and on that of the teacher and *pedagogue*. [Perhaps Karl] had not written to his uncle.]

———

And, even worse, he had promised to do it and not kept his promise

---

Karl has little feeling, and N.B. for all the knowledge he is praised for, little understanding, — that is probably the key to this otherwise really unforgivable behavior.[1]

Oliva further reported that it was not until Karl's piano-teacher gave him a canon which his uncle had composed for him that Karl expressed regret at not having seen his uncle for so long.

On another occasion Oliva complained of Karl in the boy's presence:

Your nephew imagines that I am prejudiced against him and have spoken against him to you —

Ludwig immediately called Karl to account, whereupon the boy wrote:

I only say that H[er]r v. Oliva should not talk now about what is past.

Oliva:

The young man bears me malice through no fault of mine; I was far from mentioning anything previous and in vino veritas, he spoke against me in that connection.

He had heard that I spoke against him to Blöchlinger.

To which Karl replied:

He reprimands me and tells me that I owe you the utmost gratitude, because I am lost if you withdraw your hand from me.[2]

It appears that Oliva — perhaps acting on Ludwig's instructions, but in any case expressing Ludwig's views — had complained to Blöchlinger that Karl did not show enough affection for his uncle; and that he had also exhorted Karl to gratitude. But the boy was resolved to defend himself against pressure from Oliva. The reason for this attitude in him, we learn from Blöchlinger's entries in the Conversation Book a little later:

Has not his mother appealed to the highest justice? She was here about two weeks ago and says only that it will yet come to that.

I would be glad not to let her come here any more, for the last time she told Karl: 'everything is going very well'; whereupon the boy was lost for the entire day. She said it to him only when I looked away.

Karl confided it to one of my tutors, adding that he does not believe it, he loves his uncle, but of course his mother more. The next time I shall simply tell her that I will not allow her to come any more, because [it] would be very injurious to Karl.

He works very well, last Thursday he had a written examination again, in which he did his composition without an error [;] on the 15th he has his oral examination. All boys have to be more or less forced to work.

He is still a child, and I am convinced that he is very fond of you and recognizes what you are doing for him, so far as he can at his age.[3]

Johanna, then, had told Karl of her confident hope that the court would finally award him to her. Though he had been trying to resign himself to the inevitable, this news reawakened all his feelings for his mother, all his longing for her. He was "lost" for the entire day. He did not let himself hope that he would be allowed to return to her, but he could not keep from saying that he loved her more than he did his uncle. The months of uncertainty in regard to his future, his inner struggle between submission to his uncle and longing for his mother, upset him and had a bad effect on his behavior. For now Blöchlinger too began complaining of him. Clearly, Blöchlinger had no insight into the psychological turmoil aroused in the boy by the conflict between his love for his mother and the impact of his uncle's personality. Like everyone else connected with Beethoven, Blöchlinger was deeply under the influence of his aggressive and dominating nature. Added to this was the fact that Ludwig was a source of revenue for him. We see from the Conversation Book that Blöchlinger was completely prejudiced against Johanna:

She is an unqualified canaille, I am quite convinced of it, and unfortunately the boy seems to be becoming so too.

The boy lies every time he opens his mouth. His laziness, for which

of course he has to be seriously reprimanded, leads him astray
into everything. Do you perhaps want to talk to him? —

———

If he could perhaps be sent to Salzburg, or to some more distant
place, perhaps he would improve, away from his mother's influence.

———

It has seemed to me lately that the Beethoven woman might be
pregnant, I should be very glad to know it for certain, one
would have new evidence for telling Karl that his mother was immoral, in any case he must have noticed it too when he was with
her.

———

I should very much like to be certain of it
Karl must, as you said yourself, be made to see what is what in
regard to his mother, for if he clings to her, he is lost, and in order
to make him turn from her, we must be able to prove to him that
she is immoral. I told him recently too that she was once in the
house of correction,[4] and left him to judge if what his mother had
done so far had been good for him.

———

The boy will be and must be completely without character, even
if we do manage to make him learn something worthwhile.

———

He can and must be told that she only leads him into evil, I have
proofs enough now, and I will stand before the whole world and
say the same thing.[5]

As we see, Blöchlinger had the same unpsychological notion as
Oliva and Beethoven himself — that the boy could be brought to
love his uncle instead of his mother by being constantly reminded
that his uncle's benevolence brought him all sorts of advantages
whereas his mother was "immoral." Particularly harmful, of course,
were the attempts to represent the boy's mother to him as an evil
person, corrupted and corrupting. The result was that, to a certain
extent, the boy outwardly submitted to the influence of the people
about him and attempted to suppress his feeling for his mother,
ostensibly agreeing with them in their condemnation of her. But
neither his uncle nor his uncle's allies nor the boy himself were
able to stifle his emotional relationship to his mother. It expressed
itself in two forms. First, in occasional outbreaks: the boy would
run away to her, especially when the pressure of his surroundings
became too great, or when he felt afraid, for his mother represented

comfort and protection to him, as every mother does to her child. The second was indirect: his love for his mother expressed itself in the form of an identification. Since his uncle represented his mother to be so bad, he became "bad" himself — that is, he began to lie and to neglect his schoolwork. It is as though he were unconsciously trying to say: If my mother is bad, then I am bad too, for I am still her child, and I intend to be like her because I love her. So the attempt to turn him from his mother and put him on the right path by showing him her badness, had the opposite result. There can be no doubt that he suffered continually from this inner conflict. We have only to consider the following diatribe which his uncle prepared, for his own use or for Blöchlinger's; we can easily realize what its effect on the boy would be. In one of the Conversation Books, Beethoven noted the points with which he or Blöchlinger was to reproach Karl. We see from them how greatly he was even yet preoccupied, both emotionally and intellectually, with his struggle for his nephew.

> you are little by little becoming habituated to abominable [things], the judges over you will say that you must know your mother, for you were given the best example here and, without any regard, you are becoming a recipient of charity
>
> —
>
> [An unintelligible sentence is here omitted] — now you [Blöchlinger] go through these 2 occurrences with K[arl], hear his remarks what (sic) against his mother
> say that you are as impartial as I, and take as little pleasure as I in saying anything against his mother that is not so
> Ask him how with me he was guided after the Socratic manner, how it went at his [mother's], how it happened that he could twice run away from me, tell me the truth in everything, I
> even if they did wrong?
>
> —
>
> Did you understand without a mother from childhood K[arl]
> then lead back to the griefs he has caused me, say that others had already said that they would have cast him off entirely, in my place — go through the various periods of his childhood with him —
> ah [Karl] you do everything evil with your mother, for you [it] is of evil consequence
> but what if K[arl] to exonerate himself you [Beethoven] by his mother, [The sentence is unfinished. "You" was apparently to be the direct object of the missing verb.]
> It would be the greatest corruption, and irreconcilable with *love of her*

furthermore it seems to me that the foundation of his moral improvement is to be laid on true knowledge of his mother —

. . .

Further to Karl —

already over 13 years old the good must be established anew in you — you must not hate your mother, but you must not regard her like another good m[other]
this is evident, and if become *guilty* of further offenses against *me*, you cannot become a good man, that is the same as if you rebelled against your father. —
[Karl] you know my situation in other respects I have to earn everything to provide for you, I do it with joy

. . .

how could I wish to bring you here in view of B[löchlinger's] dissatisfaction and your new running away to your mother the best [would be] that Bl[öchlinger] should come here alone with K[arl] where we can talk.

—

The faults that you pretend to have been led into by your m[other], no longer have any excuse, you are old enough to know what is good or bad
furthermore it is a question if you must be separated from her, regard her as an unreasonable woman. After all your mother has not now advised you to study badly and you have enough understanding so that you yourself must have been aware of her unreasonableness but
but it is your own inclination.

—

how I also remember that you first ran away to her — [6]

These are surges of thought in preparation for a great diatribe against his nephew. Their stormy and spasmodic character reveals the intense excitement into which Ludwig was thrown by the boy's "crime" — his love of his mother — and his grim determination to change Karl's mind. We learn the occasion for these notes from a statement of Bernard's later in the Conversation Book:

I visited Blöchl[inger] recently with Captain Baumgarten, who is putting his son in the school. I saw Karl. [Blöchlinger told me that] Karl had now admitted to him that he had only gone away to persuade his mother to plead with Blöchl[inger] so that he would receive no punishment.
Furthermore, she [Johanna] may not enter his house again. Frau

von Blöchl[inger] believes that your sister-in-law is in the family way.[7]

So Karl had once again fled to his mother for love and protection. In a later passage in the Conversation Book Blöchlinger reports the circumstances under which Karl had again run away:

We had another scene this morning. Karl had his oral examination today, but he ran away very early to his mother, because he had not learned his lessons yesterday and today. As I did not know his mother's house number, I sent my wife to her with the servant. My wife remained sitting in the carriage in the street and sent the servant to tell her to give Karl back, or I would be obliged to send the police to fetch him. At first Fr[au] Beethoven denied he was there but my wife sent the servant up a second time with the same demand. Then Frau Beethoven sent a message to my wife asking her to come up. But my wife sent back word that she had no business with her and asked her for the last time if she would give Karl back or not, whereupon she finally came down and still, with lying equivocations, denied that the boy was there. But then she finally brought him, on my wife's promise that she would persuade me not to punish him, and I went with him to the examination, in which he did fairly well.
Do you want to talk to him?
In such a case one cannot easily deal out blows, when the lawsuit matters are not entirely settled, when she has no further recourse, we can at once take another course.

———

Just within the last few days I have heard frightful things about her.

———

In any [case] we must receive immediate backing from the police, if we want to attain an end

. . .

My wife told me just now that she [Johanna] said, if she could only see Karl more often.

———

She is a canaille, her very presence poisons the boy and in my opinion he can never thrive in her atmosphere, the best would be if I should receive full authority to demand instant help from the police, with that I can easily see to the rest.
You know in any case how strongly I talked to her last year, but she is herself to blame, if she had behaved so that Karl received no injury through her, I would have been in favor of it myself, but I feel ashamed to see such a notorious whore in my house. I will

write the incidents of today's affair (in full detail) if you consider it necessary.

———

In any case I ask you to give me a warrant of full authority, for only when he sees that he can have no further refuge, he will and must yield.[8]

Again the boy had fled to his mother in fear of an examination. The fear was groundless, for he did well in the examination — in other words, had learned enough. Examinations are often the occasion for anxiety-attacks, even when the candidate is thoroughly prepared. Such fear is irrational, it derives from unconscious sources, to which reminders of its groundlessness do not reach. In view of the scanty material, we can scarcely draw conclusions as to the motivation of Karl's fear. Experiences of anxiety during the psychological troubles of puberty are a frequent phenomenon. Karl was still too young not to seek help from his mother, she who had been his protection against all fears in childhood. For Ludwig, of course, and for all those who saw things with his eyes and reacted to them with his anger, this was a horrible crime on the boy's part; for it testified to the child's deep relationship to his mother. How great was Ludwig's anger when Blöchlinger told him of the "crime," we see from his demand that Blöchlinger immediately punish the boy with blows. Blöchlinger is still educator enough to answer, "In such a case one cannot easily deal out blows"; but he has to justify this to Ludwig by pointing out that the lawsuit is not yet entirely settled. It should be remembered in this connection that when the boy, then twelve, ran away to his mother for the first time, Ludwig tried to choke him on his return. Ludwig's unbridled temperament demanded such a physical discharge for his bitter disappointment directly upon the "guilty" object.

Blöchlinger's report throws some light on Johanna's behavior. He was concerned to make her out as bad as possible — in the hope, we may suppose, of thus diverting Ludwig's anger from the school to the mother. It was, after all, the responsibility of the school to keep watch on the boy; hence we must regard Blöchlinger's account as prejudiced. Nevertheless, we do not learn that Johanna did anything which any good mother would not have done under such circumstances. Her child had fled to her in fear; she surrendered him after she was assured that he would not be punished, and the only complaint she made was "if only she could see him more often!"

Johanna's pregnancy, to which Blöchlinger reacted by calling her a "canaille" and a "notorious whore," need not necessarily be regarded as evidence of extreme corruption, if we bear in mind that illegitimate children were by no means unusual in this period without contraceptives. In addition, Viennese morality was rather lax at the time, and an illegitimate child was by no means such a disgrace as, in itself, to brand Johanna as a whore and unworthy to be a mother. In any case, her behavior when Karl ran away shows that all her reactions were those which would be expected from a loving mother.

We do not know how Karl reacted to his mother's bearing a second child. He was long past the age when the birth of a little brother or sister produces a traumatic effect. At first he seems to have been angry with his mother. We can conclude this from the fact that for a time he shared Ludwig's hostility to Johanna. But in the end his relationship to his mother seems not to have been essentially changed by the event.

How greatly the entire staff of Blöchlinger's Institute was prejudiced against Johanna through Beethoven's influence appears from the entries of one of Karl's teachers in the Conversation Book. His name was Joseph Köferle; he taught Karl geography, history, and religion. He came to Beethoven to ask him for a recommendation to the Exchequer. On this occasion he wrote in the Conversation Book:

> Karl has his examination soon — he would very much have liked to be able to go out with me yesterday but —
> So far as I am concerned, I give geography, and history and religion, earlier I had
> taught him everything, I am very satisfied. —
> In Greek and Latin and perhaps in other subjects he is not yet quite up to the mark — but there is no doubt that it will go well. His mother alone (I am convinced of this) is to blame for his entirely changed nature. For his whole behavior changed to the utmost laxity, because he broods about things that distract him from everything else. I know him well — he was always fond of me — and hence, as I am constantly with him, I can judge him

rightly. And I said to H[er]r v. Blöchlinger, as soon as he went: he is nowhere but at his mother's — for symptoms and some secret urge are clear to see all over the boy. His mother must never come to him, for her look and her talk (although pleasantly attractive to the child) are poison.
I know from H[er]r von Blöchl[inger] that she may no longer come to him under any circumstances, for he says he will speak to her quite categorically. And that is the only way and best of all. —
I say: from the boy's own statements, she has led him entirely into an evil course.
As to order, I believe that it is attended to as well as possible here, for Blöchlinger is strict, affectionate at the right time and always present.
His eye sees everything. —
We were having the geography lesson on the Kingdom of Hungary, I told him that it was regarded as a foreign country because it is so difficult to get fugitives back. Perhaps he took in the idea. — They learn nothing but — corruption of morals — evil of all kinds and that would be to put him precisely in the situation which would be most agreeable to his mother and himself.

. . .

What was the name of the lawyer his mother had? I think I know him . . . I offer my most humble thanks for the high grace of being allowed to eat at your table, and once again repeat my most humble request for a recommendation to the Director . . . So I thank you again most humbly and will attempt, in but a small measure, to recompense this great favor in the person of your nephew.[9]

It is very curious that the teacher refers to his geography lesson on the "foreign country" Hungary as having suggested Karl's flight and that the much more natural explanation — that Karl sought his mother's protection — never occurs to him. Immediately after these entries, Beethoven wrote, addressing himself:

We must now also bear in mind to practice humanity toward her but recollect how you yourself discovered everything — in respect to her sending the police.
here too K[arl] was
with me for some time quite different —

Then, addressing someone else:

But if she comes do not listen to her, and drive her away home — [10]

From which it appears that he did not seriously intend to practice humanity toward Johanna.

Elsewhere in the Conversation Books of this period we find entries by Karl himself, which tell us of his little joys and griefs, his toothaches, his willingness to have teeth extracted:

> but if the pain stops, perhaps I could still keep the tooth. There isn't one next to it and it has had a cavity for 3 years.[11]

And again:

> now 6 are to be pulled

Then he comforts himself:

> he [the dentist] said that I will get very fine teeth.[12]

And with childish simplicity he tells his uncle about his little garden:

> I have planted Turkish pinks, but they have not grown yet, for I only just got the garden.[13]

What was going on within him we can deduce from further events. Johanna's appeal to the Emperor was rejected early in July. A few days later the Magistracy informed Johanna, Peters, and Nussböck of the Emperor's adverse decision.[14] With this, Beethoven's outward struggle for possession of the boy ended once and for all; no one could ever again dispute his claim to his child.

Schindler vividly describes Ludwig's triumph over this new victory:

> . . . because of sheer joy and bliss at the successful victory over evil and intrigue, but also because of the presumed saving of his talented nephew from physical and spiritual perils, little or almost no work was accomplished throughout this summer . . .[15]

At first Ludwig wanted to separate mother and child completely and, if possible, never let them meet again. Dr. Bach had to advise him to be moderate and reasonable:

> . . . to forbid the mother all communication with her child through the Appellate Court cannot be done because his mother, until she is legally proved to have committed a misdemeanor or even a crime, is still permitted to see her son. — But then what would

be stopped by it? All secret meetings and all secret letters. But a designing woman will contrive these even if they are forbidden her by the court itself, because evil always slinks in darkness and does its monstrous deeds in secret.[16]

But the impulsive uncle refused to be constrained by such reasonable considerations; he insisted upon limiting the meetings between mother and son to the greatest possible extent.

But "joy and bliss" over his uncontested possession of his nephew could only be brief, for Ludwig's emotional attitude to Karl was far too intense, posses,ive, and ambivalent for a stable relationship between uncle and nephew to be possible. As early as August, Ludwig felt seriously offended by his nephew. He received no name-day letter from him. It was a hard blow to him to be forced to recognize that the decision of the court, even though confirmed by the Emperor, was not finally valid for the boy's heart and mind. He must have complained to Oliva of his nephew's lack of affection, for Oliva tried to soothe him:

> There were examinations Friday and Saturday, perhaps that is the reason and he will write today . . .[17]

Later Oliva wrote:

> he [Blöchlinger] was very much upset when he learned that it was your name-day, and he admitted that the fault on his side was greater than on Karl's; in any case, he thinks that the examination was to blame that Karl forgot it, he will go into it with him and make him write today, so I did not want to talk to Karl.
> Bl[öchlinger] wrote you day-before-yesterday to Mödling that the examination came out extremely well; —
> Karl was the best in the entire school at the Piarists'; —
>
> . . .
>
> he [Blöchlinger] wrote to you at length and will inform the police of several more things against the mother,
>
> ———
>
> he [Karl] has made extraordinary progress in Greek to the astonishment of the priests.[18]

Still offended, Ludwig decided to punish Karl by not seeing him for some time; on this, Oliva remarked:

> When he sees that you do not come for a week he will be very different [19].

Yet not very long afterward, perhaps a few days later, Karl wrote in the Conversation Book:

> I have the Homer [book] already [20]

So Ludwig must have visited his nephew during that week. Schindler added immediately afterward:

> Karl is diligent, all his teachers say so [21]

Karl's successes at school were gratifying, as we also learn from other sources. Thus Oliva wrote:

> For the last 3 weeks Karl has translated 110 lines of Homer into German every day.[22]

Since at this time Beethoven had already gone to the country, to Mödling, he did not see his nephew very often — in any case, not often enough to satisfy his longing. His friends tried to bring Karl with them whenever they visited Ludwig at Mödling. When Beethoven came to the city, he naturally wanted to be with his Karl. On one such occasion he could not see Karl, because, Ludwig not having been expected, the boy had been allowed to go to the theater with other pupils. Ludwig was deeply disappointed and at once ready to blame Karl; Bernard, however, tried to excuse him:

> No one thought that you would come so late in the afternoon, and in any case Karl cannot do anything about it.[23]

This little incident, trivial as it may be, deserves to be considered, for it shows how vulnerable Ludwig was to his nephew, how sensitively he reacted even to little failures such as are unavoidable in every human relationship. The slightest disappointment was followed by bitterness and aggression out of all proportion to the occasion. We see from this how great was Ludwig's proclivity for negative reactions to the boy, whom he nevertheless loved deeply and who was the only human being who was close to him. But this love was so ambivalent that the slightest occasion undermined its positive elements. Love then became disillusionment, offense, and reproach, and, at a later stage and increasingly, an attitude that was almost hostility. In discussing Ludwig's relationship to his brother Karl, we pointed out to what an extent Ludwig experi-

enced his brother as his possession and what difficulties grew out
of this. In his relationship to his nephew Karl, which in so many
respects represented an intensification of his relationship to his
brother Karl, this experience of the love-object as possession became more and more pronounced. With this, his aggressiveness,
particularly in the form of mental torture of his beloved nephew,
increased to a degree which the boy found more and more difficult to bear. These features of Ludwig's relationship to his child
are signs of the regression in his erotic development, to which
we referred in Chapter VII.

Karl apparently continued to do well at Blöchlinger's Institute,
especially during the time when Ludwig was away at Mödling.
The intelligent, childishly alert way in which he speaks up to his
uncle when the latter once visited him at the Institute is extremely
refreshing. The Conversation Book has the following entries in
Karl's hand:

> My Greek teacher gives me two h[ours] a day and gets 600
> fl[orins]. He [Dr. Smetana] said that I must wear the truss only
> for a year after the operation.

> The professors at the gymnasium get 80 fl[orins] a year. Day be-
> fore yesterday at the maneuvers at the Schmelz [training ground]
> the Crown Prince had his horse shot under him.

> Several people said so in the stage-coach.
> Everything has to be paid in silver now

> Before we always had big rolls for breakfast that cost 3 xr[kreuzer],
> but now we must get little ones, one of which costs 1 xr Conv. M.
> [kreuzer, Convention currency]; because the big ones cost 6
> [kreuzer] now [24]

But this time too, Ludwig could not wholly enjoy the visit. For
he learned, perhaps from Karl himself, that the boy had given one
of his teachers a pocket-book. This at once aroused Ludwig's
jealousy, for the boy had obviously become very fond of this
teacher. Jealousy, in turn, instantly made Ludwig suspect the boy's
motives. Blöchlinger tried to allay his suspicions:

> It may be that he gave it to him out of fondness; his teacher is
> really a splendid man, who has every fine and great gift. [25]

But this was only to pour oil on the flame. Since Ludwig was not satisfied, Blöchlinger questioned Karl further and reported:

> He says that he gave it to him because other pupils gave him little presents of maps, so he put this pocket-book in with them, and his teacher was very much pleased.[26]

This confirmation of Karl's fondness for his teacher greatly troubled Ludwig. He must have discussed the matter with Oliva and consulted him as to possible methods of preventing such occurrences, his assumption being that Karl had procured the pocket-book by underhanded means. Oliva agreed with him in almost Mephistophelian fashion:

> but how can you guard him when there are such seeds in him. The boy has an unfortunate secretiveness and duplicity, the continuing result of his first impressions as a child.[27]

Apparently Ludwig also wanted to question the teacher on the subject, for Blöchlinger wrote, two pages later:

> The teacher will come early tomorrow morning, in regard to the pocket-book.[28]

The poor boy! First his mother was taken from him, then his fondness for a beloved teacher, something so natural, desirable, and valuable in school-life, was denounced as a crime by his uncle and his uncle's friends. He was certainly given a hard time, and it is greatly to his credit that he nevertheless continued to make good progress in school.

Since it throws much light on his relation to his nephew, it will be useful at this point to say something more about Beethoven's emotional constitution during the last years of his life. There can be no doubt that during this period of involution, Beethoven underwent a psychological deterioration. It was even manifested in his outward appearance; he neglected himself to such an extent that once in Wiener Neustadt he was jailed as a tramp until the burgomaster, to his horror, discovered on whom the local police had laid hands.[29] A Dr. Müller describes Beethoven's appearance at this time:

> Everything about his exterior was strong, very coarse — as the bony construction of his face, with a high, broad forehead, a short

squarish nose, with hair bristling upward and divided into thick locks. — But he is endowed with a delicate mouth and beautiful expressive eyes, in which his rapidly changing thoughts and feelings are constantly mirrored — pleasant, winning, wild, threatening wrath, terrible . . .[30]

Haslinger says of him at this period:

> . . . sometimes he is overcome with the most lively gaiety, more often with the heaviest depression, all of a sudden, for no reason, and which he cannot resist . . .[31]

Composing became more and more an effort to him. But even his attitude toward his creative mission, and to work planned or in progress, was full of inner contradictions and reveals the struggle between the duty to create, as the highest command laid upon the artist, and the refusal to compose, to give forth the thing formed, to exteriorize it as a work.

This struggle is visible in all its painfulness in the planning of one of his greatest masterpieces, the *Missa Solemnis*. Beethoven had scheduled the performance of it for March 20, 1820, to celebrate the enthronement of his great, indulgent patron, Archduke Rudolf, as Archbishop of Olmütz. But meeting a deadline, and the fact that the Mass was dedicated to His Imperial and Royal Highness, called up all the inward resistance which was so characteristic of the great rebel. By the date set for the performance, nothing was ready but sketches for the first part of the Mass, the Credo. For this lack of finished work, Ludwig substituted an illusion, which acquired a considerable measure of reality for him. He started negotiations with several publishers for the publication of the Mass, thus giving them the impression that the work was almost or entirely finished. Since this was by no means the case, and as he had promised the Mass to several publishers at the same time, Ludwig was driven to perpetual evasions. For years he had to maintain an almost impenetrable tissue of intrigues, in order to quiet the publishers as their demands for the Mass became more and more pressing. When the manuscript of the Mass was at last ready, Ludwig decided to give it to none of the five publishers to whom, together with exclusive rights, he had promised it, but instead to offer it to the various courts of Europe, hoping thus to get a higher figure for it. The subscription unfortunately did not produce the result he had hoped for; only ten courts subscribed. It must have been particularly mortifying to him that a long letter which he wrote to Goethe and in which he asked him to support his undertaking at court, was never answered and that the court of Weimar was not among the subscribers. The Mass was not published until 1827, the year of his death, by Schott.

Ludwig's inner struggle over the Mass, his efforts to explain the delay, and the network of intrigue with which he surrounded its publication, show that at this period, when he was achieving his last and most profound creations, his personality had changed for the worse in many respects. The difficulty in producing was itself a symptom of a retreat from the free bounty of the creative genius to a withholding, an almost anxious inward hoarding. He met the pressure of the outside world with evasions and fantasies which show that his capacity for truth had diminished. His concern over money, even if justified by his long creative block, was still excessive. He had become so irresponsible with regard to keeping his word and fulfilling his promises that one can almost speak of a breakdown of the ethical structure of his personality. His inability to make decisions markedly increased, greatly to the despair of his friends. This breakdown of his personality had a most unfortunate effect on his relationship to his nephew.

Karl, now fourteen, remained the whole year of 1821 at Blöchlinger's Institute, apparently doing very well in his studies. No Conversation Books from this period are extant, but we have no knowledge of any untoward occurrence. During these years Ludwig turned his interest to another dear relative, and renewed the struggle for him which, many years before, he had made in vain. His brother Johann begins to appear more frequently in letters and conversations. Since 1812, when Ludwig's violent interference had forced Johann into a hasty marriage, this brother had remained entirely in the background. He reappeared at the time of the second suit, only to be included in the network of suspicions with which Ludwig surrounded Johanna, and Ludwig had accused him of bribing the judges (see Chapter IX). For Johann had money. He was able to live on the income from the fortune he had acquired by supplying the army in 1809. He spent the summer on his estate in Gneixendorf, but lived in Vienna during the winter months. He kept a carriage and was able to afford many other luxuries. Gerhard von Breuning has left a description of his dandified appearance.[32]

Breuning also mentions that he had seen Johann taking the air in the Prater in an old-fashioned phaeton with two or four horses, either driving himself or lounging back with two liveried footmen behind.[33] In one of the Conversation Books, Count Lichnowsky ridiculed Johann for trying to ape the aristocracy: "Everyone laughs at him; we call him the Chevalier." [34] But these judgments stem from people who were under Ludwig's influence and, as far as possible, copied his attitude toward Johann. Karl refers to Johann's avariciousness in two passages in the Conversation Books:

> Your brother sent 2 very old hats to the hat-maker and wanted to get a *new* one for them.

> I felt really ashamed when the hat-maker said he had plenty of old hats like that lying around on the floor.[35]

And:

> . . . you are not as stingy as your brother; the baker's daughter [36] had a good piano-teacher, but he would be too expensive for your brother.

> I have no doubt of his wealth, and as little of his stinginess.[37]

It is apparent from many conversations that Johann's views on music were primitive and crude, and that, in his coarse way, he envied his great brother for his music. Schindler wrote:

> We are discussing conducting, your brother says that it is not hard to conduct, and if he had started 6 years ago, he could tell now if a mistake was made.

And Karl continues:

> Your brother says that he would give half what he has to be able to judge when the orchestra makes a mistake in a composition.

> He wants to study the piano even now. Is not that impossible. The fingers?

Then Schindler:

> He still wants to learn to conduct your symphonies . . .

And Karl again:

> He says that, in 2 months, he will be as able as I am to tell what key is being played in upstairs on the 3rd floor.

> ———

> He claims that he can recognize a mistake if I make one in playing. So I sat down, and to fool him, made not one mistake; but he said he had heard a mistake.[38]

That Johann had a certain naive conceit is clear from these passages. But it seems unjustified to represent him as the evil principle of Ludwig's last years. Almost all the biographers agree that he wanted only to exploit his brother and insisted upon intruding into all his affairs. The Conversation Books testify against any such interpretation of Johann's role.

We learn from the Conversation Books of March and April, 1822, that Johann invited his brother to stay with him in the country; that he tried to be helpful to him in selling the Mass; he also tried to find him a lodging — no small task in view of Ludwig's increasing inability to make decisions. He offered to supply his brother with wine, and gave him medical advice.

It is impossible not to feel a certain astonishment when Johann's wife Therese, toward whom Ludwig had behaved so outrageously in 1812, appears in the Conversation Books for 1822. We learn that she had undertaken to procure a cook for him; and, in her conversation with him on the subject, at which Johann was also present, her attitude toward her famous brother-in-law was most respectful.[39] But Frau van Beethoven was no more successful than Frau Streicher had been in her various attempts to find servants for Ludwig.

Ludwig spent the first part of the summer of 1822 in Oberdöbling. From there he wrote several letters to Johann, who was then in Vienna. One of the letters reads:

> I hope surely to see you — but in vain. — By Staudenheim's advice, I still have to take medicine constantly, and must not even bestir myself too much. — I ask you, instead of driving in the Prater today, to come here to me with your wife and [her] daughter. — I have nothing against your wife, I only wish she would see how much for your existence too can be gained with me,[40] and let all the miserable pettinesses of life cause no disturbances.

Postscript. Peace, peace be with us, God grant that the most natural bond between brothers be not again unnaturally sundered; in any case my life might not last much longer. I say again that I have nothing against your wife, although her behavior toward me struck me as very strange a number of times lately, and in any case, because of my ailing condition, now of three and a half months standing, I am very, indeed extremely sensitive and irritable. Away with everything which cannot promote the goal, so that I and my good Karl can enter upon a more regular life which is particularly necessary to me. — Only look at my lodging here, and you will see the consequence, what happens when I, especially in sickness, have to entrust myself to strange people, not to mention other matters which in any case we have discussed already. — In case you come today, you could fetch Karl, hence I enclose this unsealed letter to H. v. Blöchlinger, which you can at once send to him.[41]

Ludwig is unmistakably courting his brother in this letter. He even tries to get on with Therese and her daughter, so that he can come closer to his brother. He had, then, undergone a distinct change of heart. His wish for close human companionship, which, because of inner impediments, he was never able to attain, is now turned upon his brother. Johann rented the lodging next to his own in the Kothgasse for Ludwig. But Ludwig's immediate reaction to this was to suspect Johann's motives:

. . . As to the lodging, since it is already taken, let it rest as it is, but whether it is good for me is a question. The rooms open on the garden, but garden air is the most injurious to me, then the entrance is through the kitchen, which is very inconvenient and intolerable; and now I have to pay a quarter for nothing; in return, Karl and I, when possible, will come to stay with you at Krems, and live in high style, until this money is made up . . .[42]

In the same letter he asked Johann to come and visit him for a week at Baden, where he was to take the baths.

A letter to Johann of July 31, 1822, is the first which Ludwig dictated to his nephew, thus giving the boy the new role of secretary:

Best little brother! Mighty landlord! I wrote to you yesterday, but I was exhausted by many efforts and much business, and with a bad pen it may be hard for you to read.
Write me first how quickly the mails go back and forth from you

to me and from me to you; [a passage concerning business with publishers follows] . . . I should be glad if you would write me whether you can spare something, so that I shall not be prevented from going to Baden before it is too late, where I must stay for at least a month. You see that there is no uncertainty here, even as you shall receive back the 200 fl[orins] in September with thanks. Please return the enclosed note to me at once. Besides, you as a merchant are always a good counsellor. The Steiners are also driving me into a corner. They insist upon having it in writing that I will give them all my works. They are willing to pay for every printed sheet, but I have said that I will not enter into such an agreement with them until they cancel the debt. For this I have proposed two works to them, which I wrote for Hungary and which can be regarded as two little operas, from which they have already taken four pieces. The debt amounts to about 3000 fl[orins] but they have abominably added interest, to which I do not agree. In this connection I have taken over part of Karl's mother's debts, for I gladly show her every kindness, in so far as Karl is not thereby endangered. If you were here, these matters would soon be settled; only need forces me to this sort of selling one's soul. If you could come, and go with me to Baden for a week, it would be splendid, only you must write at once what you think you will do. Meanwhile put kitchen and cellar in the best order, for presumably I and my little son will set up our headquarters with you, and we have taken the noble resolve to eat you out of house and home. It goes without saying that only September is in question.

Now fare well, best little brother! Read the Gospels every day; take the Epistles of Peter and Paul to heart, travel to Rome and kiss the Pope's slipper. Give my heartfelt greetings to your family. Write soon. I embrace you from my heart

Your faithful brother
Ludwig

I, the secretary, also embrace you from my heart and hope soon to see you again.

Karl.

N.B. I do not enclose the note for 300 fl[orins] for I fear something might happen to it.[43]

This letter shows a surprisingly strong emotional relationship toward Johann on Ludwig's part. The feeling is almost ardent. The affectionate terms with which the letter begins and ends sufficiently reveal this. He acquaints him with his business affairs and flatters him as a good adviser; he had previously got 200 florins out of

him, and now wants to borrow more, offering as security his fee
for the Mass, which was nowhere near finished at the time. His
benevolent reference to Johanna, to whom he "gladly shows every
kindness," is remarkable; but this surprising attitude will find its
explanation later.

In further letters,[44] Ludwig expressed his concern at not hearing from Johann and feared that Johann was angry because he
had not yet paid his debt to him. To one of these, Karl added:

> I have had to stay in bed now for two days because of a little
> cough, but I am quite well again and so can resume my position as
> secretary to my dear uncle. Please be so good as to write about my
> overcoat too.
>
> Your most loving Karl
>
> N.B. My dear uncle asks you, for your answer, to use the tempo
> known as prestissimo.[45]

Karl, who was now almost sixteen, must during this period have
spent many weekends, and perhaps his holidays too, with his uncle,
as we may conclude from his secretarial activities. From one of
the Conversation Books we learn that Karl now matriculated at
the University. From this long conversation we shall cite a few passages which evidence the degree of development that he had
reached. We find him in high spirits, he shows himself boyishly
rebellious to all authority, superciliously despises generally accepted values, and is vastly impressed by his own cleverness. In
regard to his matriculation at the University, he says:

> The gentlemen are horribly boorish, when I entered, the Vice-
> Director asked: What's up?
>
> ────
>
> But it was only because I entered with a deep bow; with others,
> who are boorish, he is polite at once.[46]

On the professors:

> I do not permit people to speak to me in that way; I am addressed
> as Herr.
> Now the Professor has to say — *gentlemen*.[47]

And again:

> Now we are a little more politely treated than in the preparatory

schools, where the gentlemen do not even condescend to look at us.[48]

On his uncle Johann:

Meanwhile I am convinced that he doesn't squander everything on women because he is well aware that it would soon be all spent.[49]

The note of youthful superiority is particularly strong in the following statements:

Austrian poems are rubbish (*Knödl,* literally "dumplings") [50]

and

We, Herr Carl van Beethoven foresee with our clear eyes that a transition easily possible in such a conversation can lead to things that are not to be heard by everyone, particularly by suspect persons; the more so as all pay attention as soon as anyone says such things.

The person who just left wishes everyone an *obedient good-night.*[51] Tomorrow I shall go to no professor, for I will get up only after 10 hours sleep.[52]

He had already adopted Ludwig's unfavorable opinion of the Austrian aristocracy:

He seems to be a very good man; better than *our* noblemen [53]

And he finds fault with the servants and the food, just like his uncle. He had even adopted his uncle's attitude toward the opposite sex:

I have seen the same maid for several days now standing at the entrance with her lover. In general our house is full of common people.[54]

In Vienna it was a daily occurrence to see a maid standing at the door of a house with her lover. The indignant comment that this meant that the house was full of common people shows that here the uncle is speaking through the nephew. Throughout, we see that the lad had adopted his uncle's value-judgments. We can conclude from this that his relationship to his uncle at this period was markedly positive. He as it were formed his ego-ideal after him.

Yet he is by no means wholly submissive to his uncle. For he defends himself vigorously when Ludwig accuses him of being lazy:

> That is not the question, it is the injustice of your reproach that I *am lazy* [55]

His appearance must have changed greatly at this time, for, in relating a visit to Giannatasio, he wrote:

> Giannatasio showed me to his family asking if none of them knew me. And they all looked at me open-eyed and said that they had never seen me. Their astonishment when they heard my name was indescribable. They asked me to come very soon again, preferably in the evening, when the whole family were together.[56]

He exhibits his learning by reciting Greek epigrams to his uncle. The general impression of Karl which this conversation gives is that of a lively, pleasantly intelligent youth in the bloom of adolescence, with the increased self-esteem and typical arrogance of this period of self-discovery and of rebellion against the stigmata of childhood.

The conversation from which we have quoted was held at a tavern. This appears from the fact that Karl had to taste Ludwig's wine for him. He wrote:

> it strikes me as stronger than the Erlauer [a Lower Austrian type of wine] at the Camel [57]

Having wine or food tasted for him beforehand in this way, by his nephew or his friends, occurs with increasing frequency during Beethoven's last years. Especially later, it becomes unmistakably clear that this represents a measure of protection against being poisoned. On another occasion during this period Karl wrote:

> Too much water.
> Too much water that is all.
> — too weak
> — Be so good as to let Dr. Staudenheimer taste the soup, if you please.
> Then you must not get angry if I am of a different opinion, or else simply not ask me.
> I am also convinced that it [the soup] is better.
> There is too much water in it; but it does not have a bad taste.

I see nothing wrong with the soup except that there is too much water.

Then you ought never to ask for my opinion.[58]

We see how naggingly Ludwig insisted upon an expression of a conforming opinion.

At this time Ludwig was living in the Kothgasse in the same house with his brother Johann. He had moved there after taking the cure at Baden. Having seen the instability of Beethoven's other human relationships, we know that this fulfillment of his longing to be near to his brother was bound to end in distrust, suspicion, disillusionment, and suffering.

Ludwig's loving and exacting wooing of his brother was incomprehensible and distasteful to the latter, if for no other reason simply because he regarded such advances on his brother's part as unnatural. The strong unconscious homosexual component was so apparent that it must at times have put Johann on the defensive. This is also strikingly present in Ludwig's relationship to other males. In his relationship to his nephew the maternal attitude predominated, but in his relationship to his brother Johann the homosexual trend is unmistakable. Ludwig's unconscious homosexuality also broke through suddenly and violently on several occasions when he made the acquaintance of an attractive young man. The clearest evidence for this is the reports which many of these young men have left of their encounters with Beethoven.

In the "Notes on the Friendship between Ludwig van Beethoven and Karl Friedrich Amenda compiled from oral tradition," [59] we read:

> Amenda . . . receives an invitation from a friendly family and there plays first violin in a quartet. While he was playing somebody turned the pages for him, and when he turned about at the finish he was frightened to see Beethoven, who had taken the trouble to do this and now withdrew with a bow. The next day the extremely amiable host at the evening party appeared and cried out: 'What have you done? You have captured Beethoven's heart! B. requests that you rejoice him with your company.' A., much pleased, hurries to B., who at once asks him to play with him. This is done and when, after several hours, A. takes his leave, B. accompanies him to his quarters, where there was music again. As B. finally prepared to go he said to A.: 'I suppose you can accom-

pany me.' This is done, and B. kept A. till evening and went with him to his home late at night. From that time the mutual visits became more and more numerous and the two took walks together, so that the people in the streets when they saw only one of them in the street at once called out: 'Where is the other one?' [60]

Baron de Trémont says of his meeting with Beethoven:

I admired his genius and had a thorough knowledge of his works when, in 1809, as auditor to the Council of State, I was charged to convey the Council's decisions to Napoleon, who was campaigning in Austria. Despite my hasty departure, it occurred to me that, in case Vienna should fall, I should not want to miss the opportunity of seeing Beethoven there. So I asked Cherubini for a letter of introduction to him. 'I will give you one to Haydn,' said he. 'That excellent man will welcome you; but under no circumstances will I write to Beethoven. I should be inconsolable if he did not receive someone whom I had recommended to him. He is an unlicked bear.'

I applied to Reicha, who, however, said: 'I am afraid my letter would be of no use to you. Since France has become an Empire, Beethoven despises the Emperor and the French to such an extent that Rode, the first violinist in Europe, spent a week in Vienna on his way to Russia without being received by him. He is shy and bad-tempered, a misanthropist, and to give you an idea of how little he stands on ceremony, it will be enough to tell you that the Empress [Princess of Bavaria, second wife of Franz II] once summoned him to an audience. He answered that he would be busy the whole day, but would try to come the next.'

This information made me certain that any effort on my part to make Beethoven's acquaintance would fail. I had neither rank nor reputation to procure me credit, and I had all the more reason to fear a refusal because I reached Vienna when the city was for the second time being bombarded by the French army, and, in addition, I was a member of Napoleon's Council of State. Yet I determined to try. I went to see the inaccessible composer, and at the door I thought that my day was ill chosen. As I had to make an official call, I was wearing the Council of State undress uniform. In addition, he unfortunately lived on the Wall, and since Napoleon had ordered its destruction, a mine had been laid under his window.

His neighbors pointed out his lodging to me. 'He is at home,' they said: 'but at present he has no servants; for he changes every moment. It is doubtful if he will open the door.' I rang three times and was on the point of leaving when an extremely ugly man, obviously in a bad temper, opened the door and asked me what

I wanted. 'Have I the honor of addressing Herr Beethoven?' 'Yes, sir, but I warn you,' he answered in German, 'that I understand French very poorly.' 'I understand German no better, sir, but my business is only to bring you a letter from Paris from Herr Reicha.'

He looked at me, took the letter, and asked me to come in. I expected that, after reading the letter, he would dismiss me and that therewith our acquaintance would unfortunately be at an end. I had seen the bear in his lair; it was more than I could hope. I was therefore extremely surprised when he continued to stare at me, laid the letter on the table without opening it, and offered me a chair — and still more astonished when he began to chat with me. He asked about my uniform, my position, my age, the object of my journey — whether I was a musician, whether I should be remaining in Vienna. I answered that Reicha's letter would tell him all that, and better than I could.

'No, no; please just talk,' he said, 'but slowly, for I am very hard of hearing; I will soon understand you.' I made incredible efforts to express myself, and he did his best to do likewise, it was the strangest mixture of bad German and bad French. In short: we understood each other, the visit lasted almost three-quarters of an hour, and I had to promise him that I would come again.

I went out more proudly than Napoleon had entered Vienna; I had conquered Beethoven! But when I asked myself how? I could find no answer. The reason is to be found only in his wonderful character. I was young, meek, and polite; I was unknown to him, and his opposite. Out of caprice, for some reason inexplicable to me, he was pleased with me. And since in crotchety people these sudden fondnesses are seldom shy, he arranged to meet me frequently during my stay in Vienna and improvised, for me alone, for as long as two hours, on one piece after another.

Some musicians whom I knew would hardly believe it. 'Will you believe me,' I said to them, 'if I show you a note he has written me in French?' 'French? Impossible; he hardly understands it and doesn't even write German so it can be read! He is incapable of such an effort!' I handed them the proof. 'Then he has a real passion for you,' said they, 'what an inexplicable man!'

This note, which for me is a precious document, I have had framed.[61]

Trémont even succeeded in persuading Beethoven to go to Paris with him. Owing to a change in the Baron's plans, however, the journey did not take place.

Karl Maria von Weber, another good-looking young man, reports his visit to Beethoven as follows:

He received me with an affection which was touching; he em-
braced me most heartily at least six or seven times and finally ex-
claimed enthusiastically: 'Indeed, you're a devil of a fellow! — a
good fellow!' We spent the afternoon very merrily and contentedly.
This rough, repellent man actually paid court to me, served me at
table as if I had been his lady . . .[62]

The intensity and the type of attraction exhibited in his friendship to Karl Holz, who was very much younger than himself, are
also indicative of a strong unconscious homosexual component.[62a]

The few devoted friends Ludwig still had at this time found the
loving intensity with which he turned to Johann inexplicable and
indeed repellent. It was with deep concern that they witnessed
Ludwig's courting of his brother, his overvaluation of him, and
his efforts to draw Johann into his business affairs. Schindler, who
at this time was attempting to acquire an influential position in
Beethoven's councils, was assailed by real jealousy. It expressed itself in his efforts to undermine Johann at every opportunity, to
belittle him, and to sow distrust of him in the fertile soil afforded
by Ludwig's ambivalent attitude. Schindler partly took over Oliva's
role; he wrote the innumerable notes and letters necessitated by
the attempt to obtain subscriptions for the Mass, and tried to raise
money for Ludwig, as the following letter to him from Ludwig
shows:

Very best optimus optime! I send you herewith the Calendar; where
the paper is inserted all the embassies here are indicated. If you
would shortly draw up a list of courts for me from this, the matter
could be expedited. In addition I ask you, if my brother takes a
hand in it, to cooperate with him, otherwise we might come to
grief instead of joy. —
See if you cannot scare up a humanitarian who will lend me on
a share of bank stock, so that in the first place I may not too greatly
try the generosity of my only friends, the v. B., and, through the
delay of this money, shall not myself fall into the need for which
I have to thank my dear brother's elegant arrangements and pro-
visos. — It would be nice if you would appear at Maria Hilf this
afternoon about half past three or even this morning. —
It must absolutely not be known that the money is wanted. — [63]

We see from this letter that distrust of Johann is beginning to
grow. Johann had doubtless refused to listen to Ludwig's request

for a further loan, since Ludwig had not yet paid back the 200 florins.

Schindler's attitude, however, was different from the submissiveness which people like Oliva and Bernard so diligently practiced toward Ludwig. His reverence and admiration for the master are great and genuine; as a musician, he was much better equipped to understand and sense Beethoven's genius. But he was a self-willed, often almost intractable man, and he had the courage to speak up to the master and even to criticize him. He tried to restrain Ludwig's exaggerated outbursts of emotion and to force him out of his indecisiveness. Ludwig hated him for it; only of Johann did he say such monstrous things as he said of Schindler. At times he could not bear Schindler, with his pedantry and his citing of facts which went against Ludwig's fantastic distortion of reality. Schindler grimly and stolidly withstood Ludwig's attacks, and held out indomitably to the end. His services made him indispensable; yet during his last years Ludwig was glad to replace him for a time by a warmer and more genial friend — Karl Holz. Ludwig's mistreatment of Schindler naturally aroused aggressiveness in the latter, but he turned it on Ludwig's circle, on Johann, on Johanna, and often on Karl. When hatred filled him, his judgments were emotionally determined to a very high degree. He is largely responsible for the misrepresentations regarding the characters of Beethoven's intimates which we encounter so frequently in Beethoven literature. His lack of objectivity entirely unfitted him to be a biographer. But he was the only person who dared to speak up to the great man and say such things as: "Don't be so irresolute, my dear master!" [64] or "God, what a bad mood you are in again today — I will not put up with it." [65] The exaggerated flattery of the "dear master," which Schindler often uses, must in itself have got on Ludwig's nerves. On another occasion, Schindler wrote: "How far have you got with the music? I hear you were in a terrible fury again the other night, is that true?" [66] Indeed, he had courage enough to write: "Don't lock yourself in at night, for no stranger enters your room, and the housekeeper often has to go in" — "then you must put up with having all the dishes spoiled and cooked to pieces and inedible, and not thunder. (hear! hear!)" [67]

Schindler hardly ever missed an opportunity to say or suggest something unpleasant about Johann.[68] He seems to have been particularly offended that Beethoven entrusted some of his business to his brother; as a musician, Schindler felt himself a far more suitable person than Johann to deal with various publishers for Beethoven's musical creations. Thus he retails gossip about Johann:

> He told Gallenberg [69] that he had come to Vienna simply to accommodate you, to pay your debts, because you were buried in them.[70]

Or, provocatively:

> Doesn't your brother come to see you at all? — I am certainly a thorn in his eye, for I help to expose his insufficiency, he must and shall know that.[71]

It is easy to imagine what an effect such insinuations against his brother aroused in Ludwig, for we know how accessible to such provocations his ambivalence made him. Schindler was not the only one who, from jealousy or from real concern over Ludwig's exaggerated affection for his brother, campaigned against Johann. Prince Lichnowsky seized every opportunity to denigrate Johann to Ludwig.[72] Bernard did his share too, though he remained objective enough to admit:

> If you have signed the declaration, he believes that he can sell everything as he sees best, for through the declaration he perhaps considers himself authorized to be able to take all these steps.[73]

Karl too puts in his word against Johann, repeating Schindler's and Bernard's views:

> Schindler says that a complete separation would be the only way. Nothing good will come of it.

> He [Johann] wants to give another ball.

> He invited him, and Schindler did not dance the whole time, so that they were even angry with him; he only went out of politeness.

> About the ball, he told me too that he wished he might not go, but he did not want to offend him.

Bernard thinks that there is only a misunderstanding here; and though your brother is mercenary, he is not a traitor.

He says himself that he thinks a complete separation would be best.

As soon as I read the letter I said to Schindler; if he had written that to *me*, I would have beaten him, for he says not much less than that you have deceived him.[74]

Karl's outspoken hostility to Johann is in all probability to be attributed to jealousy too. When Beethoven's friends spoke against Johann, they included Karl in the conversation, for Schindler wrote, immediately after this, in Karl's presence:

Let us drop these scoundrelly acts for the present — the right way will be found, and your brother, let us hope, frightened out of such deceitfulness. He is too paltry.[75]

Beethoven himself may have provoked many of these suspicions against Johann in his friends; as we know, he was particularly distrustful in money matters. His friends seized the opportunity to exacerbate his distrust. From a letter to Ries it appears that Ludwig finally believed that he had been deceived and defrauded by Johann:

One more request:
My brother, who keeps a carriage, has wanted to fleece me too, and so, without asking me, has offered these overtures to a publisher [named] Boosey in London. Just let him wait, that it cannot be decided at present if he can have the overtures [*sic*], I will soon write to him about it. In this matter everything depends upon the Philharmonic Society. Just be so kind as to say that my brother was mistaken in regard to the overtures; in regard to other works, about which he wrote to him, he could certainly have those. He bought them from me in order to profit exorbitantly, as I see. O frater!! [76]

How strong the negative feeling in his relationship to his brother became at times, appears from the following letter to Dr. Bach, written when Ludwig was still living in the same house with Johann:

. . . that I declare my beloved nephew Karl van Beethoven my sole heir, and that everything without exception, that can even be

supposed to be a possession of mine, shall after my death belong
solely to him. — I appoint you his Curator, and should no other
will follow except this, you are also empowered and requested
to choose a guardian for my beloved nephew K. v. Beethoven —
excluding my brother Johann van Beethoven — and to appoint the
same for him according to the established laws.
I declare this document to be as valid for all time as if it were
my last will before my death. — I embrace you heartily. — [77]

This may have been his reaction to Schindler's informing him
that Johann had proposed that Ludwig put up his shares of bank
stock as security for a loan he wanted Johann to make him. For, to
Ludwig, this was like asking for a piece of his body — so precious
and important had the possession of money become to him at this
time. Schindler, by no means a stupid observer, was so struck by
this steadily increasing preoccupation with money at this period
that, in his biography of Beethoven, he discusses the subject at
length. He says:

> . . . it now becomes necessary to elucidate matters most of which
> took place before my eyes and for most of which documentary
> evidence lies before me. From this there emerges a hardly believ-
> able change of maxims and principles in our master, such as would
> inspire the psychologist to unravel its complex causes. The indi-
> vidual had obviously separated into two essentially disconnected
> parts of intellectual life, which however meet at a certain point
> and, under certain circumstances, complete each other. After the
> Ninth Symphony, that supreme triumph of instrumental music
> perhaps for all time, the spontaneity of creation seems to be stricken
> by atrophy. In addition, reflection is accorded an extensive do-
> main, indeed it almost entirely dominates the artist who, previously,
> had always freely created beyond its limits. On the other hand
> arithmetic had so strikingly taken possession of the master that
> the room which was opened to artistic reflection was taken up by
> mercantile speculation. For a third interest, there was hardly any-
> thing left, if newspaper reading and politics be disregarded.
> This strange turning point in his essential self became fully mani-
> fest during the course of the year 1824, after many premonitions
> of it had appeared during the two previous years, even in his artistic
> productions (see the second movement of the Sonata, Opus 111).
> A material proof of it is found in the figure-scrawled window shut-
> ters of the Schlosser house in Baden, in addition to still extant
> large-folio sheets likewise scrawled over with figures. Every half-
> way suitable surface was covered with long columns of figures.

Only a family misfortune which occurred in the year 1826 was able to call a categorically imperative 'Halt!' to the master, sunk as he was in speculations. He did not fail to hear the summons and again raise himself, in word and deed, to the innate sentiment proper to his rank as an artist; but for many things, unfortunately, this reawakening came too late.[78]

The depth-psychologist is not surprised to learn that Ludwig exhibited an increased interest in his intestinal functions at this time. The following report speaks for itself; it bears witness to the connection between the highest and the lowest production:

In the same house it also happened that a woman who lived on the same storey wanted to go to the privy, but found it shut. She waited a quarter of an hour, and since the door still could not be opened, she asked the housekeeper if the lock was defective. A violent knocking was now tried, and the answer came: 'There, there! I am coming now!' — Beethoven emerged, and on the door lines were found, drawn in pencil and filled with notes! [79]

In February — that is, before writing the letter to Dr. Bach cited above — Ludwig had paid Johann back the 200 florins he owed him, as he himself recorded in the Conversation Book:

I gave my bro[ther] Cain his 200 fl. today.[80]

But Ludwig owed him still more, and it was for this reason that Johann demanded the security. Wrath and resentment thereupon reached an apogee, as an entry in the Conversation Book shows:

Everything was done to keep him from this shameful connection — in vain, but, as I know him, he deserves nothing better.
he always sought out the most vulgar. —
he was better, he was spoiled under the French and here.
He brought me to the Kothgasse, what I have endured so far is unbelievable, for now I am parting from him again.
il est barbare and has the unhappy propensity d'être riche.[81]

But Ludwig's resentment against his brother had yet another cause. When he moved into the house in which his brother lived, he cherished the hope that his intimacy with him would lead to an estrangement between Johann and his wife Therese. It was a fresh attempt to rescue his brother from the peril of woman. He was unsuccessful, for Johann was very devoted to his wife. This made Ludwig extremely bitter against his brother, and above all against Therese and the daughter she had brought to Johann when they married. For Therese he at this time used a curious derogatory nickname, whose meaning is not entirely clear. He called her "Fettlümmerl." [82] Among other things it was doubtless an allusion to her full figure and her demeanor. For her daughter he used the name "Bastardl," [83] since she had been born out of wedlock.

From Johann's own entries in the Conversation Books during this period, we see that the reproaches with which he was assailed by Beethoven's friends and biographers were wholly unjustified.

If Schindler told Ludwig that Johann "is only concerned to make you [Beethoven] a rich man," [84] Johann, after all, was doing nothing but what Ludwig would have been glad to do for himself. There is no basis for assuming that Johann had an eye to his own profit when he undertook to sell Beethoven's works. Nor can it be made a reproach to him if he thought he could sell them better than many others might; after all he had made a fortune in business, and like most men who have acquired wealth, he had a high opinion of his mercantile ability. Thayer, the most important of Beethoven's biographers, recognized the injustice which Schindler and other biographers had done to Johann, and attempted in an essay published separately in 1877 ("Ein kritischer Beitrag zur Beethoven Literatur") to restore Johann's much maligned honor.[85] Johann's remarks, in the Conversation Books, on the subject of Beethoven's business affairs impress one as thoroughly sensible, if a little primitive. Thus he advised Ludwig to sell his works more cheaply; [86] Ludwig asked far higher prices than were usual at the time. The consideration that his works were incomparably more valuable than the works of other contemporary composers is inadmissible here. The publishers of the period estimated them according to what was then their "market value." If Johann wrote in a Conversation Book, "But you must put the price of the Variations in writing for me"; [87] if, in May, 1823, he proposed to Ludwig, "I will take everything from you, I will give you what the highest [highest-bidding publisher] will give here, and you can also sell it for yourself in London, then everything will be settled," [88] we really cannot see what "insufficiencies" Schindler could have "exposed."

The Conversation Books also show that Johann was honestly, if somewhat stupidly, concerned for Ludwig's health, and gave him a great deal of medical advice, which his experience as an apothecary to a certain extent entitled him to do. It sounds like genuine concern for Ludwig's well-being when Johann writes: "I will take Karl home, you stay at home here, the weather is too bad for you." [89]

Karl was at this time devoting himself entirely to his studies at the University. It appears that Ludwig was so occupied with his relationship to Johann, his financial difficulties, and his struggle over the Mass, that the lad could devote himself to his studies more or less without interference. He was living at Blöchlinger's, where his uncle now considered him comparatively safe. Yet Ludwig's distrustfulness was by no means extinguished. Toward the end of January, 1823 Karl reported in the Conversation Book that he was to take an examination at the University and had to prepare a poetical essay and a Latin composition.[90] Hence he could not see his uncle so often. Schindler had to soothe Ludwig:

> Karl sends you affectionate greetings and kisses, and much as he wished to see you today, he cannot spare a minute, for he has much still to [do] before Wednesday.

> In general, but where is Karl, that this should be feared of him

---

> For misconduct, every place is the most dangerous.[91]

After the examination Karl was laid up; the winter weather had brought on his old malady, chilblains, again. Schindler reported to Ludwig:

> I visited Karl yesterday evening to see how he is. He sends you greetings and kisses and tomorrow we shall both come to see you, arriving in a carriage in high style about 1 o'clock, for he cannot walk yet.[92]

As it was quite a time before Karl was able to make the trip on foot, Schindler had again to allay Ludwig's suspicion that the lad was using his sore foot as an excuse and that he really did not want to visit his uncle:

> Karl greets you affectionately, his foot is getting better [93]

and:

> You have no reason to suspect Karl of anything, [it is] only that
> it [comes] hard to him to put you to expense for the carriage, he
> told me this long ago.[94]

Karl too had to defend himself against his uncle's suspicion:

> Suspicion does not help matters. They are quite all right now, it
> is just that my overshoe still presses on one toe.
> I'll be able to walk a week from today.[95]

In the same conversation, Karl gives one of the reasons why he
likes to visit his uncle:

> On Monday everybody is always surprised that I have got fatter.[96]

The food at his uncle's must have tasted better to him than the
food at the Institute.

On the whole, however, the relationship between uncle and
nephew was now comparatively untroubled. Karl's general adop-
tion of his uncle's views and value-judgments somewhat allayed
Ludwig's suspicions. For a time, he was even a little more mildly
inclined towards Johanna, possibly because he had found a better
object for his misogyny in Therese. Financially, Johanna was in a
really pitiable situation: she had to give half of her small pension to
Ludwig for Karl's education, and she did not know how to use the
remainder frugally. Early in January, 1823, Bernard even warned
him not to be so generous to Johanna:

> It might perhaps be that she is only in want for the moment. In
> any case, it would be better for you to inform yourself of her
> situation before you do anything. Or give it to the doctor. . . .
> Besides, it is more humane only to consider the viewpoint that she
> is Karl's mother, and he will perhaps always remember that she
> had to live in need for a time, even if she is herself to blame.[97]

Ludwig also discussed the subject with Schindler, who wrote on
the next page:

> all the same it must be put down on paper, so that you will be safe,
> however bad she may be, she does after all belong to the family
> and hence must be regarded as a member of it. unfortunately! [98]

At the beginning of March, Ludwig wrote down an account
which apparently had to do with Johanna's pension and her con-

tribution toward Karl's education. For, immediately following it in the Conversation Book, Karl wrote:

> I do not think that you should bind yourself forever to leave her the pension.[99]

We see from this that, at times, the boy adopted Ludwig's attitude toward Johanna, and even persisted in it when Ludwig was more mildly inclined. But Karl varied in his attitude toward his mother, for when Bernard reported that things were going very badly for her and that she could not pay for medicine, Karl advocated helping her. But when it appeared that her illness might be connected with the birth of an illegitimate child, he expressed himself very strongly against her. He was naturally resentful of his mother because he was no longer the only child. In his resentment, he repeated all the accusations he had heard on the subject of Johanna's "badness." He wrote:

> He [presumably his uncle Johann] says that he recently talked with Hofbauer himself and the latter told him that, with the child, she had already cost him 30,000 fl[orins], and that he now still gives her 40 fl[orins] a month.[100]

And later:

> The child, your brother says, is by Raicz, a Hungarian who was studying medicine here, and was a *roomer* with us even in my father's lifetime; but Hofbauer does not know this and believes it is his.

> Although she is my mother, I must admit that I think you should first inquire fully into her circumstances. For it could easily be that such a contribution would enable her even more to continue her evil life; and in that way it would be more an encouragement to her passions than a good deed.

> Your brother says that he thinks Bernard goes running to her too.

> Your brother says that my mother was earlier always to be seen in all public places with notorious whores.[101]

Yet this occurrence seems not to have exercised any disturbing influence on his studies, as we can conclude from his successfully taking his examinations at the University. Both he and Peters report on this in the Conversation Book.[102]

Conditions for a tranquil relationship between uncle and nephew were comparatively favorable at the time. Johanna was obviously out of the picture, so that Ludwig was more mildly disposed toward her; Karl was prepared to ally himself more closely with his uncle, since he was angry with Johanna over her illegitimate child. His behavior and his progress with his studies were satisfactory. But the eternal conflict in Ludwig did not cease. His distrust of the boy he loved, even though he was now safely in possession of him, was still active. It was the expression of his ambivalence, which became more acute with the passing years. The kind of distrust which was always alive in Ludwig had no justification in the facts, as our study has already abundantly shown. His distrust was a pathological phenomenon, not a reaction to outward causes, but arising from an inner need, and hence inaccessible to reasonable arguments. His deafness had markedly contributed to increasing it. But it must again be emphasized that Ludwig's distrust did not first manifest itself after he began to grow deaf, but preceded his deafness by many years. The nature of it also indicates that it was not principally caused by his deafness. For it increasingly expressed itself in the form of jealousy of his nephew. Erotic jealousy, which played the principal role in Ludwig's relationships, is hardly a factor in the pathological behavior which is referable to deafness. As always in the case of pathological jealousy, in Ludwig too it expressed itself in the form of a sadism which literally martyrizes its object. In Ludwig's case Karl was naturally the unfortunate victim. We shall cite Karl's part in a conversation with his uncle during this period, or rather Karl's defense against his uncle's accusations. We may assume that this scene was not an isolated occurrence. When things got too bad, Schindler doubtless saw to it that the record should not reach posterity. The occasion of the following conversation was the fact that the housekeeper ("the old woman") had done the washing on Friday instead of on a later day. This may have been a misunderstanding; it is also possible that Ludwig had told her to do it on Friday. He had violently reproached the old woman, and she had complained bitterly to Karl. Karl defended her against his uncle's unjustified scolding. He wrote:

You said that you had to have them at once.

———

You ordered her to wash on Friday

———

I do not know what you are angry about. I cannot remember having laughed. At any rate, I must say that on the way she wept and complained that you torture her greatly and that she would rather go than to be so mistreated any longer in her old age. If you ordered her to wash, she only did her duty. She admits, however, that she may have misunderstood

———

She could find no one

———

I believed, when I told you my opinion, that it would not be taken wrongly if I spoke honestly; and I am

Here Ludwig interrupted him, obviously with bitter reproaches, so that Karl began to cry. Then Ludwig tried to force him to eat, for Karl wrote:

I cannot eat until I have finished crying; it would be poison if I tried to eat in this state of vexation.

Schindler must have come in at this point; Karl seems to have left the room for a moment, whereupon Ludwig told Schindler that he suspected Karl of protecting the housekeeper because he took an erotic interest in her. Schindler wrote:

I do not believe it, and I am firmly convinced that you misunderstand Karl at such a person's expense [sic]. The woman is old.

———

But you have already said 'it is forgotten,' [103] do not make his heart so heavy.

When Karl came back, Ludwig continued his reproaches, for Karl wrote:

I tried to write down the reason for my behavior earlier, but you would not let me write, and I also kept quiet in the belief that, according to your own promise, there would be no more discussion of the subject. But since I now see that, out of dislike, you will not even bestow a look on me, I see myself forced to tell you why I behaved as I did. I thought, as I said before, that I could speak as I think; besides I said not a word in the old woman's presence which could have shown her that I considered her right, and you

have also completely misunderstood what I wrote to you. I did not say that the old woman was right, I only wrote down her *own words* with the intention of saying nothing. But since you yourself urged me to speak, I said what I thought, in the certain conviction that you would not forbid me to speak freely; for, had I foreseen that you would feel hurt if I spoke as I thought, I would have had no choice and I would have had to say: *You are right.* But I thought that I could speak my opinion fearlessly, and so I said, if what she says is *true,* that you had yourself ordered [her] to wash *immediately,* then she had done her duty. —
But in future I shall certainly be careful not even *to say that,* if I see that it hurts you.

————

You are better able to know her than I; and I do not say that she is not malicious, I only said that, if what she said was so, I do not find her so culpable.

————

You did not say that until just now

————

I do not defend her at all, the less so, as I know how the matter stands, I only thought you had been rather too violent, and were mistaken, the more so as she clamored to me this morning that you misunderstand her and are unjust to her.

————

In her presence I said nothing at all, but only, after she had gone, expressed my honest opinion to you; and she herself must admit that this morning I said to her that you are certainly never unjust to her but that she herself is to blame if you scold her. My shirts are torn too, and she does not mend them.

————

She asks you to forgive her; she misunderstood you, and promises to do better.[104]

It is unmistakable what torture his uncle's distrust and his stubbornly repeated reproaches inflicted upon Karl. We also see from the Conversation Books how cautiously Karl dealt with his uncle, how he tried to divine his wishes, and how seriously concerned he was to avoid any outward troubling of their relationship.

Ludwig became more and more difficult to deal with. The Conversation Books show what trouble his friends had to make him come to any decision. Since he was considering writing a second opera, they exerted themselves to procure librettos for him. But his indecision made it impossible for him to make a choice. As summer approached, and plans had to be made for him to go to the country, Schindler and Lichnowsky especially had the greatest difficulty in bringing him to a choice: he hesitated over every detail, considered every expenditure too high, and only a white lie on Prince Lichnowsky's part — who said that, if Beethoven did not take the lodging, he would take it himself — brought Ludwig to the point of moving into particularly fine quarters in Baron Pronay's house at Hetzendorf, near Vienna. Schindler moved into Beethoven's lodging in the Kothgasse for the summer.

Karl helped his uncle to move, and since Ludwig was suffering from an ocular affection at this time, and had to spare his eyes, the lad had many letters to write for him. In May Karl had to take examinations at the University again; it is not known what marks he received. His numerous conversations with Ludwig show that Karl had now acquired considerable self-assurance; it made him outspokenly critical of other people, particularly of Johann, of whom Ludwig had nothing good to say at this time. Karl made fun of Johann for dying his hair black to preserve his youthful appearance, and wrote a satirical poem on the subject in the Conversation Book:

> You show yourself, a youth, with black-dyed hair,
> You, who but recently a gray-head were?
> Men you deceive, but you deceive not death;
> He from your aged face the mask will strip.[105]

On another occasion he characterized Johann quite mordantly:

> I always have to laugh at your brother when he says something to which I have reason to object that it can be done better some other way; then he usually says: My dear Karl, in your book of experience most of the pages are still empty, but mine will soon be full. He needs everyone, and so tries to win everyone over; but as he has few other means, he chooses to set himself up as a universal information bureau.[106]

Karl also expressed himself cuttingly on the subject of Johann's avarice and uncleanliness:

> He will not even buy a glass for 6 xr [kreuzer], and washes in an old pan that a dog has always eaten out of beforehand; I think that when one carries uncleanliness so far, one does not deserve to improve.

How can he possibly rinse out his mouth when he does not buy a glass?
___
Good that we learned to know him in time.[107]

Ludwig's indecisiveness obliged Karl to attend to his menu, to provisioning the household, to supervising the servants. He also had frequently to taste Ludwig's wine for him, and thus acquired a more extensive knowledge of alcoholic beverages than is perhaps good for a seventeen-year-old. In one of the Conversation Books he quotes the well-known German proverb: "You are not a real man if you have never been drunk."

At times his relationship to his uncle was affectionate and intimate, even though he was careful to avoid scenes. He was concerned about Ludwig's health, reported to him intelligently and alertly after attending concerts or the theater, brought him news of the musical world. Hence the recorded conversations with Karl are on a higher level than those with Ludwig's other intimates. In addition to the classical languages, Karl studied English, French, and Italian. His attitude toward Blöchlinger's Institute became more critical; he was doubtless outgrowing the limitations of a boy's school. When Blöchlinger asked his pupils for a contribution for his wife's name-day, Karl's critical attitude asserted itself. He calls Frau Blöchlinger "his illustrious consort," [108] says that she is a bad mother, unworthy of such an expenditure, and reports that Blöchlinger used the occasion to drink all night.[109] He complained of the increasingly poor food at the school:

> Before, we could have bread, as much as we wanted. Each of us was given a big piece at 11 o'clock, and at meals each as much as he pleased. Now we cannot have any bread in the morning, but have to stay fasting from 7 to 1, and then at table can eat only 2 pieces, and at supper only 1; although often the bread is what we like best in the meal. The time I had scarlet fever, I should soon have gone hungry if you had not sent me food.
> ___
> I am hungriest in the morning, because I only eat a small roll about 7 o'clock.[110]

He added resignedly:

> If I have managed so far, I suppose I can still manage. Anyway it will soon be over.[111]

He told his uncle of Blöchlinger's highly unpsychological treatment of his pupils in dealing out canings at regular intervals — which, as Karl rightly observed, only made the boys more refractory.[112] Karl's comprehension of the psychological problem of a bed-wetter is at least greater than Blöchlinger's:

> There is one there, for example, a very little boy, who often pisses in bed. As often as it happens, he gets a terrible thrashing, but it does not help.
>
> ———
>
> He knows nothing about it, in his sleep.[113]

Karl was very modest in his demands upon his uncle. He disliked having to ask him for money for Frau Blöchlinger's nameday celebration, for he wrote:

> It cost me almost more of a struggle to tell it to you than for him [Blöchlinger] to ask it.[114]

He spent most of his weekends with his uncle, and, aside from occasionally going to a concert or the theater, we do not hear of his being allowed any pleasures. He gave up his wish for a butterfly net after he had learned the price of one:

> The butterfly nets that I mentioned today are very well made, and hence very dear too; I do not think one could be bought under 10 fl[orins]. I would rather be allowed to use a part of that amount for a pair of stilts, which many [of the boys] at[?] Bl[öchlinger's] have now, and which I like very much; a pair costs 4 fl[orins].[115]

How far Karl sometimes went in imitating his uncle appears from his having joined him in hatching a plan to beat the chambermaid. The following entries are in Karl's hand:

> Your brother said it would certainly help if you beat her a little.
>
> ———
>
> Anyway nothing else helps
>
> ———
>
> Nothing will happen to us; for she will not defend herself strongly against the two of us.
>
> ———
>
> I am not afraid for myself.
>
> ———
>
> If only no one comes to help her.[116]

It may be assumed that Karl's great effort to submit to his uncle and imitate him was only possible through the suppression of hostile feelings toward him. His uncle had taken his mother from him, regarded him as a possession, wanted to determine the course of his life, tortured him by his distrust and by forcing him to act as secretary, errand-boy, and companion in his free time. Under these circumstances, a considerable resentment must have accumulated in Karl, which doubtless only partly reached the threshold of consciousness, for at the same time he was emotionally bound to his uncle. Yet once, under the influence of alcohol, his aggression against his uncle must have broken through. For in the Conversation Book for 1823 we find an entry in Karl's hand from which we must conclude that, in his intoxicated state, Karl insulted his uncle or perhaps even assaulted him physically. His contrition for this aggression is unmistakable and genuine:

> Dearest Father, you can be convinced that the hurt I caused you distresses me more than it does you. Anxiety has restored my reason to me, and I see what I have done. If I had to think that you believe that I purposely acted in this way, I should be inconsolable. It just happened in drunkenness. If you can forgive me, I promise you that I will surely drink not another drop of wine, so that I shall never get into such a condition again. But that you can have such thoughts of me causes me great distress. What kind of a person I would have to be if I had the most remote intention of causing you hurt. Forgive me only this once! I will surely drink no more wine, it was all because of it that I could no longer contain myself and did not know where I was. Again I beg you, forgive me! [117]

It appears that this was a wholly isolated occurrence.

Soon after Ludwig had moved to Hetzendorf, his brother Johann, who was still in Vienna, living in the Kothgasse with his wife and stepdaughter, fell ill. It must have been a rather serious illness; in any case, he was confined to bed for several weeks and had to be looked after. Since Schindler had moved into Ludwig's lodging in the same house in the Kothgasse, he had an opportunity to observe what went on in the Johann van Beethoven family; at Ludwig's request, he visited Johann regularly. In a letter dated July 3, 1823,[118] Schindler undoubtedly made the facts blacker than they were. But even allowing for his exaggerations, his report shows Therese, Johann's wife, in a highly unfavorable light. She

left her sick husband to himself, and amused herself with another
man. The stepdaughter knew it, and expressed no disapproval. We
see from Schindler's account that he made every effort to stir up
Ludwig's wrath against Therese. The Conversation Books ac-
quaint us with Ludwig's reaction to Schindler's letter. He there
drafted a letter to Johann:

> At last you have undergone fine experiences, I am informed of
> everything, keep Schindler with you, he is useful to me, that I can
> have news of you, and also help you. — *You see how right I* was
> to keep you from *these* etc, come to me and stay with us, I need
> nothing from you, how terrible if you had to *give up* the ghost
> under such hands —
>
> —
>
> if you want to come, come alone, for I will not have her —
>
> —
>
> I advise you to come out, and to stay here entirely, and later *to live
> with us* entirely, how could you live more happily, with a splendid
> youth like Karl, like *your brother* I [*sic*] you would have bliss on
> earth — what iniquity, the mother herself leads the daughter to
> clandestine love [to be] the guardian of her lust.[119]

Karl too was informed of the sick Johann's unpleasant circumstances, as the following entries in his hand show:

> Your brother is now really to be pitied; all alone among those
> beasts, badly cared for; in addition the slightest shock now has the
> worst effect on him; but Schindler was there and told me that the
> hussy, his daughter, only attends to him most grudgingly, and that
> when he wants something she only hands it to him with her face
> *turned away* and grumbling; I am glad it did not happen in front
> of me, for I could not have restrained myself from laying hands
> on her; in any case, as was to be expected, he was very glad at my
> coming and he thanks you for having gone there and for behaving
> as you did. — I think I will go to see him for a minute again tomor-
> row morning early; he is really deserving of pity; and now, I think,
> is the moment to separate him from them entirely; for he has never
> before *so* learned the difference. —
>
> ———
>
> The woman went out yesterday about 12 and did not come [back]
> until late in the evening.
> She always does that now.
>
> ———
>
> The woman told him to his face that he had nothing to expect from
> her in his sickness.
>
> ———

You ought not to go there, for I know that you will not be able to restrain yourself from beating her when you see how she treats him. They will only behave all the worse afterward.[120]

The Conversation Book shows that Schindler continued to report to Ludwig concerning the progress of events in Johann's house and Therese's callous behavior. He is not sparing of insults to both "women." Beethoven finally went to Johann himself, bent upon making a real scene, as he had done at Linz in 1812. Schindler had to lure him away, on the pretext that Johann wanted to sleep, for, when Therese heard that Ludwig was in the house:

> . . . she began to rage terribly, but then went away, but immediately afterward the nurse rushed into the room and told me that the mistress was standing in the hall with the poker and waiting for you, intending to receive you with it. I was terrified by this atrocity and did not know what to do except to keep you away by the excuse that your bro[ther] wanted to sleep . . .[121]

Therese, who had been deeply resentful of Ludwig ever since 1812, was, then, determined to prevent him from again interfering in her affairs. Ludwig wanted to take extreme measures and summon the authorities to intervene against Therese, as the following letter to Schindler shows:

> The occurrence of yesterday, which you will gather from the report to the police, is only fit to recommend this matter to the worthy police. The statements of an unnamed person are also in complete agreement with your own. Here private individuals can no longer help, only authorities invested with power.
> Your Beethoven [122]

Things did not go so far. Johann recovered and forgave his wife, upon whom, despite everything, he was extremely dependent. Ludwig was greatly embittered by the failure of this latest attempt to rescue Johann from Therese; and his impossible behavior to his host, Baron Pronay, may in part be referred to his consequent ill-humor. Unable to stomach any more of the Baron's politeness — who, it will be remembered, bowed deeply every time he met Beethoven [123] — he moved to Baden. Johann even took over some of Beethoven's business affairs again; and Ludwig made use of the consequent exchange of letters to work on him further to leave the two women and come to him. We cite one of these letters in part, because it shows in what a miserable frame of mind Ludwig was at the time and how violently he expressed his aggressions:

> Dear Brother Johann! I rejoice in your improved health. As for me, my eyes have not yet entirely recovered, and I came here with a ruined stomach and a terrible catarrh, the first from that archswine, the housekeeper, the second from a cow of a kitchenmaid, whom I once before drove away and yet took her back again; —
>
> . . .
>
> I received your letter of August 10 through that miserable scoundrel Schindler. You need only give your letters directly to the post, where I receive them all safely; for I avoid this vile, despicable man as much as possible. —
> Karl cannot come to me until the 29th of this [month], when he will write to you. You will not be entirely unaware of what the two canailles Fettlümmerl and Bastard [124] are doing to you, [you have] also received letters from me and Karl through (sic) this occasion; [125] for little as you deserve it of me, I shall never forget that you are my brother, and a good spirit will yet come over you, which will part you from these two canailles, this former and present whore, with whom during your illness her cully slept no less than three times and who, over and above that has your money entirely in her hands, oh execrable infamy, is there no spark of manhood in you?!!!! . . . Fare well. Invisibly I hover about you and work through others so that the canailles shall not noose your neck, —
>
> As ever your faithful brother [126]

Despite all this commotion, Karl was again diligently pursuing his studies at the University, especially Latin, Greek, and French. The Conversation Books present him as ambitiously and conscientiously pursuing his goal; we hear of no interests that distracted him from his studies. Ludwig's warning, in a letter,

> . . . Work now, so that everything to fit you for your Konkurs [127] will be done and be modest, so that you will show yourself to be higher and better than people think . . .[128]

seems unnecessary. And such an admonition as

> Just send your wash straight here, your gray trousers can at least still be worn at home, for, dear son, you are again very dear! [129]

must have produced an unpleasant effect on Karl. What he may have thought when, still in the same letter, he found that Ludwig had written of his faithful and helpful factotum,

> For Schindler, that despicable object, I will send you a few lines,
> for I do not like to deal directly with that wretch — [130]

we must leave open. There are similar derogatory remarks about
Schindler in other letters besides the one to Johann already quoted;
Schindler's exhortations to moderation and his audacity in con-
tradicting the master must have irritated Ludwig intensely. Thus
he wrote to Ries:

> . . . a more miserable scoundrel I have never yet met on God's
> earth, an archscoundrel, to whom I have given his walking pa-
> pers . . .[131]

and to Grillparzer:

> . . . this importunate appendix of a Schindler has long since, as
> you must have noticed at Hetzendorf, been repulsive to me to the
> utmost,— otium est vitium. — [132]

But despite everything, Schindler remained doggedly faithful.
His fanatical passion for Beethoven, his urge to idealize him, and,
in cases of conflict, to put all the blame on others, were doubtless
in large part a reaction-formation against the feelings of hatred
which the master must have aroused in him by such bad treatment
and such unconcealed expressions of contempt.

Ludwig had finally removed Karl from Blöchlinger's Institute
and had brought him to Baden at the end of August. Now that
the boy was living with him — as he was to do from then on —
Schindler's services were no longer so necessary, and Ludwig could
give free rein to his dislike of his former factotum. Ludwig stayed
at Baden until October; Karl was with him at least the greater
part of the time. In the autumn Ludwig moved to a lodging in
the Ungargasse, taking Karl with him. Karl continued to attend
the University, pursuing his philological studies. Ludwig, for his
part, was tormenting himself over the composition of the Ninth
Symphony. On what terms the two now lived together is not
known; the Conversation Books for this period are not extant.
There are, however, no indications of major conflicts. Early in
January, 1824, Ludwig wrote Karl's mother a letter which is surprising by its benevolent attitude toward the formerly hated
"Queen of the Night":

Numerous occupations even brought it about that Karl and I could not testify to our good wishes to you on New Year's Day; but I know that, even without, you expect nothing from me as well as from Karl but the purest good wishes for your welfare. —
As for your need, I would gladly have helped you out with a lump sum, but unfortunately I have too many expenses, debts, and only the expectation of various amounts, to be able instantly to show you my readiness to help you on the spot. — Meanwhile, I herewith assure you in writing that you may now permanently draw Karl's half of your pension too; we will give you the receipt each month; whereupon you can yourself collect the same, for it is no shame (and I [know?] several of my acquaintances who collect their pension every month) to collect the same monthly. If I should later be in a position to be able to give you a lump sum from my cash to improve your circumstances, it will certainly be done; the 280 fl[orins] 20 kr[euzer] which you owe Steiner I have likewise long since undertaken to pay, as you have doubtless been informed. Nor have you for some time had to pay any more interest.
You have received two months' pension from me through Schindler. — This month on the 26th or somewhat later you will receive the pension amount for this month. — As to your lawsuit I shall very soon consult Dr. Bach about it.
We wish you all conceivable good, Karl as well as I.
Yours, most ready to oblige, L. v. Beethoven [133]

It is as if at this time Therese had drawn all his hatred of women upon herself. Then too, his child was with him and he enjoyed complete possession of his "precious treasure." He believed that Johanna was forever banished from his nephew's heart, and doubtless assumed that she had found a substitute for Karl in her illegitimate child. But his possessiveness and his unchecked power over his nephew aroused new storms, incomparably more violent and disastrous than any that had gone before.

XII

MARTYRDOM

NOW began a period of great psychological suffering, which drove Karl to the catastrophic act. But it was not only Karl who suffered; Ludwig too was the victim of terrible mental torments caused by his jealousy, his distrust, the disappointment of his demand to possess the object of his love, and his growing fear of losing Karl. The uncle suffered all the fiendish torments of the thwarted and jealous lover, the nephew all the martyrdom of the victim of a love tortured by jealousy. From 1824 on, Ludwig was forced to turn almost entirely to Karl for help and companionship, for he had again estranged his brother Johann, he had dismissed Schindler as intolerable, and Bernard, for whose oratorio text he never composed music, had dropped him. Thus his nephew was the sole object of the whole gruesome power of Ludwig's emotional relationships; he had to bear the entire brunt of Ludwig's indecisiveness; he had to assume the role of factotum and business agent for his uncle. This last would by itself have been a full-time occupation, requiring all the powers of a competent and psychologically skillful man. It is astonishing how long Karl bore up under it all, in addition to his studies, until he finally collapsed.

Out of the abundant material which illuminates the whole tormented and tragic relationship between uncle and nephew during this period, we shall select only the most cogent.

Karl was now seventeen. He was studying at the University, specializing in philology; he lived with his uncle in the Ungargasse. By now Ludwig was almost totally deaf. Conversation with him was no longer possible, even by shouting into his ear. His nephew, who knew him so well, and to whom he entrusted so much, was at times his only intermediary with the outside world. The responsi-

bility which lay upon Karl was great. Yet he had very little experience of life — for, at least for the last few years, he had lived
in a boarding-school. His secretarial duties and his numerous services to his uncle were very time-consuming, as we learn from the
Conversation Books. In addition there was the chronic servant
trouble, which increased with Ludwig's intensifying distrust and
fear of being poisoned. Ludwig was very strict with his nephew,
as Holz too reports later, and gave him little freedom. The burden
of Karl's duties deprived him of time for study; it also increased the
temptation to skip lectures at the University (there was no check
on attendance at lectures). He often had to defend himself against
unjust reproaches from his uncle, who, in his impetuous way, was
quick to blame him for any trouble in the house, particularly with
the servants. Entries in the Conversation Books in Karl's hand, such
as, "Whenever you have any trouble with the servants, I have to
bear the blame; I do not know how I deserve it," [1] testify to this.
His uncle's indecisiveness must often have been a torture to him.
"If you were a man of decision, things would long since have been
different," [2] Karl wrote in the same Conversation Book.

How difficult it was to deal with Ludwig at this period, how
unreasonably and emotionally he acted, can best be seen from
the events connected with the first performance of the Ninth
Symphony. The enthusiasm of the Viennese for Rossini had greatly
embittered Ludwig at this time, and he was extremely touchy.
Hence he was determined that the première of the Ninth Symphony, which he had finished after six years of hard work, should
not take place in Vienna. He applied to Count Brühl in Berlin,
asking if the Missa Solemnis and the Ninth Symphony could be
performed there. Schindler told this to Count Moritz Lichnowsky.
Lichnowsky persuaded Beethoven's friends, and many artists, to
sign a petition to the master to arrange the première of these two
great works in Vienna. After the petition was presented to him,
Beethoven changed his mind and began to plan a concert. His
painful indecision in the choice of a suitable hall is documented
in the Conversation Books. Schindler, Beethoven's friend the violinist Schuppanzigh, his brother Johann, and Karl made suggestion after suggestion, each trying to eclipse the others by insisting that his own was a better proposal. But Beethoven, who was

basically hostile to every adviser, disapproved either of the hall
or of the proposed conductor. His friends tried to persuade him
to accept their suggestions by all sorts of flatteries and arguments
— and indeed by intrigues, like courtiers dealing with a tyrannical
potentate. He could not reach a decision. He even gave up the
whole idea of arranging a concert. It was only with difficulty that
he was persuaded to return to it. However, the concert finally
took place and was a complete success. It is touching to read that,
at the end of the Ninth Symphony, the master had to be plucked
by the sleeve to make him turn to the audience, who, aware
of his deafness, were applauding by waving shawls and handker-
chiefs. Schindler had taken precautions that the box-office receipts
should be locked up in Karl's presence; [3] he knew Beethoven's distrustfulness in money matters only too well. Despite this precaution, Ludwig was convinced that he had been cheated, as the
receipts were less than he had expected. At a meal in a restaurant,
he went so far as to tell Schindler and Schuppanzigh that a reliable source had informed him that he had been swindled.[4] His
friends resented this and immediately left the restaurant, to which
Ludwig had invited them, so that Ludwig and Karl had to eat up
the food, which had been ordered. It is obvious what an unfortunate impression his uncle's paranoiac attitude must have made
on Karl. Karl's reaction was doubtless a mixture of fear before
the great man's arbitrary rage and of superiority to such unreasonableness. After such scenes, Karl, even though his existence
depended on his uncle, could hardly regard him as a reasonable
man. It is almost astonishing to see with what respect and caution
he treated his uncle, despite everything, in order to avoid any unnecessary offense.

On May 1, 1824 Ludwig moved to summer quarters in Penzing,
a suburb of Vienna. For the sake of his studies, Karl stayed on in
the Vienna lodging. From a Conversation Book we learn that the
difficulties of life with his uncle had a deleterious effect on Karl's
work. The long conversation took place during a visit Karl paid
to his uncle at Penzing. Ludwig brought up the subject of Karl's
studies. Karl then wrote:

> I am doing all that I possibly can. — The examination *must* be, if
> I want to go on studying, for otherwise I lose a whole year; for I

cannot take the second if I have not taken the first. — I will be *entirely* frank. It has gone too far now to keep back. From the very first it was lack of pleasure in these studies which prevented me from taking proper advantage of the lecture courses, and for the same reason I cut many.

[Several words crossed out.] — I have not missed much and during that time I was in the library; Dr. Stein can tell you that too, to whom I told it. — You yourself think that the examination will not turn out well; and alas! so do I. — Begin again from the beginning? I do not think that I could bear the shame of being behind so many with whom I started together. And then what will Giannatasio and many others say about it? I shall be the object of their mockery and unfortunately not unjustifiably. How that can *harm* me, you know yourself.[5]

And further:

— In that case do you give me a free choice? —
But I will not become anything without your approval, and will, if you wish, even go on studying, or rather begin over again. — You will find my choice strange, but I will nevertheless speak freely as my inclination prompts me. And the career I should like to choose is not a *common* one. On the contrary, it requires study *too;* only of another kind; and such as I believe suitable to my inclination. — Soldier. — [6]

Apparently his uncle asked him reproachfully in what sort of company he had acquired this inclination. Karl wrote:

— In no company. — The discipline is certainly very strict. And mathematics and the science of fortification are certainly not among the lower [sciences].[7]

The whole conversation reveals Karl as significantly matured; his statements sound completely sincere and truthful. His wish to become an officer appears to be the result of ripe reflection. We learn nothing more about Ludwig's immediate reaction to Karl's intention of giving up his studies at the University and embarking on a military career, but he was obviously disappointed that his "son" was not to become the famous scholar he had already pictured him in imagination. In any case, Ludwig was against a military career, and Karl gave up the plan for the time.

The same conversation gives us the young student's daily schedule, into which his uncle inquired. Other portions of the conversation show how many business and domestic details Karl had to attend to for his uncle. He even had to arrange for the servants' time off.

We learn further that Karl asked his uncle if he might bring a friend with him the following Sunday. He was obviously very lonely when he had to spend the whole weekend with the deaf, elderly Beethoven. This need for a friend of his own age, which aroused violent distrust and suspicion in Ludwig, was later to lead to most bitter conflicts.

The lodging in Penzing did not suit Beethoven; he complained that he could not put up with people trying to look in at his windows. So on August 1 he went to Baden again, and remained there until November. Karl stayed on in Vienna, to take the special examinations [Konkurs] at the University. When he could, he came to his uncle's at Baden for the weekend. Thayer cites two conversations from this period which well exemplify the increasing difficulties between uncle and nephew. Karl had a friend named Niemetz; the friendship dated from his days at Blöchlinger's Institute. Ludwig disapproved of the association, which imperiled his sole possession of his nephew. Happening to come to Vienna, and learning that Karl, who was then nineteen, had not spent the night at home, he began asking him, most distrustfully, where he had been. Karl answered in detail. He wrote:

> At Niemetz's mother's. She was here yesterday and invited me verbally, because she saw that I sleep here so badly and am so uncomfortable, you can ask her. — I would not have accepted, but because I did not want to go to an inn and she has known me so long now, I went there. — She asked me because of a book of hers that I still had.[8]

Ludwig apparently said nothing more about Karl's friend, but instead reproached him in regard to his studies, expressing his dissatisfaction with their progress. Karl answered:

> I will take the Konkurs as soon as the time comes when it is held. In any case I shall not have lost so much in my courses, for from now on philosophy is to last only 2 years, and I shall be finished just as soon as [I] otherwise [would]. — [9]

After a time, Ludwig again nagged at Karl on the subject of his studies. Karl wrote in reply:

Even if I repeat to you that I will do everything that lies in my power to bring you to another opinion, it is of no use. So I can only ask you to have patience for a little while more. I hope you will then be convinced that my intentions are not mere *words*, but that I shall carry them out. — I see very well that you are incensed, I even have to take it as natural, unfortunately! — And yet I *still* hope that in a calmer hour you will think otherwise and will not *entirely* give me up. Do not rob me of this hope, and do not cast me down completely; I am sufficiently so as it is. Allow but a little time for [your] full conviction and I know it will be different again. — I have no girl friends. — [10]

His uncle must have expressed his suspicion that the lad was interested in girls — which to Ludwig was the bitterest of reproaches. Karl then wrote:

If I were still keeping anything back, I would tell it to you *today;* for things *cannot* be worse than they are today. — During the summer I did not use my time as badly as you believe. — As soon as it was decided that I was to repeat the year, my resolve was to take the Konkurs too, and to distinguish myself in it, which may still happen; for one can very well accomplish more than is demanded there. And this is my intention now too, and firmer than ever. Besides having read Greek and Latin with Enk, I often went to the library, and *here* too I shall make every endeavor to distinguish myself.[11]

The second conversation cited by Thayer took place some time later and is of particular interest because on this occasion Beethoven too wrote his part, so that we have both sides of it. Karl had brought his friend Niemetz with him; this aroused violent jealousy in his uncle. The conversation was held after Niemetz had left the room. Ludwig wrote:

I am very ill pleased with your choice of this friend of yours [Niemetz]. Poverty, to be sure, deserves sympathy, but not without exception. I should not like to do him injustice, but I find him a burdensome guest, completely lacking in poise and manners, which after all are somewhat necessary for well brought up youths and men. — In addition I suspect that he sides with the housekeeper rather than with me. — Besides, I like quiet, the space here is too limited for more people, since I am constantly busy, and he can hardly fish up anything of interest to me. — You are still very weak in character.[12]

Karl immediately came outspokenly to his friend's defense:

> As for my choice, I believe that four years of close association is
> quite enough to get to know a man from *all sides*, especially a boy,
> who could hardly appear in a disguise for so long. — So there can
> be no question of any lack of conviction on my part, but simply of
> the causes which led me to it, and they in a word are: the greatest
> similarity in character and inclinations. If he was unable to please
> you, you are free to send him away, but he has not deserved what
> you say of him.[13]

At this, Ludwig became more aggressive:

> I find him crude and common. Such are no friends for you.[14]

Driven into a corner by his nephew's incisive and firm answer,
Ludwig now brought out an argument which adults often use
when they feel cornered by a child's intelligent and convincing
answer. He wrote:

> You are not yet capable of discriminating.[15]

Hurt by his uncle's questioning his ability to judge, the nineteen-
year-old lad launched into a firm and detailed explanation:

> It is useless to argue over a subject, especially over a character,
> about which I will never give up my conviction, *so long as I myself
> am not to regard myself as a bad man;* for [if] there is anything
> good in me, he certainly possesses it at least to as high a degree as I
> do, and it would be unjust to be angry with him if you do not con-
> sider *me* exactly the *same*. For my part, I shall not cease to love
> him, as I could love my brother if I had one.[16]

Ludwig then turned the conversation to the food. But he could
not long suppress his dislike of Karl's friendship with Niemetz
and returned to the subject, as Karl's next answer shows. From
here on, Ludwig spoke his part of the conversation, but we can
reconstruct his stubbornly fault-finding remarks from what Karl
wrote:

> I think the best way to have no difficulties is to say nothing about
> it. — I never forced him on you. I did not expect that I would be
> met with reproaches concerning something which I have explained
> clearly enough. If he did not please you, you could have sent him
> away at once. He is too proud to beg alms and he does not *need*
> to, so he will not be a burden to you again. — You do not *need*

to quarrel. If you stop talking about it the subject will be closed. —
I have *nothing* to reflect on. — I should simply have to lie (and
that I will not do) if I should admit that I will stop loving Niemetz.
I have known him for 4 years, and hence just as well as myself,
and if he has faults, then they are certainly obscured by his
other qualities. I do not see *how* trouble could arise. I will not
bring him to you any more, and we can stop talking about it. If
you think that he is so bad, time will certainly make me notice it
too. — I shall not bring you to a harangue [against me again?] for
you shall see him no more, and I will not say another word about
him. Furthermore I should have to be too slavish indeed, if I were
willing to lie and say that his character was bad and his knowledge
despicable! [17]

It is impossible not to recognize the young man's mature de-
liberation and intelligent self-control. No one can help feeling
that in this conversation the nephew is superior in poise to the
uncle. It is obvious that this superiority of mind and emotional
control, of which Karl must have been conscious, in conjunction
with his complete dependence upon his uncle, in themselves provided the material for a conflict which must inevitably break out
in time.

Ludwig was not only jealous of Niemetz; he was above all concerned lest Karl should develop too great an interest in his friend's
mother. In general he came increasingly to fear Karl's developing
an interest in the opposite sex. He had even accused Karl's friend
Niemetz of siding with the housekeeper during his visit. In the
last analysis, however, the real cause of his jealous distrust was
still Johanna. Even during this period when he was in sole and
uncontested possession of the lad, he was still considering the idea
of sending him abroad, away from all danger threatened by the
Queen of the Night. Thus J. A. Stumpf, the London harp-manu-
facturer who visited him at this time, reports that Ludwig said to
him:

'I want to make a man of my nephew Karl, whom I bought from
his worthless mother, and I want to send him to an advanced school
in Saxony, and every gulden that I can acquire by straining my
strength is intended for his education. Karl shall learn English
too and come to you in London, to become something too, but our
clever authorities will not consent to it, he is to be and remain
in Vienna as an ordinary man.' Beethoven now asked anxiously

[Stumpf continues] what it might cost to maintain a young man, like his Karl, in London for a year.[18]

For Ludwig, Johanna remained the arch-peril, the representative of all harmful women. Every older woman who came into contact with Karl aroused Ludwig's suspicion that the lad was interested in her and had a secret erotic relationship with her. He found means to have Karl supervised and spied on by others. Before going away, he had rented a lodging in the Johannesgasse. Just before he returned to Vienna from the country, Karl and the housekeeper once came in from Baden to get the place ready for Ludwig's return. Karl stayed in Vienna for two days, but Ludwig had expected him back sooner. The idea that Karl might have spent the night in the Johannesgasse lodging with the housekeeper, or in the lodging of his friend Niemetz's mother, filled him with anxiety. He wrote to his friend, the publisher Tobias Haslinger:

> Baden, evening 6th October 1824
> Dear Tobias! I beg you most fervently to send to inquire at once in the house in the Johannesgasse into which we are moving, if Karl slept there yesterday and today, and if he is at home, to have this note given to him at once; if not, to have it left with the caretaker there to give to him. — He left here yesterday and this evening he and the housekeeper are not yet back. I am alone with one person who can neither speak nor read nor write, and I can hardly find anything to eat here outside the house. I had to go in from here to fetch Karl from Vienna once before; for where he once is, he is hard to get away. I beg you to send me whatever news possible here at once. I would gladly have spent these last few days quietly here; unfortunately I shall have to go to town about him again. In addition I beg you to let no one know anything. God is my witness, what I have already had to put up with on his account. — If no information can be got from the janitor in the Johannesgasse, then send to the Landstrasse, where I lived, to ask the janitor where Mrs. Niemetz lives and find out if he has been there or is coming there so that she [Mrs. Niemetz] can send him here at once.[19]

His letter to Haslinger the next day has a ring of joyous relief:

> Baden, the day after the 6th October 1824
> Best [Tobias]! Our Benjamin arrived here early this morning, wherefore I have had 17 and a half cannons fired. Earlier occurrences without his fault et sine mea culpa made me anxious; heaven be praised, despite my agitatos everything now goes well and as

wished. It is no wonder, considering these miserable institutions,
that one is anxious on account of a growing young man, what with
this poisonous breath of the dragons! — [20]

We may well imagine what an oppressive effect such suspicions
and supervision exercised on the already sexually mature young
man. In addition, soon after moving into the lodging in the Johannesgasse, Ludwig was given notice to quit, for the other people in the house complained of the noisy quarrels in his household.
His scenes with his nephew and the servants must, then, have
been quite outrageous. A relative of the owner of the house later
told the Beethoven scholar Frimmel that Ludwig was quite fero-
cious with his nephew and the housekeeper.[21] There is no reason
to doubt it. The household now moved into the nearby Kru-
gerstrasse.

Because of his slowness in producing, Ludwig's receipts were
rather meager at this time; hence he began to reconsider a visit
to London. His friends were all in favor of the idea; the London
publishers and his friends there promised him a considerable profit.
Karl advised him:

> You should read the letter carefully, and your own judgment, dis-
> regarding your brother's insatiable thirst for money, must make the
> decision. You must also consider how many other ways there are of
> making money in London; Neate assures [you] that you will come
> back with a sum that can make the whole rest of your life free from
> care.[22]

But Ludwig could not reach a decision; above all he did not
want to leave his nephew behind, out of his own sight and exposed to "the poisonous breath of the dragons."

Karl continued his philological work at the University, even
though, as will be remembered, he had the previous year expressed himself in favor of taking up other studies. Ludwig, then,
had not agreed to the change, and Karl had consented to continue
preparing himself for a philological career and had diligently devoted himself to his courses. In the biographies of Beethoven, it
is constantly emphasized that Karl was frivolous. Nothing in the
available documentary material indicates frivolity. His only pleasure was occasionally attending the theater. With great modesty
he once asked:

I wished to ask you if perhaps you would not object to my going to
the Italian Opera today, since it is the last opera. —
If I had known yesterday, I would have stayed at home, so as not
to go to the theater 2 days in succession. In any case, I am not miss-
ing anything, and when I once go to the Polytechnic Institute, it
will have to be very seldom anyway. But if it is not agreeable to
you, we will drop it. Otherwise I will go in the fourth balcony
where it costs 30x [kreuzer].[23]

It is here that we learn for the first time that Karl now definitely
planned a change of studies. He intended to go to the Polytechnic
Institute to prepare himself for a commercial career. In March,
1825, just before Karl was to enter the Polytechnic, Ludwig had
an attack of "intestinal inflammation" which kept him in bed for
a time. It may be assumed that the emotional agitations caused by
his relationship to his nephew contributed to this attack. Karl tried
earnestly to calm his uncle's fears concerning his new course of
study. He wrote:

It is my earnest purpose to proceed zealously on the road we have
now chosen; I also see that the subjects are really not so unattrac-
tive. Some of them, e.g. history and mathematics, in so far as they
affect commerce, will certainly be as well taught as at the University, if not better. Yet I should not like to lose Latin and Greek,
so I am going to the Greek [teacher?], and he would have come by
now, if he were not very busy at present, for he is giving re-exami-
nations.[24]

At about this same time, Karl's co-guardian was changed. Peters
was away a good deal, traveling with the Princes Lobkowitz; so
it seemed advisable to find a guardian who could better supervise
his studies. The Vice-Director of the Polytechnic Institute, Dr.
Reisser, was the appropriate man, and he was willing to assume
the office. As Ludwig was ill, his brother Johann took the necessary steps to legalize the change. Karl's entrance into the Polytechnic took place in the spring of 1825, in the middle of the
school year; hence he could not follow the course without making up what had been previously taught. We learn from the Conversation Book of this period how cautiously but firmly Karl gave
his uncle to understand that he needed a tutor for the purpose.
Ludwig became angry, presumably on account of the expense.[25]
In the course of the conversation, Karl repeatedly assured his

uncle that his intentions were good and honorable, and that all
would go well, but apparently failed to convince him. As Ludwig
was leaving for Baden at the beginning of May and wanted to be
sure that his Karl was well guarded, Dr. Reisser arranged for him
to lodge and board with a trustworthy civil servant, named Schlemmer, who lived in the Alleegasse, close to the Polytechnic. He was
to spend his holidays with his uncle at Baden.

A diary-entry in Ludwig's hand from the early days of his stay
at Baden shows that, in his imagination, the separation had increased the danger to his nephew from women. For the idea that
Karl had suffered a hemorrhage reappears. Ludwig wrote:

> Karl very pale [and] sunken, I see. — The cool mountain air may
> well be responsible for the bleeding.[26]

As Thayer rightly remarks, Ludwig blamed Karl's unhealthy appearance on his way of life and possible dissipations, not on the
intensive studying he was doing. How little Ludwig realized that
study in an advanced school was a serious and absorbing activity,
demanding quiet and an efficient distribution of time, appears
from another passage in the Conversation Book. Ludwig went to
see Karl one Saturday in Vienna and asked him to accompany
him while he did some errands and then go back to Baden with
him. Karl wrote in answer:

> To get everything finished today is absolutely impossible if I have
> to do things with you. But I will take something with me, because
> we are very much overloaded and on Sunday have to write
> everything that was given in lectures the whole week before. —
> Certainly I am glad to be going out with you today, but it is almost
> impossible to do much out there, because it is too difficult to bring
> along all the books and papers I should need; as I have to go with
> you about the lodging too, I shall have too little time left. — So
> I think that I should meet you somewhere about 12, and [then]
> go to the lodging and do other errands with you and eat with you.
> But not come out until tomorrow, so that I could have the evening
> to myself, when I can get through the most [of it]. For you cannot
> believe *how much* writing and studying there is to do, to satisfy
> the demands of the professors and especially of Reisser, who
> watches me very carefully anyway. — Then I could [come back]
> here early day after tomorrow morning and be with you all day
> tomorrow. —
> The work does not go as fast as one might think. There are too

> many subjects that have to be well understood and studied. I
> spend 5 hours daily, and twice a week 6, at lectures alone. At
> the end of every day there is nothing one can do but read up every
> subject and do the assignments for the next day. Yesterday there
> were 6 different subjects, which gave me plenty to do in the eve-
> ning too. Saturday is reserved for making a fair copy of what one
> can manage to note down of the lectures and the dictation. Today
> I took up history first, which is taught in so far as it has an influ-
> ence on commerce. — I have purposely brought with me what I
> wrote during the time when I was alone just now so that you can
> see how slowly it goes, for I have to have the maps and a textbook
> of geography at hand, and immediately look up and read up every-
> thing to do with *places*. — [27]

The careful detail in which he here set forth his obligations as a
student shows how little receptive his uncle was to the explanation.

There is yet another conversation,[28] in which Karl patiently explains to his uncle his course of study and the necessity for schedul-
ing his time properly. For Ludwig wanted Karl to be at his disposition at any moment, and he could not see why Karl could not just
as well study in Baden. Karl tried to explain to his uncle, who was
still nagging at him for having changed his curriculum, that study
at the University did not necessarily prepare one for more lucra-
tive professions than did study at the Polytechnic. He seems not to
have succeeded in reconciling his uncle to the Polytechnic.

From the period of Ludwig's stay at Baden in 1825, thirty-five
letters from him to Karl are extant. They affectingly document the
martyrdom which grew out of the uncle's strange love and jealousy
in his relationship to his nephew. In the first letter Ludwig announced that on Saturday he would send a carriage to the city
in which Karl was to come to Baden at 6 o'clock, or as early as 4
o'clock if at all possible. This was despite the fact that Karl had
explained to him that he needed Saturday evening for studying.
Ludwig could not refrain from reproaching him for his expensive
tutor:

> And do you know that this business of the tutor together with
> board and lodging come to 2000 fl[orins] a year? [29]

he wrote in this letter, and the reproach is unmistakable. It is
doubtful if such a "memento pecuniae" promoted Karl's zeal for
study.

Five further letters written to Karl from Baden on three suc-

cessive days (May 17, 18, 19) [30] give an idea of the flood of errands, complaints, and reproaches which Ludwig sometimes let
loose on poor Karl, who, after all, was busy studying. In the first
letter, Karl is to get chocolate for his uncle and give it to the housekeeper to take back to Baden. The chocolate was to help cure
Ludwig's diarrhea. Before Karl could do this errand, for he had
to attend lectures all day, he received a second letter in which Ludwig complained that the housekeeper had not yet got back; Karl
was to go at once to her family in the Kothgasse and find out if she
had started back for Baden. Ludwig complained with an under-
tone of reproach that he was dependent upon such people — that
is, had been left in the lurch by Karl. Further complaints follow
— there was no wine in the house and he had to get it from the
inn, where it was expensive and bad. The housekeeper was a
wicked old woman. The people in whose house he had lived in
Vienna, so the housekeeper told him, refused to give him back
the bell-pull which he had had put up there to call the cook; so
he suspected that the housekeeper was an accomplice of the owners
of the house and would share in the profits from the sale of the
unrightfully confiscated bell-pull. The letter ends with yet another
reproachful complaint: "What a painful situation to have to be
here thus!!" [31] "Thus" doubtless means "thus" ill and "thus" forsaken by his nephew. Then came a third letter, written the same
day, telling Karl that the housekeeper had arrived after all, not
to mention the bell-pull. The letter then closes with a long, reproachful exhortation not to let his studies make him forget his
duty to his uncle:

> . . . study diligently and rise early in the morning, with which
> you could also reconcile such things as will arise to be done for
> me; — for a young man soon to be 19 years old, it cannot be other
> than becoming that he should combine with [the fulfillment of]
> his duties to his education and future career [a corresponding at-
> titude] toward his benefactor [and] supporter. — I certainly did
> it with my parents. —
>   Most hastily your faithful Father.

The old bell-pull arrived here.[32]

From these same days, though impossible to date precisely, is a
letter in which he again reminds Karl of the chocolate and gives
him a fresh nagging on the subject of the Sunday visit:

. . . I am growing steadily thinner and feel rather badly than well, and no doctor, no sympathetic people! If you can at all on Sundays, come out, yet I do not want to keep you from anything, if I were only sure that Sunday without me would be well spent. I must wean myself of everything, if only this benefit will come to me, that my so great sacrifice will produce worthy fruits. — Where am I not wounded, torn? [33]

The third day Karl received a fifth letter ordering him to look at several lodgings — a task for which he certainly had no time.

These letters are still moderate compared with the following. A veritable storm of emotion broke with a letter of May 22nd. The day was a Sunday, — and Karl had not come to visit his uncle. The letter reads:

Until now only surmises, although I have been assured by someone that secret communications [have taken place] again between you and your mother. — Am I again to experience monstrous ingratitude?! No, if the bond is to be broken, so be it; you will be hated by all unprejudiced men who hear of this ingratitude. — My brother's remarks, and in Dr. Reissig's [34] presence, as he says, and your remark yesterday in reference to Dr. Schönauer, who must naturally have a grudge against me, for the opposite of what he wants occurred in the Landrechte, am I once again to mix in these vulgarities, no, never again. — If the compact is burdensome to you, in God's name — I resign you to divine Providence; I have done my part and can therefore appear before the highest of all judges. Do not be afraid to come to me tomorrow, as yet I only suspect [you]; God grant that none of it is true, for truly it would be impossible to see the end of your misfortune, lightly as my scoundrelly brother and perhaps your mother would take it with the old woman [the housekeeper]. I expect you without fail.[35]

All Ludwig's suspicion of a secret connection between Karl and Johanna was then reawakened. The threat that his uncle would finally withdraw his support and protection must certainly have produced a traumatic effect on Karl, if he took it halfway seriously. The next letter is dated May 31. It is cold and cutting as a knife:

Dear Son! I expect to come to town Saturday and to return here Sunday evening or Monday morning. — Hence I ask you to inquire of Dr. Bach at about what hour he is usually in for consultation, and also to have the baker [Johann's brother-in-law] give you the key, so that you can see if the room which my unbrotherly brother occupies is sufficiently furnished so that I can pass the night, if the linen is clean, etc. Since Thursday is a holiday and you will hardly come here, nor do I demand it, you could certainly do these few errands. Saturday when I arrive you can give me the information, I send you no money, for in case of necessity you can borrow a gulden in the house. Temperance is necessary for youth, and you appear not to have regarded it sufficiently, since you had money without my having known it or yet knowing from where? — Pretty behavior! It is not advisable to go to the theater now, because of the too great distraction, I believe. — the 5 florins furnished by Dr. Reissig I will meanwhile pay off punctually monthly — and with this basta. — Spoiled as you are, it will not harm you at last to apply yourself to simplicity and truth, for my heart has suffered too much from your deceitful behavior toward me, and it is hard to forget. And even if, for all that, I were willing to pull like a yoke-ox without murmuring, your behavior, if it is thus applied to others, can never procure you people who will love you. God is my witness, I dream only of being utterly separated from you and from this miserable brother and from this abominable family which has been foisted upon me. God grant what I wish, for I can trust you no more.

Unfortunately your Father or better not your Father.[36]

The question concerning Dr. Bach's hours of consultation was an indirect threat to begin proceedings toward resigning the guardianship. We have no information as to Karl's reaction to this letter. But Ludwig could not cherish his anger for more than a week, and again his longing gained the upper hand. On June 9th, he was once more impelled to ask his beloved nephew to come to him:

I wish at least that you will come here Sundays. In vain I ask for an answer, — God be with you and with me.
                                   As ever your faithful Father.
Fare well. If I am sulky with you, it is not without reason, I should not wish to have expended so much to have given the world an ordinary man. I hope to see you without fail. —
But if the intrigues have already matured, then speak out openly (and naturally), and you will find him who always remains the same in the good cause . . .
How I live here, you know, and with the cold weather to boot. The constant solitude weakens me even more, for truly my weakness often borders on faintness. Oh vex [me] no more, the grim reaper will in any case grant but little more time. — [37]

In a postscript he told Karl that he had arranged everything for him to come and return on Sunday. In his softened mood, then, he had renounced having Karl with him on Saturday too. Yet even in this letter he had to admonish and express his suspicions. He went so far as to hope that Karl could not obey his order because he had been sick and not for another reason (obviously because of a woman). The letter ends with an almost heartrending supplication and threat.[38]

The following letter to Schlemmer, with whom Karl was lodging, dates from this period:

> Sir! It is striking to me that Karl can almost never be persuaded to join an elegant circle where at this time he could enjoy himself in the most reputable manner. It could arouse the suspicion that he might perhaps be amusing himself evenings or even nights in society certainly less good. I beg you to pay attention to this and upon no pretext to allow Karl to leave the house at night, if you have not received written word from me through Karl in this respect. Once with my consent he was at Hofrat Breuning's. — In enjoining this matter, which can be indifferent neither to you nor to me, upon you, I again recommend to you the greatest attention herein. — [39]

It is impossible not to be reminded of the precautions taken by a jealous husband who wants to make sure that his wife is watched during his absence.

The next day, Ludwig wrote yet another letter concerning Karl — this time to Bernard. That he should turn to Bernard indicates how desperate he was, for Bernard was angry with him on account of the oratorio. This letter shows that the network of Ludwig's suspicion included not only Karl and Johanna but also his brother Johann and even Herr Reisser, the new co-guardian. He begged Bernard to keep an eye on Karl, who was treating him so badly that it was extremely mortifying to him and even prejudicial to his health. Karl, he said, had not written to him. (This is only too understandable after the letter of May 31.) Ludwig continued:

> I surmise that this abomination of a mother [is] again involved, and in addition the intrigues of my brainless and heartless brother, who proposes to traffic with him [presumably Karl] and who is always wanting to criticize me and teach me (as the sow did Minerva in Demosthenes), because I will have absolutely nothing to do with his whore of a Fettlümmerl and Bastard,[40] still less will live with creatures so far beneath me . . .

He insists that he had learned from his "ass of a brother" that Johanna and Reisser were trying to bring it about that Karl should no longer be with his uncle at all. This letter to Bernard likewise closes with a threat:

> . . . but should Karl again [have] secret relations with her, or should anyone help him to have them, it will be impossible to imagine what I will do, for I am at last wearied with experiencing the most shameful ingratitude for so much sacrifice and magnanimity.[41]

The remaining letters to Karl even more clearly reveal Ludwig's emotional derangement, which made him more and more incapable of respecting his nephew as an individual.[42]

Almost every one of these letters contains one or more considerable errands for Karl, who at this time was catching up on the year's work at the Polytechnic. In all there are thirty-four time-consuming errands, letters to be written, or other services which Ludwig demanded of Karl in these letters from Baden. Wafers, special matches, tailor, cobbler, cutler, bank bonds, shaving soap, copyist, piano-tuner, receipts, and finding a lodging — all these things Karl was expected to attend to, and generally "urgently"!

Some thirty of the letters contained a warning or a threat. Merely the repeated exhortations to be sure to spare his good clothes, and take them off immediately he got home, must have been highly irritating to the nineteen-year-old youth. In addition, Ludwig had a knack for making such admonitions particularly mortifying, as for example:

> I should have managed two years with the out-of-door coat, but to be sure I have the bad habit of putting on a worn coat at home but Herr Karl, oh fie, the shame, and why? — Herr L. v. B.'s money-bag is of course there just for that. — [43]

Again and again he admonished his nephew to rise early, so that he could study and do his errands:

> Let Aurora be not only the awakener, but let her give wings to your diligence . . .[44]

Karl was constantly lectured on his expenditures too:

> You always receive too much money . . . a Viennese remains a Viennese; I was happy that I could help my poor parents, what a

difference from you in your attitude to me — frivolous one, fare
well! [45]

Karl had also to keep a written account of all his expenditures.
Ludwig further accused Karl of lying, secrecy, hypocrisy, and
clandestine meetings with his uncle Johann and his mother. In
general he admonished him not to become a "Vienna no-good." [46]

"Imitate my virtues without my faults" [47] and similar phrases
occur in the letters. Karl was also to avoid everything which "could
debilitate and lessen his youthful powers," [48] a clear warning
against sexual dangers. Nor, finally, was Ludwig sparing with
threats of his own death, to oppress his nephew with a feeling of
guilt: "Someone will be found to close my eyes." [49] He had not, he
wrote in the same letter, given Karl life, but he had preserved his
life, and he earnestly implored him to walk in the one true way of
goodness and uprightness.

The third theme which fills these letters is complaints and vilifi-
cation of the housekeeper and the maid. Ludwig refers to the
latter as "the wench." His names for the housekeeper are "old
witch," "old devil," "Satan," "old beast," "wild animal without aim
or understanding, never at rest," "the old goose," "the old evil nature," "old vulgar kitchen-creature." The servants collectively are
a "pack of witches," "wicked unteachable riff-raff," "despicable
domestics," a "disgrace to culture," "scum of the people." He
"suffers and is patient like a saint under the boiling wrath and
the madness of Satan." In short, reading these letters, one would
suppose that he was surrounded by tormenting evil spirits, like
St. Anthony in the painting by Hieronymus Bosch. As we should
expect, his fear of poisoning persisted concomitantly. Thus he
wrote that he was "every moment in danger of being poisoned
daily!" [50] He ordered Karl to go with the housekeeper when she
bought seltzer water, "otherwise I might get who knows what." [51]
He also complained that the "old woman" starved him, he got "no
soup, no beef, not an egg, and finally a roast joint from the inn." [52]

Together with this abundance of negative formulations, these
letters contain expressions of the tenderest love and most intense
longing for his beloved. Exclamations like "Good night! Fare well!
fare well!" [53] or "Come soon! Come soon! Come soon!" [54] or "Je
vous baise!" [55] sound like the outcries of a lover. And "only fol-

low me, and love and bliss of soul, joined with human bliss, will be with us, and you will join an ethical life with outward life," [56] is like an exhortation to permanent union addressed to a hesitant beloved.

We leave it to the reader to conceive the effect which must have been produced upon Karl by this avalanche of negative and positive feelings, together with his responsibility for attending to all sorts of errands and business. It required a strong nature to stand up under it.

In addition to all this, Ludwig continued to have Karl spied upon. About this time, a new figure appears in Ludwig's more intimate circle. This was Karl Holz, second violinist in the Schuppanzigh Quartet. It was the first performance of the E-flat major Quartet, Opus 127, which brought Ludwig and Holz together. Karl Holz was then twenty-seven years of age, an accountant in the States' Chancellery. He was well-read, intelligent, witty, clear-headed and firm in expressing his views, attractive in nature and appearance. Ludwig rapidly developed a highly positive relationship toward him. Holz knew how to flatter him, and Ludwig found his wit and irony highly amusing. Holz was also an excellent mathematician, which Ludwig, with his incapacity for figures, found impressive. Holz soon became indispensable to Ludwig. Schindler is very critical of Holz. He tries to attribute his attraction for Ludwig solely to his mathematical capacity.[57] In his jealousy he could not admit that Holz was simply a far more entertaining companion for Ludwig, and also a much more charming person, than himself. In a short time, Holz had completely supplanted him in Ludwig's entourage.

It was this Karl Holz whom Ludwig employed to spy on Karl. Holz's attitude toward Karl was extremely variable. He distrusted him to some extent — obviously under Ludwig's influence. But when Ludwig was too hard on his nephew, he tended to stand up for him. A report on Karl by Holz appears in one of the Conversation Books. Holz wrote:

> I visited Karl Sunday, to give him your note; it was in the evening, and I learned from the maid that he had gone out early in the morning and had not even come back to the house to eat. — My plan is to become more intimate with him; I should very much

like to win him over; perhaps I shall the more easily learn to know him and his way of life; then I will give him friendly advice. — I tried to get him to go to a beer-house with me, because I [wanted] to see if he drinks much; but that seems not to be the case. Now I shall ask him once to play billiards; I shall see immediately if he has had much practice at it.[58]

Ludwig now apparently expressed his concern that, on his way to school through the city, Karl might become the victim of temptations. Holz thought this was going too far, for he wrote:

— What harm can come to him if he walks from the Alservorstadt [59] through the city. — What do other young men do? [60]

He also considered that Karl deserved some reward, although he made a reservation:

— I think that in return for his efforts and the drudgery he puts up with you should give him something at times — but not money.[61]

Karl was given no pocket-money. His uncle only once sent him two florins to go to a public bath. Yet at the same time Ludwig entrusted him with all his major business with publishers. It nowhere appears that he abused this trust. But he once borrowed 1 gulden 15 kreuzer from the housekeeper, who later debited it to Ludwig. Ludwig was furious, for to him it represented not only a theft but, at the same time, a suspicious complicity with the housekeeper. He wrote to Karl:

There seems to me to be collusion in all that has happened, in which my brother (pseudo) plays a role. — I know that later [sic] you have no desire to be with me, naturally, with me things are too clean. And the past Sunday you again borrowed 1 fl. 15 kr. from the housekeeper, that old common kitchen creature. — It had been forbidden. — [62]

Holz was intelligent enough to restrain Ludwig when he went too far in repressing his nephew: "The branch bent down by force easily springs up again"; and he tempered his wrath by saying: "One cannot be angry with him [Karl], even when one is convinced of his frivolity." [63]

We can nowhere learn in what this "frivolity" consisted; it seems to have existed only in Ludwig's fears. But Holz's warnings were of no avail.

One time in October, Ludwig must have been particularly harsh
when Karl visited him at Baden. After a stormy scene, Karl returned to Vienna. Ludwig, afraid that he had gone too far, wrote
to him the following day:

> For today it would be hardly possible to write to me, but I hope
> tomorrow to have a letter and to see you without fail Saturday. —
> I wish that you would never need to be ashamed of your unloving-
> ness toward me; I — but alas I can say nothing; I wish and hope
> that everything you alleged in order to go to Vienna, will be per-
> formed. — Be assured that at all times you can expect only all
> good from me, but should I wish this of you too? — If you see me
> stormy, ascribe it to my great care for you, since dangers easily
> threaten you. — I hope for a note from you at least tomorrow, do
> not put me in anxiety and consider my sufferings. By rights I
> should have no cares at all on this account, but what have I al-
> ready suffered?|
>   As ever your faithful Father.
>
> Consider that I sit here and can easily fall ill.[64]

Apparently Karl did not spend the night at Schlemmer's, and Ludwig somehow learned of it. The news made him really desperate,
as the following letter, of October 5, shows:

> My dear son!
> Only no more — only come to my arms, you will hear no hard
> word, O God, go not in your wretchedness. — You will be received
> lovingly, as ever, what to consider, what to do for the future, this
> we will discuss amiably; my word of honor, no reproaches, for
> they would now be fruitless, you may expect only the most loving
> help and care from me. — Only come, come to the faithful heart
> of your father. —
>   Beethoven
> Come home immediately after receiving this.
>   Si vous ne viendrez pas, vous me tuérez sûrement. Lisez la
> lettre et restez à la maison chez vous, venez m'embrasser, votre
> père vous vraiment adonné, soyez assuré, que tout cela restera
> entre nous. Only for God's sake come back home today, it could
> bring you [who] knows what danger.
> Hurry — hurry! [65]

Meanwhile, however, Karl had already written; and the joy expressed in Ludwig's answer reminds us of the jubilant "Oh welche
unnennbare Freude . . ." from *Fidelio*. He wrote to Karl again
on October 5:

Precious dear Son! I have just received your letter, already full of anxiety and resolved even today to hasten to Vienna. — God be thanked, it is not necessary; only follow me, and love and bliss of soul, coupled with human bliss, will be with us, and you will couple an ethical life with outward life. Yet better, that the former should stand first above the latter. — Il fait trop froid — so I will see you Saturday, write again, whether you will come morning or evening, so that I may hasten to meet you. —

A thousand times I embrace you and kiss you, not my lost but my new-born son. —

I wrote to Schlemmer; do not be offended, I am still too full.[66]

But by October 12, all the reproaches and dissatisfaction had returned:

I wish that your selfishness toward me would cease; it does me as little good as it sets you upon the right and best way. Only go on, you will regret it! Not that I will perhaps die earlier, since this is your wish, but in life I will entirely cut myself off from you, without on that account abandoning you and not supporting you. Seek the fool who has so sacrificed himself and so been rewarded by you and daily will be so by you. The worst are the consequences which will arise for you from your behavior. Who will believe and trust you, who hears what has happened and how you have mortally wounded me and daily wound me. Arrange to let me know how to find you, I am coming, whenever [it may be]. If I come Sunday, you can return here with me in the evening. (It is still particularly beautiful outside Baden; I take long walks, but yesterday I was in danger.) Alone! while my nephew could be here, if he had not wasted his time at billiards.

Do not become Rameau's nephew. Your faithful Father.[67]

In the next letter, however, the wind has changed again:

I send you word in greatest haste that even if it rains I shall surely come tomorrow morning, so let me surely find you — I rejoice to see you again, and if dark clouds still appear for you, do not ascribe it to deliberate unkindness, they will be wholly driven away by the better efforts you promised me for your true, pure happiness based upon diligence. In the last letter I was haunted by something which, not quite rightly, nevertheless produced a black mood; after all that has passed this is easily possible, but who will not rejoice if the erring one again treads in the right footsteps, yes this I hope to experience. — It especially pained me that Sunday you came so late and hurried away so early. I come tomorrow with the carpenter, the witch-pack shall go; it is too outrageous. Until the other housekeeper comes, I can use the

carpenter. — More by word of mouth, and you will admit that I
am right. — So expect me tomorrow without fail despite rain
etc. —

Your loving Father who clasps you to him.[68]

If the young man, constantly harassed in this way, neglected his
studies at this time, no one can blame him. His progress at the
Polytechnic was mediocre [69] — which of course gave rise to fresh
reproaches. Psychologically, the situation gradually became a
hopeless one for him.

As for Ludwig, his constant uneasiness in respect to his nephew,
his torturing fear that Karl might be unfaithful to him with a
woman and become a victim to the danger of the female sex, the
gnawing feeling of his beloved's supposed ingratitude, the fiendish
torment of perpetual jealousy, produced a disintegrating effect
upon him. He was now over fifty-five. Descriptions of his person
at this time show that this disintegration was outwardly visible.
The organist Freudenberg, who visited Beethoven during this
summer, describes him as "rather small in stature, with a wild,
somewhat distracted appearance, gray bristly hair, standing up
like a brush." [70] Even to people who did not know him well it was
obvious that Ludwig was so preoccupied by his relationship to his
nephew that his creativity was largely dependent upon it. The
Paris publisher Moritz Schlesinger, who visited Ludwig at Baden
in the summer of 1825, wrote in the Conversation Book on this
occasion:

I said that it *all depends* on your nephew what you want to write
["want to" is emended to "will"].[71]

Likewise Schuppanzigh:

no it is *up to him* [Karl] what Beethoven writes.[72]

To such an extent had his relationship to Karl absorbed Beethoven's psychic life.

On October 15 Beethoven moved to the "Schwarzspanierhaus"
in the Alservorstadt, where Stephan von Breuning, with whom he
had been intimate at Bonn, also lodged. Breuning had advised
against Ludwig's assuming the guardianship of his nephew, and
so for many years the friendship had cooled. But living in the

same house brought them together again, and Stephan proved to
be a faithful friend and helper during the last year of the master's
life. Stephan's son, Gerhard von Breuning, was eleven or twelve
years old when Ludwig moved into the Schwarzspanierhaus, and
in his thirteenth year at the time of Ludwig's death. He later published his reminiscences of the master. We owe him a description of Ludwig's appearance at this time which emphasizes
his negligent attire and his wild hair.[73] His grotesque appearance
was exaggerated by his behavior in the street, which Gerhard von
Breuning describes as follows:

> If he walked in company, he spoke very animatedly and loudly,
> and, since his companion had always to write the answer in the
> Conversation Book, there were frequent stops — a procedure suf-
> ficiently odd in itself, and which was made even more so, when
> worst came to worst, by answers expressed in mimicry. So it came
> about that most people who encountered him in the street turned
> to look at him, and the street-boys made fun of him and shouted
> after him.[74]

Gerhard continues:

> Hence his nephew Karl was ashamed to go out with him and had
> even once told him that he felt ashamed to walk in the street with
> him because of his 'foolish appearance'; he [Ludwig] expressed
> himself to us about this in a very angry and hurt fashion. I, on
> the contrary, was proud to be able to show myself with this im-
> portant man.[75]

Gerhard did not consider that a twenty-year-old has a different
reaction from a half-grown boy when his companion is stared at
by every passer-by and mocked by the street-boys.

Karl remained at Schlemmer's and continued his studies; his
uncle still plagued him with suspicions. For example, he insisted
that Karl was keeping on his tutor unnecessarily and simply to
make things easy for himself. He said that Schlemmer had said the
same thing. Karl wrote in answer:

> I have also discussed it with Schlemmer. He denies having said
> that; and he could not have done so, for he had no knowledge
> of how much I needed him or not. —
> The [tutor's] lessons are not difficult for me, and what I take with
> *him*, I could not take *earlier*, because we only take the subjects

that were taken in lecture.. — By my hours with him I save several
hours that I would have to work by myself alone.[76]

Such a gross misrepresentation of the facts as Karl here chal-
lenges must have greatly diminished his respect for his uncle. And
how much resentment must have slowly accumulated in him
against his uncle's sadistic spirit! Of course he had to set forth
his schedule of courses and his allocation of the day in full detail
to his distrustful uncle. And no sooner had he done so at great
length, in the Conversation Book, than Ludwig checked his nephew's statements by questioning Schlemmer. Schlemmer wrote:

> I can assure you that he has never yet stayed away over night.
> And I must tell you that your nephew is home in the evening
> daily, and only goes out in the morning when it is time for school,
> but if he nevertheless went out to play, it would have to be in-
> stead of school. Otherwise he is at home, and it cannot be that
> he plays. In the time that he has been here he has changed for
> the better, compared with the beginning. Today at table at noon
> he said that his tutor was not quite satisfied, he was disorderly
> during his lessons.[77]

Karl, hoping that this information would lessen the suspicion which
plagued him, now wrote:

> I am glad to have you inform yourself; any day that I stay out,
> the professors would have to know of it, for the roll is called. And
> Herr Reisser sees me daily.[78]

A pathological distrust, such as Ludwig felt for his nephew, is
fed by inner conflict and cannot be combated by reference to the
facts which contradict the suspicion. Holz too reported at this
time that Professor Reisser, who supervised Karl's studies, had
told him that Karl was behaving "as is to be expected of a reasonable person." [79] Thayer deserves the firmest contradiction when
he writes that Karl's "inclination for pleasure, for neglecting his
duties, for associating with unsuitable companions did not decrease," [80] for whatever material is investigated shows that these
inclinations were simply not present in Karl, and hence could
hardly decrease. But Thayer, otherwise so honorable, was determined to explain Ludwig's unhappy and ruptured relationship to
his nephew in terms which excluded Ludwig as the cause; hence
the blame had to fall on Karl.

Nothing more vividly shows Ludwig's pathological jealousy than his grotesque idea of accompanying his nephew to a ball during the carnival of 1826. As Karl found his uncle's "foolish appear-ance" trying, even in the street, we can imagine that all his pleas-ure in the ball would have changed to embarrassment and torture if Ludwig had really gone with him. Karl Holz had to exert every effort to talk Ludwig out of the idea by remonstrating with him against letting himself be "gaped at" by the crowd. Since Ludwig remained distrustful, Holz reassured him by saying, "I will go with him to a proper ball"; and when Ludwig even rejected this offer, since he did not trust Holz, the latter finally proposed: "When there is a ball in the Apollo Room, the so-called 'Reform Ball,' you can go there [and] be less noticed than elsewhere, which would certainly be agreeable to you." [81] Which likewise, to be sure, would have spoiled Karl's pleasure.

On the whole, however, Karl Holz appears to have exercised a mitigating influence on the conflict-fraught relationship between uncle and nephew. The mere fact that he was with Ludwig a great deal, as we know from the fact that pages of the Conversa-tion Books of this period are filled by his handwriting, took some of the pressure from Karl. Holz also did many of the errands which had formerly fallen to Karl's share and had so burdened him. To be sure, Karl also knew that his uncle used Holz to spy on him and that Holz was sometimes greatly under Ludwig's influence and at such times shared his distrust, so that the two men were allied against him. Yet Karl still found the winter bearable. Things were not to become entirely bad until spring, when he was making every effort to prepare for his decisive examinations at the Polytechnic and could not so often visit his uncle, who wanted to see him daily. Then the tension gradually became intolerable and finally led to catastrophe.

XIII

CATASTROPHE

DURING the spring and early summer of 1826 Karl was fully occupied by his work at the Polytechnic Institute, pursuing the courses which were to prepare him for a commercial career. Examinations in advanced schools require intense and thorough study, and anyone who has had to take them knows how much not only of the student's time but also of his thought they absorb. As Karl had not entered the Polytechnic until the spring of the previous year, he had much to make up. His uncle allowed him no recreation; even Ludwig's good friend Karl Holz admitted, after Ludwig's death: "Beethoven was excessively strict with his nephew and did not permit him the slightest extravagance." [1] Ludwig's brother Johann saw that Ludwig was tormenting Karl with baseless suspicions and unjustified reproaches on the subject of his studies, and therefore advised Karl to take a voluntary "honor examination," so that the result might calm his uncle. Reisser who, as Vice-Director of the Polytechnic and Karl's co-guardian, was certainly informed of his progress and interested in him, tried to soothe Ludwig by satisfactory reports on Karl and to silence his untimely demands by reminding him that the final examinations were now not far off. "It will all be over by August anyhow," [2] he wrote in the Conversation Book.

It was indeed all over in August, but in a very different sense than Reisser had intended.

Stephan von Breuning, who saw what a disturbing effect the relationship between uncle and nephew exercised on both sides, tried to persuade Ludwig to resign the guardianship, against assuming which he had advised him from the beginning. After a conversation with him, Ludwig wrote, addressing himself: "Resign the guardianship . . . it cannot go on this way." [3] But of course he did not do so, and the martyrdom continued. Karl could no longer bear the perpetual scenes, and tried to visit his uncle less often. This naturally did not improve matters, for Ludwig's distrust increased, and, when he saw Karl again, he assailed him with even worse reproaches. In his inner unrest, tortured by longing for his nephew, by distrust and jealousy, Ludwig asked his friends, and even his brother Johann, to watch Karl and find out why he no longer came to visit him so frequently. Johann brought him the following conclusive answer:

> I today seriously discussed with him why he shows his face here so seldom. — His answer was roughly as follows. He would very gladly be with you, only he fears the frequent rows and the frequent lectures on his faults in the past, likewise the frequent rows with the servants. I only ask [you] not to reproach him with this, otherwise he might lose his frankness with me. So I think it is simply up to you to draw him to you entirely.[4]

In the same conversation, Johann advised him to put Karl in a commercial firm immediately after the examinations and to transfer the guardianship to Dr. Bach. In another conversation, Karl had to defend himself against Ludwig's reproach that he did not go to see the co-guardian, Dr. Reisser, often enough; he appealed to the testimony of his tutor, with whom Holz too had had a talk which produced nothing unfavorable to Karl. Schindler, on the other hand, did his best to add fuel to the fire, for, instead of soothing Ludwig when the latter complained of Karl's badness, he wrote: "I regret to hear it, what will we go through next on Karl's account if things keep on this way." [5] At the same time he seized the opportunity to deal a blow at his rival Holz and advised Ludwig not to give Holz any role in the matter.

In June the situation was even worse. Karl really had to work very hard if he was to get through the examinations successfully.

> The professors always give so much to do over the holidays that one can hardly get through it. The fair-copying is the worst, because it takes so much time

he explained to his uncle. And

> there is much to do because the examinations are soon.[6]

It is easy to imagine how discouraging it was to Karl when, despite all his efforts to fulfill the requirements of his courses, he had to defend himself against Ludwig's harsh and unjust reproaches, as appears from the following entry in the Conversation Book:

> Those who envy you cast the shadow as it is, I need not contribute to that.[7]

We get some idea of the real torture Karl underwent when we read in the Conversation Book with what suspicions and reproaches Ludwig assailed him when a receipt for 80 florins for the month of May, which Karl had paid to Schlemmer for board and lodging, could not be found. Karl had undoubtedly given the money to Schlemmer; Ludwig had presumably got the receipt from him, but could not find it when it was time for Karl to pay Schlemmer for the month of June. The disorder in Ludwig's lodgings defies all description. For example, an important manuscript, the Kyrie of the Missa Solemnis, could not be found, until it turned out that the butter was wrapped in it! [8] Ludwig accused Karl of having misappropriated the money and used it for debauchery. Karl defended himself:

> In case the receipt is not found in my place, Schlemmer can give it to me together with the present receipt for this month. — But it will be found. —

He insisted that he only went out for walks and then occasionally took some refreshment.

> I have no other expenditures.[9]

But Ludwig continued to reproach him violently, even though the scene was taking place in Karl's room, so that other people in the house could hear it. This naturally was particularly mortifying to Karl. A few days later his uncle came again and tortured him with the same suspicions and the same reproaches. Karl now wrote:

> You consider it stubbornness that, after you have assailed me with undeserved reproaches for hours on end, literally at least this time, I cannot immediately change from the bitter feeling of pain to joking. I am not as frivolous as you believe, I can assure you that all these days, since the scene Sunday in the presence of that man, I have been so cast down that even the people in the house noticed it. The receipt for the 80 fl. which were paid in May, I gave to

you, as I know definitely and, now that I have made a search in
my place, for certain, and as I also said on Sunday; hence it must
and will be found, perhaps by chance.[10]

Upon this Ludwig began reproaching him that he did not devote
his attention to him (Ludwig) but studied instead, and that he
only worked in his presence but idled otherwise. To which Karl
replied:

> If I, while you are with me, go on working, it is not out of stub-
> bornness but because I believe that it will not offend you if I do
> not allow myself to be kept from my work, now really piled up,
> by your presence, the more so since, apart from that, we are seeing
> each other *here*, where there is time enough to discuss everything
> necessary; and you are mistaken too if you believe that I wait for
> you *to be diligent*.[11]

Beethoven now accused Karl, who had reported some piece of
derogatory gossip to him, of expressing his own opinion. Karl answered:

> Furthermore, you seem to take as my sentiments what I only *re-
> port* to you as the expression of *others*, like Haslinger's remark and
> Frau Passy's gossip. — I know well enough what to think of this
> chatter, but I considered it my duty to inform you of it. — I hope
> that what I have said will suffice to convince you of my real sen-
> timents, and to end the tension which, recently, although by no
> means on my part, has existed between you and me.[12]

Ludwig now returned to the receipt, for Karl wrote:

> This whole unpleasantness is superfluous, for it is only a matter of
> your inquiring of Schlemmer and having him give you the receipt
> for May over again. —
> You saw it, but if it should still be somewhere in my place, which
> I do not believe, you shall receive it.[13]

Uncle and nephew even came to blows, and finally Karl, in desperation, stormed out of the house. But despite everything Ludwig
continued to assail him with reproaches, until he finally drove him
to extremes.

If Ludwig tortured Karl in this and other ways, he did so out of
an inner compulsion. The great danger from which he had saved
his beloved nephew, and was determined to continue saving him,
was the poisoning woman and mother. It has been sufficiently set

forth how, in so doing, he attempted to replace Karl's mother for him, at the same time identifying himself with her. In this identification, it was at first more the positive and loving side of the mother whose image Ludwig carried within him which found expression, even though mingled with the negative traits of possessiveness, jealousy, and distrust. Gradually, however, and hand in hand with the mental regression and breakdown which took place in Ludwig, the negative traits of the mother-image acquired the upper hand. Thus he became more and more the evil, poisoning mother. As such, he was inwardly compelled to poison his nephew's life. He did so systematically, with increasing intensity and persistence, until the victim was stricken down.

Reproach followed upon reproach, the statements brought to Ludwig by prejudiced friends whom he had set to spy on Karl were distorted and thrown in the poor youth's face. The examinations were approaching; he could accomplish the necessary preparation only by devoting himself entirely to his studies. Yet his uncle robbed him of his time by errands which had always to be executed at once. In short, the pressure on Karl from all directions caused him intolerable tension. The lad felt driven to the utmost. All his attempts to free himself from suspicion and reproach were unavailing; his uncle was impelled to torture him. There was even a warning signal before the catastrophe. After a desperate scene, in which Karl had vainly tried to defend himself against the terrible network of suspicion and reproach, he rushed away, apparently threatening to kill himself. His uncle hurried after him and implored him not to go to extremes. This time he was still able to restrain Karl from the last despairing step. We can deduce this from a letter of Ludwig's which followed the scene and which, with its note of reconciliation, seems to express a revulsion of feeling:

> Simply because you at least obeyed me, all is forgiven and forgotten. . . . Today all calm. — Do not think that another thought save only your good rules in me, and judge my behavior from that. — Take no step which would make you unhappy and rob me of life earlier. I did not get to sleep until about 3 o'clock, for I coughed all night. — I embrace you lovingly and am convinced that soon you will no longer misunderstand me, thus I judge your conduct yesterday too. I expect you without fail today about 1 o'clock, only

cause me no more trouble and no more anxiety, meanwhile fare well.

> Your true and faithful Father.

We are alone, hence I will not let Holz come; the more so as I do not want anything of yesterday to become known; come — let my poor heart bleed no more.[14]

But Ludwig's baleful drive to destroy could no longer be stayed. It would have been a relief on both sides if, as in every previous year, the uncle had already gone to the country by this time. But his distrust, or rather the destructive drive which expressed itself as distrust, forced him to remain in Vienna and continue to assail his nephew. The poor lad worked on desperately, despite all the hindrances which Ludwig put in his way. He implored his uncle to leave time to study. For example:

> There are only a few weeks more and very much to do, one can scarcely get through the assignments, all the harder to prepare for the examination, and I am among the first to be examined, for it goes by the alphabet;

and

> The first examination will be in a few weeks; so it is high time that I used every hour.[15]

But his uncle renewed his reproaches, and there were constant quarrels because Karl would not spend the evenings with him. Ludwig could not bear to have Karl away from him in the evening, and Karl's absences at that time provided fresh food for Ludwig's distrust. He suspected Karl of going to a coffee-house and playing billiards in the evening. Schindler could hardly wait to substantiate the suspicion with gossip. These are the only "debaucheries" — and even so they are unproven — which all the biographers, fanatically endeavoring to represent Ludwig as his nephew's victim, can find, in their wrath, to impute to Karl.

Indeed, Ludwig did one thing more to make his nephew's situation intolerable. He constantly went to the Polytechnic to ask Reisser about Karl's progress. Reisser himself later said that Ludwig had done so far too often. In addition, he often waited in the courtyard of the Polytechnic in the afternoon until Karl came out from lectures, and then walked home with him arm in arm. We already know how reluctant Karl was to be seen with the grotesque-looking, shouting, notorious figure. And his classmates' mockery at his being fetched from school and taken home like a child cannot have been easy to bear.

Reading the Conversation Books, we see that Karl, thus hard-pressed, trapped, and tormented, was approaching a breakdown. His answers become increasingly peevish and sullen. In his despair, he turned to his mother and his friend Niemetz, whom his uncle had forbidden him to see. Ludwig reacted with volcanic anger. When the examinations began, Karl's agitation furnished the final impulse to the act of despair. In the course of time an immense quantity of aggression against his tormentor, for which he could find no outlet, must have piled up in him. It was impossible for him to vent his hatred upon the powerful man to whom he was delivered over body and soul, whose fame and greatness overwhelmed him, yet to whom he could not but feel bound to be grateful. The people with whom he was in contact were under Ludwig's influence and, as it were, his representatives. He could not express himself negatively to them in regard to his loving persecutor. It is only in a letter to Niemetz, dating from this period, that we find a hostile expression against his uncle:

> . . . I had to write in such a great hurry for terror and fear of being discovered by the old fool . . .[16]

We feel from this statement how surrounded and harassed he was. There remained only one possible way for him to vent his monstrously increasing hatred. He must turn it upon himself. Thus he began to plan suicide. He carefully prepared the act, overcame all obstacles, and on July 31, 1826, carried it out with the most serious intentions.

The events which immediately preceded the act can be reconstructed only fragmentarily. Schindler removed from the Conversation Book several pages which contained the conversations immediately after Karl's desperate action. They may well have contained the most important entries. The following facts can be ascertained:

Schlemmer, with whom Karl was living, learned — how, we do not know — that Karl was contemplating suicide, and conveyed

the information to Ludwig. Ludwig, in great agitation, hurried
to Schlemmer with Holz to learn more and to prevent the act.
There Holz wrote in the Conversation Book:

> I will fetch the police. — He must be removed from here any-
> way. He will certainly not take the examination. — Shall I have
> Schlemmer brought up? [17]

When Schlemmer arrived, he reported:

> The matter in brief, since you have already been informed through
> Herr Holz. I learned today that your nephew intended to shoot
> himself at latest next Sunday; I was given to understand only that
> it was to be on account of debts, but not quite for certain, he ad-
> mitted them only in part, as the consequence of former sins —
> I searched to see if any preparations had been made, and, sure
> enough, I found in his chest a loaded pistol, with additional lead
> and powder, I therefore informed you of the matter [so that you
> could] act as his father, the pistol is in my keeping. — Treat him
> leniently, or he will be desperate.[18]

Ludwig asked Schlemmer if Karl had spoken hostilely of his uncle.
Schlemmer wrote:

> No insults, but complaints that he was always having trouble.[19]

Ludwig now changed the subject and asked if Schlemmer considered the embezzlement of the board money the cause. Schlemmer answered:

> I have been paid in full — to the present month, but not yet for
> August.[20]

Holz looked through Karl's papers and found one referring to the
payment of the board money.

> This is not his handwriting, but everything is paid to the end of
> July [21]

he wrote, which shows beyond doubt that Karl had not embezzled
any money.

Holz now hurried to the Polytechnic to catch Karl, but Karl
escaped him there. Holz reported back to Ludwig:

> He could not be stopped; he said he would come right back to
> Schlemmer, he would only fetch his manuscripts from a friend's
> while I talked with Reisser. —
> I said that I could not wait longer than a quarter of an hour.[22]

In answer to Ludwig's rebuke for letting Karl go, Holz defended himself:

> He would have run away from you just the same. — I believe that if he intends to do himself harm, no one can stop him . . . He said, what good will it do you to keep me, if I do not get away today, it will happen another time.[23]

Karl, then, was determined to end his life. Schlemmer said that he would have someone unload a pistol he had found in Karl's room; his wife had taken charge of a second pistol. Ludwig then wrote:

> He will drown himself [24]

Since Karl did not return, Ludwig and Holz went the next day to Niemetz's, but found no one at home. Then they went to Johanna's. There they found Karl. He had a bullet wound in the left side of his head; the bullet was still lodged in it. After getting away from Holz, Karl had sold his watch and bought another pair of pistols with the proceeds. With these, he drove to Baden, where he had so often been with his uncle. The following day, a Sunday, he climbed the ruins of Rauhenstein on a cliff in the beautiful Helenenthal, and fired the pistols against his temples. One bullet missed, the other remained lodged in the skin of the head or the skull. A carter found him wounded and bleeding, carried him down the cliff, and, at his request, conveyed him to his mother in the city. His mother at once sent the carter to Ludwig, but meanwhile Ludwig and Holz had already set out in search of Karl, in the course of which they arrived at Johanna's and now learned what had taken place. Karl had written farewell letters, which he had sent to his friend Niemetz. The latter did not deliver the one addressed to Ludwig until two days after Karl had made his suicide attempt.

Thus it was in the house of the so hated "Queen of the Night" that Ludwig found his child, whom, it might be said, he had systematically driven to the desperate act. But even this did not at first make any basic change in his essential relationship to his nephew. For the first words which Karl put in the Conversation Book after Ludwig's arrival show that his uncle immediately attacked him with reproaches again. Karl wrote:

Now it has happened. Only a surgeon who can hold his tongue.
Smetana, if he is here. — Do not torment me now with reproaches
and complaints; it is past. Later everything can be arranged. —
She sent for a doctor, but he is not at home. Holz will soon bring
one.[25]

It is striking how forcefully Karl here repulses his uncle. As we
proceed, it will become even more apparent that the act brought
with it a significant turn in Karl's psychological situation.

While Holz ran for a doctor, Ludwig wrote a hasty note to
Smetana:

> Most honored Dr. Smettana! A great misfortune has happened,
> which Karl accidentally inflicted on himself; I hope he can still
> be saved, especially by you, if you will but come quickly. Karl has
> a bullet in his head, how, you will soon learn. Only quickly, for
> God's sake quickly.
> > Yours respectfully, Beethoven
> [The need for] speedy help sent him to his mother, where he now
> is: the address follows herewith.[26]

A surgeon, Dr. Dögl, arrived and applied a bandage. Dr. Smetana's assistance was found to be unnecessary. Ludwig then went
home, leaving Holz with Karl. Holz later told Ludwig what Karl
had further said to him:

> He [Karl] says: He will tear off his bandage at once if you are men-
> tioned again.[27]

Just before this Holz had written:

> He said, if he [Ludwig] would only stop his reproaches, and
> when you left, he said, if only he would never show his face
> again.[28]

There can be no doubt that the act had produced a change in
Karl which enabled him to defend himself against his uncle far
more aggressively.

Holz's indignation with Karl was unbounded; his expression of
it shows him to have been so completely under Ludwig's influence
that he was incapable of any sympathetic comprehension of Karl's
psychological situation. It is painful to read how greatly he misunderstood Karl and even urged Ludwig to cast him off entirely
and put him in the army:

Here you see ingratitude clear as day; why do you want to hold him back any longer? If he is once with the military, he will be under the strictest discipline, and if you still want to do something for him, you have only to allow him a small sum monthly. — A soldier at once.[29]

The biographers, without exception, share the lack of psychological insight which Holz here exhibits. Their reverence for the master prevented them from recognizing that Karl had been driven almost to death by him.

Since suicide was treated by the authorities as a punishable offense, the police had to be informed. By direction of the police, Karl was removed to the General Hospital. When, during the course of the police investigation, Karl was asked what had been his reason for committing the crime, he gave a clear, conclusive, and doubtless true answer:

Because my uncle harassed me so [*weil mein Onkel mich so sekkiert hat*].[30]

So now Karl was in the hospital, seriously injured and apparently unconscious at intervals; in any case, he was to be constantly watched by two nurses. Suicides being under police arrest, he was treated as a prisoner in the hospital.

On Ludwig, Karl's act produced a shattering effect, which eventually had fatal consequences. All his hope for his child was destroyed. In those days, suicide was regarded as a particularly infamous and sinful crime and, in the last analysis, the disgrace reflected upon himself. He felt that his nephew's act was a rejection of all the love and motherly solicitude which he had expended upon him. It cut him to the quick that the precious possession for which he had fought like a lion and whose conquest he had greeted with jubilation, now vanished like a phantom. For after the desperate act, the unhappy child had asked to be taken not to him but to his real mother, and wanted to hear no more of him. But what must have been most wounding of all was the new strength of mind with which Karl was able to ward off his further attacks and attempts to torture him. For it showed Ludwig that, through the act, a great inner change had begun in his nephew and was proceeding irresistibly.

Karl's attempt at suicide was the result of a process well known to psychopathology — the process referred to earlier as "turning upon oneself." Through the constant torture inflicted on him by his uncle, an intolerable excess of aggression accumulated in Karl, which, since all other means of discharging it were blocked, must necessarily lead to self-destruction. Least of all could his uncle — whom he experienced as a substitute for his own father and to whom he was still childishly bound, to whom he could not but feel deeply indebted, and of whose crushing affection he had only too many proofs — be the object of direct, conscious aggression. Holz told Ludwig, reporting what Karl had said:

> it is not hate but an entirely different feeling with which he is filled toward you.[31]

This "different feeling" was doubtless a mixture of defensiveness against Ludwig's oppressive tenderness, guilt because of unconscious hate, and conscious rebellion against the duty to love which Ludwig was constantly emphasizing.

Another psychological mechanism which plays an important part in this type of suicide is well known from the clinical study of similar cases. The turning of the aggression upon the self is regularly accompanied by an identification with the person against whom the aggression is originally directed. Such a suicide includes the killing of the person on whose account the suicide is performed; it is a murder-substitute.

Karl carried out the act, but he did not die from it. The injury to himself discharged enough aggression to allow him to free himself from the intolerable pressure which his uncle's personality had exercised on him. With his assault upon himself, Karl had also significantly diminished his feeling of guilt toward his uncle; we recognize this from the much more determined and independent attitude which he assumed toward his uncle thenceforth. Through the act he had psychologically "liquidated" his uncle. Ludwig could not help realizing this from Karl's behavior after the act.

Ludwig, to be sure, could no longer change his attitude toward his nephew; he continued to give expression to his hate-love for him. But from now on its manifestations produced no effect. He was gradually forced to see that he had lost his child forever. Karl had survived his uncle's aggressions; his suicide had immunized him against his uncle's attacks and attempts to torture him. Thereafter but one way remained open to Ludwig's destructive drive. He must turn it upon himself. His nephew's suicide thus became Beethoven's death-blow. It was as if from then on the great man knew that his death was certain. Again and again the phrase "memento mori" [32] appears in letters and notes, and in a Conversation Book of this period we find, in Beethoven's hand, the ominous allusion:

on the death of the late Beethoven.[33]

Soon afterward the illness which led to his death began.

We shall first set forth the immediate effects of Karl's act upon Ludwig. Gerhard von Breuning wrote:

The grief which he felt from this event was indescribable; he was laid low like a father who has lost a greatly loved son. Completely distracted, he met my mother on the Glacis. 'Do you know what has happened to me? My Karl has shot himself!' 'And — is he dead?' 'No, he only grazed himself, he is still alive, there is hope of being able to save him; — but the disgrace he has put upon me; and I loved him so much!' [34]

Schindler describes the effect of Karl's act on the then fifty-six-year-old composer:

The still solid man, forceful in all his movements, was gone, before us stood an old man of seventy, will-less, docile, obedient to every breath.[35]

But this description must have referred only to the first shock reaction. For Ludwig very soon found the energy to attack his nephew again with reproaches, torments, and suspicions. Even when he had seen Karl at Johanna's for the first time after the act, Karl had been obliged to halt the flood of reproach with which his uncle tried to overwhelm him. And the physician in the surgical section of the General Hospital, whose patient Karl was, later described Ludwig's first visit to Karl there:

In the late summer of 1826, just as I was starting to make my rounds, a man in a gray coat approached me whom I instantly took for an unpretending bourgeois. He asked drily: 'Are you Herr Seng? Is it to you that the reception office directed me? Is one

of your patients my nephew, the profligate, the scoundrel?' etc.
After learning the name of the person sought, I answered in the
affirmative, and replied that he was in a room in the three-gulden
section for paying patients, was bandaged for a wound, and might
I take him there? whereupon he said: 'I am Beethoven.' And while
I conducted him to the patient, he continued: 'I really did not want
to visit him, for he does not deserve it, he has made too much
trouble for me, but . . .' and then he went on talking of the
catastrophe and of his nephew's conduct and of how he had spoiled
him too much, etc.[36]

Ludwig, then, was full of rancor, and without the slightest conscious realization that he was responsible for the catastrophe. He
sought in vain to discover the motive of his nephew's act, and
wrote in his diary:

> Confusion of mind and insanity, the heat too, afflicted with head-
> aches from childhood — [37]

from which it appears that he wanted to put the blame on inheritance, the weather, and excessive strain.

During the first weeks, Karl was in real danger. Holz, who visited
him regularly at the hospital, reported to Ludwig concerning Karl's
condition and the treatment he was receiving:

> Every day 4 of the most skillful doctors come 4 times. — His care
> leaves nothing to be desired. — There is no fever yet, but when
> it does come will be the dangerous crisis. — [38]

And again:

> It is still a question if he will recover; any head wound endangers
> life, and, in case the brain was too shaken, which can still appear
> within a few days, he is lost. —
> Weariness of life! — If he should die, he must, according to the
> law, be buried at the Rabenstein.[39]

The Rabenstein was the place, outside the cemetery, where suicides were buried, as they were denied burial in consecrated
ground.

It appears that, being under arrest, Karl was more strictly treated
in the hospital than other patients. It was the law that every suicide must be reinstructed in religion, since the act was regarded
as a sin, and its commission as a proof of irreligion. A person under
arrest for attempted suicide was only released after sufficient reli-

gious instruction. Karl later told his uncle about his harsh treatment at the hospital:

> It was impossible to look outside — But in the evening there was no light, so the place was very unpleasant — I could not sleep for vermin — the commonest people — I kept to myself — [40]

Finally a priest came, convinced himself of Karl's orthodoxy by an examination, and so gave him a certificate which allowed his situation in the hospital to be improved.

Beethoven's friends were very much concerned as to what was now to be done. Naturally, they wanted Ludwig at last to keep away from his nephew. The magistrates considered it their duty to investigate the causes of the suicide attempt. Ludwig, however, regarded this as an unwarrantable interference with his rights as guardian. Both Holz and Schindler thought that Ludwig, for the sake of his health and peace of mind, should resign the guardianship; but he at first clung to it doggedly.

Karl's future was the next matter of concern. Schindler, who had resumed his intimacy with Ludwig at this time, strongly advised:

> Let it be in whatever situation it may, only away from Vienna.[41]

At first Karl was to be placed in a commercial establishment abroad; but no final decision was reached. Karl himself firmly expressed his wish to become a soldier.

But the Magistracy too had to interest itself in the whole matter of the suicide and its consequences. The case was officially investigated; Holz attended the hearings and kept Ludwig informed. In the course of the investigation, Karl stated his motive for the act to have been his "imprisonment" by his uncle; there is no reason to doubt that he was telling the truth. The court recognized Ludwig's valuable services to his nephew, but found that objection could hardly be raised if Karl expressed the wish to live with his mother, for to do so was "in accordance with natural instinct." [42] Karl, however, expressed no such wish, Holz reported to Beethoven.

Karl's examinations also came up for discussion, and both Holz and Reisser reached the conclusion that Karl need not fear them, and indeed that it was not fear of them which had driven him to attempt suicide. Karl himself said that he did not care whether he took the examinations or not. Dr. Bach, Ludwig's attorney,

urged that Karl should enter upon a business career at once. For
the time being, however, Karl had to remain in the hospital until
his wound was healed and the scar concealed by a new growth
of hair. Ludwig finally consented to resign the guardianship in
favor of someone in whom he had confidence. He at first thought
of Holz, but Holz had just become engaged and could not well
assume the burden of the guardianship. Ludwig next turned to
his old friend Councillor Stephan von Breuning, and asked him
to assume the office. After considerable hesitation, von Breuning
accepted. Ludwig entrusted his child to him in a letter which is
touching in its concern:

> With Karl there are, I believe, three points to observe, first, that
> he be not treated as a criminal, which would produce not what is
> desirable but the very opposite. — Second, in order to be helped
> to a higher condition, he must not live too poorly and shabbily. —
> Third, too great a stinting in food and drink would be hard on him.
> — I do not encroach upon you.[43]

The loss which abandoning the guardianship meant to Ludwig
finds painful expression in a letter to Holz:

> . . . I am wearied and long will joy flee from me, the suitable
> expenditures, present as well as future, must cause me care, all
> hopes vanished! To have a being about me whom I hoped to make
> resemble me, at least in my better characteristics! . . .[44]

Inwardly, of course, he could not give up Karl. At his next visit
to the hospital he could not refrain from venting his hostile attitude
toward Johanna and reproaching Karl for being friendly to his
mother when she visited him. Ludwig also expressed his concern
lest, after he was discharged from the hospital, Karl should really
wish to live with his mother. Karl's answer clearly shows the inner
transformation which he had undergone:

> I want to hear nothing about her that is derogatory to her, and
> it is absolutely not my place to pass judgment on her. If I should
> spend the little time I shall be here, with her, it would be no more
> than a small compensation for all that she has suffered on my ac-
> count, there can be no question of any harmful influence on me,
> even if it could occur, simply by reason of the shortness of the time.
> — But in no case will I treat her more coldly than has hitherto
> been the case, no matter what anyone may say.[45]

And:

> Hence during these days I can all the less deny her her wish to be with me, since presumably I shall not soon be here again; it goes without saying that this is no obstacle to our seeing each other as often as you want.[46]

Even Thayer, commenting on this, says that an inner transformation had taken place in Karl.[47]

Toward the end of September, Karl was ready to be discharged from the hospital. Breuning had prevailed upon his acquaintance Lieutenant-Fieldmarshal Stutterheim, to take Karl into his regiment, which was stationed at Iglau in Moravia. Karl's hair, however, had still to grow enough to conceal his wound, before Breuning could present him to Stutterheim. The question arose where Karl was to spend the period between his discharge from the hospital and his entrance into the army. Karl had first to be put under the supervision of a member of the Magistracy, Councillor Czapka. The following letter from Ludwig to Czapka shows that the old fear of danger from women, particularly the mother, which had been so instrumental in determining and ruining Ludwig's relation to his nephew, was as active in him as ever:

> Sir! I urgently beg you to order that, since my nephew will be well in a few days, he may leave the hospital with no one but myself and Herr v. Holz. It cannot possibly be permitted that he should be very close to his mother, that most corrupt person. Her so extremely bad and wickedly malicious character, indeed her temptation of Karl to embezzle money from me, the probability that she has divided sums with him, and was also in collusion with Karl's dissolute accomplice, the scandal she arouses with her daughter, whose father is to seek, indeed the presumption that at his mother's he would become acquainted with women anything but virtuous, justify my apprehensions and my request. Even mere habituation to the company of such a person cannot possibly lead a young man to virtue. While commending this matter to your heartfelt attention, I present my best respects to you, and only add that, although upon such a painful occasion, I was greatly delighted to make the acquaintance of a man of such excellent intellectual gifts. . . .[48]

In a second letter, Ludwig implores Czapka to put Karl in his keeping, although Karl had objected:

Sir! Herr Hofrat von Breuning and I have carefully considered what is to be done, and have always concluded that at this moment nothing else can occur but that Karl must spend a few days (preceding his departure for military service) with me. His assertions are still ebullitions of the impression which my reprimands made upon him, when he was already on the point of ending his life. But after that period he also showed himself loving toward me. Be convinced that humanity even in its fall is ever sacred to me; a warning from you would produce a good effect; it might do no harm too to let him know that he will be invisibly watched while he is with me. — Pray accept my very high esteem for you and regard me as a loving friend to humanity, who wishes only good, where it is possible.[49]

Breuning presented himself before the Magistracy, where he talked with both Czapka and Karl, who had been brought by the police. He reported back to Ludwig:

He [Karl] will not see you. — At the Magistracy I assumed the guardianship, upon which he was placed at my disposition. — I fear that, if he is here, you will talk to him too much, which would cause fresh irritation. — Because he told the police that you tormented him too much, which led him to the step. — Then let him be brought here by Holz; then on Friday I will take him to Lieutenant-Fieldmarshal Stutterheim, in five days he will be equipped and in a week he will go. — At the hospital there is much doubt whether they will take him again. If he runs away from here, he will also run away on the journey to the regiment. Referee Czapka himself said that he [Karl] will not speak with his mother. — [50]

While the question of what to do with Karl until he entered the army was being considered, Johann, who was temporarily visiting Vienna, suddenly entered the picture. He invited Ludwig and Karl to come to stay at his place in Gneixendorf for the short time until Karl left for his regiment. He proposed that they should travel back with him; but he was in a great hurry to set off:

We must start day after tomorrow morning at 5 o'clock, otherwise all my business will be ruined.[51]

Ludwig, who had accepted the invitation, since the police would not allow Karl to remain in Vienna, still wanted to put off the departure. Karl finally insisted on a start, and did his best to dispose of Ludwig's pretexts for further delay:

We will write the necessary letters now, so that we will be ready
tomorrow; for your brother absolutely refuses to wait longer than
early tomorrow morning [52]

he wrote in the Conversation Book. So, on September 29, the
brothers set off from Vienna with their nephew, and reached
Gneixendorf two days later. There Beethoven spent his last period
of close companionship with his Karl. It was a time of deep dejec-
tion and depressive apathy for him, interrupted by outbreaks of
painful anger and distrust. In Gneixendorf he worked on his last
string quartet, Opus 135.

Johann and Therese gave Ludwig a friendly reception to their
large house. He was assigned a room with a pretty view. From the
Conversation Books we learn that Johann inquired into his wishes
— for example at what hour he wanted breakfast and his morning
hot water. Therese put a bunch of flowers in his window. His
nephew took him walking in the fields, Johann in the vineyard.
The countryside, however, was comparatively flat and unwooded,
and did not provide Ludwig with the kind of Nature he so greatly
loved. From the beginning he was dissatisfied with everything,
and even regretted having come. He wrote in the Conversation
Book:

Breuning ought *not* to have let *me* go along.[53]

Karl treated him in friendly fashion, giving him detailed accounts of everything that he did; doubtless Ludwig, in his distrustful way, also inquired minutely into everything. He was well cared
for, and consideration was given to his wishes; Johann once wrote
in the Conversation Book: "Do you want eggs or Bratwürste?"
and then added, "Malaga." [54]

Certainly, Ludwig was not badly accommodated in his brother's
house. But it had no effect upon his depression and deep dissatisfaction. A passage from a letter of this period sounds like a melancholy foreboding of death:

You see that I am at Gneixendorf. The name has some resemblance
to a breaking axle. The air is healthy. Concerning the rest, one
must make the memento mori . . .[55]

He also complained that his room was unheated, although there
was an ample supply of wood for the stove. Naturally, he was ex-

tremely displeased with the food, probably at times Therese prepared it herself.

> No good beef, and on top of that a goose, Heaven help my hunger,[56]

he complained.

Since the hair took longer to grow over Karl's wound than had been anticipated, and since Johann was in financial difficulties and behind on taxes, at the end of two weeks he asked Ludwig to pay a modest amount for board. He also proposed that Ludwig should spend eight months of the year with him, for which he would charge him less than half his yearly income. It is clear, then, that he had no intention of exploiting Ludwig.

Therese, who knew from experience how hostile Ludwig was toward her, avoided being with him more than was necessary. A young man named Michael Krenn was taken on as Ludwig's personal servant. Krenn later provided much information concerning Ludwig's stay at Gneixendorf and his strange behavior there. At first the cook made his bed, but once when she could not help laughing when she saw Ludwig sitting at his table, "waving" his hands and stamping out the time with his feet and humming, he chased her out of the door. Krenn, who was also in the room, wanted to go with her, but Ludwig held him back, gave him sixty kreuzer, and said that he must thenceforth make his bed and clear up his room every day. In the evening, Krenn had to sit in Ludwig's room with him and write down what had been said about him at the family meals. Ludwig gradually came to regard Krenn as a confidant. Therese once discharged Krenn because he had lost five gulden with which he was to buy food in the neighboring town of Stein. She related the incident at lunch, when Ludwig asked for him. Ludwig became terribly excited, considering it a personal attack on him by Therese; in a great rage, he gave Therese the five gulden and insisted that Krenn should instantly return. Once when Johann had business with the bailiff in a nearby town, Ludwig went with him and, while Johann talked with the bailiff, sat for some time in the clerk's office, unaware of his surroundings. When the bailiff later asked the clerk, who was a Beethoven enthusiast, whom he had supposed the visitor to be, the clerk answered:

> Since you, sir, paid him so many compliments, his may well be an
> exceptional case, but otherwise I should have taken him for a half-
> wit.[57]

So apathetic and withdrawn had Ludwig become as a result of
the disastrous experience with his nephew.

But there was still a sufficiency of explosive material in him
when Karl was concerned. He soon began to suspect him of taking
too great an interest in Therese. Karl had brought some four-hand
marches, so that he could occasionally play them with his uncle.
It appears that he once played them with his aunt, for she wrote
in the Conversation Book:

> Karl plays very well.[58]

But Ludwig immediately interpreted this as indicating an intimate
relationship between aunt and nephew. Many of the biographers,
in their infatuation, have followed him and accused Karl of an
improper relationship with Therese.[59] Yet nothing testifies to such
an assumption except Ludwig's pathological suspicions. Ludwig
violently reproached his nephew, Karl defended himself vigorously, and there were noisy, intolerable scenes.

Ludwig could not make up his mind to return to Vienna, for it
meant his final parting from his beloved child. Still wanting to
accomplish one last thing against the female rival he so deeply
hated, he demanded of Johann that he leave his entire estate not
to his wife and step-daughter but to Karl. Needless to say, Johann
had no intention of acceding to this demand. He refused, and Ludwig was furiously embittered.

Since the stay at Gneixendorf had now lasted eight weeks —
far longer than originally planned — Johann was understandably
concerned and insisted that Karl ought to return to Vienna and
at last join his regiment. He expressed his concern to Ludwig in
a friendly letter, in which, while attempting to spare his feelings,
he reminded him of his duty to Karl and urged that he now take
him back to Vienna. He stipulated the following Monday as the
day of departure. Beethoven was furious at Johann's letter, and
Schindler reports that it led to a violent scene between the brothers,
in which Ludwig once again demanded that Johann disinherit his
family and leave his estate to Karl — which Johann again declined
to do.

At last, however, Ludwig himself urged their departure on Karl, who was enjoying himself at Gneixendorf, for Karl wrote in the Conversation Book:

> I cannot object to it, for after all we have been here longer than could be foreseen; but *Breuning* himself says that I cannot go to the Fieldmarshal until I look so that no sign of what happened can be seen in me, for he must know nothing about it. This is now almost accomplished, except for a little, and that cannot take much longer; hence I believe that we should stay at least until next week. If I had had the salve here, even that would be unnecessary. In addition, the longer we stay here, the longer we shall be together, for as soon as we are in Vienna I must naturally soon go away.[60]

Finally, however, the departure was fixed for December 2. In the interval there were several more violent scenes; during one of them, Karl rushed away, and Ludwig was afraid he might again inflict injury on himself. Therese soothed him, as appears from the Conversation Book:

> Do not worry; he will certainly be home within an hour. He appears to have your violent blood. He did not seem to me at all angry, he loves you to the point of reverence.[61]

But such scenes had lost their disastrous effect on Karl. In general, he opposes a determined resistance to his uncle's reproaches. Passages from two conversations show his attitude:

> You disgrace yourself and me by this behavior; there is no question of laughing, I only told the young man to send the servants out, because I saw the turn the conversation was taking . . .

and:

> I am asked why I do not talk — because I have had enough. You have the right to say everything to me, and I must bear it. — I can only repeat that I can answer nothing to all that you have said to me today, for I know nothing better to do than to accept it in silence, as is my duty. You must not regard this as stubbornness.[62]

In the second conversation, Ludwig too wrote a few sentences, which show the way in which he tortured his nephew:

> What is the matter with you? What are you hanging your head for now? Is the truest devotion, despite whatever faults, not enough? You are still unhappy to leave here, and I have taken it into consideration too.[63]

Yet Karl's answer makes it even clearer:

> Did you see me speak a word? Hardly — for I was in no mood to speak. — so everything that you say about intrigues requires no refutation. — So I beg you at last to leave me in peace. — If you wish to leave here, good — if you do not, good too — only I beg you again not to torment me as you do. — You could also regret it in the end; for I bear much, but what is too much I cannot bear. You did the same thing to your brother today without cause; you must remember that other people are human too. . . . These eternal unjust reproaches . . . But why are you making such a scene today? Will you not let me go for a little now? I really need it for my relaxation. I will come back later. I only want to go to my room. I am not going out, I only want to be alone for a little now — will you let me go to my room? [64]

Anyone who still doubted that Beethoven was the cause of Karl's attempted suicide would have to recognize from these sentences that it was psychological maltreatment which drove Karl to the act. But by this very act he purged himself of the destructive forces, leaving Ludwig to destroy himself. It was during these last weeks at Gneixendorf that Beethoven showed the first symptoms of vascular engorgement, caused by his affection of the liver. His legs swelled, and because of the accumulation of fluid in the abdominal cavity, he had to wear a bandage.

A few days before uncle and nephew left Gneixendorf, Therese went to Vienna in the carriage which belonged to the estate. Ludwig had presumably refused to travel with her. He began the journey with his nephew on a cold rainy evening in an open cart and had to spend the night in a village. When he reached Vienna he was seriously ill with pneumonia and was obliged to go to bed at once. He was hardly to leave it again until his death.

XIV

AFTERMATH AND AFTERTHOUGHTS

THERE the great man lay mortally ill, stricken by the fate which his own inner compulsion had forged for him. Ludwig first asked his former physician, Dr. Braunhofer, to attend him, but Braunhofer excused himself on the ground that the distance was too great. This was undoubtedly a pretext. Considering what a restless, irascible, and ungrateful patient Ludwig was, it is not surprising that his former physician did not wish to attend him. The next summons went to Dr. Staudenheimer, who promised to come, but did not. Finally, on the third day, Holz brought Dr. Wawruch to the sick man's bedside.[1] Dr. Wawruch diagnosed pneumonia. Once again Ludwig's strong constitution was able to resist the attacks of the disease. On the tenth day he could even get up, walk about, read and write. But the improvement lasted only a day. It is probable that a last conflict with his nephew disastrously checked the recovery which had begun.

Immediately after returning to Vienna, Karl was presented by Breuning to Lieutenant-Fieldmarshal von Stutterheim, who received him graciously and again assured him of a place in his regiment. When Karl reported on this visit, his uncle again expressed his disapproval of his nephew's choice of a career and questioned whether he really wished to enter the army. Karl's firm and decided answer appears in the Conversation Book:

> You are mistaken if you believe that I have become undecided. — On the contrary, I rejoice that the matter is ending so nearly in accordance with my wish, and I shall never regret my decision.[2]

Karl then reported that Stutterheim's adjutant had accompanied him to the barracks for his examination by the regimental physician, that he had himself taken the certificate to Stutterheim, and that the latter had received him "very nicely." "I shall be here

294

5–6 days longer," [3] he wrote at the end of the conversation. Ludwig, in despair at finally losing his child, thought of accompanying him to his regiment at Iglau in Moravia. But Karl rejected the proposal, and on reasonable grounds:

> We cannot in any case go together, because you will not be able to go within 6 days, as the doctor has told me. [4]

Thus the beloved youth slipped from his grasp and Ludwig was forced to recognize that he had no more power over him. Thereupon he collapsed.

It is pathetic to read Dr. Wawruch's account of the rapid deterioration which immediately followed. On December 12 he found Beethoven in an alarming condition:

> . . . greatly disturbed, jaundiced all over his body; a frightful cholerine attack had threatened to kill him the previous night. A violent rage, a deep grief over ingratitude suffered and undeserved mortification, caused the powerful explosion. Trembling and shivering, he writhed with pains which raged in his liver and intestines, and his feet, previously only moderately inflated, were now greatly swollen. [5]

The jaundice increased, the secretion of urine diminished, the dropsy grew quickly worse, necessitating repeated abdominal punctures. The cirrhosis of the liver, from which he had presumably long suffered, suddenly made more rapid progress, until he succumbed to it.

Karl's decision to go his own way was free of hostility to his uncle. His entries in the Conversation Books show that the impatient sufferer, rebellious to the doctor's orders, received loving and considerate treatment at his nephew's hands; Karl cared for him almost as an experienced, solicitous mother cares for her unreasonable sick child. In the Conversation Book, December 4–6, we read:

> If you had no opening [bowel movement] today, you ought to take an enema at night . . .
> You are to eat only soup in the evening. . . . I have already told Thekla that if there is no opening before 7 o'clock, she is to fetch the barber; they know how to go about it properly, and they have syringes. He finds you better than yesterday. But every drop of urine must be saved, so that he can see not only the quality but

the quantity. The doctor recommended the greatest warmth. At night, when you are awake, you are to take warm cloths too . . . The doctor thinks it well that someone should be near you at night, to make warm cloths for you when you are awake. So, for the few days it will be necessary, Thekla could either sleep here or outside in the [next] room . . . I gave orders to buy a bedpan and a urine flask tomorrow. The former is very comfortable, and you do not cool off so much, and the urine flask is very good too, to keep it in.[6]

Again, he was ready with advice and assistance during the administration of an enema:

The maid says that you drank water during the night, that cannot have done you good . . ./ During the enema you must hold your breath, otherwise it runs out . . ./ Take a breath./ Don't hold your breath, breathe in./ Breathe in hard, keep it up./ Now hold your breath so the enema will act.[7]

These few lines alone refute the biographers' accounts of Karl's behavior during the last days before his departure. For the biographers assert that, while the uncle lay mortally ill, the nephew neglected him and spent his time playing billiards in cafés.

The Conversation Books also show how cautiously Karl went about making his uncle understand that his military equipment would cost money and that it was absolutely necessary to tip the regimental tailor if his uniform was to fit properly.

On December 12 Karl informed his uncle that he was now enrolled, that from that day on he would receive pay and keep from the regiment, and that he would travel to Iglau by stagecoach, because the mailcoach cost 38 florins more. However, his stay in Vienna was prolonged for a time, since he was present when the first abdominal puncture was performed on Ludwig, December 20. The Conversation Book shows that he continued to deal with the servants, with whom Ludwig had difficulties to the very last. He was still in Vienna for the Christmas holidays. Once again he asked his uncle for the money for the tailor, and Johann soothed Ludwig:

You do not have to buy anything more, for he has everything.[8]

There is no report as to how they parted.

The day after Karl left, Ludwig wrote to Dr. Bach:

Honored Friend!

Before my death I declare Karl van Beethoven my beloved
nephew my sole universal heir of all my possessions and property,
whereof principally 7 bank shares and whatever cash may be on
hand.

Should the laws prescribe modifications in this, attempt to turn
it as far as possible to his advantage. — I name you his Curator
and ask you together with Councillor Breuning his guardian to
assume a father's place toward him — God preserve you — a thousand thanks for the love and friendship you have shown me. —

(L.S.) Ludwig van Beethoven m.p.[9]

On January 13 Karl wrote the following letter to his uncle:

My dear Father,

I have received your letter, written by Schindler, only I beg
you in future to have the date added, so that I can find out how
the post goes. As to the state of your health, I rejoice to know that
you are in good hands, in me too the procedure of your previous
(or still present?) doctor aroused some distrust, now it is to be
hoped that all will go well.

I wrote to the Councillor [Breuning] some days ago, and indicated what I still wished to have. I would have written to you yourself about it, if I had not wished to spare you all fatigue. H[err]
von Breuning will attend to everything in the best way.

You wish to know my circumstances in detail. The captain under
whom I am is a very cultivated man, with whom I hope to get
along very well. I do not know if I have already written that I live
in a nice room with the sergeant-major of the company, a very
fine young man. — There is no such thing as an officers' mess here.
Everyone goes to eat where he pleases. For reasons of economy
I have already changed my eating place several times, but now
a common mess for cadets is to be set up — if it ever gets done.
But in the evening everybody has to look about for something
outside barracks. I have an orderly to wait on me, who gets 1
fl[orin] C[onvention] currency monthly aside from the outlays for
white lead and chalk for cleaning uniforms. Washing comes to a
few gulden too, if one wants it clean. There is a theater here too,
to which I go with the captain's permission. — These are more
or less the principal circumstances of which I can now inform you.
— Of what I still need and have already indicated in my letter
to the Councillor, the captain can naturally provide nothing until
he has the authorization in his hands, hence I ask you to mention

it to H[er]r v. Breuning. If you would send me something extra
on account of the expenses which I could not avoid and which I
also indicated, it would be very kind. I also counted on receiving
my pay from the day of my enrollment (Dec. 12, 1826), but this
has not been the case, for the enrollment list is still in Vienna.
Hence I must still live economically now. — And now another request. A first lieutenant of the regiment, who loves music and
particularly your works, wants within the next few days to have
the Concert pour le pianoforte dedié à Mr. Charles Nickel, Oeuvre
19. Vienne chez Hoffmeister Comp. performed at his quarters. By
an accident, however, the flute part has been lost, and so he has
turned to me. So I ask you to arrange to get the flute part and send
it to me very soon. — My address is of little importance. I receive
letters through the regimental adjutant. — Write to me again very
soon. I embrace you heartily. My regards to the Herr Councillor.

Your loving son
Carl.

P.S.

You must not think that the little privations to which I am now
subjected make my lot distasteful to me, rather be convinced that
I am happy in this life and only regret being so far from you. But
with time that too will be different.

As you see, I have myself attended to getting a seal with my
name.[10]

Karl apparently did not write at all during February; he was
doubtless too much occupied with his duties. Schindler seized the
occasion for last bitter reproaches against Karl; they are preserved in the Conversation Book. Ludwig was visibly depressed
because Karl had failed to answer a request from him to translate
a letter into English. Johann, trying to encourage him, took his turn
at attacking Karl:

You must be more cheerful, for sorrow hinders your recovery. —
The carnival at Iglau must be preventing him.[11]

Finally, on March 4, the long desired letter from Karl arrived. He
had previously sent the translation. This is the last letter that Karl
wrote to his uncle:

My dear Father.

I am just in receipt of the boots, which have been delivered to
me, and I thank you very much for them.

You will have received the translation of the letter to Smart; I
do not doubt that it will have a successful result.

Just today a cadet returned to the battalion who was on leave
in Vienna for some time, he says that he heard you had been saved
by some sherbet and that you are feeling very well. I only hope
that the latter is true, whatever the means may have been.

There is little new to tell about me, duty goes on in its usual
way, with only the difference that the weather is much milder and
hence guard-duty easier to bear.

Write me very soon how your health progresses; and please give
my warm regards to the Herr Councillor. I kiss you,

Your loving son Carl.

P.S.

Please frank your letters, because I have to pay much postage here,
and have a hard time making my account balance as it is.[12]

Karl apparently was not aware how serious his uncle's condition
was. What effect this letter had on the dying man, we do not know.

The final weeks of his illness were lightened for Beethoven by
a new relationship, which he developed to a boy about thirteen;
it shone through the darkness of his last days like a soothing reflection of his tormented passion for Karl. The boy was his friend
Stephan von Breuning's son, Gerhard. Ludwig first got to know
him when he moved into the Schwarzspanierhaus and was reconciled with Stephan. Even before the visit to Gneixendorf, Ludwig
had procured Clementi's pianoforte studies for Gerhard and in
other ways shown some interest in his musical education. Now as
the master lay in bed mortally ill, Gerhard regularly came in his
free time and entertained him, writing industriously on the slate
or in the Conversation Book. Gerhard later recounted his friendship with the dying Beethoven in his reminiscences, *Aus dem
Schwarzspanierhause*. The child was utterly devoted to the great
man, of whom he had heard so much, and in whose fame he indirectly shared through the relationship. He took much pride in
pleasing him; his greatest wish was to be allowed to address him
by the familiar "Du"; and he was overjoyed when Beethoven permitted it. He prattled on, criticizing the cook and the food, Ludwig's favorite and inexhaustible subject, promised to bring an
insecticide against the bedbugs which kept the master awake at
night, gave him accounts of concerts and plays, brought him
books, and solicitously inquired how he felt. In his relationship
to this bright, vivacious boy Ludwig re-experienced his relation-

ship to Karl to such a degree that he called him "trouser-button." He had used the same playful designation in his first letter to his nephew, as an expression of close physical relationship.

Yet his concern for Karl's future and welfare did not cease. The majority of Ludwig's letters during these last weeks were written to friends in England and contain requests for financial assistance. In particular, he begged his London admirers, Smart and Moscheles, to get up a benefit concert for him, on the ground that he was lying sick and completely destitute. This was a last gross misrepresentation of the facts, for Ludwig was still drawing his salary and in addition owned the seven shares of bank stock, whose value was 7441 florins. There was no question of destitution or even of great poverty; both Schindler and Breuning were opposed to Ludwig's misrepresenting his real situation. But Ludwig wanted to save the bank stocks for his beloved Karl, and did not mind falsifying the facts for the purpose. The London Philharmonic Society immediately granted him a hundred pounds, which were sent on March 1 and which he received on March 18, a week before his death. It testifies to the highmindedness of these English music-lovers that they at once came to Beethoven's assistance, although he had placed himself in no favorable light by the sale of the three unusable overtures in 1815. The certainty that he had saved the bank stocks for his beloved child must have been a great satisfaction to the master during his last days of suffering.

After the fifth abdominal puncture, the patient rapidly sank; he himself, as well as the doctors and his friends, had given up all hope of his recovery after the fourth operation. He died on March 26, during a thunderstorm. A flash of lightning, accompanied by loud thunder, suddenly illuminated the room with glaring light. At that moment the great man's Promethean nature once again asserted itself. He opened his eyes, raised his right hand, and, his fist clenched, looked upward for several seconds with a very serious, threatening expression.[13] It was a last act of rebellion at the moment of death. When he let the raised hand sink, his eyes closed forever. Therese — the last, hated female rival — was the only member of the family present at his death. Karl, who hurried to Vienna immediately upon receiving the news, arrived too late for the funeral; his daughters report that he still regretted it, even late in life.

Of Karl's further history, there is little to relate. He became an
excellent officer. He was officially described as: "able, well-
informed, of good and cheerful disposition, gentlemanly in his
behavior to civilians, accommodating in the regiment, kindly and
patient with his subordinates." [14] He left the service after five
years, being permitted to retain his status as an officer. In August,
1832 he married. His wife bore him four daughters and a son.
He had become heir to both of his uncles, for Johann's wife outlived Ludwig by only a year. So he was able to spend the rest of
his life as a man of leisure in Vienna. He was an irreproachable
husband and a good father who devoted himself entirely to bringing up his children. He is said to have improvised beautifully at
the piano. It is astonishing that the traumatic experiences of his
youth had no perceptible ill effect on the development of his
personality. Whether this is to be ascribed more to his strong
psychological constitution or to the good foundation of emotional
stability which the much maligned Johanna had been able to give
him in his early childhood, must remain an open question.

Karl van Beethoven never defended himself against the accusations of Beethoven's biographers. In silence, he allowed them
to invest the man Ludwig van Beethoven with a nimbus of glory
at his expense and the expense of truth. He cannot be denied the
credit due him for his behavior and attitude. He died in 1858, at
the age of fifty-two.

His children were less willing to accept the abuse and calumny
with which the biographers had distorted their father's image.
An otherwise totally unknown author, named Heinrich Heinemann,
wrote a play entitled "Beethoven and His Nephew." It represented
Karl with all the distortions which Beethoven's biographers had
imagined in the course of the years. In the *Wiener Tagblatt* of
March 17, 1903, Karl van Beethoven's children published a letter
to the author in which they emphatically stated that the play contained misrepresentations of their father. They raised the question:

> . . . at what period is our father supposed to have behaved so
> frivolously; for if in other cases it goes hand in hand, so to speak,
> that such profligate youths also show poor progress in their studies,
> we, on the contrary, are in possession of all his certificates, all
> of which are first-class, that is, 'eminent.' Before his open grave,

his former headmaster, as well as the Professor of Music Herr Bokler, pronounced eulogies in which both gentlemen described him as their best and most able pupil. In addition, during his military career he enjoyed the best conduct-rating; an honorable discharge from the same, which is likewise in our hands, may serve as proof. . . . But even granting that there was such a period in our father's life, would it not rather be admirable than blameworthy, and certainly not to be made a reproach to him even beyond the grave, that by moral force he escaped from it and still became the strong-principled, steadfast, and highly regarded man which, in the strictest sense of the word, he was . . .[15]

The play had very few performances.

Johanna too received yet another rehabilitation after Beethoven's death. Since a new guardian had to be appointed to replace Ludwig, she approached Dr. Bach, Ludwig's attorney, with the request that he arrange that the court name her brother-in-law Hotschevar, whom we have had occasion to mention before, to the post. Dr. Bach at once agreed and obtained the appointment. This shows that Dr. Bach had formerly acted against Johanna only under pressure from Ludwig, and that he saw no reason for objecting to her choice of a guardian concerning whom Ludwig, for his part, had expressed himself most insultingly. Dr. Bach, then, felt that Ludwig's hostility to Johanna was objectively groundless. With Beethoven's death, his motive for thwarting Johanna's wish had ceased to exist. Johanna outlived her son by many years; she died in poverty at the age of eighty-two. The van Beethoven family has since died out.

This concludes our presentation of the long tragedy of love which the great master underwent with his nephew and which finally killed him. No one who follows it with sympathy and comprehension can escape its terrible pathos.

Our presentation differs in essential respects from that of the usual Beethoven biographers. It attempts, as far as possible, to avoid evaluations, and, uninfluenced by his works, to recognize the psychological drives which are to be found in Beethoven's human relationships, especially in the most important of them, his relationship to his nephew. Such an undertaking is bound to encounter strong inner resistances. The reader must certainly have been aware of such resistances in himself to accepting the conclusions of our study.

For most people it is surprising — for many, indeed, it is painful — to learn that the ideal image of Beethoven which they have gained from the literature and formed in themselves from their experience of his works is in such contradiction to his real personality. For the partly conscious, but in greater measure unconscious, need in mankind to believe in ethically higher figures, paramount and superhuman, affects not only biographers; it is common to all men. They stubbornly defend the illusion of the ideal figure against the reality. In our culture this need for an ideal figure finds one of its typical forms of expression in overevaluation of the human personality of the artist. This idealization of the creative artist as a man is significantly reinforced from two interrelated sources.

The first is the experience of the work of art itself. The briefest résumé of the findings of depth-psychology in regard to the effect of art will suffice here. The work of art does not affect us only by producing conscious esthetic pleasure, but primarily because, on the basis of Fechner's "principle of esthetic enhancement," it opens suppressed sources of pleasure which, particularly in music, depend upon a regression to otherwise long abandoned, deeply repressed possibilities of enjoyment.[16] This "latent" factor in the enjoyment of art is far greater than the conscious esthetic factor.

The essential power of the great work of art and the intensity of the feelings which it releases must be primarily ascribed to the latent factor in its effect. He who, through his work, produces this effect in us is felt by us to be a man equipped with higher magical-supernatural powers beyond our experience; he becomes a conjurer and hero.

The hero is a mythological figure; hence his personality is the object of typical myth-formation. It is indicative of the early and intense heroization of Beethoven that such myths about him appeared even during his lifetime. A characteristic legend which early formed around him is based on the well-known "myth of the birth of the hero." [17] This myth serves to deny the hero's humble ancestry by relating that his parents were only foster-parents; in reality he is of far higher and more illustrious lineage. A king or ruler is a particularly frequent choice for the father. This or the like is what their legends relate of Cyrus, Romulus, Oedipus, Paris, Perseus, Hercules, Gilgamesh, and many other heroes. Now we learn from Wegeler and Ries [18] that Fayolle and Choron in their encyclopedia [19] assert that Beethoven was an illegitimate son of Friedrich Wilhelm II. Wegeler and Ries also report that Frederick the Great of Prussia was named as Ludwig's real father.[20] Despite the solicitations of his friends, Beethoven refused publicly to deny these legends of his exalted origin.

The second legend told of Beethoven likewise reflects a myth formed around the hero's childhood. This myth tells how an elder rival, recognizing future extraordinary characteristics in the hero as a boy, or learning of his future greatness through a prophecy, immediately attempts to do away with him or render him harmless. It is related that when Ludwig, still a child, was traveling with his mother in Holland, a pianist, jealous of the prodigy's playing, attempted to mutilate his fingers with a knife. As with all typical legends, no one knows what the sources of these two stories were.[21]

Nothing more clearly shows the imperious need to make a hero of the genius than the large number of idealizing portraits for which Beethoven posed to various painters — for example, the well-known portrait by Stieler. On the other hand, the greatest Viennese portrait-painter of Beethoven's time, Ferdinand G. Waldmüller, represented the composer as he might be supposed to have looked on the basis of our presentation of his relationship to his nephew. To be sure, his friends and contemporaries were outraged by Waldmüller's canvas, for it sadly shattered their illusion of the unity between work and personality.

The second source of the heroization of the artist in our culture is due to the increasing secularization of intellectual life from the end of the Middle Ages. Secularization led to the freeing of art and the artist from subservience to religion. It is observable that since this liberation from religious bonds, and with the growing assertion of the individual, the creative artist has been increasingly experienced and represented as an ethical figure. It is as if the inner need for ethically higher figures, which, with the growth of secularization, could no longer find full satisfaction in the realm of religion, was transferred to the realm of art. Thus, in a certain sense, the creative artist becomes the substitute for the saint. And in fact, with their eulogies of the ethical perfection of the genius, the biographies of artists often read like hagiographies — not least, many of the biographies of Beethoven.

In the case of no other genius, certainly, did idealizing biography find it more of a problem to distort the facts than in dealing with Beethoven.[22]

Heroization seeks to bridge over the contradiction between work and man, which in Beethoven's case was felt to be particularly strong and painful. But the contradiction itself can only be a matter of appearance. Basically, there must be unity between man and work. After all, it is the same personality which creates the works and reveals itself in human relationships; the same psychological motivations and drives impel the creator to produce his works and determine his conduct. The same inner conflicts are manifested in both.

Our presentation has shown what principles were at war in Beethoven and led to the immense conflict which he was unable to solve in his personal life. It is the *polarity between the male and female principle,* which he vainly sought to reconcile in his behavior. The assumption remains sound that the same polarity was also the basis of his work, and indeed the strongest incentive for his production. But we have no way of proving this; for here we reach the limits of present-day psychological knowledge. Two unscalable walls bar even a speculative psychological advance into the unexplored realm of the musical work. The first wall specifically surrounds the musical work of art. It consists in the non-objectiveness of music. This cardinal characteristic of music makes the methods employed by depth-psychology in the investigation of works of art impossible in the case of music. In general, the works of the other arts are copies of reality. The choice of the real prototype and the specific alteration to which it is subjected in the work of art are determined, among other things, by the given psychological content and psychological powers of the individual creative artist. From the distortion which reality undergoes in the work of art, from knowledge of the psychological structures and motivations common to all mankind, and from the special forms and contents which, on the basis of the particular circumstances of the individual artist's life, these structures and motivations are assumed to have in the particular case, depth-psychology attempts to draw conclusions as to the latent, i.e., unconscious, content of the work of art. This method cannot be applied in the realm of music, where the work of art is not a copy of reality. At most, it might be possible to find, in the *form* of the musical work of art, correspondences with the psychological formations and drives deducible from the artist's biography; but all such formulations must be undertaken with the utmost caution.

In any case, the authors of this book are not competent to undertake an investigation of the form of Beethoven's compositions and to compare the results with the dynamic structures elicited by the application of depth-psychology to the investigation of Beethoven's personality. We shall, however, remark that certain musicologists who apply Guido Adler's method of stylistic criticism to Beethoven's works arrive at results which agree with our presentation of his inner conflict. Thus Ernest Newman finds that a *principle of polarity* underlies Beethoven's production during all of his three periods. Newman speaks of a tendency in Beethoven's entire work "to conceive and manipulate things in antitheses." According to Newman an "inner crisis" is the predetermining and necessary basis of Beethoven's creation.[23]

We shall hardly err in assuming that "polarity" and "antithesis" in Beethoven's work correspond to the conflict between the male and female principle which we have been led to deduce from his conduct. This conflict was certainly one of the most important dynamic motivations of his creation; to be sure, this assumption in no wise explains what enables the creator to produce the work of art from the conflict.

Here we meet the second barrier which opposes psychological penetration into the secret of the work of art. As yet we know nothing of the artist's mysterious gift which enables him to shape a work of art from the drives, defenses, and conflicts which fight for expression in him. Before the work of art, Freud says, "analysis must, alas, lay down its arms." [24]

It is possible, however, that a recent direction in research may provide further understanding of this mysterious ability of the creative artist. This youngest branch of modern psychological investigation is "ego-psychology." [25] It too is based upon Sigmund Freud's great discoveries and is a continuation of them. As its name implies, ego-psychology concerns itself with the ego, its dynamic factors, and the mechanisms operative in it. Psychoanalysis employs the term "ego" to designate the relatively organized part of the psychological personality, the part which is directed toward reality. Consciousness and feeling of self are bound up with the ego. One of the most important functions of the ego is to adjudicate between the claims laid on the life of the psyche by basic drives, external reality, and the moral component of the personality, to dismiss unrealizable demands or to keep them at bay by various kinds of defenses.

Study of the ego has shown that it is capable of isolating from one another different areas and possibilities of expression for a psychological conflict. The result of the conflict may be entirely different in different areas. We must assume that the same conflict which remains irresolvable in the life of the creative genius — and indeed, in Beethoven's case, led to his death — can be brought to an entirely different issue in a different area of ego-activity, that of artistic sublimation. If the conflict is transferred to the autonomous ego-area of artistic creation, it is thereby freed from the original dichotomy of irreconcilable opposites. Hence, by the aid of the creative gift, it can be integrated, brought into harmony, and shaped into a work of art. We may expect that the surprising fact that work and conduct, while in such contrast, are yet produced by the same motivations, will become more comprehensible through increasing knowledge of the ego-mechanisms. On the basis of a recognition of the possibilities of such an autonomization of certain activities and areas of expression of the ego, we can find it understandable that a deeply disturbed, even psychotic, artist creates most perfect works of art. To be sure, this does not "explain" the work of art. The narrow limits of our present psychological knowledge will not permit us to go beyond this simple indication of the common basis for conduct and creation in the form of the motivating inner conflict. But all extension of our understanding of artistic creation must depend upon an insight into the fundamental structure of the psychological content and dynamisms of the artist's personality. It is these which, in Beethoven's case, we have sought to exhibit in this book.

APPENDICES

I

LETTER TO THE IMPERIAL-ROYAL LOWER-AUSTRIAN LANDRECHTE [1]

Vienna, Sept. 25,1818.

When the summons of the I.-R. L.-A. Landrechte of the 22nd of this month was sent to me at my present place of residence Mödling, it happened that I was in Vienna on business and on account of this circumstance could not obey the same at the appointed time. Hence I avail myself of the means of a written explanation, which I herewith present to an I.-R. L.-A. Landrechte.

The mother of my ward, who on account of her moral incapacity was entirely and strictly excluded from his education by the I.-R. L.-A. Landrechte, has again, after several unsuccessful attempts to hinder by her interference the plan of education outlined and followed by me, presumed to take a step to which as exclusively appointed guardian of my nephew Karl van Beethoven I can by no means give my consent.

In order to attain her end she has recourse to means which in and of themselves testify to base-mindedness, for naturally she seizes upon my deafness, as she calls it, and my alleged ill-health, as a pretext to cast a disadvantageous light on the education of my nephew.

As regards the first point, by all who know me at all intimately it is too well known that every verbal communication between me and my nephew, as well as between [me and] other persons is carried on in the easiest manner, for any obstacle to arise from this. In addition, my health was never better than now and from this side too there is no reason that my nephew's education could be endangered.

After having had him instructed in Herr Giannatasio's educational institution for two years entirely at my expense, I now took him home with me, in order to observe whether he possessed more inclination to music or to the sciences.

Here under my eyes he had every opportunity to develop his talent for music, in which I myself daily instructed him for two and a half hours, likewise at the same time to continue his school studies.

I found that he has more inclination to the sciences. That throughout this past summer in the country with me he worked as diligently as in Vienna to keep up his studies, is most adequately confirmed by the certificates Exhibit A herewith, which I ask to have returned. As regards the intention of the mother of my ward, to place him in the Konvikt, I must most definitely declare myself against this proposal on the following grounds: I. Those conditions which the court prescribed to exclude the mother not only from the guardianship but also from all influence upon education and communication with the ward are still in force. II. The ward's being placed in the Konvikt would itself frustrate the precaution of the court, since the special restrictions in regard to this mother cannot be acknowledged there so that she would easily manage to ask for the boy and take him home with her in her company. She has dared to make attempts of this sort even at my home by bribing the servants and leading the boy to untruth and deceit, despite the fact that she is free to see and speak with her son in my presence, if only she expresses her wish to do so and if circumstances permit it. III. That the mother of my ward already made such secret attempts during his residence at the Institute and that her communication with the ward was recognized as in the highest degree injurious to him by the principal of the Institute, is sufficiently shown by Exhibits B and C. IV. Since the time when the I.-R. Landrechte entrusted the exclusive guardianship of my nephew to me, I have not only paid all the costs of his education myself (— for the small contribution from the mother, only recently begun to be received as indemnification, can hardly enter into consideration in this connection —), but also constantly taken all care and trouble to have him instructed as well as possible in everything requisite to become a good and useful citizen of the state, so much so indeed that the tenderest father cannot better care for his own child. — For this I do not expect the mother's thanks, but I hope for the appreciation of the high guardianship. V. The plan for the future higher education of my nephew has long been outlined and followed. Hence only a very harmful disturbance in the continuing course of his education would arise if, suddenly, a change in conformity with other views should result.

Furthermore I shall give proper notice to the I.-R. L.-A. Landrechte on the occasion of every proposed change with regard to my nephew, in order to embark upon what is fitting in unison with the same, in which respect it might become more and more necessary, in order to avoid every possible disturbance and impediment, to exclude the boy's mother from all influence, not only as, in the case affecting her, it is stipulated by Paragraph 191 of the Civil Law Code — certainly a very wise stipulation — but also because, in view of her intellectual and moral characteristics, now that the boy is growing older, she appears less and less suited to mingle in his education for manhood.

But in such a manner Frau Johanna van Beethoven following the procedure of the Court by which as morally incompetent she was excluded from his education and from communication with her child, as well as after the decision of the I.-R. L.-A. Landrechte of January 19, 1816, through which the education of my nephew is entrusted solely and exclusively to me as guardian — how, I say, she can dare to present herself as guardian of her minor son is somewhat explicable to me from her bold behavior in all circumstances.

Ludwig van Beethoven
as guardian of my nephew Karl van Beethoven

II

EXTRACT FROM PROTOCOL OF THE IMPERIAL-ROYAL LOWER-AUSTRIAN LANDRECHTE [2]

Ludwig van Beethoven examined:

How did his nephew leave him?

He did not know exactly; his nephew had made himself culpable; he had charged him with it and the same day in the evening he had received a note of farewell. He could not tell the cause of his departure; his mother may have asked him to come to her the day before, but it might have been fear of punishment.

What had his nephew done?

He had a housekeeper who had been recommended to him by Giannatasio; two of her letters to Miss Giannatasio and one of the latter's had fallen into his hands; in them it was stated that his nephew had called the servants abusive names, had withheld money and spent it on sweetmeats.

In whose care was his nephew?

He had provided him with a Correpetitor for pianoforte playing, French and drawing who came to the house; these studies occupied all the leisure time of his nephew so completely that he needed no care, moreover, he could not trust any of his servants with the supervision of his nephew, as they had been bribed by the boy's mother; he had placed him in the hands of a priest for the development of his musical talent, but the mother had got into an agreement with him also. He would place his ward in the Convict, but the supervision was not strict enough there among so many pupils.

Did he have any testimonials touching his nephew's studies?

He had appended them to his last examination.

Had his nephew not spoken disrespectfully of his mother in his presence?

No; besides, he had admonished him to speak nothing but the truth; he had asked his nephew if he was fond of his mother and he answered in the negative.

How did he get the boy back?

With the help of the police. He had gone to the mother in the forenoon to demand him of her, but she would promise nothing except that she would deliver him back in the evening; he had feared that she intended to take him to Linz, where his brother lived, or to Hungary; for that reason he had gone to the police; as soon as he got him back he placed him in the care of Giannatasio.

What were his objections to having his nephew sent to the Convict?

It was not advisable at present because, as the professor had said, there were too many pupils there and the supervision over a boy like his ward was not adequate.

What means did he purpose to employ in the education of his ward?

His ward's greatest talent was in study and to this he would be held. His means of subsistence were the half of his mother's pension and the interest on 2,000 florins. Heretofore the difference between this sum and the cost had been paid by him and he was willing to assume it in the future if the matter could but once be put in order. As it was not practicable to place his nephew in the Konvikt now, he knew only of two courses open to him: to keep a steward for him who should always be with him, or to send him for the winter to Giannatasio. After half a year he would send him to the Mölker Konvikt, which he had heard highly commended, or if he were but of noble birth, give him to the Theresianum.

Were he and his brother of the nobility and did he have documents to prove it?

"Van" was a Dutch predicate which was not exclusively applied to the nobility; he had neither a diploma nor any other proof of his nobility.

III

EXTRACT FROM PROTOCOL OF THE IMPERIAL-ROYAL LOWER-AUSTRIAN LANDRECHTE [3]

Johanna van Beethoven examined:

How did her son come to her from the house of his guardian?

He had come to her in the evening for fear of punishment and because he did not like to live with his uncle.

Had she advised him to return to his uncle?

Yes; but her son did not want to do so because he feared maltreatment.

It looked as if she had concealed her son?

She had written to her brother-in-law that she would send her son back to him, but she had not seen him for a long time and was therefore glad to have him with her for awhile, and for this reason she had not sent him back at once.

Had she been forbidden to see her son?

Her wish to do so had been frustrated by telling her of different places where she might see him, but when she went to the places he was not there.

Had her son been taken from her by the police?

She had herself taken him to the police at 4 o'clock.

How did she learn of the plan to send her son out of the country?

Giannatasio had disclosed the project to the police.

Did she consider that her son had been well treated at his uncle's?

She thought it unsuitable for the reasons given in her former application. She wished to say in particular that v. Beethoven had only one servant and that one could not rely on servants; he was deaf and could not converse with his ward; there was nobody to look after the wants of her son satisfactorily; his cleanliness was neglected and supervision of his clothing and washing; persons who had brought him clean linen had been turned back by his guardian.

What prospects had she for caring for her son?

She had previously had the assurance of Count von Dietrichstein that her son would be accepted at the Konvikt; she had not been to him since because her application [to the Court] had been rejected.

In whose presence had her son spoken disrespectfully of her?

She had not herself heard him do so, nor could she mention the names of persons who had heard him.

From what source would she meet the deficiency in her income which would have to be applied to the support of her son?

She had no fortune herself but the Hofconcipist Hotschevar would defray the expenses.

Was her husband of noble birth?

So the brothers had said; the documentary proof of nobility was said to be in the possession of the oldest brother, the composer. At the legal hearing on the death of her husband, proofs of nobility had been demanded; she herself had no document bearing on the subject.

IV

APPEAL BY HOTSCHEVAR [4]

Right Honorable I.-R. Lower-Austrian Landrechte.

Frau Johanna v. Beethoven, widow of the late I.-R. Cashier, has under same date submitted to this high court a petition wherein she repeatedly asks the supreme guardianship to grant her permission to enter her only son, Carl v. Beethoven — at present under the tutelage of his uncle and guardian, Herr Ludwig v. Beethoven, musical composer — for board and training in the I.-R. University Konvikt.

Weighty reasons prompt me to use the present report to draw the attention of the Right Honorable I.-R. L.-A. Landrechte to a number of circumstances which may be expected to be deemed qualified to lend support to the petition of Frau v. Beethoven.

Before anything else I beg leave to state the reasons which induced me to undertake the present representation in writing. The *first* reason is the relations of kinship which exist between myself and Frau v. Beethoven. My wife and the late mother of Frau v. Beethoven were step-sisters; which fact suffices to explain that a man, especially when requested to do so and seeing a passionate pursuit of the matter carried to extremes, will not hesitate to embrace by a public act the cause of a hard-pressed person who has received ample punishment for her long since superannuated misconduct, and indeed that he will rather feel it to be even his duty to do so for this additional reason, that *secondly* everyone who has the rights of humanity at heart must be allowed, and in accordance with § 217 of our General Civil Code expressly is allowed in the cases referred to in said paragraph, to employ his good services to intercede with the legal authorities and thus, since the present matter comes under the jurisdiction of this high court, to intercede with this supreme guardianship authority.

Thirdly, it seems hardly possible that it should be considered blameworthy on my part if I, having been for several years tutor and educator in noble houses, employ, on behalf of a boy to whom I am related if not by blood at least by marriage and whose talents attract attention at first sight, the pedagogical and psychological knowledge which I have gathered, and if I present to the supreme guardianship authority, which cannot possibly enter into matters pertaining to the domestic conditions of its wards except in so far as complaints are filed against them, a few notable circumstances for its august consideration.

Accordingly I claim

1. that the widow Johanna v. Beethoven was unrightfully deprived of the complete influence on her child, partly with the knowledge and partly without the knowledge of this high and noble [court].

2. that there is no doubt that the talented twelve-year-old boy Carl v. Beethoven cannot in any way be allowed to remain *under the exclusive* influence of his uncle and guardian, Herr Ludwig v. Beethoven, except at great risk to his well-being and with the danger of being morally and physically warped.

I proceed to explain myself in greater detail, to wit with reference to 1. Every mother, provided there is no superseding guardianship established in the [father's] last will and testament, has a claim next to the paternal grandfather to the guardianship over her child if she is not excluded therefrom by legal obstacles. There were to my knowledge three Messrs. v. Beethoven who were brothers. Their excellent qualities notwithstanding, all three of them are eccentric minds, not excepting the late Carl v. Beethoven. This truthful and frank statement cannot detract

from the honor of Messrs. v. Beethoven but it does prove incontroverti-
bly that, overpowered by their temperaments, they do not in all their
actions and undertakings set to work with the requisite circumspection
and calm dispassionateness, and often go to extremes which in a certain type of endeavor are most disadvantageous to the ends to be gained.
That Messrs. Ludwig and Carl v. Beethoven were eccentrics is a point
to which I can bear witness as an impartial and calm observer and
I can corroborate it by written evidence; for Messrs. Ludwig and Carl v.
Beethoven were brothers, but in their relations they were more enemies
than friends, and it will not be asserting too much if I say that Herr
Carl v. Beethoven was only on good terms with his brother, Herr Ludwig v. Beethoven, when he was in need of money; indeed, one is
tempted to assert that the boy Carl v. Beethoven and the rights of
future proprietorship in him in course of time became an object of bargaining between the two brothers. This is in part proven by the text
of the will which Frau v. Beethoven cites under A in her petition and
by the codicil B, but still more by the holograph letter drafts herewith
submitted, Nos. 1 and 2, in which the fact is expressly touched upon
that Herr Carl v. Beethoven agrees to a certain composition in respect
to payment of 1500 fr. [*sic*] only on condition that his brother, Herr
Ludwig v. Beethoven, return the written instrument relative to the
guardianship over the boy Carl. "*Never,*" says the father, "would I have
drawn up an instrument of this kind if my long illness had not caused
me great expenses; it is only in consideration of these that I could, *under
compulsion,* sign this instrument; but at the time I was determined to
demand the return of same at an opportune moment or to invalidate it
by another instrument, for my brother is too much a composer and hence
can *never,* according to my idea, and with my consent, become my son's
guardian."
    Let no one object that these drafts are without date or signature and
hence prove nothing. It suffices that Herr Carl v. Beethoven's own hand
cannot be denied, and it appears from them that Herr Carl v. Beethoven saw that the guardianship over his child could not well be entrusted
to Herr Ludwig v. Beethoven, and further that Herr Carl v. Beethoven
himself deserves to be called an eccentric person.
    It is true that Herr Ludwig v. Beethoven received the guardianship
under the will, but Herr Carl v. Beethoven still had enough clarity of
mind to provide on his deathbed through the codicil to his will B dated
November 14, 1815, that, since he has observed that Herr Ludwig v.
Beethoven wishes after the demise to take the boy Carl *wholly* in
charge and withdraw same *wholly* from his mother's supervision and
training, and since, furthermore, not the best harmony prevails between
Herr Ludwig v. Beethoven and Frau v. Beethoven, he has considered
it necessary to stipulate that it is by no means his wish that his son Carl
be taken away from his mother but rather that same is always to remain

with his mother as long as his future career permits, hence she quite as much as Herr Ludwig v. Beethoven is to exercise the guardianship (thus Herr Ludwig v. Beethoven is to be only co-guardian).

"Only by unity," his still active paternal feeling says on his deathbed, "can the object which I had in view in appointing my brother guardian of my son be attained; wherefore, for the *welfare of my child,* I recommend compliance to my wife and *more moderation* to my brother. God permit them to be harmonious for the sake of my child's welfare. This is the last wish of the dying husband and brother."

Little knowledge of psychology is required to judge — since the express voice of the dying brother and husband, dictating to the pen his last words and natural instincts for the welfare of a promising son, confirmed it — how little Herr Ludwig v. Beethoven, despite his unmistakable good and indeed best will and the magnanimity he otherwise displays in dealing with the boy, is qualified to exercise the guardianship. Thus it is not at all in keeping with the spirit of the will and was not the intent of Herr Carl v. Beethoven to entrust the guardianship *exclusively* to his brother whom he urged on his deathbed to moderation in his passionate and eccentric behavior.

Far rather it was and must have been the intent of the father to accord the mother too a *joint* influence on the education and guardianship of the boy Carl v. Beethoven [*sic*].

According to exhibits A and B accompanying Frau v. Beethoven's petition, Herr Ludwig v. Beethoven found means to arrogate to himself the exclusive guardianship. His trump card was an investigation which was to be ascribed rather to her husband than to Frau v. Beethoven and which in no case could have any bearing on the son Carl and can have such bearing even less at this time when it is a superannuated affair. Partly by means of a planned course of action on his own part, partly by means of officious scandalmongers, Herr Ludwig v. Beethoven managed to induce even a supreme guardianship authority to agree to a termination of the mother's influence on the conduct of the affairs of the guardianship. This termination would appear severe, much too severe, if one more closely considers the circumstances as they were previously set forth. Yet the high Landrechte permitted the mother to visit her child from time to time. But the guardian managed, through his adviser and scandalmonger Giannatasio del Rio, to make certain that, in accordance with letters E and F of her petition, she was never able to see her son. This was certainly not the intent of the high court, and such a treatment clearly conflicts with the advice issued by the Landrechte on February 20, 1816. It sounds strangely in letter E, written by Giannatasio del Rio, manager of an educational institution, when he writes to a mother who wants to visit her child: "I consequently request that you will not again trouble yourself to come to my house because in that case you would expose yourself to the *most unpleasant scenes.*"

No wonder then that the eccentric guardian, as the parish priest
Fröhlich confirms, expressed delight when the boy, against his own
wishes and simply to flatter his guardian, called his mother a raven-
mother. There is therefore no denying that Herr Ludwig v. Beethoven
did achieve his purpose of *completely* depriving Frau v. Beethoven of
every kind of influence on her child, against the express will of her
husband, against the legal decrees, and against the high will of the
supreme guardianship authority.

With reference to 2., Frau v. Beethoven has already demonstrated in
her petition and its exhibits, and especially the testimony H contributed
by the parish priest Fröhlich of Mödling, that the boy Carl v. Beethoven
will be warped in his physical and moral development, and that it would
be of the greatest detriment to him, if Herr Ludwig v. Beethoven is any
longer allowed the *sole* guardianship and *all* the influence on the boy's
education. No more seems needed than the fact that the dying father
made it sufficiently clear in the codicil to his will and in his letters that
Herr Ludwig v. Beethoven was not fit on account of his exaggerated
and eccentric ideas to be the *sole* guardian.

In general I can state with full conviction that in accordance with
my psychological and pedagogical knowledge and experience Carl v.
Beethoven is greatly neglected — or, to put it more plainly, misdi-
rected — in his physical and moral upbringing.

In support of this, Frau v. Beethoven has already furnished some
specific data in her representation, especially the trustworthy testimony
H of the parish priest Fröhlich. But in addition I too am in a position
to assure this high court from my own experience that I have personally
satisfied myself as to the behavior of the boy Carl v. Beethoven and
that, upon seeing him only once, when he recently ran away from his
guardian, I deduced the following sad conditions. Namely, the boy
Carl v. Beethoven is not well cared for *physically;* his hands and feet
are frost-bitten, he has no winter clothes; he seems not to change his
underwear in weeks; for a handkerchief, a piece of blotting paper often
has to serve, and since Herr v. Beethoven is a bachelor, little thought
seems to be given to cleanliness of clothes and body. That his *moral*
training is in a bad state is evident from the parish priest Fröhlich's
testimony. From all this it is clear that the boy was led to entertain
in increased measure the enmity which for years, and indeed from the
very beginning, prevailed between Herr Ludwig and Frau Johanna v.
Beethoven, to smother all filial affection, and completely to disavow
a child's duties to his mother. In religion the boy holds warped ideas,
as witness the manifest evidence furnished by his actions and demeanor in church, in school, and in the street, or he has little respect
for the teachings of our faith. In his general behavior he is a hypocrite,
he says that he must lie and equivocate, for if he were to tell the truth,
his guardian would not believe him, he must always speak otherwise
than he thinks, than the facts are. He voices bold views in regard to

freedom and license, has a tendency to pilferings, of which he has
already been guilty toward his guardian; in short, under the exclusive
supervision and guidance of a guardian whose very physical condition
disqualifies him for the task, the boy Carl v. Beethoven runs the risk
of degenerating completely and of becoming a dangerous member of
society, for, being spirited and perversely inclined, he is not held within
the proper bounds and cannot be by his unfit guardian, rather, indeed,
he unfortunately finds too much opportunity for his perverse inclinations and too much food for degenerating further, he learns to ignore
filial duties and religion and is, generally speaking, spoiled both physically and morally, in part because from the beginning the guardian
was principally concerned with trying to smother in him his filial affection for his mother, in part because the guardian is physically and
morally incapable of putting into effect his fundamentally good intentions by other than wrong means.

It is unmistakable that Herr v. Beethoven — not considering the
enmity between himself and the mother, which he entertains partly
from his own passionateness, partly at the promptings of officious
scandalmongers — has the best intention to care for the boy. However,
the choice of appropriate means is always but a burden for him, because
he has managed to exclude all other influence on the guardianship and
especially that of the mother. No one begrudges him the praise which
the periodical "Janus," No. 1, October 3, 1818, recently meted out to
him. Yet it is only right if we likewise quote Janus in exclaiming: "Let
it be hoped that the results will not contradict his expectations."

How little moderation Herr Ludwig v. Beethoven possesses and how
he may rightly be called cynical (cf. Janus, p. 6), appears from the attached letter No. 3; and I say once again that one is glad to grant his
magnanimity in dealing with the boy, but yet I must, together with
the mother who has been deeply hurt and all too severely and passionately treated, most urgently implore him — since the boy, despite the
magnanimity and good intentions of his uncle, is in danger of being
completely corrupted — either to heed the clear indications of his late
brother and entirely resign the exercise of the guardianship, or at least
— though in view of his exaggerated ideas there is unfortunately little
hope of this — to concede to the mother, or to someone better qualified,
the kind of joint dispassionate influence in the matter which is indis-
pensably necessary to save the boy from imminent ruin.

After this frank but unfortunately true analysis, which cannot in any
way detract from the fame and kindheartedness of Herr Ludwig v. Beethoven because it does not fail to recognize his excellent intentions but
merely reproves his exaggerated ideas and choice of wrong means —
and rightly so, since the matter at stake is the salvation of a talented boy
— I join the deeply hurt mother and with a quiet heart leave to the
august judgment of this high and noble court the decision as to what
it will graciously see fit to decree in regard to the future education of

the boy and the exercise of the guardianship over him, in consideration of the fact that the foregoing makes plain that Herr Ludwig v. Beethoven should be considered physically and morally unfit to exercise the same.

Vienna, December 11, 1818   Jacob Hotschevar

                              I.-R. Hofconcipist

V

MEMORANDUM [5]

To the I.-R. L.-A. Landrechte

                                 December 15, 1818

It first appeared to me superfluous further to inform an I.-R. L-A. Landrechte. But after the recent events, which, as I am more and more convinced, are brought about by machinations in order to effect a separation of my ward from me, I find it expedient and necessary to explain in further detail the method I have hitherto followed. That hence the strictest truth prevails [herein] is guaranteed by my views and my publicly recognized moral character. The following enclosures will furnish the most conclusive proofs in this respect.

Enclosure A contains the desired school certificates for my ward. They sufficiently show his progress and moral conduct, but in a few branches of science would perhaps have been still more favorable, if the continual disturbances on the part of his mother had not caused impediments. — The two letters of the servants are at the moment no longer to be found among my papers. Their contents are wretched and for the most part exaggerated common gossip, as for instance that my ward almost pulled down the caretaker's bell, that he put a capon among the wood, where it was suffocated, that he kept back 30 kreuzer from a purchase and bought himself sweets, abused the servants, etc. As these letters came to me, so that I might reproach my ward for this behavior, exactly on the day when by connivance he left my house in the evening, it is evident what the intention in writing or perhaps even dictating them was, namely, to furnish a pretext for his departure. Pray, how could servants presume to enter into correspondence with third persons of higher station concerning the behavior of my ward.

Enclosures B give the small contributions from the pension of my ward's mother toward his education as well as the expenses which I paid for the same purpose from my own funds. From this it is clearly apparent that it would have been impossible to give him a decent life and adequate education, if I had not willingly made such a great sacrifice.

Enclosure C contains two letters to me from the Principal of the Institute, Herr von Giannatasio del Rio, where my ward was formerly. They amply show how harmful he considered the mixing of the mother in the matter of my ward's education, and, in view of the sufficiently recognized circumstances, require no further discussion.

In addition to the very considerable expenses for the Institute, I further, as enclosures show, paid the attorney and solicitor on my nephew's behalf out of my open pocket, undertook a journey to Retz on his business at my expense, privately paid masters for his instruction in science and in music, and, in addition to other unforeseen expenses which it would be tedious to mention here, also bore the considerable costs of an operation for rupture successfully performed on my nephew. On the other hand, the contribution from the half of the mother's pension was very inconsiderable, and in addition I first received the same only very late, and actually at present have received nothing at all for the last half year.

So much for the economic side of my guardianship. So far as the scientific and moral education of my ward is concerned, I have before all things therein endeavored, by word and example, to bring him up to be a good man and a capable citizen, and to enable him to acquire the necessary knowledge.

Hence I first put him in the Institute of Herr von Giannatasio del Rio, which, however, in course of time did not suffice for me. Last summer I accordingly took my ward to live with me under the superintendence of an excellent tutor at my expense and, since the time was approaching when a decision must be made as to his future profession, took him with me to the country in order to see how far his inclination for music would develop under my own direction, without his school studies being set aside, as the certificates show; for here too I kept a tutor. Although he showed no little aptitude for it [music], yet finally his inclination was more to science and from that moment my intention was to let him enjoy public school instruction.

On returning to town I at once sent him to public school, and at home had him enjoy the necessary private instruction, both in preparation for school, and in music, French and drawing. After the last sad interruption by the mother, I immediately placed him in the Giannatasio Institute.

At present, since he sees and repents his faults, and only begs to be allowed to remain with me, he is once more with me in my house under the direction of an experienced tutor and myself, who [i.e., the tutor] accompanies him to and from school, and at home constantly attends to his instruction and supervision jointly with myself, and for this I do not spare the considerable expense of 600 fl. per annum without [reckoning] other emoluments for this tutor.

And so I shall continue further to overcome all obstacles which might be placed in my way, having in view only the best for my ward and mindful of the wishes of my deceased brother, as well as of the duty which my legal guardianship, my relationship, and humanity impose on me in this difficult matter, in connection with which, in view of my honest efforts, the purity of my intentions and my purpose, I shall be ready at any moment to render to the worshipful I-R. L.-A. Landrechte, as the supreme guardian, an accounting in the most satisfactory manner.

Ludwig van Beethoven,
Guardian of my nephew, Carl van Beethoven

VI

MEMORIAL [6]

Vienna, Feb. 18, 1820.

Information concerning Frau Beethoven. It is painful for one of my sort to be obliged even in the least to sully himself with a person like Frau B.; but as this is the last attempt to save my nephew, I for his sake accept this humiliation. Lite abstine, nam vincens, multum amiseris. (Abstain from strife, for even if you conquer, you will lose much.) How much the rather would I be guided by this, but the good of a third person does not permit it to me.

Frau B. had no education, her parents, bourgeois upholsterers by profession, left her mostly to herself, hence even in her early years she developed evil propensities. Even while still in her parents' house she had to appear before the police authorities because she had accused their maid of being the perpetrator of something of which she was herself the tool, and the maid was found entirely innocent, however the police let her go out of [certain] considerations, with the promise to improve.

In 1811, when, already a wife and mother, though as such highly frivolous and lax, headstrong and malicious, she had already partly sacrificed her good name, she committed a new more frightful crime, which even brought her before the Criminal Court; here too she again calmly alleged that entirely innocent persons were involved in her crime. Finally she had to admit that she was the sole perpetrator. Only through the greatest efforts of her husband and my friends was she, if not unpunished, at least spared from the most shameful punishment and again set free.

This most terrible occurrence brought a severe illness upon my late brother, through which he had always to lead a sickly life. Only my beneficent support spared him his life a while longer. Some time before his death, she took a considerable sum of money, without his knowledge. This led him to wish to divorce her, but the grim reaper came and divorced him from — life, November 15, 1815; — The day before his death he appointed me, at the same time thanking me as his benefactor in his will, to be sole guardian of his son. Hardly had I left him for a few hours the same day, than my brother told me, when I returned to him, that during my absence something else had been added, which he had been misled into signing. (It was the codicil, in which she got herself declared guardian as well as I.) He asked me to get this back from the lawyer at once, but he was not to be found that day, although at my brother's request I several times presented myself at his lodging. The next morning early about 5 o'clock my brother was no more. — Nevertheless all that was lacking was a witness to testify that my brother had wanted to destroy the codicil, if it had not already lost its force through § 191 of the Civil Law Code, according to which the worthy Landrechte too appear to have granted it no validity, since they confirmed me as sole guardian.

It is obvious that in 1815 she had yet taken no step toward her moral improvement. After what has been related above, her dishonesty to her son was revealed anew in the inventory. I remained silent, for I wished only to save my nephew's soul. Immediately after the death of my brother, she was in secret commerce with a lover, through which alone the modesty of her innocent son was injured, she was to be found on all dance-floors and at merrymakings, while her son had not even what is needful and was left alone by her to a miserable maid. What would have become of him, if I had not taken his situation to heart?!

That from 1815–1820 she likewise always showed herself to be a corrupt, extremely designing person, practicing the art of dissimulation to the highest degree, is proved by the following: Whenever she possibly could, wherever my nephew might be, with me or in the Institute, she attempted to impart erroneous ideas to him, [to maintain] secret contacts with him [and] to instruct him in everything abominable, such as deceit and lies. She even tried to lead him astray with money and again gave him money to abuse other people for her evil ends. A few times, when he had worst transgressed, she was able to entice him to her, where he was then told that such a thing was of no importance. Me, his benefactor, support and stay, in short, his father in the true sense of the word, she attempted to vilify by the most abominable intrigues, cabals, slanders, and to infuse her moral poison into all, even the most innocent. Finally her hellish and yet imprudent activity reached a new apogee under the worthy supreme guardianship of the Magistracy, for at the time of the coming Easter examination in 1819 she drove my nephew to bring it about that he should go into the second or third class, on which account he could not be removed from here. In me she had always found a dam which she vainly sought to demolish. But as guardian Herr von Tuscher was little listened to and regarded by the magisterial supreme guardianship. The latter took a particular pleasure in enjoying certain infernal dainties with this amiable woman, and hence my nephew has to be eternally grateful to her that he has lost a whole year of his educational life through the liking which this respected supreme guardianship took to his loving mother. One may well imagine that this worthy supreme guardianship naturally backed its favorite according to her deserts, hence we see her from October 1819 until now, February 1820, guardian of her son, and the true and only guardian, benefactor, support, stay of his deceased brother and the father of my nephew [sic], as of my nephew himself, abased in the basest, most vulgar way. But we have now reached the information concerning the supreme guardianship on the part of the Vienna Magistracy.

No chance more odious and more full of evil consequences could befall my nephew than unfortunately from lack of nobility to fall to this supreme guardianship, and I [i.e., to me], the guardian, support, stay, promoter of everything good in him. Frau B.'s hypocritical nature, her mendacity, seem to have found a good place there.

Mendatio comites tenebrae. (Lying is the companion of darkness.) The principles of the worthy Landrechte were immediately departed from, according to which she was not only allowed no influence on the [boy's] education [sic]. Since it also once happened that while the Magistracy had the supreme guardianship, I once in exasperation pulled my nephew from his chair, because he had done something very bad, and since he also, after the operation for a hernia performed two years earlier still had to wear a truss, this in the rapid turning around caused him some pain at the most sensitive spot. I immediately sent for Herr v. Smettana and he at once declared it was of no consequence and that not the slightest damage was done. The same accident had already occurred to him once when he was playing with other boys, on which occasion too Herr v. Smettana was called; but I immediately had Smettana put in writing for me what the situation was. One can well imagine that such a man would not lie to please me, still less did his duty allow him to pass an actual injury over in silence. He laughed when I asked him for a certificate. "It is not worth talking about," he said, but I well knew why I needed it. I conveyed it to the supreme guardianship. That this precaution was necessary was shown by the papers conveyed by the supreme guardianship to the subsequent guardian, chosen by me, Herr v. Tuscher. Among these there was also a letter from Frau B. to the then Referee, in which it was said that I had inflicted a physical injury on her son, on which account he must stay in bed for three months. Imagine the frightful lie, since the boy went out as always, and Herr v. Smettana's testimony was certainly true. From this alone it is to be seen how this matter too was perhaps presented by the supreme guardianship authority, and how very necessary it is to hear myself and my nephew in regard to everything.

(I grant that one should never let oneself be carried away by anger, for I too am a man, harried on all sides like a wild beast, misunderstood, often treated in the basest way by this vulgar authority; with so many cares, with the constant battle against this monster of a mother, who always attempted to stifle any good brought forth, one who knows human nature will excuse me; however, let Herr von Smettana be now summoned, and it will transpire that everything even in the least said about an injury is wholly unjust and false.)

It also occurred that Frau B. accused me to the supreme guardianship of having written a letter to my nephew against confession. Herr von Tuscher himself read the same and hence showed it to these gentlemen, and even their eyes, he declared, were wet with tears at the truly religious, paternal exhortations in respect to this solemn act. But it will soon be found that Frau B.'s slander was not thereby expunged, despite the fact that it was proved that my nephew on the same day (he being no longer with me) went from the Institute to her instead of to confession, for which reason I myself later took him to confession to the worthy intelligent Abbot of St. Michael. — Perhaps this false assertion will again appear in the report.

I now think it incumbent upon me to make a few more brief historical representations in respect to the supreme guardianship authority down to the present time. Immediately after coming from the Landrechte to this Magisterial tribunal, I was, since in obedience to the Landrechte I as far as possible warded off the influences and evil impressions of Frau B. on my nephew, regarded as the cause of a family squabble. Indeed it appeared that the matter was not understood a priori, meanwhile the mother's machinations grew steadily worse. It became intolerable. She contrived to entice my nephew to her for the second time. I chose Herr v. Tuscher as guardian of my nephew and likewise under these conditions and in general did not wish [to have] him [Karl] with me any more, for in these circumstances the cares were too great. Hence in March 1819 he entered the Institute of H[err] Kudlich. I was not particularly well impressed by it, and would have preferred him to be with Giannatasio, but it was known how decidedly the latter was against the mother, since he regarded the removal of the same from her son as of the highest consequence in the upbringing of my nephew, and it was wished that he should rather be where the mother would perhaps receive more favorable treatment. Although as formerly I was the one who bore the expense, I had to allow it to take place, since I was no longer guardian. In the meantime there had reached me a proposal from the celebrated worthy scholar and cleric, S. M. Sailer, that he would receive my nephew at Landshut and supervise his education. The worthy Abbot of St. Michael said that this was the greatest good fortune that could befall my nephew, as other enlightened men [said] the same. Even His Imperial Highness, the present Archbishop of Olmütz, declared himself in favor of it and exerted himself for it. Herr von Tuscher also agreed that this plan best pleased him, for through my nephew's removal from here the further breaking of the commandment "Honor thy father and thy mother," into which he was always being led, would be entirely prevented, which [is] impossible in her presence. Although the boy has known his mother thoroughly from childhood, avoidance of all scandal would certainly be more expedient; further he would thereby be entirely removed from his mother's disturbances; but without the consent of the supreme guardianship this could not be. The same was therefore applied to, and one can imagine — what logic, what principles, what philosophy! The mother was now invited to protest against it! In brief, the whole plan fell through. Herr von Tuscher was now regarded as partisan. The Referee, who had finally come to know Frau B. completely and also considered the removal of her son the best thing, was given an associate Referee, being likewise accused of partisanship, hence he himself resigned the refereeship. During this my nephew could absent himself from the Institute at any time, the mother had free access, my nephew was inwardly and outwardly dealt with so that he was no longer recognizable, and it now occurred that the mother advised him to fix matters so that he would go into the second or third class, whereby he could not be removed from here. This he did, and now has to remain in the same class through a whole year more. It may be imagined that the guardian, already suspected of partisanship, could not act as energetically as necessary. Despite this the Institute received an order according to which she was forbidden to associate with my nephew. A few weeks later another was received, according to which my nephew was to show his respect for her on her name-day and to pass the same with her. The order seemed to be left to the headmaster whether he should obey it or not. The man was then sick and did not trust himself to protest. He himself could not go along, the teachers had no time, my nephew therefore made the journey alone from the Landstrasse [quarter] to his mother's in the Tiefe Graben, stayed there the whole day and over the following night, stuffed himself with food and strong drinks, which his mother, as incomprehensible as she is corrupt, gave him, and the next morning, when he could hardly stir, he had, already ill, to make the return journey to the Institute. On the very same day I came in from the country to see him, and found him lying in bed. The medicines seemed to me unsuitable for his condition, for she had sent a bungler of a doctor. I therefore immediately brought Dr. Hasenöhrl to him and there proved to be a hemorrhage. I made all arrangements for him to have the best possible care. Nevertheless she stormed into the Institute like a raging Medea. She had contrived to obtain permission by her false allegations, and at risk of life despite Dr. H.'s disapproval she took her son home with her. She was afraid of the discovery of the true cause of the sickness, and her evil genius would have been glad to escape the predicament by putting the blame on me. She had already tried to do so to Herr v. Tuscher and who knows what may again appear on the subject in the Magistracy's report. But such will-o'-the-wisps are soon extinguished among upright men. He now spent three weeks in bed. During this Herr von Tuscher communicated to me his decision to resign the guardianship. There was no honor to be reaped from it. Ill-supported by the guardianship [authority, as he found himself to be], Frau B. daily grew bolder, calumniated and imposed upon him in all ways, and even threatened him if he did not conform with her wishes. Everything good underwent a fresh defeat every instant. I myself saw that it was impossible for him to proceed upon this boggy water, and that merely by reason of everything being paid from my purse, I could be a stronger steersman. I therefore undertook and we agreed upon one and the same day [sic], on which Herr von Tuscher resigned the guardianship before the Magistracy and I on the same day sent a statement to the Magistracy that I had resumed it. The said statement was accepted. My nephew had now been recovered for three weeks, and on good grounds I put him in the present Institute of Herr Blöchlinger on July 22, 1819. Both the headmaster and I had adopted the system that a curtain should be drawn for my nephew over all that had passed, so that he would forget it. And in any case the memories of these catastrophes were not agreeable for him. But my nephew was immediately to [be taken away] from his settled situation again [to] appear before a commission. The headmaster wrote to me of his embarrassment in this respect. I wrote to him that he should refer himself to me as guardian, that I did not consider this expedient now, since my nephew was still partly to be regarded as a convalescent, in body and soul, but that I was ready at any moment to go to the supreme guardianship in order to give it information concerning anything it might wish. This was held sufficient. But since I could suppose that perhaps a new summons might come, I wrote to one of my friends, to inform me of it, as the letter Exhibit A shows. But again there came a new summons that my nephew should come before a commission, and I charged my friend [to present] my reasons why both I at present and the headmaster found it wholly inexpedient that my nephew should come to a commission, since in any case, as has been seen above, he had been mishandled, which occasioned the letter to me of August 20, Exhibit B. Let but the underlined passages be considered. Again, then, the letter against confession, which Herr von Tuscher had already shown them, was brought up. But none of the gentlemen were at this time disposed to remember it. Nor could I show the same to them, for I could no longer find it. Furthermore it clearly appears from Exhibit B what an influence

Frau B. had here, that her gossip against me was always given a hearing. It is visible how the Referee himself sought to know this person, and yet on the other side everything was to be valid again which she alleged against me. After receiving this letter I immediately sent my nephew to the Referee, Herr P.[iuk]. My friend told me that the latter had said to my nephew, "that he should be obedient to me in everything, how much gratitude he must acknowledge to me for all that I had done and do for him, that it was only through my support that he could learn all this" and so forth. To the request of the Referee that I again transfer the guardianship to someone else, I answered that I would never do so again, since experience showed that this only occurred to the detriment of my nephew. Also I did not want to employ such considerable sums only that a third person should botch everything for me again. This was not in the least intended to reflect on Herr Tuscher. But with such a supreme guardianship as this, the guardian is only a creature. It has been seen how, despite Hr. von Tuscher's favoring the removal of the boy from here, the overguardianship nevertheless had the mother appear to protest against it. Which procedure [is] contrary [to what obtains] with the Landrechte, where the guardian, since after all he has the responsibility, can speak against something that seems to him not good, and not only is heard, but his opinion decides the issue. Now as the case is here, precisely only a guardian who at the same time has such means as I is advantageous to his ward; not to pass over the fact that the guardianship over my nephew is never again rightfully to be denied to me, the closest relative and the guardian appointed by my brother himself in his will, the benefactor of father, son. And what stranger will so concern himself over his ward as the closest relative? A hundred thousand people would count it a good fortune to be able to give their children to such an uncle and guardian!

Once again in my communication cited above I asked Herr Referee P. [iuk] for peace for myself and my nephew. That I had already been accepted as guardian and was immediately regarded as such, there is no doubt. But the intrigues of Fr. B. continued ceaselessly, and even in September she wrote to Herr v. Blöchlinger that she was appointed my co-guardian. Nothing was said and the whole thing was taken as one of her usual tricks to impose on the headmaster. Finally in October appeared a communication from Fr. B. to Herr v. Blöchlinger signed by her own hand and by the Magistracy, "in which she stated herself to be guardian and Herr Nussböck to be co-guardian.[7] It was said in the communication that I was physically and morally unfit for the guardianship, that her son was never to be given to me from the Institute, because I wanted to take him with me to Olmütz, with the present Archbishop His Imperial Highness Archduke Rudolf (likewise a monstrous lie)" etc. To this nonsense was added the fact that at the Institute she was presented

by Herr Nussböck to the headmaster Herr v. Blöchlinger and to my
nephew as guardian!!!

Now compare the way Herr Referee P. himself expressed himself
concerning Fr. B. in the above [cited] letter, Exhibit B; but let it not
be believed that he took this so very seriously, for this Herr Referee
said at Herr Blöchlinger's, when he was entirely alone with him, that
this nuisance would not last, as soon as I should take a lawyer. Yet in
Fr. B.'s presence at Herr Blöchlinger's he tuned quite other strings, in
short, he said precisely the contrary of what he had said to him alone.
In general I have made the observation that there is something in the
character of the said Magisterial personage which never allows him
[to hold] firm opinions. That is up today which will be down tomorrow,
and vice versa. If today he said this was so, tomorrow it was overturned
by a diametrically opposing authority. I therefore did not take the
least time to speak with one of the said Referees, because I knew in
any case that even if I were admitted to be right today, it would be
considered wrong tomorrow. God preserve all men from such an authority.

Hardly had I come in from the country and entrusted this matter to
Dr. Bach than co-guardian Nussböck came to the Institute and stated
that in a few days he would remove my nephew from the Institute to
place him somewhere else. "It was believed that I would appeal, he
was in great perplexity, he did not know where he was to take him, he
had no money, and did not know how to get any. In any case, he added,
he was only doing what Herr Referee Piuk told him to." Consider the
fatherly care of this supreme guardianship for its ward. What a monument of barbarity, this supreme guardianship: first in respect to my removal as guardian, what an evil example of ingratitude it is on the
part of an authority which should properly be philanthropic-pedagog-
ical; and again what frivolity to want to entrust my nephew to chance
or even to put him in his mother's hands. Who knows if this was not
the intention. I immediately stated that I would in no case tolerate my
nephew being taken away from his present Institute, and as before so
now I continued to pay everything for him.

Dr. Bach now appeared before the Magistracy and Herr Referee P.
immediately again brought the above hackneyed complaints of Fr. B.
against me, among others even "that I was in love with her," and more
such claptrap. As Dr. Bach informed me that because of my deafness
it was in accordance with law to choose a co-guardian, this too was
done. Here Fr. B. was again invited by the Magistracy to give her consent thereto. What is to be said to this? Yet again there was a session,
at which I myself appeared with the chosen co-guardian Herr Peters.
Here again there was talk of the too fine clothes which I had given my
nephew etc. such claptrap. — Then again came a meaningless decision.
This is the information concerning this Magisterial supreme guardianship.

Information concerning my nephew and his school certificates.

It is not yet time to attribute a definite character to a boy of thirteen or even at a younger age. These are the years when one cannot attribute and still less speak finally. Until his eighth year my nephew was chiefly with his mother; his father had business concerns, and toward the end his constant ill-health prevented him from paying much attention to him. From this alone it is clear that, under his mother, much must have crept in which could not be got rid of immediately upon his leaving her. After all she had taught him to lie and equivocate and had mistreated him generally. This sort of thing was discovered even while he was at H[err] Giannatasio's. I discussed the matter several times with H. v. G., he was of the opinion that probably several years would be required before he would entirely lose all past impressions. Even here there were frequent complaints of his behavior. Neither I nor anyone else ascribed this to H. v. G., but things were entirely different when I took my nephew to live with me, which really came about because of his great talent for music, and who knows what a great musician he might have become under me, without the evil intrigues of his corrupt mother; now the same behavior as at H. v. G.'s was ascribed solely to me. It is easy to imagine how everything was falsified and exaggerated through this perpetual opponent. How she herself led him astray has already been shown in the information given above. Yes, she obviously exaggerated everything only in order to be able to ascribe the blame for it to me. Let him be called today, and let it be inquired how he was exhorted to the fear of God and to religion by me. In the Institute too I constantly took part in his education; when with me, he was never without a tutor or coach, and the character of his studies was always adapted to his nature. I can give the reasons for my procedure at any moment. In addition, this could only occur under a guardianship so little perceptive and so partisan, and under a guardian who, such being the guardianship, could never really regard himself as such.

As for H. v. Giannatasio's opinion that my nephew would need several years before the impressions of his childhood would be lost, [it] appears to be confirmed. Nature, furthermore, seldom makes leaps. H. von Blöchlinger is now very satisfied both with his diligence and his conduct. The gardener has patience with his plants, he tends them, lets them grow freely, binds them again, and shall not a man have it with the young human plant?! Here too the obscurantism of this Magistracy was revealed, which transplanted him into unfavorable circumstances with his raven-mother; and also passed judgment on him in the most warped, injurious and unfeeling manner. It was even wished to determine a definite character in these years. Thank heaven, I have only gratifying things to say and relate of him now.

Information concerning what I have done for my nephew. For five years I had for the most part paid for his education at my expense and borne cares for him like few fathers. In all circumstances I never lost the true aim, to make my nephew a sound, intelligent, and orderly citizen, both when I was guardian and when I was not, and even now, when I am in litigation over it, I continue and only consolidate my nephew's good.

Throughout two years, from 1816–1818 he was at the Giannatasio Institute entirely at my expense, where he also had his own piano-teacher privately, his hernia was operated upon, on his account a private attorney was kept here and in Prague. Likewise in connection with his estate I traveled to Retz etc. etc. — These two years may well be estimated at 4000 fl. W.W. [florins, Vienna valuation]. The accounts could if necessary easily be produced; it was not until this time that some payment was received as will be seen in more detail in the information concerning his estate. During the time he was with me, then in March 1819 went to Kudlich's Institute until his leaving there, he cost me at least 2000 fl. W.W. — From July 22, 1820 on he entered Herr Blöchlinger's Institute. Since these are the shortest accounts, I submit them herewith. — See Exhibit C. — In all this many other necessities, such as clothing, sicknesses, are not reckoned at all.

There can be few uncles and guardians in the Monarchy who care so liberally for their dependents, and so entirely without profit to themselves; — at least I have no other profit than that of regarding myself as the originator of something good, and of moulding a better human nature.

Information as to my nephew's fortune. This consists of 4000 fl. W.W., of which the mother has the usufruct during her lifetime; for my nephew is sole heir of his grandmother. It is apparent that the latter was wiser than the Magistracy, since she did not wish to put this fortune in her [Johanna's] hands, but what is even more, the Magistracy even put my nephew's soul into her hands as guardian.

Further, of 2000 fl. W.W. which serve as compensation for surrender of his inheritance, and for his education; to which I added enough so that it now makes 2200 fl. [in] two and one-half per cent treasury bonds. — Half of Frau B.'s pension, 66 fl. C. M. (Convention currency) annually, which likewise serves as compensation for his entirely renounced inheritance — cannot properly be counted as capital, but simply as a contribution to his education, for when she dies he loses it.

The interest from the coupons from the 2200 fl. yielded a sum toward education but did not become liquidable until February 1, 1818 — they yield $27\frac{1}{2}$ in silver semiannually. The first receipts from the pension also did not come in until the end of May 1818.

The half of the pension together with the interest give at the rate of 250 about 450 fl. W.W. annually. Of this I have to date received in all about four quarters, for it is now 13 months since I have received a heller of this pension. What motherly solicitude and what support of my nephew by this supreme guardianship, which is low enough to have perhaps combined with her so that this sum should not [come] to me for him!

Since even before 1816 immediately after my brother's death I provided [my nephew's] education at my expense, it is easy to reckon what I have gained. It was not until 1818 that the contributions came, as shown above.

Consideration has been given to my nephew's future too: 4000 fl. C.M. are on deposit in the Austr[ian] National Bank from me as an inheritance for him. — If one takes the interest of the 400 [sic] fl. C.M. in the bank and the interest on the treasury bonds, which yield at least 1058 fl. W.W. and something [be] added to that, this is already a considerable reserve for any case. Supposing that his mother should die, when the usufruct of the 7000 fl. W.W. would devolve to him, the interest on his capital would come to at least 1408 fl. W.W.

Conclusion. In view of the frightful gossip and tittle-tattle of the Magistracy and Fr. B.'s everlasting machinations and slanders in respect to me, I have thought that a presentation which includes almost all sides of this guardianship matter would not be inexpedient. In connection with the Magistracy's report, this presentation can serve as a handbook does at the lectures of a — professor!!

I must admit that I am weary, and if one must suffer for the sake of good, I believe that I have done my share therein. It is high time that Fr. B. was put in her place by the high Appellate Court and learned that no further cabals can overthrow what has been firmly established by the worthy L.R. [Landrechte] and remains established, for it is at least four years that she has been pursuing this plan of having her son with her and having the guardianship over him; hence she must be rendered entirely incapable of doing harm. Not until then can humanity and consideration demand their rights, although this was always the case with me in respect to her. Except where the good of my nephew demanded that her stubbornness be bent by legal means, yet she has never been willing to endure either consideration or magnanimity or true goodness.

Let no one believe that, as she says, I am guided by private hatred of her or vengeance against her. It is painful to me to be obliged to discuss her, and were it not for my nephew I should never think of her, or speak of her, or act against her.

May the high Appellate Court now grant my request and decide whether Fr. B. and Sequestrator Nussböck are to retain the guardianship of my nephew, or I, the guardian appointed in the will (with my co-guardian, chosen by me, and extremely suitable for me and profitable for my nephew), I who for five years have been at once the benefactor, support and stay of my nephew.

The decision will bring my nephew weal or woe; the latter certainly if it results against me. — For my nephew needs me, not I him. Not only from the pecuniary point of view would it be harmful to him but through it his whole moral existence will suffer a detrimental change.

This matter has in any case fallen into such bad hands that, if it remains on this footing, I could no longer concern myself with it, and would have to commend my nephew to the protection of Providence. — If on the contrary, as I hope, his entire weal and woe is again entrusted to me, I will continue to meet the expenses of his education as I have until now, which in any case I would always have done. How I have sought to provide for his future, has already been seen, and in this respect still more might be done. — And if, as a human being, I have once erred, or should my hearing be taken into consideration, a father's children are not taken away from him for these two reasons, — and such I have always been to my nephew, both his father and a benefactor!

God bless my work, I commend the weal and woe of an orphan to the heart and the prevailing wisdom of the high Appellate Court! — Sapienti honestas lex est, libido lex est malis! (Uprightness is the law of the wise, the law of the wicked is passion.)

Most obediently.

Supplement. Since, as has already been seen from the information concerning Fr. B., even in her parents' house, the urge appeared to ascribe her own misdemeanors to innocent persons, as in 1811 she accused innocent persons of her crime, or at least knew that they were innocently brought in, without having any part in her crime, and since from the information concerning the Magistracy it has likewise been seen what false facts she has ascribed to me and how she has always slandered me, it is to be expected of this Magistracy that in its reports it will dish up more of the like against me, of which I know nothing. Since perhaps the Magistracy will come against me armed with the papers alleged! to emanate from the priest of Mödling, a clearing up of this matter is not out of place.

It was in May 1818, that, having taken my nephew from H. v. Giannatasio to live with me in February 1818, I also took him to the country with me. Being a student, his then tutor could not accompany us to the country, I believed that here in Mödling too I should find the necessary time to develop my nephew's musical talent. The priest there was highly spoken of to me as an instructor of boys, and so I entrusted my nephew to him.

Unfortunately I soon found that I had been very much mistaken in this priest. On Monday this reverend gentleman had not yet slept off his Sunday carouse, and was then like a wild beast. Yes, I felt ashamed for our religion, that this person should represent a man of the Gospel.

My nephew could not be prevailed upon to render him respect and obedience. Naturally, for he gave him the most brutal, rough treatment over every trivial thing, made his pupils lie down on the bench like soldiers, and the strongest of them had to play the corporal and thrash the culprit with a stick. I entirely forbade the use of this method with my nephew, nor did I allow my nephew to go to church in the morning with his [the priest's] pupils, since I had observed their unseemly behavior and did not wish to have my nephew with this rabble. It can be imagined that this in itself served for an accusation that I had no religion or was not bringing up my nephew religiously.

Since I saw through the crookedness of this man only too well, after a few weeks I no longer let my nephew go to him, and had a better teacher for him come from the city. That nothing was neglected is shown by his good certificate of August 26, 1818, the last under the supreme guardianship of the worthy L.R. and my guardianship, which [certificate] is even better than the previous one.

It can be imagined that the removal of my nephew from the priest offended his vanity. To this was added the intrigues of Fr. B., for it was known that His Reverence was not indifferent toward the fair sex. In this respect things were told about His Reverence — which we poor but well-bred laymen would both refrain from and be ashamed of. In general he was neither loved nor respected by his congregation, nor by other clergymen. This man was not ashamed to become a new tool against me in the hands of Fr. B. He had (according to her) written an essay to please her in which several false accusations against me appeared, and which, it seemed, was taken into consideration by the L.R. on the occasion of the last commission, although the record must show that nothing was proved against me. It can be imagined that the Magistracy will not fail to bring this sort of thing up again. It is apparent how from March 1819 on, when my nephew was not with me and I was no longer guardian, things went, how his morals grew worse, how his mother took him out with her more and more, he in turn ran out of the Institute when he pleased, and merely by this fact no good examination was to be expected.

Now in addition came Fr. B.'s unholy counsel that my nephew should diligently try to get into the second or third class; and this occurred, as the record of the Easter examination, 1819, shows. Finally he even had another hemorrhage on account of her.

Since after June 1819 I again regarded myself as guardian and have acted as the same, I suppose that the difference between the better and the worse can easily be seen; for with energy and dignity, as befits me, I have opposed all further misdoings of the Magistracy, and stated "that I once for all insist upon knowing that the money I give is used in absolute accordance with the end." This declaration, which I was finally forced to make against an authority which at all times stubbornly opposed all good contemplated by me, aroused its vengeance against me, and its vulgarity easily joined with this corrupt Fr. B. and through the same became the tool whereby, again as ever, to undermine my nephew and to humiliate me in all ways. But I hope: convitia hominum turpium laudes puta! (Regard the calumnies of bad men as praise!)

I appeal to the Almighty as witness, who sees my inmost heart, that I have never acted and concerned myself in respect to my nephew during more than five years other than according to the best and most upright principles. Furthermore I have always laid it upon myself as a duty never to relinquish my nephew; but I have been thoroughly disabused by the Magistracy, but I hope that the high Appellate Court will be of my opinion herein. Finally I must add that it seems to me that it has by no means been proven if I am to regard the Magistracy as a competent guardianship authority! [7]

NOTES FOR CHAPTER I

1. *Leonardo da Vinci*, transl. by A. A. Brill, Dodd, Mead & Co., New York 1932, p. 115.
2. Ibid., p. 125.
3. Her brother supplied Beethoven with firewood. See also letters to Gleichenstein, Emerich Kastner, *L. v. Beethovens Briefe*, new edition, by Julius Kapp, Hesse and Becker, Leipzig 1923, Nos. 163 and 164, p. 121.
4. Anton Schindler, *Biographie von Ludwig van Beethoven*, 1st ed., Münster 1840.
5. *Ludwig van Beethovens Konversationshefte*, ed. Georg Schünemann, vols I–III, Max Hesse Verlag, Berlin 1941.
6. New York *Times:* "BERLIN, Sept. 14, 1951 — The priceless 'conversation books' recording Beethoven's talks with his friends during his final years of deafness have disappeared from the former Prussian State Library on Unter den Linden in the Soviet sector of Berlin. Rumor of this loss was confirmed when Carleton Smith, director of the National Arts Foundation, was told he could not see

them when he visited the collection yesterday. He did peruse other gems in the musical documents collection, such as the original score of Bach's 'Saint Matthew Passion.'
"One of the library's senior curators, Dr. Joachim Kruger-Riebow, disappeared late this spring at about the same time that the absence of the precious five-foot shelf of notebooks was first noted. Dr. Kruger-Riebow, who had the reputation of being a loyal Socialist Unity (Communist) party member until he absconded, is presumed to be working his passage home with these treasures of Germany's musical heritage."
7. J. G. Prod'homme, *Les cahiers de conversation de Beethoven*. Éditions Corrêa, Paris 1946.
8. A. Schindler, *Biographie von L. v. Beethoven* (abridged and annotated edition by Stephan Ley), Glöckner Verlag, Bonn 1949, p. 235.
9. Schindler, ed. Ley, p. 30. (Italics ours.)
10. Schindler, 1st ed., p. 14.

NOTES FOR CHAPTER II

1. Ludwig's original petition to the Elector is not extant, but A. W. Thayer (*L. v. Beethovens Leben*, Leipzig 1917, Vol. I, p. 236) cites the decree. By its terms: "as requested," only 100 Rheinthaler of the father's yearly stipend are to be paid

to him in future, the other 100 Rheinthaler are to be given to the son "in addition to his present stipend and together with the 24 bushels of grain per annum for the rearing of his brothers." At the same time his father is ordered to change his place of residence to some village in the neighborhood of Bonn. This stipulation, however, was not enforced. He continued to live in Bonn with his sons.

2. This is Ludwig's second stay in Vienna. He had also been sent there to study at seventeen, at which time he became acquainted with Mozart. But his mother's illness prematurely interrupted the earlier stay in Vienna after a few months.

3. Thayer II, p. 6.

4. Dr. Max Vancsa, *Beethovens Neffe*. Supplement to the *Allgemeine Zeitung*, Munich, Feb. 6 and 7, 1901.

5. florins: *Gulden.*

6. Schindler, ed. Ley, p. 91.

7. *Industrie Comptoir.*

8. Thayer II, p. 399.

9. Wegeler and Ries, *Biographische Notizen über Ludwig van Beethoven*, Coblenz 1838 (reprint edited by Dr. A. C. Kalischer, Leipzig 1906, p. 147): ". . . All sorts of trifles and many things which he never wished to publish because he thought them unworthy of his name, came surreptitiously into

the world through his brother. Thus songs which he wrote years before he moved to Vienna, when he was still in Bonn, first became public when he had already reached a high degree of fame. Even little compositions which he had written in albums were purloined and printed in this way."

10. Kastner, No. 85, p. 73.

11. Wegeler and Ries, p. 113.

12. Ibid., p. 116.

13. Schindler (ed. Ley), p. 53.

14. Ibid., p. 204.

15. Ibid., p. 89.

16. Beethoven wrote a memorandum, obviously addressed to himself, on a sketch sheet: "For all works, as now for the violincello sonata, reserve the right to fix the day of publication for the publisher, without the publishers in London and Germany so to speak knowing about each other, because otherwise they give less, and anyway it is not necessary; you can give as excuse that someone else ordered the composition from you." Kastner, No. 606, p. 362.

17. Thayer III, p. 545.

18. Ibid., p. 547.

19. Wegeler and Ries, p. 105.

20. Here the second brother's name was evidently omitted.

21. Here the second brother's name was again omitted.

22. Thayer II, p. 333. (Translation: Thayer-Krehbiel I, pp. 352–354.)

NOTES FOR CHAPTER III

1. "und wahrscheinlich der andere, den der Rachegeist gegen mich beseelt, auch an ihm." This passage is equally unintelligible in all editions and has not been explained. Perhaps it means: "and I shall take vengeance on my other brother too, who did not support my request."
2. Kastner, No. 138, p. 107.
3. F. Kerst: *Die Erinnerungen an Beethoven*, Hoffmann, Stuttgart 1913, Vol. I, p. 124.
4. Kastner, No. 175, p. 126.
5. Kerst I, p. 48.
6. Kastner, No. 190, p. 136.
7. Wegeler and Ries, p. 143.
8. Kastner, No. 226, p. 156.
9. Ibid., No. 250, p. 169.
10. Thayer I, p. 350.
11. Stephan Ley, *Aus Beethovens Erdentagen*, Glöckner, Bonn 1948, p. 21.
12. Kastner, No. 335, p. 221.
13. Thayer III, p. 343.
14. Kastner, No. 353, p. 233.
15. Thayer III, p. 344.
16. Of the 105 letters which Beethoven wrote to the Archduke 70 are letters in which he excuses himself for lessons not given.
17. Kastner, No. 359, p. 237.
18. Kerst I, p. 196.
19. Ibid., p. 197.
20. Kastner, No. 363, p. 238.

21. Thayer III, p. 363.
22. Vancsa, *Beethovens Neffe*. Supplement to the *Allgemeine Zeitung*, Munich, Feb. 6 and 7, 1900.
23. Thayer III, pp. 363–364. For further details concerning Karl's conferring the guardianship on Ludwig, see our summary of Hotschevar's statement, p. 145.
24. Kastner, No. 384, p. 251.
25. Ibid., No. 385, p. 251.
26. Ibid., No. 482, p. 300.
27. Ibid., No. 524, p. 322.
28. Ibid., No. 531, p. 325.
29. Ibid., No. 485, p. 302.
30. Ibid., No. 505, p. 314. (The queried interpolation in square brackets is sheer conjecture. Here and elsewhere, the original is incoherent. — Translator.)
31. Ludwig Nohl, *Beethovens Leben*, Günther, Leipzig 1867, Vol. II, p. 482.
32. Kastner, No. 513, p. 317.
33. Ibid., No. 481, p. 299.
34. Ibid., No. 550, p. 332.
35. Ibid., No. 496 (printed in italics).
36. Thayer III, p. 517. (Translation from: Thayer-Krehbiel II, 320.)
37. Ibid. III, p. 518. (Translation from: Thayer-Krehbiel II, 321.)

NOTES FOR CHAPTER IV

1. Kastner, No. 540, p. 328.
2. Thayer III, p. 519.
3. Kastner, No. 542, p. 329.
4. Ibid., No. 602, p. 361.
5. Ibid., No. 553, p. 333.
6. Thayer III, p. 520.
7. Ibid., p. 538.
8. Nohl III, p. 33.
9. Ibid., p. 814.
10. Thayer III, p. 538. (Translation from: Thayer-Krehbiel II, 331.)
11. Kastner, No. 603, p. 361.
12. Salomon had been a violinist in the Elector's orchestra at Bonn.
13. Salomon's.
14. Kastner, No. 569, p. 340.
15. This refers to events narrated in the following chapter.
16. Kastner, No. 582, p. 347.
17. Ibid., No. 600, p. 359. (Italics ours.)

NOTES FOR CHAPTER V

1. Baron de Trémont, Kerst I, p. 135.
2. Gerhard von Breuning: *Aus dem Schwarzspanierhause*, Vienna 1874, p. 61.
3. Mölk (Melk) is on the Danube, halfway between Vienna and Linz, and was famed for its Benedictine monastery, in which there was an excellent school for boys.
4. Kastner, No. 561, p. 337.
5. Of 28 letters to Giannatasio, 17 contain similar attacks on Johanna.
6. Kastner, No. 562, p. 337.
7. Thayer III, p. 540.
8. Ibid.
9. Kastner, No. 568, p. 340.
10. Thayer III, p. 540.
11. Ibid.
12. Kastner, No. 571, p. 341.
13. Thayer III, p. 541.
14. Friedrich Stärcke, Kerst I, p. 241.
15. Kerst II, p. 102.
16. Thayer IV, p. 528.
17. Ibid., p. 529.
18. Kastner, No. 581, p. 346.
19. Ibid., No. 592, p. 354.
20. Johanna's.
21. Thayer IV, p. 531.
22. Kastner, No. 597, p. 358.
23. Ibid., No. 604, p. 362.
24. Breuning, *Aus dem Schwarzspanierhause*, p. 63.
25. Kastner, No. 609, p. 363.
26. Ibid., No. 612, p. 365.
27. Ibid., No. 611, p. 364.
28. The surgeon.
29. Kastner, No. 613, p. 365.
30. Ibid., No. 619, p. 368.
31. Bursy, Kerst I, p. 200.
32. The word is here used as the equivalent of August Aichhorn's term *Verwahrlosung*, to signify asocial behavior by the young. (August Aichhorn, *Verwahrloste Jugend*, Internationaler Psychoanalytischer Verlag, Vienna 1925.)
33. Kastner, No. 620, p. 369.

34. Ibid., No. 654, p. 385.
35. Kastner, No. 658, p. 387. (A translation will be found in Kalischer-Shedlock II, p. 8.)
36. Kastner, No. 736, No. 737, p. 417.
37. Ibid., No. 657, p. 386.
38. In a letter from the period preceding the second court action, Ludwig himself admits exercising influence on the officials concerned in the guardianship proceedings:
"To S. Steiner and Co.
Best Lieutenant-General!
Please send some vocal duets, trios, quartets from various operas, as well as some transcriptions of the same for violin quartet or quintet and the 'Merkenstein' song, 'Der Mann von Wort,' 'An die Hoffnung,' and 'An die ferne Geliebte.' I beg you to have them reach me all together at latest by this afternoon, for there is an opportunity to send them on. *The Lieutenant-General must grease the General, the General others in turn;* were it not for the Lieutenant-General's vast mines and the General's head, we should long since have been lost. *The guardianship obliges me to such gifts, so that the wagon wheels may be duly greased to 'reach house and home.'"* (Kastner, No. 687, p. 396.) (Italics ours.)
39. Kastner, No. 659, p. 387.
40. Fanny Giannatasio, Kerst I, p. 214.
41. Kastner, No. 724, p. 412.
42. Ibid., No. 663, p. 389.
43. Ibid., No. 736, p. 416.

NOTES FOR CHAPTER VI

1. Kastner, No. 675, p. 392; No. 676, p. 392; No. 678, p. 393; No. 679, p. 393.
2. Ibid., No. 664, p. 389.
3. Nohl III, p. 42.
4. Kerst I, p. 265.
5. Kastner, No. 745, p. 422. (Italics ours.)
6. Ibid., No. 2, p. 14. (Italics ours.)
7. Gottfried Fischer's statement, Thayer I, p. 467.
8. Id., ibid.
9. Id., ibid., p. 451.
10. Ibid., p. 145.
11. Bernhard Mäurer, Kerst I, p. 10.
12. G. Fischer, Kerst I, p. 4.
13. Id., ibid. I, p. 7.
14. Id., ibid. I, p. 6.
15. Id., ibid. I, p. 8.
16. Thayer I, p. 346.
17. Closson, *L'élément flamand dans Beethoven,* 1944, p. 237.
18. G. Fischer, Kerst I, p. 3.
19. Thayer I, p. 138.
20. G. Fischer, Kerst I, p. 5.
21. Gerhard v. Breuning, *Aus dem Schwarzspanierhause,* p. 12.
22. Wegeler and Ries, p. 144.
23. Thayer I, p. 203.
24. Wegeler and Ries, p. 24.
25. Ibid., p. 49.

26. Ley, *Aus Beethovens Erdentagen*, Glöckner, Bonn 1948, pp. 21, 22, 23.
27. Thayer II, p. 484.
28. Kerst I, p. 155.
29. Thayer III, p. 321. (Translation from: Thayer-Krehbiel II, p. 29.)
30. Stephan Ley, *Beethovens Charakter*, Röhrscheid, Bonn 1948, p. 26.
31. Kerst I, p. 134.
32. Ibid., p. 232.
33. Ibid., p. 205.
34. Wegeler and Ries, p. 24.
35. Ley, *Beethovens Charakter*, p. 7.
36. Kerst I, pp. 124, 125.
37. Ley, *Beethovens Charakter*, p. 61.
38. Kerst I, p. 71.
39. Hermann von Pückler-Muskau, Kerst I, p. 154.
40. Kastner, No. 323, p. 216.
41. Ibid., No. 927, p. 532.
42. Kerst I, p. 165.
43. Kastner, No. 300, p. 205.
44. Ibid., No. 1073, p. 642.
45. Ibid., No. 987, p. 592.
46. Ibid., No. 844, p. 468.
47. Breuning, *Aus dem Schwarzspanierhause*, p. 44.
48. Ley, *Beethovens Charakter*, p. 64.
49. Kastner, No. 740, p. 419.
50. Cf. E. Buenzod, *Pouvoirs de Beethoven*, Lausanne 1947, p. 7: "Beethoven a ceci de fatal qu'il ne plaît ni ne charme: il envoûte, il subjugue. Il oblige à prendre parti violemment pour le héros contre l'homme, pour la grandeur contre la mesure, pour le surhumain contre l'humain."
51. Kastner, No. 1329, p. 784.
52. Ibid., No. 24, p. 28.
53. Ibid., No. 453, p. 282.
54. Thayer III, p. 195.
55. Kastner, No. 456, p. 283.
56. As early as 1801 Beethoven wrote to his friend Amenda concerning two other friends: "I regard him and . . . . . as mere instruments, upon which I play when I please; . . . I rate them only in accordance with what they do for me" (Kastner, No. 50, p. 43).
57. Kerst II, p. 121.
58. Ley, *Beethovens Charakter*, p. 61.
59. Freud, *Moses and Monotheism*, A. Knopf, New York 1939, p. 171. (Italics ours.)
60. Ibid., p. 172, 173.
61. "Beethoven after a hundred years," *Musical Quarterly*, 1927.

NOTES FOR CHAPTER VII

1. Wegeler and Ries, p. 54.
2. Kerst II, p. 101.
3. Wegeler and Ries, p. 139.
4. Thayer II, p. 298.
5. Ibid.
6. *Beethoven Studien*, 1832, p. 13.
7. Kastner, No. 3, p. 15.
8. Ibid., No. 7, p. 17. (Translation from: A. C. Kalischer, *Beethoven's Letters*, trans. J. S. Shedlock, London and New York 1909, I, pp. 7–9.)
9. Helene Deutsch, "Zur Psycho-

logie des Misstrauens," *Imago*
VII, 1921.

10. Kastner, No. 31, p. 30.
11. Ibid., No. 245, p. 165. (Italics ours.)
12. Ibid., No. 55, pp. 50 ff.
13. In his analysis of the letter, Romain Rolland reaches a similar conclusion. But he attributes it to Ludwig's maturity, practical sense, and reflectiveness instead of to inner impediments. Romain Rolland, *Les Aimées de Beethoven*, Editions du Sablier, Paris 1949.
14. Thayer was also of this opinion, III, p. 341.
15. Thayer IV, p. 534.
16. Kastner, No. 581, p. 346.
17. Ibid., No. 343, p. 229; No. 344, p. 229; No. 345, p. 230; No. 347, p. 230; No. 349, p. 231.
18. Ibid., No. 351, p. 232.
19. Ley, *Beethovens Charakter*, p. 32.
20. Ibid.
21. Ibid., p. 42.
22. Thayer III, p. 136.
23. Ibid., p. 185.
24. Beethoven broke off his former close friendship with an excellent composer and conductor in Vienna, and carried the break so far that he hardly

answered the latter's salutations with the customary politeness. Schindler says that his only reason for this was the fact that his former friend was having an illicit relationship with another man's wife. (Thayer II, p. 150.)
25. Kastner, No. 160, p. 119. (Translation from: Thayer-Krehbiel II, 85.)
26. A. B. Marx, *Ludwig van Beethovens Schaffen*, Berlin 1875, II, p. 110. On the other hand, we may remember how indignant Beethoven was because Johanna had attended a masked ball! See Chapter V.
27. Nohl III, p. 828.
28. Franz Grillparzer, "Erinnerungen an Beethoven," Kerst II, p. 44.
29. Kerst I, p. 20.
30. Ibid. II, p. 186.
31. Kastner, No. 7, p. 26.
32. Ibid., No. 597, p. 358.
33. Ibid., No. 631, p. 375.
34. Ibid., No. 685, p. 395 (cf. the perils of the bottomless road at night, in the letter to the Immortal Beloved).
35. Ibid., No. 525, p. 323.
36. Kerst II, p. 125.
37. Thayer IV, p. 540.

NOTES FOR CHAPTER VIII

1. Thayer III, p. 371.
2. Kastner, No. 745, p. 422.
3. Ibid., No. 791, p. 444.
4. Ibid., No. 542, p. 329.
5. Ibid., No. 581, p. 346.
6. Wegeler and Ries, p. 147.

7. Kastner, No. 585, p. 349.
8. Thayer IV, p. 3.
9. Ibid. IV, p. 75.
10. Nottebohm, *Beethoveniana*, ed. Mandyczewski, Leipzig 1887, Introduction.

11. Thayer III, p. 568.
12. Kastner, No. 554, p. 334.
13. Ibid., No. 736, p. 416.
14. Thayer III, p. 558.
15. Schindler, ed. Ley, p. 235.
16. Schünemann II, p. 120.
17. Kastner, No. 826, p. 458.
18. Schünemann II, p. 30.
19. Reinitz (*Beethoven im Kampfe mit dem Schicksal*, Rikola Verlag, Vienna 1924) says of the letters to Frau Streicher: "If written by a housewife, they would be perfectly appropriate" (p. 64).
20. Kastner, No. 826, p. 457.
21. Ibid., No. 790, p. 444.
22. Ibid., No. 738, p. 418.
23. Ibid., No. 764, p. 433.
24. Kalischer, *Beethovens sämtliche Briefe*, Schuster & Loeffler, Berlin 1907, III, No. 518, p. 50.
25. Kastner, No. 827, p. 458. A translation of this letter, in which Beethoven says that he has "made short work" of the housekeeper's "infernal tricks" by throwing "my heavy chair by my bed" at her, will be found in Kalischer-Shedlock II, pp. 14–15.
26. Kastner, No. 798, p. 448.
27. Ibid., No. 826, p. 457.

28. Thayer III, p. 566.
29. Kastner, No. 753, p. 428.
30. Ibid., No. 754, p. 428.
31. Ibid., No. 653, p. 384.
32. Ibid., No. 661, p. 388.
33. Ibid., No. 705, p. 403.
34. Ibid., No. 752, p. 412.
35. Thayer IV, p. 11.
36. Ibid., p. 10.
37. Kastner, No. 742, p. 420.
38. Ibid., No. 752, p. 427.
39. Ibid., No. 734, p. 415.
40. Thayer IV, pp. 36–37.
41. Kastner, No. 761, p. 431.
42. Ibid., No. 732, p. 414.
43. Ibid., No. 771, p. 437.
44. Ibid., No. 794, p. 445.
45. Ibid., No. 824, p. 456.
46. Ibid., No. 827, p. 459.
47. Ibid., No. 825, p. 456.
48. Thayer IV, p. 91.
49. Kastner, No. 826, p. 457.
50. Ibid., No. 826, p. 458.
51. Ibid., No. 829, p. 460.
52. Ibid., No. 830, p. 461.
53. Ibid., No. 840, p. 465.
54. Thayer IV, p. 96.
55. Kastner, No. 847, p. 470.
56. Ibid., No. 857, p. 475. (A translation of the entire letter can be consulted in Thayer-Krehbiel II, 394–95.)
57. Thayer IV, p. 97.

NOTES FOR CHAPTER IX

1. See Appendix, p. 309.
2. Kastner, No. 821, p. 455.
3. Thayer IV, p. 110.
4. Ibid., p. 112.
5. Ibid., p. 110.
6. Ibid., p. 111.
7. Underlined in the original.
8. Thayer IV, p. 112.

9. Ibid., p. 551.
10. See Appendix, p. 311.
11. Schindler, ed. Ley, p. 228.
12. See Appendix, p. 312.
13. See Appendix, p. 313.
14. Thayer IV, p. 548. Italics ours.
15. See Appendix, p. 319.

16. Thayer IV, p. 554.
17. Kastner, No. 881, p. 490.
18. Schindler, ed. Ley, p. 228.
19. Schünemann I, p. 215.
20. Ibid., p. 247. The last phrase is written in large letters and underlined.
21. Thayer IV, p. 116.
22. Ibid.
23. Ibid., p. 137.
24. Kastner No. 883, p. 493. (A translation of this letter will be found in Kalischer-Shedlock II, pp. 124–29.)
25. Director of the private school which Karl attended as a day-pupil.
26. J. M. Sailer, Professor of Ethics and Pastoral Theology at Landshut.
27. Schünemann I, pp. 30–31. Schünemann transcribes the originals of the conversations exactly. We omit non-essential passages and make slight changes to facilitate comprehension. The dashes stem from Beethoven's partners in the conversations. They usually indicate the point at which Beethoven, reading the words as they were written, broke in on his partner without waiting for him to finish. Dashes between the individual speeches indicate interruptions in the conversations. Underlinings (represented by italics) are those which appear in the MSS. Schünemann's interpolations are in parentheses; our explanatory interpolations are in square brackets. The names of the more important speakers were written in the Conversation Books by Schindler; Schünemann, using infor-mation from letters and other documents, added a few more.

28. Schünemann I, p. 32.
29. Thayer IV, p. 140.
30. Schünemann I, pp. 36, 37, 40, 42.
31. Ibid., p. 40 f.
32. Thayer IV, p. 141.
33. Schünemann I, p. 63.
34. Ibid., p. 65.
35. Kastner, No. 895, p. 506. (The letter is summarized in Thayer-Krehbiel III, p. 6, and translated in full in Kalischer-Shedlock II, p. 134.)
36. Thayer IV, p. 141.
37. Kastner, No. 884, p. 500.
38. Ibid., No. 887, p. 502.
39. Ibid., No. 888, p. 503.
40. Ibid., No. 891, p. 504.
41. Thayer IV, p. 144.
42. Kastner, No. 897, p. 508. (A translation will be found in Kalischer-Shedlock II, pp. 136–37.)
43. Ibid., No. 898, p. 510.
44. Frimmel, *Beethoven Forschungen, Lose Blätter* I, p. 14.
45. "Ober A[r]s[ch] Hinterschaft," Ludwig's scornful designation for the guardianship authorities (*Vormundschaftsbehörde*).
46. Kastner, No. 901, p. 512.
47. This passage is crossed out in pencil in the original letter!
48. Kastner, No. 901, p. 513.
49. Ibid., No. 904, p. 515.
50. Ibid., No. 932, p. 534.
51. Ibid., No. 885, p. 500.
52. Ibid., No. 910, p. 520.
53. Ibid., No. 911, p. 521.
54. Thayer IV, p. 145 (Thayer-Krehbiel III, 8).
55. Kastner, No. 902, p. 514.

NOTES FOR CHAPTER X

1. Kastner, No. 916, p. 522.
2. Ibid., No. 920, p. 525.
3. Ibid., No. 931, p. 534.
4. Ibid., No. 945, p. 543.
5. Ibid., No. 944, p. 542.
6. An allusion to the fact that Blöchlinger was Swiss.
7. Italics ours.
8. Italics ours.
9. Chief surgeon of St. John's Hospital at Salzburg and an enthusiastic admirer of Beethoven.
10. Kastner, No. 943, p. 541.
11. Ibid., No. 924, p. 530.
12. Ibid., No. 934, p. 537.
13. Judges of the Landrechte.
14. Schünemann I, p. 75.
15. Ibid., p. 108.
16. Ibid., pp. 79–80.
17. Ibid., p. 81.
18. Ibid., p. 119.
19. Ibid., p. 85.
20. Karl or Blöchlinger.
21. Schünemann I, p. 86.
22. Peters always writes "Plechlinger" for "Blöchlinger."
23. Schünemann I, p. 113.
24. Ibid., pp. 128–29, 133.
25. Ibid., p. 151.
26. Ibid., pp. 133–34.
27. Beethoven's share of Johanna's pension is meant.
28. Karl again protests against his uncle's suspicion that he sees his mother.
29. Schünemann I, p. 112. (The italicized words were underlined by Karl.)
30. Ibid., p. 162.
31. Ibid., p. 157.
32. Kastner, No. 949, p. 544. (A translation will be found in

Kalischer-Shedlock II, pp. 164–66 ["North" in the superscription should be altered to "Lower."]. See also note 44 below.)
33. Schünemann I, p. 204. Winter was the Referee for the case.
34. Ibid., p. 185.
35. Ibid., p. 195. (Karl's underlining.)
36. Thayer IV, p. 143.
37. Schünemann I, p. 198.
38. Ibid., p. 199.
39. Ibid., p. 211.
40. Ibid.
41. Ibid., p. 212.
42. Ibid., p. 210.
43. Ibid., p. 229. For further evidence of Peters's interest in Karl's studies, see ibid., p. 251.
44. Thayer IV, p. 563. "ad 2dum": In his appeal of Jan. 7 to the Appellate Court, Beethoven had written: "My nephew is now reaching the years in which he must be provided with a higher education. Neither the mother nor the former guardian is fit to guide the boy along this scientific path. Not the former, because she is a woman . . . Not the latter, because . . . as a former paper-manufacturer, I cannot grant him the necessary insight and the proper judgment for a scientific education." (Kastner, No. 949, p. 544).
45. Refers to a law concerning the rights and duties of a guardian.
46. Refers to the intended order of the memorial.

47. The name of a street.
48. Properly "Smetana." He was the surgeon who operated on Karl. This notation becomes intelligible in the light of the Memorial. (See Appendix, p. 323.)
49. Beethoven's copyist.
50. Schünemann I, pp. 187–89.
51. Kastner, No. 955, p. 569.
52. See this chapter, p. 175.
53. Schünemann I, p. 189.
54. Thayer IV, p. 564. (Italics ours.)
55. Kastner, No. 956, p. 569.
56. Schünemann I, p. 353.
57. Ibid., p. 268.
58. Ibid., p. 269.
59. Ibid., p. 270.
60. I.e., Beethoven's maid.
61. I.e., Beethoven's maid.
62. Ibid., pp. 278–79. (Karl's underlining.)
63. Ibid., pp. 322, 329, 339.
64. Ibid., p. 352.
65. Ibid., p. 380.
66. Ibid., p. 382.
67. Thayer IV, p. 566.
68. Schünemann I, p. 391.
69. Ibid., p. 395.
70. Ibid. II, p. 4.
71. Ibid.
72. Ibid.
73. Ibid., p. 9.
74. Ibid., p. 10.
75. Ibid., p. 14.
76. Ibid., p. 16. (Beethoven's underlining.)
77. Ibid., p. 17.
78. Ibid., p. 28.
79. Ibid., p. 71.
80. Ibid., p. 34.
81. Thayer IV, p. 566.
82. Secretary to Count Palffy.
83. Kastner, No. 975, p. 585.

NOTES FOR CHAPTER XI

1. Schünemann II, p. 88.
2. Ibid., p. 125.
3. Ibid., p. 126.
4. The statement was untrue. Johanna had only been sentenced to a house-arrest.
5. Schünemann II, p. 153 f.
6. Ibid., p. 155 ff.
7. Ibid., p. 167.
8. Ibid., p. 175.
9. Ibid., p. 189.
10. Ibid., p. 192.
11. Ibid., p. 124.
12. Ibid., p. 125.
13. Ibid., p. 126.
14. Thayer (IV, p. 567) gives the document.
15. Schindler, ed. Ley, p. 243.
16. Schünemann II, p. 202.
17. Ibid., p. 228.
18. Ibid., p. 230.
19. Ibid., p. 231.
20. Ibid., p. 235.
21. Ibid.
22. Ibid., p. 231.
23. Ibid., p. 252.
24. Ibid., p. 256.
25. Ibid., p. 257.
26. Ibid., p. 258.
27. Ibid., p. 259.
28. Ibid., p. 261.
29. Thayer IV, p. 224.
30. Ibid., p. 207.
31. Ibid., p. 283.

32. Ibid., p. 264. (A translation
    will be found in Thayer-Kreh-
    biel III, pp. 66–67.)
33. *Aus dem Schwarzspanier-
    hause*, p. 126.
34. Schünemann II, p. 396.
35. Ibid. III, p. 247. Karl's under-
    lining.
36. Johann's brother-in-law was a
    baker.
37. Schünemann III, p. 307.
38. Ibid., p. 265.
39. Schünemann II, 272, 273,
    275, 276, 277.
40. I.e., that it would also be ad-
    vantageous for you to be closely
    associated with me.
41. Kastner, No. 1094, p. 656.
42. Ibid., No. 1023, p. 612. ("at
    Krems," i.e., at Johann's estate
    at Gneixendorf, near Krems.)
43. Ibid., No. 1024, p. 612.
44. Ibid., Nos. 1032, 1034, 1035,
    pp. 619, 620, 621.
45. Ibid., No. 1034, p. 620.
46. Schünemann II, p. 284.
47. Ibid. (Karl's underlining.)
48. Ibid., p. 287.
49. Ibid., p. 286.
50. Ibid.
51. *Gehorsame Nacht* (Karl's
    underlining). Karl is apparently
    making fun of a slip on the
    speaker's part.
52. Schünemann II, p. 286.
53. Ibid., p. 288. (Karl's under-
    lining.)
54. Ibid., p. 301.
55. Ibid., p. 288. (Karl's under-
    lining.)
56. Ibid., p. 304.
57. Ibid., p. 288.
58. Kalischer IV, p. 225.
59. Amenda was in Vienna in
    1798–99.

60. Kerst I, p. 33. (Translation
    from: Thayer-Krehbiel I, pp.
    233–34.)
61. Kerst I, p. 133.
62. Ibid., p. 66. (Translation
    from Thayer-Krehbiel III, p.
    137.)
62a. On this late relationship, see
    the following chapter.
63. Kastner, No. 1058, p. 634.
64. Schünemann II, p. 325.
65. Ibid. III, p. 154.
66. Ibid. II, p. 262.
67. Ibid., p. 263. The last two
    words are in English in the
    original.
68. To make sure that they would
    not be overlooked in the
    Conversation Books, Schindler
    rewrote in ink the pas-
    sages in which Beethoven
    complains of Johann and his
    marriage. See, for example,
    Schünemann III, pp. 158, 169,
    170, 171.
69. Count Gallenberg.
70. Schünemann II, p. 382.
71. Ibid., p. 389.
72. Ibid., p. 396.
73. Ibid., pp. 399–400.
74. Ibid., p. 402.
75. Ibid.
76. Kastner, No. 1067, p. 637.
77. Ibid., No. 1081, p. 648.
78. Schindler, ed. Ley, pp. 325–
    26.
79. Kerst II, p. 179.
80. Schünemann III, p. 12.
81. Ibid., pp. 170–71.
82. Literally "fat" plus something
    like "little dangler."
83. "Little bastard."
84. Schünemann II, p. 376.
85. Thayer IV, p. 265. (Thayer's
    exoneration of Johann is acces-

sible in English in Thayer-
Krehbiel III, p. 68 f.)
86. Schünemann III, p. 141.
87. Ibid., p. 140.
88. Ibid., p. 256.
89. Ibid. II, p. 317.
90. Ibid., pp. 334, 337.
91. Ibid., p. 358.
92. Ibid., p. 394.
93. Ibid. III, p. 30.
94. Ibid.
95. Ibid., p. 67.
96. Ibid.
97. Ibid. II, p. 307.
98. Ibid., p. 308.
99. Ibid. III, p. 75.
100. Ibid., p. 116.
101. Ibid., pp. 118, 119, 122.
(Karl's underlining.)
102. Ibid., p. 159.
103. These and the following italics represent underlinings in the
original.
104. Schünemann III, pp. 162,
164, 165 f.
105. Ibid., p. 264.
106. Ibid., p. 288.
107. Ibid., p. 308.
108. Ibid., p. 325.
109. Ibid., p. 326.
110. Ibid., pp. 336–37.
111. Ibid., p. 337.
112. Ibid., p. 301.
113. Ibid.

114. Ibid., p. 325.
115. Ibid., p. 302.
116. Ibid., p. 346.
117. Kerst II, p. 304.
118. Thayer IV, p. 577. (Translated in part in Thayer-Krehbiel III, p. 132, note 1.)
119. Schünemann III, p. 339.
(Beethoven's underlining.)
120. Ibid., p. 344. (Karl's underlining.)
121. Ibid., p. 363.
122. Kastner, No. 1152, p. 685.
123. See Chapter VI.
124. Cf. footnotes 82 and 83 to
this chapter.
125. The sentence up to this point
is grammatically impossible;
hence the translation is only con-
jectural. The meaning might
also be: "What [ever] the two
canailles . . . do to you, you
will not be entirely unwatched,
and will receive letters," etc.
126. Kastner, No. 458, p. 689.
127. A special examination for
which Karl was preparing.
128. Kastner, No. 1157, p. 688.
129. Ibid.
130. Ibid.
131. Ibid., No. 1165, p. 694.
132. Ibid., No. 1174, p. 697.
133. Ibid., No. 1183, p. 701.

NOTES FOR CHAPTER XII

1. Thayer V, p. 8.
2. Ibid.
3. Ibid., p. 92.
4. Ibid., p. 94.
5. Ibid. V, p. 505. This and the
following conversations, which

are preserved only in Thayer,
are given in the form in which
he prints them. Italics represent
underlinings in the originals.
Dashes represent breaks in the
conversations.

6. Ibid. (Karl's underlining.)
7. Ibid.
8. Ibid., p. 507.
9. Ibid.
10. Ibid. (Karl's underlining.)
11. Ibid. (Karl's underlining.)
12. Ibid., p. 509.
13. Ibid. (Karl's underlining.)
14. Ibid.
15. Ibid.
16. Ibid. (Karl's underlining.)
17. Ibid. (Karl's underlining.)
18. Kerst II, p. 87.
19. Kastner, No. 1245, p. 729.
20. Ibid., No. 1246, p. 730.
21. Thayer V, p. 157.
22. Ibid., p. 162.
23. Ibid., p. 510.
24. Ibid., p. 511.
25. Ibid.
26. Ibid., p. 513.
27. Ibid., p. 514. (Karl's underlining.)
28. Ibid., p. 515.
29. Kastner, No. 1292, p. 760.
30. Ibid., Nos. 1294–1298, pp 760–62.
31. Ibid., No. 1295, p. 761.
32. Ibid., No. 1296, p. 762.
33. Ibid., No. 1297, p. 762.
34. Beethoven frequently writes "Reissig" instead of "Reisser."
35. Ibid., No. 1299, p. 763.
36. Ibid., No. 1302, p. 764.
37. Ibid., No. 1305, p. 766
38. In discussing the Heiligenstadt Will in Chapter II, we pointed out that Ludwig had already addressed such death-threats to his brother Karl.
39. Kastner, No. 1300, p. 763.
40. See notes 82 and 83 to Chapter XI.
41. Kastner, No. 1224, p. 716.
42. Kalischer says of Beethoven's letters to his nephew during this period: "The master's agitation and distress become more and more terrible; an indication of this is the increasingly faulty sentence-construction, the greatly increased use of abbreviations, and both the quantity and the quality of the breaks in thought (indicated by dashes), some of them real monstrosities!" A. C. Kalischer, *Beethovens Sämtliche Briefe*, Vol. V, p. 192.
43. Kastner, No. 1343, p. 791.
44. Ibid., No. 1306, p. 767.
45. Ibid., No. 1316, p. 774.
46. "Wiener Früchtel" Ibid., No. 1308, p. 768.
47. Ibid., No. 1329, p. 784.
48. Ibid., No. 1313, p. 772.
49. Ibid., No. 1343, p. 790.
50. Ibid., No. 1313, p. 772.
51. Ibid., No. 1311, p. 770.
52. Ibid., No. 1313, p. 772.
53. Ibid., No. 1307, p. 768.
54. Ibid., No. 1310, p. 769.
55. Ibid., No. 1311, p. 770.
56. Ibid., No. 1349, p. 794.
57. Schindler, ed. Ley, pp. 332–33.
58. Thayer V, p. 518.
59. The suburb in which Karl was living.
60. Thayer V, p. 518.
61. Ibid.
62. Kastner, No. 1343, p. 790.
63. Thayer V, p. 519.
64. Kastner, No. 1347, p. 792.
65. Ibid., No. 1348, p. 793.
66. Ibid., No. 1349, p. 794.
67. Ibid., No. 1350, p. 794.
68. Ibid., No. 1351, p. 795.
69. Thayer V, p. 217.
70. Ibid., p. 225.

71. Conversation Book of 1825, ed. Frimmel, in *Beethoven Jahrbuch*, II, Munich 1909. (Schlesinger's underlining.)
72. Ibid. (Schuppanzigh's underlining.)
73. G. von Breuning, *Aus dem Schwarzspanierhause*, p. 64.
74. Ibid., p. 63.

75. Ibid., p. 64.
76. Thayer V, p. 521. (Karl's underlining.)
77. Ibid., p. 521.
78. Ibid.
79. Ibid., p. 344.
80. Ibid., p. 284.
81. Ibid., p. 344.

NOTES FOR CHAPTER XIII

1. Thayer V, p. 353.
2. Ibid., p. 345.
3. Ibid.
4. Ibid., p. 346.
5. Ibid., p. 347.
6. Ibid.
7. Ibid. Beethoven seems to have reproachfully told Karl that his behavior cast a "shadow" on his honorable name.
8. Breuning, p. 35.
9. Thayer V, p. 347.
10. Ibid.
11. Ibid., p. 348. (Karl's underlining.)
12. Ibid. (Karl's underlining.)
13. Ibid.
14. Kastner, No. 1392, p. 811.
15. Thayer V, p. 351.
16. Ibid., p. 353.
17. Ibid., p. 355.
18. Ibid.
19. Ibid., p. 353.
20. Ibid., p. 355.
21. Ibid.
22. Ibid.
23. Ibid., p. 356.
24. Ibid.
25. Ibid.
26. Kastner, No. 1403, p. 815.
27. Thayer V, p. 358.

28. Ibid., pp. 357-58.
29. Ibid., p. 358.
30. Ibid., p. 353.
31. Ibid., p. 358.
32. Ibid., p. 375.
33. Ibid.
34. Breuning, p. 78.
35. Thayer V, p. 360.
36. Ibid., p. 361.
37. Nohl III, p. 705.
38. Thayer V, p. 361.
39. Nohl III, p. 705.
40. Ibid., p. 714.
41. Thayer V, p. 363.
42. Ibid., p. 364.
43. Kastner, No. 1425, p. 821.
44. Ibid., No. 1424, p. 821.
45. Thayer V, p. 378.
46. Ibid.
47. Ibid.
48. Kastner, No. 1415, p. 818.
49. Ibid., No. 1416, p. 818.
50. Thayer V, p. 380.
51. Ibid., p. 381.
52. Ibid., p. 382.
53. Ibid. p. 383. (Ludwig's underlining.)
54. Ibid., p. 388.
55. Ley, *Beethoven, Sein Leben in Selbstzeugnissen, Briefen und Berichten*, Berlin 1939, p. 336

56. Thayer V, p. 387.
57. Ibid., p. 389.
58. Ibid., p. 410.
59. Grove, for example, writes concerning Karl at Gneixendorf: "the ne'er-do-well nephew, intensely selfish and ready to make game of his uncle or make love to his aunt." *Dictionary of* *Music and Musicians*, 1911, Vol. I, p. 257.
60. Thayer V, p. 413. (Karl's underlining.)
61. Ley, op. cit., p. 338.
62. Ibid., p. 337.
63. Ibid., p. 338.
64. Ibid.

NOTES FOR CHAPTER XIV

1. Schindler's account that Karl was playing billiards at a café and asked the scorer to find a doctor for his uncle is dismissed by Thayer as sheer invention (Thayer V, p. 419).
2. Ibid., p. 426.
3. Ibid.
4. Ibid.
5. Ibid., p. 422.
6. Ley, *Aus Beethovens Erdentagen*, p. 207.
7. Ibid., p. 208.
8. Thayer V, p. 428.
9. Ibid., p. 439.
10. Ibid., p. 440.
11. Ibid., p. 422.
12. Ibid.
13. Ibid., p. 491.
14. Vancsa, *Beethovens Neffe*, p. 7.
15. Heinrich Rietsch, "Nochmals Johann van Beethoven und anderes," Sandberger, *Beethoven Jahrbuch*, Series III, 1927.
16. See Richard Sterba: "Das Problem des Kunstwerks bei Freud," *Psychoanalytische Bewegung*, I, 1929, p. 197. *Idem:* "Zur Problematik des musikalischen Geschehens," *Interna-* *tionale Zeitschrift für Psychoanalyse und Imago*, XXIV, 1939, p. 428.
17. See Otto Rank: "Der Mythos von der Geburt des Helden," *Schriften zur angewandten Seelenkunde*, Vienna, F. Deuticke, Heft 5, 1922.
18. Wegeler and Ries, p. 7.
19. 5th edition, p. 621.
20. Wegeler and Ries, pp. 8–9.
21. Thayer I, p. 146.
22. Recently, to be sure, a contrary trend, against the idealizing of the master as a man, has been perceptible in Beethoven literature. Thus the well-known Beethoven scholar Ernest Newman, in his *The Unconscious Beethoven* (Alfred A. Knopf, New York, 1930) takes the biographers to task for their heroization:

"At a certain stage of his posthumous career the great musician passes into the hands of the showmen-biographers, and, they being an incurably romantic-minded race, he generally emerges from their hands so changed that his contemporaries would hardly recognize him" (p. 4).

He is no less outspokenly critical of the practice of representing Beethoven as an ethical figure: "Beethoven became, for the late nineteenth century, not a mere musician, the value of whose work should be judged by the purely aesthetic tests we would apply to that of any other composer, but a man with a message, a seer, an oracle whose plenary inspiration on all occasions it were blasphemic to doubt. His music was admired not simply in terms of music but as an achievement in morality" (pp. 5–6).

And:

"He became the subject of all sorts of romantic fictions invented to support the theory that the man Beethoven who walked the streets of Vienna habitually lived on the heights of ethical grandeur that he attained in his music" (pp. 10–11).

But in making these strictures, Newman does not take into consideration the fact that such heroization satisfies the strong, unconscious, common human wish for an ideal figure. In addition, Newman attempts to explain the negative traits in Beethoven's character and behavior — which he presents in a tone of polemic disapproval — as the reaction to syphilis acquired in youth. Such a hypothesis contributes nothing essential to the interpretation of the peculiar characteristics of Beethoven's personal relationships; these can be better understood, without any forcing, from the inner conflicts he had undergone from early childhood.

23. Ernest Newman, "Beethoven: The Last Phase," *Atlantic Monthly*, March 1953.

24. Freud, "Dostojewski and Parricide," *Collected Papers* V, p. 222, ed. by James Strachey, Hogarth Press and the Institute of Psycho-Analysis, London 1950.

25. Among many, Anna Freud, Heinz Hartmann, Rudolph Loewenstein, Wilhelm Hoffer should be named as authors who have contributed to the development of ego-psychology, particularly Ernest Kris, in "Psychoanalytic Explorations in Art." International University Press, New York, 1951.

NOTES FOR APPENDICES

1. Kastner, No. 869, p. 481.
2. Thayer IV, p. 551. (Translation from: Thayer-Krehbiel II, pp. 403–04.)
3. Thayer IV, pp. 553–54. (Translation from: Thayer-Krehbiel II, pp. 407–08.)
4. Thayer IV, pp. 543 ff.
5. Kastner, No. 870, pp. 484 ff.
6. Kastner, No. 954, p. 550.
7. Johanna had miswritten "Mitvormunder" for "Mitvormund," and Beethoven appends an ironical "(*sic!*)."